Connecting with History

A Guide to Salvation History
Early Church Through Early Medieval

Companion Reader

Volume 2

Connecting with History
A Guide to Salvation History: Early Church Through Early Medieval
Companion Reader
Volume 2

Compiled and Edited by Sonya Romens and Anna Gonzalez

Book Design by Anna Gonzalez

Cover Design by Anna Gonzalez

RC History
www.rchistory.com

Introduction

Welcome to the second book in the Connecting with History Companion Reader series. The books in this series are anthologies of articles about cultures, places and events from history, stories to illustrate themes contained in the *Connecting with History* units, and short historical stories written in a friendly, conversational style about real people and events.

One of the goals of the *Connecting with History* program is to help young people encounter history from many different angles. Rather than reading one book written in one author's style, we provide a variety of voices, each with a story to tell in his or her own way.

We believe that this method deepens the reader's interest, enjoyment, and understanding of history. This also recognizes that some children respond to one type of writing over another. Some prefer informational articles while another child learns better from a storytelling approach.

Each chapter of this book corresponds to a unit in *Connecting with History, Volume Two: Early Church through Early Medieval*. To make them more easily incorporated into your history studies, most of the stories are organized to correspond with the Volume Two Daily Lesson Plans. Because this is an anthology, at times the transition from one subject to another may seem abrupt. There may be a longer selection to read on one day and on the next just a few short paragraphs. The purpose of the book is not to present every fact and date in a given time period, but to present an introduction, to be followed by more detailed activities. It is one part of the process of learning.

This book has been arranged into two sections based on the age levels in the *Connecting with History* program: the first for Beginner and Grammar level students, the second for Logic level students. Each section contains stories and articles that correspond with one another according to the Daily Lesson Plan assignments. For instance, a student in the Grammar level and a student in the Logic level will each read an article about Alfred the Great, written at his or her own level. Because each child is at a different level of maturity in their reading and comprehension, you, the parent, can decide which section to assign to your child. You might also wish to read some or all of the book aloud to your children. This emphasis on flexibility and family learning are hallmarks of the *Connecting with History* approach to education.

After long searching and sifting through classic books, we have edited them to update any archaic language, punctuation, and spelling while being careful to retain the author's voice. When necessary, historical facts have been updated. In some cases, we have combined two or more sources into one story or article. It has been widely recognized that writing from one hundred or more years ago assumed a higher reading level than what is written for children today. The authors use a rich vocabulary, speak directly to the child, respect his intelligence, and never talk down to him.

Above all, the purpose of this book is to make history come to life: to make it interesting, relevant to a child's daily life, and enjoyable. Approach it, not as a textbook, but as part of the fascination of learning about different places and times in which very real people lived.

Sonya Romens

Note that Unit Two is omitted from the Logic level section. This is intentional and due to the comprehensive amount of reading assignments already included in the Daily Lesson Plans for that unit.

Contents

Contents

Section One:

Beginner and Grammar Levels

Unit One:
Preparation for the King,
End of the Roman Republic

THEME: PREPARE THE WAY

Introduction to Rome

by Rev. Monsignor Edmund J. Goebel Ph. D.

Near the center of Italy, there arose, on the famous seven hills, the "Eternal City"–Rome. In this unit, you will read how the Latins founded Rome, how they defeated the neighboring tribes, and how they built up the great Roman Empire.

As you read the story of Rome, try to picture the columns of Romans soldiers marching along the Roman roads. Try to picture Roman lawyers pleading their cases in the courts. Try to picture Roman boys hurrying off to school and Roman laborers constructing temples, bridges, and aqueducts.

The growth of the Roman Empire and the flow of great wealth into Rome brought about many changes in the character of the Roman people. They lost the sturdy qualities that had made them great. They became less attentive to their religious duties and were unwilling to engage in hard labor or military service. They even lost the ability to govern themselves in an orderly manner. Soon Rome was under the control of one man – the emperor.

However, pagan Rome has a significant place in the progress of civilization. The Romans preserved Greek civilization and made important contributions of their own. The Latin language carried Roman ideas on law, justice, and government throughout the vast extent of the Roman Empire.

The Geography of Italy. The homeland of the Romans was a peninsula jutting out into the Mediterranean Sea. This peninsula, which is shaped like a boot, controls the Mediterranean Sea.

Italy has two mountain ranges of importance. The mighty Alps on the north keep out the cold winter winds. This protective fence gives Italy a mild, pleasant climate. The Apennines run along the east coast of Italy. This gives the country a wide plain on the western side. Most of the ports are on the west coast also.

The great plain of Italy was important for the people. They were able to raise more grain at home than the Greeks could. The high areas near the mountains were well suited for the olive trees and grapevines which the farmers cultivated. There was plenty of room also for large flocks of sheep to graze.

The great plain was important in another way also. There were no natural barriers to keep the people divided into small states as in Greece. The people could be expected to unite into one great nation.

To the west of Italy are two large islands, Corsica and Sardinia. To the south is still another island, Sicily, which was very important to Italy. It almost forms a land bridge across the Mediterranean Sea to Africa.

The City of the Seven Hills. If ever a city was destined for greatness by its location, it was Rome. Just as Italy was located near the center of the Mediterranean Sea, so Rome was located near the center of Italy. Rome was to become master of Italy and later of the whole Mediterranean world.

Rome was located on the Tiber River, about twelve miles from the sea. It was built around seven hills. Just south of Rome was the plain of Latium. The people who lived here called themselves Latins. After the Latin tribes made Rome their capital, they became known as Romans.

The Latins had made stories and legends that told of the founding of Rome. One of their favorite tales was that of Aeneas, who with his family escaped from the burning city of Troy. After many difficulties, he settled in Latium to become the father of the Latin people.

Another legend told of the twin brothers, Romulus and Remus, who had disputed over the name of the city which they had founded on the hills near the Tiber River. Romulus won the dispute, and the city was called "Rome" in his honor.

The Etruscan Neighbors. The neighbors of the Romans just north of the Tiber River were the Etruscans. We wish we knew more about the Etruscan people, but no one has yet discovered a master clue to Etruscan writing. From the remains found in their cities, however, we know that the Etruscans were skilled at building aqueducts, bridges, canals, and roads. The Romans were quick to master these skills.

Later, the Romans studied the Etruscan method of pottery making, painting, astronomy, and even medicine. From the Etruscans came Rome's first lessons in collecting and training an army for warfare.

The Greek Neighbors. The Greeks had many colonies in southern Italy and Sicily. These Greeks came to the Tiber River to trade with the Romans. From them, the Roman farmers and shepherds learned improved methods of trading. They learned to measure and to weigh articles which they bought and sold. Until the Greeks showed them how to make and to use coins, the Romans had never used coined money. The Greeks also taught the Romans how to make ships and sail the seas.

The Latin Language. The Latins also began to use the alphabet which the Greeks had learned from the Phoenicians. As the Romans conquered the lands about them, the Latin language was spread to other nations. In time, Latin became the language of the educated classes throughout most of Europe. The Romans used these letters not only to write but also to count. Roman numbers are actually letters of the alphabet put together in certain combinations. You have probably learned some of the Roman numbers.

Roman Religion. The Romans also borrowed many of their ideas about religion from the Greeks. Both Greeks and Romans worshipped the same gods, although the names were frequently different.

The Romans had one god who was different from any of the Greek gods. This was Janus, who was believed to guard the gate of every Roman city and the door of every Roman home. This god was supposed to have two faces, one to watch each side of the gate or door. The month of January is named for the Roman god Janus.

Of all the gods, the Romans especially honored Vesta, the goddess of the hearth and home. The Romans built a temple to Vesta, where a fire burned continually. Six beautiful maidens called Vestal Virgins were chosen to spend all their time in the service of this goddess.

The Kings of Rome. In the early days of the city of Rome, an Etruscan ruler led his army across the Tiber River. He drove out the Roman chiefs and set himself up as the king of the Romans. For the next two hundred and fifty years, Rome was ruled by Etruscan kings.

Some of these Etruscan kings helped to improve the city of Rome. They drained the nearby swamps and constructed a sewage system for the city. They built a protective wall around the seven hills. They built docks along the Tiber River to encourage trade.

Unfortunately, some of the Etruscan rulers were cruel men. This was especially true of one king, Tarquin the Proud. He became so unjust that the people drove him from the city.

The Roman Republic

by Rev. Monsignor Edmund J. Goebel Ph. D.

The Meaning of "Republic." The government of America is a republic. "Republic" is from a Latin word that means "public things" or "public affairs." In a republic, the people should be interested in all the affairs of the government. In a republic, the people elect their chief officials.

When the Romans drove out their last king, they set up a republic. Although some of the Roman officials had the same titles as American officials now have, their government was quite different from ours.

The Consuls. The Romans had as their chief officials two consuls. They were elected for terms of one year. There were two of them so that no one man might have all the power in his own hands. The Romans thought that each consul could watch the other and keep him from getting too much power. The consuls had charge of the Roman army.

The Roman Dictator. In times of war, it would not be wise to have two men at the head of the government. The enemy might win the war before the two consuls could agree on a course of action. So, the Romans used to choose a dictator in times of crisis. This one man then had all the power in Rome. Even the consuls had to obey him. However, no man could be dictator for more than six months at a time.

You can see from this that the Romans did not want any one man to secure control of the government for too long a time. They liked to tell the story of Cincinnatus, a dictator, who defeated the enemy in sixteen days. As soon as the war was over, he resigned his position and returned to his farm. He was a patriotic man who used his power as dictator for the good of his city.

The Patricians. The earliest settlers of Rome, or "the first families," as they might be called, kept control of the government for a long time. They became the nobles of the city and were usually called *patricians.* Only patricians could be elected to the chief offices of the government.

The Romans had a senate that made the laws, declared war, and made alliances. It was the senate that actually ruled Rome. Since all the senators were patricians, the nobles were able to hold the power in Rome for a long time.

The Plebeians. The people who settled in Rome later than the patrician families were called *plebeians.* The word "plebeians" is from the Latin word meaning "the common people." The plebeians were freemen but had few privileges. They could not hold office, and they could not marry into a patrician family. They were the workmen of the city and the owners of small farms.

The plebeians were forced to serve in the army without pay. They were also obliged to pay taxes, even though they could not vote. If a plebeian went off to war, he might find on his return that his farm or business was in debt. To pay the debt, he would have to borrow money from patricians.

The Struggle of the Plebeians for Equality. The plebeians were constantly trying to better their position. They began to struggle to secure equality with the patricians. This struggle went on in Rome for over a hundred years. The first victory of the plebeians was secured by "a strike." The patricians needed them to fight a war and promised that all plebeian debtors would be released from prison. When the war was over, the patrician senate refused to fulfill the promise. So, the plebeians left the city and settled on a hill about three miles away.

To win the plebeians back to Rome, the patricians gave them a part in the government. The plebeians were allowed to elect some of their own members to the office of tribune. The tribunes were permitted to have a place just outside the door of the senate. If the senate tried to pass a law that was unfavorable to the people, a tribune could shout "Veto," which means "I forbid." Then the Senate could not pass the law.

The plebeians next demanded written laws. In ancient Babylon, and later in Athens, the common people also demanded that the laws be written down. In Rome, the laws were carved on twelve tablets. Then the tablets were set up in the Forum, the marketplace of

Rome, where all the citizens could read them. These laws applied to patricians and plebeians alike. All citizens in Rome were now equal before the law. One of the great contributions of Rome to civilization was the Roman system of law, which began in these laws of the twelve tablets.

Gradually the plebeians gained other rights. They were permitted to marry patricians. Then at last a law was passed which said that at least one of the Roman consuls must be a plebeian. After the plebeians were permitted to become senators, priests, and generals.

Roman Character. Rome did not become great because of her laws or her armies or her language. Rather, her laws were great and her armies were great because of the character of her people. Her language has always been held in renown because of the noble ideas expressed by her people.

The Romans were simple, frugal, honest people who were not afraid of hard work. They showed their loyalty to their city in many practical ways. They were very proud to be Romans and were careful not to commit any dishonorable act.

The character of the Romans was developed in their family life. The father insisted on strict obedience, honesty, and hard work from the members of the family. These virtues were also practiced in the life of the city.

The Punic Wars

by Rev. Monsignor Edmund J. Goebel Ph. D.

Master of Italy. Rome now began a policy of conquest. At first, the wars were waged in self-defense. Rome needed protection from her neighbors, especially the Etruscans, who lived just north of Rome, and from the Italian tribes of central Italy. One by one, these neighboring states were brought under the control of Rome. Then the Roman armies conquered the Greek cities of southern Italy. Rome became master throughout the entire peninsula of Italy.

The Romans adopted a wise policy of governing these conquered states. The people were admitted to many of the privileges of Roman citizens. Rome now gave them full protection against all other enemies. Each city was also permitted to govern itself in local matters. This policy made the cities of Italy very loyal to Rome.

The Romans also built a series of roads connecting the great cities of Italy with Rome. In this way, troops could be sent quickly against any city that might decide to revolt. The Romans also drained swamps, dug tunnels through mountains, and built bridges across rivers. The Roman highways were so well built that some of them are still in use today.

Carthage, Rival to Rome. Roman expansion into southern Italy brought Rome in conflict with another great power of the Mediterranean area, Carthage. Carthage had a favorable location in North Africa. The city had been founded by the Phoenicians as a colony for trading purposes. It had grown to become the most powerful and prosperous city in the whole Mediterranean world.

Carthage, in turn, had established other trading colonies in many important places. She controlled the lands along the coast of North Africa and Spain. The islands of Corsica and Sardinia were in the power of Carthage, as well as half the Island of Sicily. The Carthaginians held the Strait of Gibraltar and permitted no ship to enter or leave the Mediterranean Sea without their permission. When Carthage captured the city of Messina in Sicily, the Carthaginians became a real threat to Rome. They could prevent Rome from sending ships to her cities along the Adriatic coast.

The Punic Wars. Rome fought three long wars with Carthage. These are usually called the Punic Wars, from the Roman name for the Phoenician founders of Carthage. By the end of the First Punic War, Rome had driven the Carthaginians from Sicily, Corsica, and Sardinia.

After more than twenty years of peace, war again broke out between Rome and Carthage. In the Second Punic War, the Carthaginian general, Hannibal, set out from Spain with a huge army and invaded Italy. He performed the mighty task of crossing the Alps in about two weeks. However, he lost half of his army in this difficult venture.

Hannibal defeated the Romans in several battles but was never able to crush the Romans completely. When a Roman army crossed over to North Africa and threatened the city of Carthage, Hannibal was called home to protect the city. But the Romans captured Carthage and sent Hannibal into exile.

This time of peace lasted fifty years. Finally, in the Third Punic War, Rome completely destroyed the city of Carthage. The city was burned to the ground. The land was plowed up and sown with salt so that nothing would grow there.

Rome, Master of the Mediterranean. With the fall of Carthage, Rome was master of the western half of the Mediterranean world. All the possessions of Carthage now became Roman provinces.

Rome had also turned her attention to the countries of the East. The empire of Alexander the Great had broken up into several parts. One by one, Rome seized control of these countries – Macedonia, Greece, Syria, and Egypt. By the year 146 B.C., every country in the Mediterranean area was included within the Roman Empire or had become an "ally" of Rome.

Decline of the Republic

by Rev. Monsignor Edmund J. Goebel Ph. D.

Roman Expansion. Rome continued its expansion far beyond the borders of Italy, expanding into what are now France, Spain, Germany, and beyond. However, it was a great problem for Rome to govern these distant lands. These remote conquests were called provinces, and Rome did not apply the same wise policies to provinces as she had to the cities of Italy. Provinces were instead governed harshly. They were placed under the control of a governor sent from Rome. The people had no part in the government. Neither did they have any of the privileges of Roman citizens. They were forced to pay huge taxes to Rome. The taxes were collected by a group of men called publicans. As you can imagine, the Romans were not well-liked by the people of the provinces. Therefore, it was necessary to keep a large Roman army in the provinces to prevent revolts.

The long wars had brought about many changes at home for the Romans also. Thousands of the finest young Romans had been killed in the wars. Others had been in the army so long that they did not know how to earn a living as civilians.

Great wealth poured into Rome. Some of the Romans became so wealthy that they lived like kings. The virtues that had helped to make Rome great – simple living and hard work – began to disappear.

At the same time, a large number of Romans were becoming poorer and poorer. The small farmers had lost everything they had owned. For one thing, they had been kept busy fighting for a great many years. While they were away from home, they could not care for their farms. They had to borrow from the wealthy. When they were unable to pay their debts, they lost their farms to the wealthy, who already had more land than they could use. Then these men who had lost their farms went to Rome to find work. But they could find no work to do, and Rome became filled with large numbers of families who were without homes and work.

The situation at Rome was made worse by the presence of thousands of slaves. These had been captured during the wars. There were so many slaves that they could be bought for very little money. Most families could afford to have three or four slaves, and the very wealthy homes had hundreds of slaves. This was not good for the Romans. In fact, slavery is not good for any country. The poor could find no work because slaves would do the work more cheaply.

Bread and Games. More and more families moved into the city of Rome. But none of them could find work. As citizens, they still had the right to vote. So, the generals and other rich men who wanted to get the votes of the idle mob gave them free grain for bread. In this way, even the poor were able to live without working. Some of the wealthy even entertained the poor with free games and shows. These were exciting contests, such as boxing matches and chariot races. Sometimes there were fights between men and wild beasts.

This idle mob helped to destroy the republic. They were no longer interested in the affairs of the government. They voted for the man who provided them with the most free food or the most exciting entertainment. With this condition, only the wealthy could afford to run for public office.

The Efforts of the Gracchi. The fine ideals of the Roman Republic were never entirely wiped out. At times, men came into prominence who tried to restore the republic to its original ways. Among these were the Gracchi, two brothers – members of a noble Roman family – who took up the cause of the poor against the rich. The older brother, Tiberius

Gracchus, was elected tribune. He got a law passed to break up the large pieces of public lands into small farms. But before he could carry out the plan, he was killed by a mob of angry senators.

Ten years later, Gaius Gracchus, the younger brother of Tiberius, was elected tribune. He took up the work started by his older brother and tried to carry out his plans. He wanted the government to build roads and public buildings and so permit the unemployed to earn a living. But Gaius, too, was killed by a mob.

From the story of these brothers, you can see that Rome had changed a great deal. In the old days, people obeyed the laws and honored their leaders. Now the power in Rome went to those who could get a large section of the mob to follow them. When the mobs began to fight one another, Rome was left without any real government.

INTRODUCTION TO JULIUS CAESAR

by Rev. Monsignor Edmund J. Goebel Ph. D.

Caesar Comes to Power. In the midst of all this confusion at Rome, a young noble attracted favorable attention. He was Julius Caesar, who was born about 100 B.C. He became popular by the usual methods of free shows, games, and athletic contests for the people. He was elected consul, the highest office in Rome. He knew that the bad conditions of Rome would have to be corrected. But his term as consul was too short. He also realized that he needed an army to protect him or he, too, would be murdered like the Gracchi.

Caesar, the Conqueror. When his term as consul came to an end, he had himself appointed governor of the Province of Gaul, which was located north of the Po River. Caesar now had an army that he trained into a mighty force. He endured all the hardships of his soldiers, and they were ready to follow him anywhere. He led his army through what is now modern France and Belgium and even crossed over into England. He had extended the boundary of the Roman state to the river Rhine.

Caesar, the Statesman. Caesar returned to Rome at the head of a conquering army. His popularity increased to such an extent that the people made him dictator for ten years. Later they made him dictator for life. They offered him a crown, but this he refused. Caesar knew that the Romans did not like the idea of having a king. He did not need the title of king, anyway. He had all the power of a king without the title. Rome was now ruled by one man – Julius Caesar.

Caesar did accept the title of imperator, which meant commander or general. From this title, we get the word "emperor," which is the title we give to the successors of Julius Caesar.

Caesar was obliged to fight other wars in the East. But he always returned to Rome as a conquering hero. He had many plans to improve the conditions in Rome and throughout the empire. He wanted to send colonies of poor Romans into the provinces. He tried to encourage the farmers so that Italy might produce enough grain to feed the people of the cities. He started a program of public building to reduce the number of unemployed men and at the same time improve the city of Rome.

Julius Caesar also changed and corrected the calendar. He introduced the idea of the leap year – an extra day every four years. He divided the year into twelve months. One of the months he renamed for himself – July. The calendar as changed by Julius Caesar is the calendar we use today, with later corrections made by Pope Gregory the Thirteenth.

Julius Caesar in Britain

By Charlotte M. Yonge

The soldiers Caesar led to battle were very strong and conquered the people wherever they went. They had no gun or gunpowder then; but they had swords and spears, and, to prevent themselves from being hurt, they had helmets or brazen caps on their heads, with long tufts of horse-hair upon them for ornament; and breast-plates of brass on their chests; and on their arms, they carried a sort of screen, made of strong leather. One of them carried a brass figure of an eagle on a long pole, with a scarlet flag flying below, and wherever the eagle was seen, they all followed and fought so bravely that nothing could long stand against them.

When Julius Caesar rode at their head, with his keen, pale, hook-nosed face, and the scarlet cloak that the general always wore, they were so proud of him and so fond of him, that there was nothing they would not do for him.

Julius Caesar heard that a little way off, there was a country nobody knew anything about, except that the people were very fierce and savage. He could not bear that there should be any place that his own people, the Romans, did not know and conquer. So, he commanded the ships to be prepared, and he and his soldiers embarked, watching the white cliffs on the other side of the sea grow higher and higher as he came nearer and nearer.

When he came quite close to them, he thought they appeared savage indeed. They were tall men, with long red streaming hair, and what few clothes they had were woolen and checked like plaid; but many had their arms and chests naked and painted all over in blue patterns. They yelled and brandished their darts, to make Julius Caesar and his Roman soldiers keep away; but he simply went on to a place where the shore was not quite so steep, and there commanded his soldiers to land. The savages had run along the shore too, and there was a terrible fight; but at last, the man who carried the eagle jumped down into the middle of the natives, calling out to his fellows that they must come after him, or they would lose their eagle. They all came rushing and leaping down, and thus they managed to force back the savages and make their way to the shore.

There was not much worth having when they had made their way there. Though they came again the next year and forced their way a good deal farther into the country, they saw mostly bare downs, or heaths, or thick woods. The few houses were little more than piles of stones, and the people were rough and wild. The men hunted wild boars, and wolves and stags, and the women dug the ground and raised a little corn, which they ground to flour between two stones to make bread; and they spun the wool of their sheep, dyed it with bright colors, and wove it into dresses. They had some strong places in the woods, with trunks of trees, cut down to shut them in from the enemy, with all their flocks and cattle; but Caesar did not get into any of these. He only made the natives give him some of their pearls, which were found in the shells of mussels which lived in the rivers and call the Romans their masters, and then he went back to his ships, and none of the savages who were alive when he came saw him or his Romans again.

Do you know who these savages were who fought with Julius Caesar? They were called Britons. And the country he came to see? That was the island of England, only it was not called so then. And the place where Julius Caesar landed is called Deal, and, if you look at a map where England and France most nearly touch one another, I think you will see the name Deal, and remember it was there Julius Caesar landed, and fought with the Britons.

It was fifty-five years before our blessed Savior was born that the Romans came to Briton.

The Reign of Caesar

By James J. Reynolds, Mary A Horn, and Phoebe Mizell

Julius Caesar was made consul after he had proved himself to be a great soldier by winning for Rome many victories in Spain. When he returned, he found things in the city of Rome were very bad. The rich people had too much money. They were lazy and idle and wasted their money. They had slaves to do all their work.

Julius Caesar loved Rome. He knew what a great empire it governed. He wanted to make things better. Caesar asked Pompey and Crassus, two of his friends, to help him. They agreed. The three men became rulers of the Roman provinces. Caesar took France, which was then called Gaul, Pompey took Spain, and Crassus took Asia.

The people had a large meeting place in Rome called the Forum. There they gathered every day to hear the news of the day. They had no newspapers, and even their books had to be written by hand. They learned the news of battles from messengers who were sent back on horse or on foot from the armies. You may imagine the excitement in the Forum when news came that Caesar had won another battle in Gaul, or that he was sending back a group of slaves.

The Germans at that time wanted to come across the Rhine into Gaul because the land was better there. Caesar had a hard time keeping them back, but he did so. He ruled the Gauls kindly. He showed them how to grow grapes in the sunny valleys, to build roads and bridges, and to make a better home.

In a short time, Pompey became jealous of Caesar and of the great things he was doing. He told the people Caesar was plotting against Rome. The Senate finally sent word to Caesar that he must give up his army by a certain time or be counted a traitor. Caesar knew he had done nothing to harm his beloved Rome and would not give up. His soldiers stood by him.

One day Caesar came with his army to the bank of a river called the Rubicon. Anyone who crossed the Rubicon with an army was considered an enemy of Rome. But Caesar plunged into the river on his horse and crossed to the other side. This meant, "On to Rome!"

Caesar reached Rome. Pompey fled, and was later killed in Egypt. Caesar was now the greatest man in Rome. Celebrations were held in the city for him. The coins had his image on them. The month of July was named for him. A golden chair was set up in the Senate for him.

Caesar made wise laws. He taught the people that they must work. He made the rich governors stop robbing the poor, and he taught the people to be less cruel to the slaves.

Again, Caesar's friends became jealous of him. They were afraid he would make all Rome a great kingdom, and that he himself would become the king. They thought the only way to conquer him was to kill him.

They waited for him one day in the Senate, with their daggers ready. He did not come. Then they sent one of their number for him. His wife begged him not to go to the Senate, for she had dreamed he would be killed. He went anyway. As he entered, one after another leaped upon and stabbed him. While he was dying of his wounds, he looked up and saw that one of those who had stabbed him was his dear friend, Brutus. His heart was broken. With the words, "And you, too, Brutus!" on his lips, he died.

HOLY MARY

By Mother Mary Loyola

Have you ever watched the clouds on a wild day hiding the sun? They move along, a dark, heavy mass as if determined to keep his light from the waiting world. At times through the rifts, you catch a glimpse of him; or there is a golden border which shows he is somewhere near. You think he must be coming soon. But no, it is all too dark for him yet. Suddenly, in the midst of the gloom appears a little white cloud. It grows bright, brighter, and brighter as he fills it with his glory. Yes, surely he is there; only his splendor could make it shine like that. A few moments at most and he must show himself; a few moments and he will scatter the darkness and flood the earth with light.

Hidden among the mountains of Galilee, amid a profusion of wildflowers, lies the village of Nazareth. The houses, small, low, with flat roofs, look like little white boxes set on the slope of the hill. That one, half cottage, half rock, the lowest in the steep street, is the home of Joseph, the carpenter of the place. All things are quiet silence. Night is in the midst of her course. No light anywhere except the stars overhead, and they shine out brightly in the clear, frosty air, for it is the month of March. Look! A lamp is burning in that last house. Who can be the watcher there when all the village is asleep? Let us go in noiselessly and see.

Alone in her little room kneels a girl of fourteen. What a wonderful face! So grave and yet so sweet, so childlike and innocent, and still so full of dignity. She must be very near to God. A great reverence comes over us as we gaze upon her, and we fall on our knees. This can be no ordinary child. Let us go back fourteen years and learn what we can about her.

Her name is Miriam, or Mary, which means "Lady," and also "Star of the Sea." Her holy parents, Joachim and Anne, had prayed long and earnestly for a child to gladden their old age before this blessed child was given them. Who shall ever tell what she was to them! They were never tired of watching her at prayer or play, even when she thought herself alone. They soon discovered that she knew more about God and holy things than they could tell her. It seemed to them that God Himself was her Teacher, and they reverenced her as one very precious in His sight. What would have been their awe and joy had they known that she was to be the Mother of His only Son! Yes, she was to be the woman promised long ago in Paradise who was to crush the serpent's head, the Mother of Him who was to redeem the world, the Mother of God. And God was getting her ready for this. Think what a preparation it must have been.

Solomon's Temple was many years building because everything in it had to be of such costly material – marbles, and sweet-scented, incorruptible cedar, and precious stones, all "artfully wrought and carved. The floor of the house was overlaid with gold within and without, and there was nothing in the Temple that was not gold or covered with gold – the altar of gold, and the table of gold, and the golden candlesticks of pure gold, and flowers like lilies, and the lamps over them of gold, and golden snuffers, and censers of most pure gold, and the hinges for the doors of the inner house of the Holy of Holies gold, pure gold, most pure gold" (III Kings vi., vii). Why? Because everything about this house of God must be as far as possible worthy of Him. Yet the Temple of Jerusalem, with its Holy of Holies, its Ark of the Covenant, and its Tables of the Law, what was it compared with that Blessed One whom He had chosen to be His Mother? What must He do to make her worthy, as far as she could be worthy, to have God for her Son?

First of all, there must be no sin. When we are going to embroider richly on white satin, we take care to see that it is spotless. It would be wasting our silk and our gold thread to lay them on what is soiled or ever has been soiled. God prizes spotlessness more than we do. He was going to enrich His Mother with His best gifts, and the first must be a perfect purity. No stains of sin must so much as come near her. She must be more dazzling in her whiteness than the Angels who come nearest His throne.

But what about original sin? Was not Mary a child of Adam? Yes, and she would have been stained with Adam's sin had not God kept her free because of her nearness to Himself. She was not cleansed from original sin as babies are when they have been baptized, for no sin of any kind ever touched her.

Some people cannot understand why Mary should have had this perfect freedom from sin which we call the Immaculate Conception. It would be clear as day to them if they would think who Mary is. A Protestant lady, who had this difficulty, was asked,

"Do you believe that Jesus Christ the Son of Mary is truly God?"

"I do," she answered reverently.

"And is there anything God could do for His Mother that He would not for His own sake be bound to do?"

She was silent for a moment, and then said, "I do not think there is."

It was the Precious Blood that saved Mary so grandly and did so even before our Lord came into the world. It preserved her from the sin that has spoilt everything else. "My spirit hath rejoiced in God my Savior," she says. "For He that is mighty hath done great things for me."

Imagine a burning mountain throwing up flames and volumes of smoke; the burning lava pouring down the sides, destroying fields, vineyards, cottages, cattle. Down it rushes, leaving everything a black ruin behind it. Down, down, till it is suddenly checked before a fair garden that lies in its way; checked and turned aside, so that no harm is done, and the trees and flowers and fruit look all the more lovely for all the desolation around.

So it was that the torrent of original sin halted when it came to Mary.

When the little Mary was three years old, she was carried by her parents to the Temple to be solemnly offered to God. She understood quite well what she was going to do. She knew that God had done great things for her, and she wanted to give herself entirely to Him, that He might do just as He liked with her always, whether it was what she liked or not. With her hands joined, her face bright with holy joy, she went alone up the fifteen steps, her parents looking on with admiration and gladness. And with sorrow too. For they were going to leave her in the Temple to be brought up with other Jewish girls, and they thought how sad and lonely they would be without her.

As she grew, Mary spent her time in prayer, in working for the Temple, and in studying the Holy Scriptures. The parts she liked best were the prophesies which told of the promised Redeemer. She knew His time was come. Perhaps He was even now upon earth. Perhaps His Mother might be in want of a little servant. Oh, how happy she would be to wait upon them both!

When she was about fourteen years old, she left her home in the Temple to be espoused to Joseph, a carpenter, and to take care of the little home of her own at Nazareth. Her life was different now. No more glorious services morning and evening, but a life of work, and very humble work. But she was content, more than content; she was quite happy, and she made Joseph happy by her brightness, her tenderness, her sweet, unselfish ways. As he came to know her more and more, he was filled with the deepest reverence for her, child though she was. And he was worthy of her, for he came next to her in holiness and nearness to God. He was trusted with the greatest treasure God had on earth, and he was about to be trusted with One more precious still.

Augustus

by Rev. Monsignor Edmund J. Goebel Ph. D.

Caesar's Heir. After the death of Julius Caesar, the people had difficulty in deciding upon a new ruler. Caesar had adopted his grandnephew, Octavian, and had made him his heir, but Octavian was only eighteen years old at the time of Caesar's death. It took him about thirteen years to defeat his enemies and make himself master of Rome.

Octavian, like Julius Caesar before him, refused to become king. He kept all the offices of the republic and was elected to most of them. Like his uncle, he accepted the title of "emperor." He also received several new titles. One of these was princeps or prince, which meant "first citizen."

Augustus Caesar. The most important title he received was Augustus. It had never before been given to any man. Until then it had been used only in speaking of the gods. This title became the one by which Octavian was generally known. It is from this title that the month of August got its name.

Good Government. After 27 B.C., Augustus was the sole ruler of the vast Roman Empire. Fortunately for the empire, he was a just and wise ruler. For the first time in two hundred years, Rome was at peace. The people of the empire lived happily under Roman law and order.

Augustus ruled the Roman Empire for over forty years after he became the sole ruler. This gave him an opportunity to improve the conditions throughout the empire. He sent capable and honest governors to rule the provinces. He had a census taken of the empire and gave the provinces a fairer tax system.

The Golden Age Of Rome. Athens had reached her highest degree of civilization during the Ages of Pericles after the Persian Wars. The long rule of Augustus had a similar place in the history of Rome. It was a period of peace after a long series of wars. Augustus himself encouraged the artists, the architects, and the writers. He gave them support from the public treasury. He showered them with honors.

Augustus planned to make Rome a city of great beauty, as Pericles had done at Athens. A new forum, a new theater, and many splendid temples were erected in Rome. In fact, Augustus made the city so beautiful that it is said, "He found a city built of brick and left it built of marble."

Our Debt to Rome

Adapted from the work of Eva March Tappan, Ph. D. and Rev. Monsignor Edmund J. Goebel Ph. D.

A Real Debt. The world we live in would be vastly different if the Romans had not made their contributions to civilization. Rome made a lasting impression on the vast empire which she governed. But we in America, too, are heirs of the great Roman civilization which was developed long before our land was discovered.

Spread of Greek Civilization. Most conquering armies destroy a civilization that is strange to them. The Roman armies destroyed whatever civilization there was at Carthage because they thought it was not a good civilization. But they did not destroy the civilization of the Greeks, because it was a civilization that they admired. In fact, the Romans did what they could to preserve Greek civilization.

After Rome conquered Greece, thousands of Greeks were brought back to Rome as slaves. A large number of these were so well educated that many Roman boys had Greek tutors or were sent to schools where the teachers were Greek. In this way, the Romans were taught to admire and preserve the civilization of their teachers, even though the teachers were their slaves.

As the Romans developed their own civilization, they borrowed many ideas from the Greeks in religion, architecture, language, and literature. They permitted the Greek university at Alexandria in Egypt to continue. One of the great scholars at Alexandria in the days of the Roman Empire was Ptolemy. He was a student of astronomy and geography. His studies and his maps were used by Columbus in preparing for his voyage to America.

The Romans did more than preserve the valuable civilizations of the Greeks. They helped spread Greek culture in the lands of the West that at this time knew little about the Greeks – Spain, France, and England. These countries, in turn, were the nations that brought Greek and Roman ideas to America.

Architecture and Engineering. The Romans themselves also gave the world many useful and beautiful gifts. We have already seen that they had a remarkable system of good roads. They also had knowledge and skill in erecting buildings. They made Rome one of the most beautiful cities the world has ever known. Many of the cities in the provinces also had fine buildings.

Some of these buildings are still standing today, and a few are still in use. Others are partially in ruins but provide enough clues to indicate what the buildings were like originally. In southern Italy, the town of Pompeii was completely covered by soot, ashes, and lava when the volcano of Mt. Vesuvius erupted in the early years of the Roman Empire. Archaeologists have excavated the town in our own day, and so we have a complete picture of what a Roman town was like.

The center of Roman life was the Forum. This was originally the marketplace but later was used by the citizens as a gathering place for public meetings. Here speakers addressed the people from a mounted platform called the Rostra. Around the Forum were some of the chief temples of Rome. Here also was the Senate House.

The Romans learned how to use the arch in many of their buildings. To bring pure water from the hills to Rome, fourteen aqueducts were constructed. These consisted of a series of arches which carried the water over high and low places into the city. These aqueducts were so well built that some of them are still standing.

The arch was also prominent in the amphitheaters, which were like our stadiums of today. The most famous of these was the Colosseum in Rome, which could seat 50,000 people for the games and shows. The arch may also be seen in the triumphal arches which conquering emperors erected at Rome in honor of their victories.

The Romans developed the arch into the dome to give a new feature to their buildings. The Pantheon, a temple which Augustus erected to all the gods, is the best example of this difficult construction. Perhaps your own state capitol has a dome.

The Romans had another type of large building which was called a basilica. It was similar to certain of the Greek buildings except that the columns were inside. The basilica was used by the judges and the merchants. The Christians found the basilicas very suitable as churches, and today some of the great Catholic churches throughout the world are called basilicas.

Language and Literature. Latin was the language spoken in business and government throughout the Roman Empire. From London to Babylon, men of different tribes could talk to one another in Latin. At the time that Christ founded His Church, Latin was the language that could be understood in all the countries of the civilized world. After St. Peter, the Head of the Church, became Bishop of Rome, it was natural that the ceremonies of the Church and the writings of the Popes should be in the Latin language.

The people of Italy, Romania, France, Spain, and Portugal today speak languages that developed from Latin. More than half of the people in the Western Hemisphere speak one of the "Romance" languages. All the land south of the Rio Grande is called "Latin America." Even our English language would be very different if we had not taken thousands of words from Latin.

The literature of the Romans, written in Latin, is still read and studied in our schools and colleges. Julius Caesar wrote a valuable account of his campaigns in Gaul and Britain. His "Commentaries" is perhaps the best-known Latin book today. Cicero, the great orator, who lived at the time of Caesar, is studied by people who wish to become great speakers.

Augustus cared a great deal about good literature. Authors cannot write very well when they are afraid of losing their heads any day; but with a strong, kind ruler who kept the land peaceful and was deeply interested in their work, they did their best.

It was in this reign that Virgil lived, who wrote about the adventures of Aeneas. The name of Aeneas's son Ascanius was said to have been changed to Julus, or Julius, after he reached Italy; Augustus liked to think that Julius Caesar and he himself were among his descendants. Horace lived at that time and wrote charming and graceful poems. He did not attempt to tell stories, like Virgil, but he understood so well how people think and feel that his poems seem as if they might have been written yesterday. Another poet was Ovid, who wrote the old tales of the gods, such as the story of King Midas, who received the "golden touch," the stealing of Proserpina by Pluto, the attempt of Daedalus and his son to make wings and fly, and many others. Livy was another of the famous authors of the day. He wrote a history of Rome, much of which is as interesting as any storybook.

These were the best of the Latin writers, and therefore the Golden Age of Augustus is also called the Augustan Age, of Latin literature. This reign might be called "Golden" for another and a greater reason. The Romans had carried on warfare with hardly a break for seven hundred years; but during the times of Augustus, there were three periods of peace, and it was during one of these that Jesus was born in the faraway province of Judea, in the little town of Bethlehem.

Unit Two: Arrival of the King, the Roman Empire

Theme: Incarnation: The Word Became Flesh

Fulfillment of the Prophecy

by Rev. Monsignor Edmund J. Goebel Ph. D.

When Augustus ordered that a census should be taken of all the people throughout the Roman Empire, he did not know how important his edict would be. An event was to take place in a far-off section of the empire which would be the most important event in all history.

Judea, the land of the Jews, was at this time under control of the Romans. King Herod, who came from a land south of Judea, ruled for the Romans in Jerusalem. Now the prophets had foretold that when a stranger became ruler of Jerusalem, the Jews could expect the Messiah. Pious Jews began to look for the Messiah, who was to be the Savior.

Augustus helped to fulfill some of the other prophesies about the birth of Christ. St. Joseph and the Blessed Virgin Mary were descended from King David. It was necessary for them to journey from their home in Nazareth to Bethlehem, which was the city of David, in order to be enrolled in the census. There, in a stable in which Joseph and Mary had sought refuge for the night, Jesus Christ, the Son of God, was born. All these details had been foretold by the prophet Isaiah.

The birth of Christ is the central point in all history. We date all previous events as so many years B.C., that is, Before Christ. All events after the birth of Christ are dated with the label A.D. This is an abbreviation for two Latin words, "Anno Domini," which mean "In the Year of Our Lord."

The coming of the Son of God into the world changed the lives of men. His teachings affected their ideas, their beliefs, and their actions.

The Divine Maternity of Mary

by James Joseph Baxter, selected and arranged by the Rev. Francis Spirago

The whole doctrine of Christianity depends on the truth of the Incarnation – that is, that in the single person of Jesus Christ, the divine and human natures were united. The value of all His words and works, of all His teachings and example, of His life and sufferings and death, depend on the fact that He, one person, was both God and man. And that is why no other doctrine has been so much insisted on and so much attacked. Even in the time of the apostles, some heretics taught that Christ was not God; others, that he was God but not man; others, that His body was only a body in appearance; others, that He took possession of His body after its birth, and left it before its death; others, that in Him there were two persons, etc.

"I don't see," said a Protestant to a Catholic friend, "why you Catholics make such a fuss over your devotion to the Virgin." "It is," was the reply, "because Mary, the Mother of God is the most fundamental dogma of our faith." And such, in truth, it is. Eve sought to make Adam equal to God; but to the new Eve, Mary, it fell to make man God Himself.

The Foundation of the Church

by the Sisters of Notre Dame

The divine head and founder of the Church is our Lord and Savior Jesus Christ. During thirty years of hidden life at Nazareth, followed by three years of teaching and miracles, and ending with His passion and death, Jesus gave us the example of a life of perfect virtue. During the three years of His public ministry, Jesus also taught us all the truths of salvation.

Many disciples followed Jesus as he preached throughout Israel and the surrounding regions. From among these Jesus chose twelve Apostles - **Peter**, **Andrew**, **James**, and his brother **John**, **Philip** and **Bartholomew**, **Thomas**, **Matthew**, **James of Alpheus**, **Thaddeus** who also called Jude, and his brother **Simon**, and **Judas Iscariot**, who betrayed Him. The Apostles were with Jesus throughout His public ministry and He gave them special teaching and training. He commanded them to bring His message of salvation to all nations and gave them the power to work miracles in His name to prove the truth of their teaching. He gave them His own divine authority, saying, "As the Father has sent me, so I send you" (John 20:21).

The Apostles were the first bishops, consecrated by Jesus Himself, and to provide unity after He had ascended into heaven, Jesus chose Peter to be their leader. St. Peter was the first Pope, shepherd, and teacher of the one flock of Christ. Jesus gave him the keys of the kingdom of Heaven and promised him infallibility, which means that the Pope cannot teach any error when he proclaims to all the faithful a doctrine of faith or morals.

These powers did not end with the twelve Apostles. They were to consecrate and appoint other bishops and priests, to whom they were to hand down all the teaching and authority given to them by Jesus. They received power to consecrate the Eucharist, to absolve sin, and to administer the other sacraments.

Jesus promised the Apostles that the Holy Spirit would come to them and teach them all truth and that He would remain with His Church forever.

All the truths taught by Jesus to His Apostles, and that the Apostles handed down to their successors to this day, constitute Christian Doctrine, the Catholic Faith.

The Four Marks of the Church. The Church founded by Christ is *One*, *Holy*, *Catholic*, and *Apostolic*.

One, because she has one founder and head, Jesus Christ, the Son of the one, true, living God, represented on earth by His Vicar the Pope, the successor of St. Peter. She teaches the one same faith, whole and entire, which Jesus gave to His Apostles. She administers the same sacraments He gave them the power to administer.

Holy, because her founder is God, the Holy One Himself; and because by following the teaching of Christ which the Church has passed down, men and women can enter into heaven and become saints.

Catholic, which means Universal, because Jesus said that His Apostles were to bring the Gospel message to all nations. He promised that the Church would last through all time to the end of the world and that the Holy Spirit would teach her all truth.

Apostolic, because Jesus taught His Apostles the truths which they have handed down to us; and because He gave the Apostles power to ordain other bishops and priests, and to hand them on to the orders and the mission they had received from Him. This unbroken chain of Apostolic succession will go on in the Church until the end of time.

History of the Church. Jesus told His apostles that when they carried the Gospel into the world, many people would not receive it. He said that persecutions would arise and that not all members of the Church would remain faithful to His teachings. He promised that the powers of evil would never overcome the Church and that, despite terrible struggles, God would always conquer and that His Church would be triumphant over all her enemies.

Church history is the story of the Apostles and their successors who have carried the Catholic Faith into the entire world. It is the story of the difficulties they have encountered, the people who have opposed the Church, others who have fallen away, and of how, despite it all, the Church remains victorious and continues to be the mother to multitudes of saints.

The study of Church history shows again and again how the words of Jesus have been proved true: "The Gates of Hell shall not prevail against My Church,"(Matthew 16:18) and how much reason we have to say, "the truth abides in us and will be with us forever" (2 John 1:2).

The Sermon on the Mount

By Mary E. Doyle. Story by Mother Mary Loyola

One day a vast multitude follows our Blessed Lord up a mountainside. They come trooping after Him, men, women, and children; their hopes, their business, all the cares of this life, by common consent left behind. Now He has stopped and turned around, facing them. He waits long and patiently as they come toiling up, guiding them with His hand to go here and there where they may hear Him best.

It is His first great Sermon that He is going to preach, this Sermon on the Mount, and it is not only for the numbers beyond all reckoning gathered together here but for all that shall come into this world and have to be taught what they must do to save their souls. Therefore, He would speak so solemnly and from such a lofty place. He sits down, and the Twelve come and stand around Him, or sit on the ground at His feet. The people press round as close as they can, and when all are seated and quiet. He begins to speak.

What will the text of this great Preacher be? What is the thought uppermost in His mind and heart? This – to teach us what we must do to be happy. He knows that we are made for happiness and that we long to be happy. But He knows, too, that very many try to find happiness in things that will not satisfy them, in the riches, pleasures, and honors of this world which can never content our hearts. And so, He tells us at the beginning of His Sermon on the Mount who are truly blessed or happy.

"Blessed are the poor in spirit, for theirs is the kingdom of Heaven.

"Blessed are the meek, for they shall possess the land.

"Blessed are they that mourn, for they shall be comforted.

"Blessed are they that hunger and thirst after jus tice, for they shall have their fill.

"Blessed are the merciful, for they shall obtain mercy.

"Blessed are the clean of heart, for they shall see God.

"Blessed are the peacemakers, for they shall be called the children of God.

"Blessed are they that suffer persecution for jus tice' sake, for theirs is the kingdom of Heaven.

"Blessed the sufferers for whom Heaven is waiting!"

The poor in spirit are those who, having little of the good things of this life, are content with what God has given them, and do not envy those who are better off. Those, too, who having a sufficiency or an abundance of the pleasant things of this world, do not let their hearts get too fond of them, are ready to give them up if God should take them away, and are generous in sharing them with those in need. To the poor, such as these, our Lord promises all the riches of Heaven by and by.

The meek are those who have gained mastery over anger and revengeful thoughts. They possess as conquerors three lands - the land of their own soul, which they control as lords and masters, the Land of Heaven, where nothing will trouble them any more, and, strange to say, that very land in which they seemed to be over come. For in the little difficulties and differences in daily life, it is those that yield who are really victors. How many conquests has meekness made!

The mourners are those who all their lives long have a quiet, loving sorrow for their sins – not as though they were unforgiven, but just because they are forgiven because they have offended Him who forgives so readily and so often. Those, too, are blessed mourners who remember when sorrow comes that He who loves them only permits it for their good and that in a very little while He will wipe away all tears from their eyes, and they shall be comforted, "nor mourning, nor crying, nor sorrow shall be any more."

Who hunger and thirst after justice. The soul, like the body, has its hunger and thirst. Our Lord says those are blessed who take care to feed it with those things which keep it alive in the grace of God, with prayer, and instruction, and the Sacraments. Blessed are those who hunger after this spiritual food, who are always trying to get more and more of God's grace, who go hungry to prayer, Confession, and Communion. Almighty God says, "Open thy mouth and I will fill it." And our Blessed Lady sings in her canticle, "He has fed the hungry with good things."

It was because all the saints hungered like this that so much was given them.

The merciful. There is nothing our Lord tells us so often and so plainly as this – that to obtain mercy from God we must ourselves be merciful. If we wish Him to judge us kindly and to forgive our many faults, we must be forgiving and kind. "Be merciful," He says, "as your Heavenly Father is merciful." He tells us that at the Last Day He will say "Come" to those who have been merciful to others for His sake, and "Depart from Me" to those who have been unmerciful to the poor and needy, and therefore to Him. For what we do to His least brethren He counts as done to Himself. If then, we want to hear His sweet invitation on that dreadful Day, we know how to secure it –"Blessed are the merciful, for they shall obtain mercy.""

The clean of heart. The reward and the joy of the next life are to see God. There are many joys in Heaven – freedom from pain and care, the delights of the glorified body, the society of the Angels and Saints, reunion with those we loved on earth. But all these are as nothing compared with the Vision of God. It is this that makes Heaven what it is. Without this, all the rest would not satisfy us. But to see the All-Holy God we must be holy. In Heaven, all are clothed with white robes, and the nearer they approach the Great White Throne, the more dazzlingly white is the raiment. We must be getting ready to join that spotless throng. How? By taking as many pains to keep our soul free from stain as we do to prevent soiling our dress when we go along a miry road; by shunning with care all mortal sin and deliberate venial sin; by being careful in our examination of conscience, and often cleansing our soul in the Sacrament of Penance, and by frequent acts of contrition. If we do this we shall be among the clean of heart, and one day we shall see God.

The peacemakers. "Some there are who are neither at peace with themselves nor suffer others to be at peace. And some there are who keep themselves in peace and study to restore peace to others." Gladness goes with these peacemakers; they turn aside little words and jokes that would give pain, and come among us like our Blessed Lord, whose favorite word of greeting was, "Peace be to you." They are so like their Father who is in Heaven that they deserve to be called in a special way His children.

The persecuted. If our Lord had not told us these are blessed, should we ever have guessed it? To be persecuted seems such a terrible thing, and so indeed it is unless we can bring ourselves to think more of Him for whose sake we suffer than of the suffering itself. Perhaps we may have known the quiet happiness of being by the side of one we loved who was in pain. The thought that our presence and our sympathy soothed that dear one was greater joy than any pleasure to be found elsewhere. Something like this is the gladness those have even now who for our Lord's sake are hated and persecuted. They know that if they are like Him in His suffering, they will be like Him one day in His glory. Are they not blessed then?

And now let us stop awhile to look at our dear Master and His hearers. The Twelve are listening with reverent and fixed attention, their eyes riveted on His blessed face. The people gaze at Him in amazement and delight. They have been taught to hate their enemies, to seek revenge, to think that poverty and suffering are the signs of God's anger, that an abundance of corn and wine and cattle are the rewards for which a good man must hope.

Their beatitudes would have been, "Blessed are the rich and the successful, those that laugh and are held in honor by men." How unlike these to the blessed ones of Jesus of Nazareth! His way to happiness was a hard way, but they knew as they looked up into His face that it was the right way. And they felt that He could not only teach but help them. Had they known the story of His life as we do, they would have seen that He had first practiced all He taught. He was so poor that He had not where to lay His head. He was meek and humble of heart, the Man of sorrows, the great Peacemaker.

After the Sermon our Lord comes down from the Mount, conversing familiarly with His disciples, His simple congregation flocking after Him, trying to get near Him, all so refreshed by His company and His words. Hear them talking of Him among themselves, saying, "We never heard the like."

Oh, if we had seen our Blessed Lord as these happy people saw Him, if we had followed Him about with the crowd, had sat at His feet as He taught, and watched Him as He laid His hands on the eyes of the blind and the sores of the poor lepers - how we should have loved Him!

Unit Three: Spread of the Kingdom, Age of the Apostles

THEME: SHARING THE FAITH

THE BEGINNING OF THE CHURCH

by Rev. Monsignor Edmund J. Goebel Ph. D.

The history of the Church began with the first Pentecost. Ten days after the Ascension of Our Lord, the Holy Ghost descended upon the apostles. They were filled with great courage and began at once to preach to the people of Jerusalem. They won three thousand converts the first day.

The apostles at first preached only to the Jews in Judea and the neighboring countries. But they remembered that Christ had told them to "go and teach all nations." They gradually left Jerusalem and journeyed throughout the Roman Empire. From the very earliest days, the religion of Christ was Catholic, which means "universal."

SPREAD OF THE FAITH IN JERUSALEM

by the Sisters of Notre Dame

Forty days after He rose from the dead, Jesus ascended into Heaven. As the Apostles stood on Mount Olivet, two angels in shining garments came and spoke to them, saying, "Men of Galilee, why do you stand looking up toward heaven? This Jesus, who has been taken up from you into heaven, will come in the same way as you saw him go into heaven" (Acts 1:11). Reassured, the Apostles went back to Jerusalem, and gathered in the Upper Room where they had celebrated the Last Supper with Jesus and witnessed the institution of the Holy Eucharist. Together with the Blessed Mother, they waited there for the coming of the Holy Spirit.

Gathered in the upper room, a hundred and twenty persons represented the Church, which was to spread over the whole earth like a mighty tree growing from a tiny mustard seed. The eleven Apostles were there as the pastors and teachers of the faithful, but the place of Judas was still vacant. Peter proposed that the assembly should choose a twelfth Apostle. Barsabas and Matthias were named equally worthy, and, after prayer, lots were cast, with the result that Matthias was added to the eleven Apostles (Acts 1:1-26).

Ten days after the Ascension, while our Lady and the Apostles and disciples were gathered in prayer, there was a noise as of a mighty wind coming, which filled the whole house, and the Holy Spirit descended upon each person in the form of tongues of fire (Acts 2: 1-4). At once they were all filled with the Spirit of God, and going out into the city, they began to preach to the people

It was Pentecost, one of the three great festivals for which Jews from all over the world came to Jerusalem to worship in the Temple. Crowds gathered around the Apostles, who spoke in their own language, but each person heard what the Apostles said in their own native language. The people were amazed, and because of this miracle, they believed that God truly was with the Apostles. Three thousand people were baptized that day and Pentecost is still celebrated as the birthday of the Church (Acts 2:5-41).

Many people in Jerusalem heard about the miracle of Pentecost and their hearts and minds were opened to hear the message of the Apostles. A few days after Pentecost, Peter and John went to the Temple, and there they healed a man who had been crippled since birth. After this new miracle, many more people came to listen to the Apostles. Peter preached to them and five thousand people were baptized that day (Act 3:4).

Until this point, no one had opposed the Apostles or their message. But as more people came to the Apostles to be baptized, the Jewish priests became angry and jealous of their influence and powerful works. They had Peter and John thrown into prison and then brought them before the Sanhedrin (the Jewish council for settling religious affairs). There the Apostles were forbidden to teach in the name of Jesus Christ. Peter and John answered by declaring that they must obey God, rather than men. The Jewish leaders were afraid of the popularity of the Apostles and couldn't find a reason to keep them imprisoned, so they had to let them go. The Apostles immediately resumed their preaching with even greater enthusiasm.

Many of the first Christians lived their faith so devotedly that they inspired everyone around them, and their example influenced both Jews and Gentiles even more than the miracles performed by the Apostles. The newly baptized listened attentively to the Word of God and were faithful in prayer, and in the Breaking of Bread, as the Eucharist was then called. They were known for their great virtue, especially their piety and charity to all around them. They lived in community and shared their resources; the rich sold their belongings and "they laid it at the Apostles' feet, and it was distributed to each as any had need" (Acts 4:35).

The Apostles continued to work many miracles. The sick were brought out into the streets so that, when Peter's shadow passed over them, they were cured. Every day more people were baptized and brought into the Church. The chief priests and Sadducees were still looking for a way to stop the Apostles and they had all twelve thrown into prison. During the night, an angel came and set them free, and sent them to preach in the Temple. They were arrested again and brought before the Sanhedrin where they boldly declared that they would never cease preaching in the name of Jesus. The leaders were furious and wanted to have them put to death. But Gamaliel, one of the doctors of the law, said, "keep away from these men and let them alone; because if this plan or this undertaking is of human origin, it will fail; but if it is of God, you will not be able to overthrow them – in that case, you may even be found fighting against God!" (Acts 5:38-39). And so the Sanhedrin had the Apostles scourged and then released, again commanding them to stop preaching in the name of Jesus. The Apostles left, praising God for being allowed to suffer for His sake, and continued to teach both in private and in the Temple.

The number of Christians increased so much that the Apostles were no longer able to attend to all their needs. And so, they chose seven holy men to help them. These men were called deacons and were responsible for looking after the poor and distributing alms.

St. Stephen was one of these deacons and his passion for the faith brought about many new conversions. Because of his zeal, he was brought before the Jewish High Priest and accused of blasphemy. Stephen boldly defended the truth, but when he said he saw the heavens opened above him, and Jesus standing at the right hand of God, they covered up their ears and dragged him outside the city and stoned him to death. Just before he died, Stephen prayed, "Lord, do not hold this sin against them" (Acts 7:60). St. Stephen was the first martyr, and his fearless witness lead to even more conversions.

Saul of Tarsus, who later became the great Apostle St. Paul, was not only present at the stoning of St. Stephen but helped by holding the coats of the men who killed him. Before his conversion to Christianity, he persecuted the Church and had many men and women thrown into prison for their faith.

The Labors of St. Peter

Adapted from the work of Rev. Monsignor Edmund J. Goebel Ph. D. and the Sisters of Notre Dame

It was clear as soon as Christ began to select His apostles that St. Peter was to be their leader. In fact, Jesus changed his name from Simon to Peter, a word that means "rock." Christ said to him, "You are Peter (the rock) and upon this rock, I will build My Church."

After the Ascension of our Lord, it was St. Peter who proposed the election of St. Matthias; it was he who delivered the first public sermon after the coming of the Holy Spirit; he who worked the first miracle by curing the lame man before the Beautiful Gate. It was St. Peter, again, who answered the Sanhedrin, and who received the first Gentile convert, Cornelius, into the church. He presided at the Council of Jerusalem and was the first to make a visitation of the Churches founded by the other Apostles. We see him everywhere acting as the shepherd of the flock of Christ.

St. Peter's first work was the foundation of the Church in Jerusalem and the neighboring provinces of Judea. He and St. John were twice cast into prison by the Jewish leaders. The second time, they were released by an angel, but the persecution continued, and they were obliged to leave Jerusalem. St. Peter's mission was principally to the Jews, whom he evangelized throughout Syria, though he did not shut out the Gentiles from his sermons. After fixing his See at Antioch, St. Peter, with St. Mark as his companion and evangelist, preached throughout Pontus, Cappadocia, Galatia, and Bithynia.

After preaching in many cities of the East, Peter went to the most important city in the world – Rome, the capital of the Roman Empire and of the pagan world. Peter now made it the capital of the new Church of Christ. He was the Bishop of Rome. Since his time, the Bishops of Rome have been the heads of the Church. They have the title of "Pope." This word means "father." The Pope serves as a loving father for the whole Church. We often call the Pope "the Holy Father."

Peter continued to govern the Church for twenty-five years, although he did not always live in Rome. When the persecution under Nero broke out, it is said that the faithful implored St. Peter to leave Rome. The legend goes on to say that he did so, but on his way, he had a vision of our Lord bearing His Cross as though going to be crucified again. St. Peter remembered our Lord's prophecy, "When you were young, you fastened your own belt and walked where you would; but when you are old, you will stretch out your hands, and another will fasten your belt for you and carry you where you do not wish to go" (John 21:18), and understood that it was now to be fulfilled. He returned to the city, where he was cast into prison with St. Paul. They converted St. Processus and St. Martinian, captains of the guard, and forty-seven others. After eight months' imprisonment, St. Peter was martyred, near Nero's palace on the Vatican Hill. He was crucified, like Christ; but he asked to be crucified upside down, as he did not feel worthy to die in the same manner as Christ. This was about 67 A.D, and he was buried near the same spot over which the Church of St. Peter now stands.

The Work of St. Paul

Adapted from the work of Rev. Monsignor Edmund J. Goebel Ph. D. and the Sisters of Notre Dame

Foremost among the early persecutors of the Church was a young Pharisee called Saul of Tarsus. He hated the Christians, as the followers of Christ were called, and was present at the death of St. Stephen, the first martyr. But God called him to be a great apostle and would make him the greatest preacher of the early Church.

Having procured letters authorizing his persecutions, Saul was on his way to Damascus, when suddenly a bright light appearing in the heavens struck him and his company to the earth. At the same time a voice was heard saying, "Saul, Saul, why do you persecute me?" And to Saul's question, "Who are you, Lord?" it replied, "I am Jesus of Nazareth, Whom you are persecuting." Then Saul cried out, "Lord, what will you have me do?" to which the answer came, "Arise, go into the city, and there it shall be told to you what you must do." Though struck blind, he obeyed and spent three days in fasting and prayer. In the meantime, God sent a vision to Ananias, a disciple in Damascus, and told him to go to Saul and cure his blindness. As soon as Ananias had laid his hands on him, the scales fell from the eyes of Saul, who, rising up, was instructed and baptized.

After his baptism, he became known as Paul. He very soon began to preach the word of God in the synagogues, to the astonishment of all who heard him and who knew how bitterly he had persecuted the Christian but a short time before. This change in St. Paul and the number of converts he made angered the Jewish leaders against him so that he was obliged to leave Damascus for Jerusalem. There he was received into the number of the Apostles. However, the leaders of the Jews continued to persecute him, so that he left Jerusalem and went to Caesarea and Tarsus, and St. Barnabas brought him afterward to Antioch.

St. Paul earned the title "Apostle of the Gentiles." This means that he devoted himself to preaching the gospel of Christ to the people who were not Jews. He was a man of great energy and was filled with a great love for God. He stirred the converts to great enthusiasm for the teachings of Christ. He founded churches in many cities of the Roman Empire. He wrote numerous letters to these churches while he journeyed throughout the Mediterranean area. Fourteen of these have come down to us and are known as the Epistles, which are read daily in the Mass. St. Peter, St. James, and St. John also wrote Epistles.

St. Paul's travels can be divided into three great missions. On his first mission, he was accompanied by St. Barnabas. They preached in Cyprus and the south of Asia Minor, returning to Antioch, and then Jerusalem for the Council held there in A.D. 50.

About the year A.D. 52, St. Paul started with Silas and preached the Gospel in Syria and nearly all the countries in Asia Minor. At Lystra, he took St. Timothy as his disciple, and at Troas, he was joined by St. Luke, who became his chronicler and evangelist. St. Paul afterward crossed to Macedonia but was driven from Thessalonica by persecution. At Athens, he preached in the Areopagus the knowledge of the "Unknown God," adored by the Greeks. After visiting Corinth, St. Paul returned to Antioch (A.D. 54) by Ephesus, Caesarea, and Jerusalem.

The third mission was undertaken by St. Paul to revisit the Churches he had founded in Asia Minor. Driven out of Ephesus, he continued his work in Macedonia and Achaia, from which he returned to Jerusalem.

There he was immediately arrested, but he claimed his rights as a Roman citizen, and so was sent to Rome to be judged in A.D. 61. Here he was kept a captive for two years, though allowed to preach freely. Some say that St. Paul after he was set at liberty, visited Spain, and preached in the churches of Italy. It is certain that he was in Rome in A.D. 65, for he was then arrested and thrown into prison by Nero. St. Paul was martyred on the same day as St. Peter. He was beheaded, for, as a Roman citizen, he could not be crucified. His martyrdom took place outside Rome, where the church of the Three Fountains now stands.

The Apostles Preach to the Nations

by the Sisters of Notre Dame

The Apostles went far and wide, preaching the Faith to Jew and Gentile.

Asia. All the Apostles, except St. Peter and St. Paul, St. Andrew and St. Simon, remained in Asia. Asia Minor, Arabia, Syria, Parthia, Judea – that is, all the important countries of the East – were visited by them. St. Thomas preached in Parthia, India, Media, and Persia.

Africa. It is not known who founded the Church in Africa, but it is certain that St. Mark the Evangelist was the first Bishop of the magnificent city of Alexandria in Egypt. The faith spread rapidly, and soon all the North of Africa was filled with Christians. Later, during the years of the persecutions, many brave African martyrs suffered for their religion. Not two hundred years after the first preaching, there were seventy or eighty bishops in the land.

Europe. It was to St. Peter and St. Paul that Rome owed the faith. St. Paul preached in that part of Europe we now call the Balkan Peninsula and in Greece.

South Russia was evangelized by St. Andrew. The Spaniards claim St. James the Greater as their first Apostle, but it is not quite certain that this is true. All that is known is that the Church in Spain is one of the oldest in Europe. St. James is the patron of the country, and his shrine at Compostela is a famous place of pilgrimage.

Old traditions tell us that some years after the Ascension of our Divine Lord, when the Christians dispersed on account of the persecution in Palestine, Lazarus and his sisters, Martha and Mary Magdalen, went to the South of France, that Lazarus became first Bishop of Marseilles, and that St. Mary Magdalen lived and died in a cavern near the city. Other disciples of the Lord preached in France, and some say that St. Luke, and St. Pauls' convert, St. Dionysius and Areopagite, were among them.

But some of these brave missionaries went further still. Old stories tell us that St. Peter came to Britain, but they probably meant that the faith of St. Peter was brought to our forefathers. St. Joseph of Arimathea is also supposed to have preached to the Britons. What is quite certain is that Britain was very early converted to the faith.

Besides these first teachers, there were many others who continued their work of converting the nations. The faith spread so fast that St. Paul says it was spoken of in the whole world (Romans 1:8). Besides this, many writers, both Christian and pagan, speak of the multitudes of Christians who were to be found everywhere. We can see how true this was when we come to read the story of the martyrs, who belonged to every nation, and who died in thousands for the faith. When St. Ignatius of Antioch was sent to Rome to be put to death, he was greeted at every place where he stopped by troops of Christians, headed by their bishops and priests. In the Catacombs of Rome, there are innumerable tombs, all of Christians buried during the first four centuries.

Nero

by Eva March Tappan, Ph. D.

Nero became emperor at the age of seventeen. Despite the wickedness of his mother, Agrippina, he had been carefully trained, for the writer Seneca had been his teacher. Seneca tried his best to make him kind and good. "Life is short, therefore live peaceably with all men," he said. "Live so that all will love you, and then they will mourn for you when you die." For a few years, Nero obeyed him. This did not please Agrippina, and she threatened to induce the soldiers to make Nero's half-brother emperor. But Nero's nature was brutal and cruel, and he slew both the half-brother and his mother. When he had been reigning ten years, a fire broke out in Rome which swept away the greater part of the city. Nero did all that he could to help the people who had lost everything. He put up buildings for them, threw open his gardens that they might have a refuge, and ordered grain to be sold at an extremely low price. Nevertheless, it was said that he had kindled the fire and had played on his lyre and sung while it was burning. Whether this was true or not, Nero was frightened and looked about him for someone to blame.

The religion of Christ had been preached in Rome, and there were many Christians in the city. The Romans could not understand a worship without images or temples, and they looked upon the followers of Jesus as heathen. The Christians believed it wrong to join in the worship of the gods and the Roman festivals in their honor, and therefore the Romans called them, "Men who hate their fellow men." It had become a custom to worship the emperor as a god and to burn incense before his statue. Christians could not take part in this, and therefore the Romans said they were not loyal. If any misfortune came upon the state, the Christians were often given the blame, for it was said that they neglected what was due to the gods. Nero laid the burning of the city on them and put large numbers of them to death. Some he crucified; some he turned over to wild beasts; others he burned at the stake so that even the cruel Romans pitied them.

After the fire, the city was rebuilt. Money and treasures and statues of the gods were taken from the temples or wherever they could be found, whether in the provinces or in Italy itself and brought to Rome to beautify the new city. Nero built himself a magnificent house with a long portico. Its vestibule was lofty enough to house a statue of the emperor one hundred and twenty feet high. His banqueting room had pipes by which perfumes might be showered over the guests, and the ceiling was so curiously made that at a touch, flowers were scattered among them. Everything was encrusted with gems and mother of pearl. Around the house stretched vineyards and woods and pools so beautifully laid out and giving such extensive views that the historian Tacitus declared they were more wonderful than the buildings. Nero called his dwelling his Golden House. When it was finished, he boasted that at last, he had a home that was fit for a man to live in.

With Nero's extravagance grew his cruelty, and he grew worse and worse – if a man as bad as he could grow any worse. Plots were formed against him, and he put his own tutor,

Seneca, to death on the charge of having joined in one of them. The armies in the provinces revolted, the praetorian guard refused to protect him, and finally, the senate gave its allegiance to a rival ruler, decreeing that Nero should be executed. The cruel emperor fled in fear and took his own life.

Pompeii and Roman Life

by the Franciscan Sisters of Perpetual Adoration

Daily Life of the Romans. We have already learned something of the public buildings, aqueducts, and roads which the Romans built wherever their rule was established. We have also seen something of their public games and the triumphal processions with which they honored their victorious generals. Let us now try to learn what we can of the ordinary life of the citizens - their houses, and shops, and schools, and the training which the boys received.

The roads, bridges, and walls which the Romans built can now be traced over a great part of Europe; and at Rome, a few ruined structures still stand, to give us an idea of the grandeur of the ancient city. Moreover, by a strange chance, a whole city has been preserved for us in Italy - that of Pompeii - very much as it was toward the close of the first century after Christ. From this, we can gain a very good idea of the life of the people in a Roman city eighteen hundred years ago.

Eruption of Mount Vesuvius. Overlooking the Bay of Naples, on the coast of Italy south of Rome, is Mount Vesuvius. Today it is one of the most active volcanoes of the world; but until the first century after Christ, the Romans supposed that its fires were extinguished, and cities were built at its very foot. In the year A.D. 79, the fires of Vesuvius burst forth again, after their long quiet, and wrought fearful destruction. When the eruption had ceased, it was found that a thick layer of ashes and mud was spread over the surrounding country. As the years went by, other eruptions came and added to the thickness of this covering. Then the top layer was gradually changed to a fine loam, and vegetation sprang up and covered all that lay beneath.

How Pompeii Was Uncovered. For sixteen hundred years the buried towns about Mount Vesuvius remained lost to sight. Then a well, deeper than usual, happened to be dug above one of them, and ancient statues were unearthed, and bits of sculptured marble. Scholars then remembered the story of the buried cities and began the work of uncovering them. From that time to this, the work has gone slowly forward. Several museums are now filled with the pictures, statues, and household furniture which have been taken from beneath the ashes of Vesuvius.

The removal of the earth over the town of Pompeii has shown that the city had a forum, surrounded by temples and law courts, and other public buildings; and this, as at Rome, was the most splendid part of the city. It is not for the public buildings, however, that we care most; for ancient temples, and other public buildings, as well preserved as these, may be found in other places. But the glimpse which we get here into the private houses of the town, and into the life of the people in the streets and shops, we can get nowhere else. It is this which makes our interest in Pompeii so great.

Streets of Pompeii. The first thing that strikes the traveler is the narrowness of the streets. In some of the broadest of these, two chariots could scarcely have passed one another. The pavements are formed of large pieces of stone, joined together with great care, and the ruts worn by the passing wheels can still be seen in some of them. The houses along these cramped streets were built - as are the houses in many warm countries today - about one or more inner courtyards, upon which most of the rooms opened. Often the street side was occupied by shops which were rented out by the owner, and which had no connection with the life of the house itself.

Interior of a House. Upon entering such a dwelling we are likely to find, on the floor of the entry, the Latin word for "Welcome" formed of bits of stone in mosaic work. Crossing this, we enter the large public reception hall. Here the master of the house received the visitors who came to see him. If they came from a distance they might be lodged overnight in the small rooms which open off from the hall on either side. The walls of the large room are decorated with paintings and drawings, and here and there are pedestals where statues once stood. The floor, all through the lower story of the house, is formed of blocks of marble or other stone, and usually, these are selected of different colors and are arranged to form a pattern of some sort.

In the center of the floor of the main room is a square basin, several feet deep, which caught the rain from an opening in the roof directly above. This opening in the roof also served to let out the smoke and fumes from the fires, for none of the houses had chimneys, and the fireplaces were only metal pots or pans in which charcoal might be burned.

Leaving the public hall, the visitor comes through another passage to the private part of the house, where the women and children lived, and where no guest might enter without a special invitation from the master. Here is another court, with rows of slender, graceful columns about it. Opening from this are small, low bedrooms, which we should think very uncomfortable; and here, too, is the dining room, where the master of the house entertained his friends at dinner. Above this court, also, there was an opening in the roof, with a basin below to catch the water; and about the basin, and among the columns, there perhaps grew beds of blooming flowers and clumps of evergreens.

Only the ground floor remains of most of the houses of Pompeii, but there must have been a second story to all of the better houses, and sometimes even a third. The upper part of the house was for the use of the slaves and dependents of the family, and could not have been so well arranged, or so beautiful, as the lower floor.

Roman Furniture. When these houses were first uncovered, many pieces of furniture remained in them; but the Roman rooms must have been too bare for our ideas of comfort. We should have found only a few chairs, some small tables, three couches in the dining room, some beds or couches in the bedrooms and here and there high stands for their strange oil lamps. The form of these articles, however, was often most graceful; and at times they were made of rich material and with great skill of workmanship. Besides such larger pieces of furniture, many smaller articles have been found among them being cooking vessels, vases, cups and fine glasses, combs, hairpins, polished metal mirrors, and pieces of jewelry.

The Shops of Pompeii. The shops of Pompeii are as interesting as the private houses. Most of these are only small rooms in the front of the houses and are entirely open toward the street. Usually, each shop displayed a sign; the milk store, a wooden goat (for it was goat's milk that was sold), and the wine shop a large jar. A snake before another shop shows that it was a drug store, and a row of hams is the sign of an eating house. A washing and dyeing shop has also been found, for the care of woolen garments, which were almost the only kind worn. Pictures on the walls of this shop show men standing in stone tubs and washing the garments by stamping on them with their bare feet.

Writings on the Walls. In at least one way the people of Pompeii were very much like boys of our own time. They loved to write and draw on the walls of the houses of the town. Here we find verses from the poets, and there letters of the Greek alphabet, written by boys too small to reach high up on the walls. In many places advertisements are scratched in the plastering, some of them announcing gladiatorial fights and performances in the theater. Occasionally we find comic pictures such as the one in which a gladiator is seen coming down the steps of the amphitheater, with a palm leaf of victory in his right hand. Such drawings and inscriptions are often found on the ancient buildings of Rome also. They must have been the work of the common people and the young boys, for the writers are usually very uncertain in their grammar and spelling.

How Caligula and Claudius Conquered Britain

by Henrietta E. Marshall

After the second coming of Julius Caesar, years passed during which the Romans left the Britons in peace. But they had by no means forgotten about the little green island in the blue sea.

Julius Caesar had been dead many years when a Roman emperor called Caligula said he would go to Britain and thoroughly conquer the island. He did not mean to land and fight in one small part of it as Julius Caesar had done. He meant to march over the island, north, south, east, and west, and bring it all under the power of Rome. That is what he said he was going to do. What he really did was something quite different.

He gathered a great army and marched from Italy right through France till be reached the coast. There news came to him that Guilderius, the king of Britain, had heard of his coming and had also gathered his soldiers together.

Caligula must have been afraid when he heard that the brave Britons were ready to fight him, for this is how he conquered Britain.

He drew his soldiers up in battle array upon the shore. Then he himself went into his galley and told his sailors to row him out to sea. After they had rowed him a short way, he told them to return. When he had landed again, he climbed into a high seat, which he had built on the sands. Then he sounded a trumpet and ordered his soldiers to advance as if to battle.

But there was no enemy there. In front of the soldiers, there was nothing, but the blue sea and the sandy shore covered with shells. They could not fight against the waves and the sand, and the brave Britons, whom they had come to fight, were far away on the other side of the water and quite out of reach. So, the soldiers stood and wondered what to do. Then Caligula ordered them to kneel upon the sand and gather as many shells as they could.

The first thing a Roman was taught, was to obey. So now the soldiers did as their general commanded and gathered the cockle shells which lay around in hundreds. It must have been a curious sight to see all these strong soldiers, armed with sword, shield, and helmet, picking up shells upon the seashore.

When they had gathered a great quantity, Caligula made a speech. He thanked the soldiers as if they had done him some great service. He told them that now he had conquered the ocean and the islands in it and that these shells were the spoils of war. He praised the soldiers for their bravery and said that the shells should be placed in the temples of Rome in remembrance of it. Then he rewarded them richly and they marched home again.

That was how Caligula conquered Britain.

After the death of Caligula, another Roman called Claudius tried to conquer Britain. He sent generals and came himself, but he could not thoroughly subdue the Britons. A few chiefs indeed declared themselves beaten, but others would not. They would rather die than be slaves of Rome, they said.

Among those who would not yield was a brave man called Caratacus. A great many of the Britons joined him and fought under his orders. Caratacus and his men fought well and bravely, but in the end, the Romans defeated them.

After many battles, Caratacus chose for his camp a place on the top of a hill on the borders of Shropshire, Cheshire, and Lancashire. There he made a very strong fortress surrounded by three walls and a deep ditch. The walls were so well built that after all these long years they can still be seen quite plainly today.

When the Roman soldiers came to the foot of the hill, Caratacus prepared for battle. He called his soldiers together and made a speech to them. "Show yourselves to be men! he said." "Today is either the beginning of Liberty or eternal bondage. Remember how your forefathers fought against Julius Caesar, and fight now for your homes, as they did for theirs."

Then all the Britons called out, "We will die for our country." The noise of their shouts was carried by the wind to the camp of the Romans. It sounded to them as if the Britons were rejoicing. The Romans feared Caratacus. They knew how brave he and his men were. They knew that it would be very difficult to take his strong fortress. Yet they felt quite sure of taking it in the end, and they wondered what cause the Britons had for rejoicing.

And it happened as the Romans expected. After fierce fighting and great slaughter on both sides, the camp was taken. Caratacus, his wife and daughter, and all his brothers were made prisoners and led in chains to Rome, and there was great sorrow in Britain.

Whenever a Roman emperor returned from battle and victory, he used to have what was called a Triumph. Everyone in Rome had a holiday; the streets were gay with flowers and green wreaths. The conqueror, dressed in beautiful robes and wearing a crown of bay leaves, rode through the streets. He was followed by his soldiers, servants, and friends. Then came a long train of the captives he had made during the war, with the armor, weapons, jewels, and other riches he had taken from the conquered people.

After the war with Britain was over Claudius had a Triumph. The fame of Caratacus had already reached Rome, and when it became known that he had been taken prisoner and would walk in the Triumph there was great excitement. The people crowded into the streets eager to see this brave warrior. And although in chains, he looked so proud and noble that many even of the Romans were sorry for him.

When he was brought before the Emperor and Empress, Claudius and Agrippina, he did not behave like a slave or a captive, but like the freeborn king and Briton he was.

"I am as nobly born as you," he said proudly to Claudius. "I had men and horses, lands, and great riches. Is it a wonder that I wished to keep them? You fight to gain possession of the whole world and make all men your slaves, but I fought for my own land and for freedom. Kill me now and people will think little of you, but if you grant me my life, all men will know that you are not only powerful but merciful."

Instead of being angry, Claudius was pleased with the proud words of Caratacus. He was so pleased that he set him at liberty with his wife and all his family. But whether Caratacus ever returned to his dear country, or whether he died in that far-off land, we do not know. We do not hear anything more about him.

The Warrior Queen

by Henrietta E. Marshall

Although the Britons had lost their great general Caratacus, still they would not yield to the Roman tyrants.

Soon another brave leader arose. This leader was a woman. Her name was Boudicca, and she was a queen. She ruled over that part of the country which is now called Norfolk and Suffolk.

The Romans wanted to take away the freedom of Britain and make the island into a Roman province. They also wanted to get all the money and possessions which belonged to the Britons for themselves.

The husband of Boudicca knew how greedy the Romans were, and when he was about to die, he became very sad. He was afraid that the Roman Emperor would rob his wife and daughters of all their money when he was no longer there to take care of them. So, to prevent this, he made the Emperor a present of half of his money and lands and gave the other half to his wife and children. Then he died happy, thinking that his dear ones would be left in peace.

But the Romans were not pleased with only half of the dead king's wealth. They wanted it all. So, they came and took it by force. Boudicca was a very brave woman. She was not afraid of the Romans, and she tried to make them give back what they had stolen from her.

Then these cruel, wicked men laughed at her. And because she was a woman and had, they thought, no one to protect her, they beat her with rods and were rude to her daughters.

But although the Romans were clever, they sometimes did stupid things. They thought very little of their own women, and they did not understand that many of the women of Britain were as brave and as wise as the men, and quite as difficult to conquer.

After Boudicca had been so cruelly and unjustly treated, she burned with anger against the Romans. Her heart was full only of thoughts of revenge. She called her people together, and, standing on a mound of earth, so that they could see and hear her, she made a speech to them. She told them first how shamefully the Romans had behaved to her, their Queen. Then, like Caratacus, she reminded them how their forefathers had fought against Julius Caesar and had driven the Romans away for a time at least.

"Is it not better to be poor and free than to have great wealth and be slaves?" she asked. "And the Romans take not only our freedom but our wealth. They want to make us both slaves and beggars. Let us rise. O brothers and sisters let us rise and drive these robbers out of our land! Let us kill them every one! Let us teach them that they are no better than hares and foxes, and no match for greyhounds! We will fight, and if we cannot conquer, then let us die yes, every one of us die, rather than submit."

Queen Boudicca looked so beautiful and fierce as she stood there, with her eyes flashing, and her hair blowing round her in the wind, that the hearts of her people were filled with love for her, and anger against the Romans. As she spoke, fierce desires for revenge grew in them. They had hated their Roman conquerors before, now the hatred became a madness.

When Boudicca had finished speaking, a cry of rage rose from the Britons. They beat upon their shields with their swords and swore to avenge their Queen, to fight and die for her and for their country.

Then Boudicca, leaning with one hand upon her spear and lifting the other to heaven prayed. She prayed to the goddess of war, and her prayer was as fierce as her speech, for she had never heard of a God who taught men to forgive their enemies.

As she stood there praying, Boudicca looked more beautiful than ever. Her proud head was thrown back and the sun shone upon her lovely hair and upon the golden band which bound her forehead. Her dark cloak, slipping from her shoulders, showed the splendid robe she wore beneath, and the thick and heavy chain of gold around her neck. At her feet knelt her daughters, sobbing with hope and fear. It was a grand and awful moment, and deep silence fell upon the warriors as they listened to the solemn words.

Then, with wild cries, they marched forward to battle, forgetful of everything but revenge.

The battles which followed were terrible indeed. The words of Queen Boudicca had stirred the Britons until they were mad with thoughts of revenge and hopes of freedom. They gave no mercy, and they asked none. They utterly destroyed the towns of London and St. Albans, or Verulamium as it was then called, killing everyone, man, woman, and child.

Again and again, the Romans were defeated, till it almost seemed as if the Britons really would succeed in driving them out of the country. Boudicca herself led the soldiers, encouraging them with her brave words.

"It is better to die with honor than to live in slavery," she said. "I am a woman, but I would rather die than yield. Will you follow me, men?" and of course, the men followed her gladly.

At last, the Roman leader was so downcast with his many defeats that he went himself to the British camp, bearing in his hand a green branch as a sign of peace. When Boudicca was told that an ambassador from the Romans wished to speak to her, she replied proudly, "My sword alone shall speak to the Romans"

And when the Roman leader asked for peace, she answered, "You shall have peace, peace, but no submission. A British heart will choose death rather than lose liberty. There can be peace only if you promise to leave the country."

Of course, the Romans would not promise to go away from Britain, so the war continued, and for a time the Britons triumphed.

But their triumph did not last long. The Roman soldiers were better armed and better drilled than the British. There came a dark day when the Britons were utterly defeated, and many thousands were slain.

When Boudicca saw that all hope was gone, she called her daughters to her. "My children," she said sadly, as she took them by the hand and drew them towards her, "my children, it has not pleased the gods of battle to deliver us from the power of the Romans. But there is yet one way of escape." Tears were in her blue eyes as she kissed her daughters. She was no longer a queen of fury but a loving mother.

When the Roman soldiers burst in upon them, they found the great queen dead.

The Romans Settle Britain

by Eva March Tappan, Ph. D.

The Romans founded colonies in Britain and fought until they conquered the people who opposed the new rule. The Britons were good fighters, but they had not the military drill and training of the Roman soldiers; and although they often rebelled, the Romans were, at last, the victors. The conquerors built forty or fifty walled towns; and wherever a town has today a name ending in *chester* or *cester* or *caster*, like *Dorchester* or *Worcester* or *Lancaster*, we may be sure that it is on the site of an old military settlement because the Roman word for *camp* was *castra*. If the modern name of a place ends in *coln*, like *Lincoln*, that, too, is of Roman origin, because the Roman word for *colony* was *colonia*.

The Romans built large, handsome country houses. The walls were beautifully painted, and the floors were paved with marble of many colors. Around these houses were spacious gardens, adorned with statues, and rich in all kinds of fruit that could be made to grow on the island. Even today, in digging in different parts of England, people often find pieces of statuary and vases, and ornaments of gold or silver, that were once used to beautify the British homes of the Romans.

The conquerors were living in luxury, but the native Britons were obliged to pay enormous taxes to support all this comfort and elegance. Many of them had to work in the mines or on the roads and to live in little mud hovels. Thousands were made to enter the Roman army and some few, who were sons of chiefs, learned the Roman language and became officers.

The Romans wished to be able to send troops quickly wherever there was need of them and so they built two long roads across Britain in the shape of an X, besides several shorter ones. They were often troubled by the attacks of the Scots from the north of Ireland and the Picts, or "painted people," who lived in what is now Scotland and also by the coming of the Saxons from Denmark and the countries near it. To shut off the Picts, they built a line of forts across Scotland; but before many years they found that they could not defend their possessions so far north and then they built a solid wall. On this wall, there were stone strongholds and watchtowers; once in every four miles, there was a fort where soldiers were always stationed. To keep away the Danes, there was a whole line of forts built, extending around the southeastern coast of Britain.

Unit Four: Seeds of the Kingdom, Martyrs and Fathers of the Church

THEME: TRADITION AND SACRIFICE

THE CHRISTIANS ARE PERSECUTED

by Rev. Monsignor Edmund J. Goebel Ph. D.

Even during the lifetime of the apostles, the companions of Christ, the Church grew to a remarkable extent. It grew so large that it aroused the hatred and hostility of the Romans. The emperors began to fear and hate the Christians. The Christians would not go to the temples and worship the pagan gods of Rome. Many of the emperors after Augustus wished to be worshipped as gods. The Christians said that there was but one true God.

So, the emperors began to persecute the Christians. There were ten serious persecutions in all. The first was under the cruel emperor Nero. During his reign, both St. Peter and St. Paul suffered martyrdom. The Christians, however, faced death with courage and even with joy. The apostles themselves had given the example of willingness to die for Christ and His teachings. All the apostles died as martyrs except St. John. Even he suffered many tortures. By a miracle, he escaped from a cauldron of burning oil in Rome.

The Romans thought that they could make the Christians give up their religion. They forced the followers of Christ to suffer the most horrible and inhumane punishments.

During the worst of the persecutions, the Christians were forced to go underground. They took refuge in passageways and rooms which they hollowed out under the city of Rome. Here, in these underground rooms called catacombs, the priest said Mass, and the faithful received Holy Communion. Here, too, the Christians buried their dead.

We have a reminder of the catacombs in each of our churches today. In the catacombs, the priest usually said Mass over the tomb of a martyr. Today, in the center of each altar is an altar stone which contains the relics of some martyr.

History of the Catacombs

by the Sisters of Notre Dame

In reading the stories of the martyrs we shall often see the Catacombs mentioned. So much are they mixed up with the early history of the Church that it is important we should know something about them.

Stretching out from Rome in all directions are still to be seen the old paved roads made by the Romans, some of them dating back quite to the earliest days of the city.

Near almost all of these roads, but outside the walls of the city, there are openings leading down by stairs into underground galleries, dark, narrow, and intricate. Some of these give entrance into little rooms which, like the galleries, have niches cut into their walls. Niches, galleries, and rooms are all dug out of the solid rock; only where it is soft and crumbling are there to be seen remains of brickwork keeping up the roof.

Passing through gallery after gallery, we may come to a staircase, and, going down, we shall find, on a lower level underneath the former, a new set of passages and chambers.

Here and there a long, narrow opening to the surface above lets in light and air, otherwise all is dark and gloomy. Perhaps we shall find another staircase leading lower down, and still another, for in some places there are four or even five sets of galleries, one below the other. But everywhere in the walls of both passages and rooms are the same long, low, narrow niches cut back into the rock. Sometimes they are open and empty; sometimes bones may be seen in them; sometimes they are closed with a slab, on which a little bird with an olive branch, or an inscription, or a cross, may be made out.

Some of the rooms have one large tomb, with an arch over it, let into the wall at the end, and round the walls, there are stone benches. These chambers are often decorated, paintings, and inscriptions covering the walls and ceilings. Most of the decorations have a hidden meaning, representing symbolically the great mysteries of religion, and proving that the faith of the early Christians was identical with our own.

These wonderful underground dwellings of the dead are the Catacombs. There are so many of them that if all the galleries were put in one straight line, they would reach from one end of Italy to the other. They were almost all made by the Christians of Rome during the days of persecution.

At first, they were used only to bury the dead for the niches are all graves, some of martyrs, the others of those who did not die for the faith but wished to be buried near those who had. Some families made a room for themselves as a family vault, or in honor of some important martyr. But later, when it was not safe for the faithful to meet for Holy Mass in the houses of the richer Christians, as they had at first done, they made the little rooms larger and used them as churches. As all the Romans were very careful about burial and had laws protecting cemeteries, the Christians were at first quite safe in the Catacombs.

But we shall see, as time went on, that even here they were discovered and put to death, and that the faithful were forbidden to go to the Catacombs again, while the openings to them were sometimes walled up.

When the persecutions were over, burials still went on for nearly a hundred years. Gradually, however, this was given up, but people still went down as to a place of pilgrimage.

During the barbarian invasions from the fifth to the ninth centuries, the bodies of the Saints were removed to the churches above ground, and little by little the Catacombs were forgotten.

For six hundred years only an occasional pilgrim visited the neglected Catacombs, but in the sixteenth century, they were discovered anew. Little was done except to destroy what was found, until, nearer our own days, they have been opened again and carefully examined. The chambers and galleries have been cleared of the rubbish that had accumulated during ages of neglect.

Staircases have been made or repaired, and now anyone who wishes may go down to pray on the very spot where the Saints and martyrs of old heard Holy Mass and received Holy Communion, and so strengthened themselves for the hard combat awaiting them before they could attain the crown of everlasting life.

The Growth of Christianity

by Rev. Monsignor Edmund J. Goebel Ph. D.

The Christian Martyrs. Despite the persecutions, the Christians continued to grow in numbers. Hundreds might be martyred, but thousands became converted. When the Romans saw that the Christians were ready to suffer torture and even death because of their belief in God, many came to realize that the Christian religion was the true religion. "The blood of the martyrs is the seed of the Church" became a famous saying.

What Christ Taught. The teachings of Christ attracted people to the Church which He had founded. For the peoples conquered by the Romans, and for all those who had been made slaves, Christ had a message of hope, "Come to me you who are heavily burdened and I will refresh you." Christ taught that all human beings were equal in the sight of God. The slave was equal to his master, the wife to her husband, and no man was better than another.

Under the pagan governments, women were considered to be inferior to men. Their fathers or their husbands had absolute control over them. But Christ taught that they had the same rights and privileges as men. The honor paid to the Blessed Mother brought a new respect for womanhood. One of the first results of Christianity was an improvement in the position of women.

Christ made it clear that He came to save all people. He gave the commandment, "Love thy neighbor as thyself." He explained that the members of the whole human race should be considered as one's neighbors. From the beginning of the Church, the faithful gave help to the needy.

The peoples of the ancient world, when at war, had always taken "an eye for an eye, and a tooth for a tooth." But Christ commanded, "Love your enemies, do good to them that hate you … so that you may be children of your Father in heaven."

Although Christ had given a great deal of attention to the poor and oppressed, many of the proud and noble Romans were attracted to His Church. Army leaders, businessmen, and advisers of the emperors, as well as common people and slaves, became Christians.

The Growth of the Church. The teachings of Christ and His Church had an important influence on the lives of those who became Christians. They were inspired to lead pure and holy lives. In fact, the good example that the early Christians gave to their neighbors and fellow workers was one of the main reasons for the rapid growth of the Church.

In several practical ways, the Roman Empire itself helped the spread of Christianity. All the peoples of the known world were united under the rule of Rome, and the world was at peace. This meant that it was easier for the apostles to spread the teachings of Christ because there were no wars to prevent them from going where they wished. The great network of Roman roads provided safe and quick travel.

The common use of two languages, Greek and Latin, by all the nations of the Roman Empire made it easier for the early Christians to spread the gospel. For instance, St. Paul spoke Greek very well. In his wonderful sermons at Athens and Corinth, he could be understood by all the people.

Rulers and Persecutors

By Charlotte M. Yonge

Domitian. Domitian is called the last of the twelve Caesars, though all who came after him called themselves Caesar. He tried to restore the old Roman pride, but he thought Christianity was only a superstition. He announced that all should die who would not offer incense to the gods. Among those who died was St. Ignatius, Bishop of Antioch, who had been taught by the Apostles. He was taken to Rome, saw his friend St. Polycarp, Bishop of Smyrna, on the way, and wrote a letter to him which remains to this day. He was then thrown to the lions in the Colosseum.

It seems strange that the good Emperors were often worse persecutors than the bad ones, but the fact was that the bad ones let the people do as they pleased, as long as they did not offend them; while the good ones were trying to bring back what they read about Rome's history, of plain living and high thinking. They shut their ears to knowing more about the Christians than that they were people who did not worship the gods.

In Rome, the chief refuge of the Christians was the catacombs, or quarries of limestone, from which the city was chiefly built, and which were hollowed out in long galleries. Slaves and convicts worked in them, and they were thus made known to the Christians, who buried their dead in places hollowed at the sides, used the galleries for their churches, and often hid there when they were hunted.

Trajan. Trajan, who began to reign in the year A.D. 98, did not persecute actively, but there were laws in force against the Christians. Pliny the Younger, a Proconsul in Asia Minor, wrote to ask the Emperor what to do about the Christians. He told the Emperor what he had been able to find out about them, namely that they met together at night or early morning to sing together and eat what he called a harmless social meal. Trajan answered that he need not try to hunt them out, but that, if they were brought before him, the law must take its course.

Trajan was so good a ruler that he bears the title of *Optimus*, the Best, as no one else has ever done. The Roman empire was at its very largest in his reign. He was not only a great conqueror but a very great builder and improver so that one of his successors called him a wall-flower because his name was everywhere to be seen on walls and bridges and roads. Some of these still remain, as does his tall column at Rome, with a spiral line of his conquests engraved round it from top to bottom. He was on his way back from the East when, in A.D. 117, he died, leaving the empire to another brave warrior, Hadrian, who took the command with great vigor.

Hadrian. Hadrian came to Britain, where the Roman settlements were tormented by the Picts. There, he built the famous Roman wall from sea to sea to keep them out. He was wonderfully active, hastening from one end of the empire to the other wherever his presence was needed. There was a revolt of the Jews in the far East, under a man who pretended to be the Messiah, and called himself the Son of a Star. This was put down most severely, and no Jew was allowed to come near Jerusalem, over which a new city was built, and called after the Emperor's second name, Aelia Capitolina; and to drive the Jews further away, a temple to Jupiter was built where the Temple had been, and one to Venus on Mount Calvary.

But Hadrian did not persecute and listened kindly to an explanation of the faith, which was shown him at Athens by Quadratus, a Christian philosopher. Hadrian built himself a grand tower-like monument in Rome, surrounded by stages of columns and arches, which was called the Mole of Hadrian, and still stands. It is now topped with a statue of Saint Michael the Archangel and is called Castel Sant'Angelo.

Antoninus. Before his death, in A.D. 138, Hadrian had chosen his successor, Antoninus, a good, upright man, cared greatly for his people's welfare. He avoided wars, only fighting to defend the empire. He was a great builder, for he raised another rampart in Britain, much further north, set up another column at Rome, and in Gaul built a great amphitheater, and raised the wonderful aqueduct which is still standing, and is called the Pont du Gard.

Saint Polycarp, Bishop and Martyr

Edited By John Gilmary Shea, LL.D.

St. Polycarp, Bishop of Smyrna, was a disciple of St. John. He wrote to the Philippians, urging them to love one another and follow the true faith. St. Polycarp was a Saint most loving and most charitable, and specially noted for his compassion to sinners. In the year 167, persecution broke out in Smyrna, a city in Greece that Saint Paul had visited in his journeys. When Polycarp heard that his pursuers were at the door, he said, "The will of God be done;" and meeting them, he begged to be left alone for a little time, which he spent in prayer for "the catholic church throughout the world."

He was brought to Smyrna early on Holy Saturday; and, as he entered, a voice was heard from heaven, "Polycarp, be strong." When the proconsul asked him to curse Christ and go free, Polycarp answered, "Eighty-six years I have served Him, and He never did me wrong; how can I blaspheme my King and Savior?" When he was threatened with fire, Polycarp told him this fire of theirs lasted but a little, while the fire prepared for the wicked lasted forever. At the stake, he thanked God aloud for letting him drink of Christ's chalice. The fire was lighted, but it did him no harm; so, he was killed with the spear. "Then," say the writers of his acts, "we took up the bones, more precious than the richest jewels or gold, and deposited them in a fitting place, at which may God grant us to assemble with joy to celebrate the birthday of the martyr to his life in heaven!"

Marcus Aurelius

by Charlotte M. Yonge

Antoninus' son-in-law, who succeeded him as emperor, is commonly called Marcus Aurelius. He had an earnest longing for truth and virtue, though he did not know how to seek them or where they could be found. When earthquakes, plagues, and war fell on his empire, and the people thought the gods were offended, he let them persecute the Christians, because the hope of the Resurrection and of Heaven seemed weak and foolish to him compared with his stern, proud, hopeless beliefs. So, the aged Polycarp, Bishop of Smyrna, the last pupil of the Apostles themselves, was sentenced to be burnt in the theater of his own city, though as the fire curled around him in a curtain of flame without touching him, he was actually slain with the sword.

Aurelius was fighting hard with the German tribes, who gave him no rest and threatened to break into the empire. While pursuing them, he and his army were shut into a stronghold where they could get no water. They were perishing of thirst when a whole legion of Christian soldiers knelt and prayed. A cloud came and showered rain on the thirsty army. It is said that afterward this division was named the Thundering Legion, although on the column built by Aurelius it is Jupiter who is shown sending rain on the army. After this, there was less persecution of the Christians, but every sort of trouble – plague, earthquake, famine, and war – afflicted the empire, and the Emperor worked in vain against these troubles. He wrote meditations that show how sad and sick at heart he was, and how little comfort his pagan beliefs gave him, while his eyes were blind to the truth. He died of fever in his camp, while still in the prime of life, and with him ended the period of good Emperors, which the Romans called the age of the Antonines.

Marcus Aurelius, the Philosopher Emperor

by Eva March Tappan, Ph. D.

A Roman emperor was thinking over his childhood one day, and he concluded that he had been an exceedingly fortunate boy. His father died when he was a baby, it was true, but he wrote in his notebook that he had "good grandfathers, good parents, a good sister, good teachers, good associates, good kinsmen, and friends." About his teachers, he wrote a great deal more. He did not say that one taught him arithmetic, one poetry, and so on; but he said that from one he had learned not to meddle with other people's affairs, from another not to spend his time on trifles, from another to be willing to forgive; and from the others to keep himself from fault-finding, to be cheerful, to love truth and justice, not to declare often that he had no leisure, and not to excuse neglect of his duties to others by saying that he was busy.

This emperor's name as a boy was Marcus Annius Verus. He belonged to a noble family and was noticed by the emperor Hadrian when he was a little fellow. The child was so noble and upright that Hadrian said his name ought not to be Verus (true), but Verissimus (truest).

When this young Marcus was about twelve, he became interested in a kind of philosophy known as stoicism. He made up his mind that its teachings were good and that he would follow them as long as he lived; and, what is more, he did not change his belief. Some of the teachings of stoicism are as follows: One ought never to complain, but to yield to necessity calmly and serenely; one ought not to allow himself to be overwhelmed with grief or enraptured with joy; one should never make pleasure his aim. The stoics dressed simply and lived plainly. They were taught to treat all men alike, whether great or small. They were to work hard, to practice self-denial, and never to listen to slander.

All this time the emperor Hadrian was watching the young stoic. He had no son, and he was trying to decide who should follow him as emperor. Marcus was only seventeen, or probably Hadrian would have chosen him. He did choose Antoninus, an uncle of the boy, a man of about fifty years. He was upright and just and with gentle, kindly manners. He was not eager to undertake so great a labor as the care of a mighty empire, but finally, he yielded. Hadrian made one condition to Antoninus' becoming his heir, and this was that he should adopt as his successors the young Marcus and also one Verus, whose father had been a friend of Hadrian. Soon after the agreement was made, Hadrian died, and Antoninus took his place.

For more than twenty years, Marcus Aurelius Antoninus, as he was now called, lived with his uncle. Antoninus loved him like a father and gave him a large part in the government and honored him in every way in his power. Antoninus was a good man. He always tried to be at peace with everyone and to treat everyone justly. He kept the empire in order, kept himself cheerful and serene, and he was greatly loved by his nephew.

When the time came that Antoninus knew he must die, he called together the chief men of Rome to talk about who should be his successor. He had two sons of his own, but he did not try to win the empire for them. He recommended that the Senate should choose Marcus. Evidently, he could not make up his mind to recommend Verus also. The Senate agreed with him and asked Marcus Aurelius to become the sole emperor. He knew that it was Hadrian's wish that Verus should reign with him, and he insisted that this should be done. Verus was somewhat weak in character and had little idea of self-control, but he did have great respect for Marcus Aurelius and was always ready to follow his advice. They ruled together in perfect harmony until the death of Verus.

All sorts of troubles afflicted the empire. First, there was a terrible flood. Much of Rome was swept away, fields and crops were destroyed, and cattle were drowned. There were fires, and there were earthquakes. Worst of all, there was war; and Marcus Aurelius had a horror of war. He thought that it was a shame and disgrace. Nevertheless, he was emperor, and he had to protect his empire. The Parthians in the east revolted. They were overcome in battle, but when the army returned, a dreadful pestilence came with them. It spread from region to region. "It is the end of the empire," people whispered fearfully; but at length, the plague disappeared. Then there was danger from the Germans, and Marcus Aurelius remained in camp and on the battlefield for three years before they were subdued.

This emperor fought because it was necessary, but he loved quiet thought, and wherever he was, he carried with him a little notebook, and in it, he wrote any thoughts that came to him about the noblest way to live. It was at this time that he jotted down between battles his memories of his childhood and of the goodness of his friends and teachers. He wrote that of course, he must expect to meet ungrateful, envious, deceitful people; but that they could not really do him any harm, and that the only reason why they were of such character was that they did not fully understand what was good and what was bad. This little notebook of the busy emperor is very interesting. He tells people that they ought not to waste their lives in wondering what others are saying and thinking and that their own thoughts ought always to be so kindly that if anyone asked, "What are you thinking about?" they would not be at all afraid to answer honestly. He says that when anyone wants to feel happy, it is an excellent plan to think of his friends and call to mind their good qualities. Think more of the good things you have than of those you have not, he advises. Another thought is that the best way to avenge one's self is to be careful not to become like the wrong-doer. He makes it seem not only wrong, but exceedingly silly to continue in ill-doing, for he says, "It is a ridiculous thing for a man not to fly from his own badness, which is indeed possible, but to fly from other men's badness, which is impossible."

Marcus Aurelius would have liked to spend his time thinking about life and setting down his thoughts in this way and in being with his family and his friends, but he could spare only stray moments for such pleasures. He had to give his days either to war or to thinking how to take care of the roads, how to manage the city at less expense, how to get enough soldiers and how to pay those that he already had, and how to answer the hundred and one questions that came up every day for his decision. It is no wonder that he had to rise early in the morning and work till after midnight. He was obliged to show himself at the games and the fights of the gladiators; but while he was there, he usually read or had someone read to him.

During the reign of Marcus Aurelius, the Christians were terribly persecuted. It often happened that the most bitter persecutions took place during the reigns of the best emperors; so it was with Marcus Aurelius. Although his ideas were much like those of Christianity, he probably knew nothing of the Christian belief and was a sincere worshiper of the gods. When any trouble came upon the state, the first thought of both him and his people was that the state worship had not been carried on properly, and so the gods were angry. The Christians would not even burn a few grains of incense on the heathen altars; and therefore, when flood or sickness afflicted the city, the Romans believed that they were to blame and ought to be persecuted.

When Marcus Aurelius was nearly sixty years old, an epidemic made its appearance in the army; and soon the Romans were grieving over the loss of their ruler. It had become the custom for the senate to pass a decree at the death of an emperor, declaring that he was now one of the gods; but in this case, the people did not wait for any decree of the senate, they made a god of him at once; for many years incense was burned before his statue and prayers were offered up to the emperor whom they loved so sincerely.

Saint Alban, First Martyr of Britain

by Amy Steedman

Long years ago, when Rome was the mistress of the world and her soldiers and citizens were to be found everywhere, even the little island of Britain had its place among the colonies of the great empire. Here the Romans laid their roads and planted their towns, built temples to their gods, and ruled the barbarians with a firm, strong hand. Many noble Roman families lived in Britain in those days, and although life was ruder and rougher than what they were accustomed to in the wonderful city of Rome, still they made their houses as luxurious and comfortable as they could and tried to be content.

It was in one of these well-built houses, with inlaid floors and marble baths, that the little Alban was born, heir to a great Roman family. The parents had settled in the town of Verulam, on the banks of the little river Ver, but they always looked upon Britain as a land of exile and planned to send their boy back to Rome as soon as he should be old enough to be taught and trained to be a Roman citizen.

But the child himself was very happy in his island home. The little stream that ran past the town was in his eyes a wonderful river that would carry his boats far out to sea. The green hill on the opposite bank was a playground fit for the gods, with its carpet of golden-eyed daisies and yellow buttercups, and the smooth grassy slopes that were so soft to roll upon. The great forests that looked so dark and gloomy held him spellbound, and he loved to watch the grey mists come rolling over the marshy land, turning everything into a world of mystery.

Never was there a happier child in all the world, but the reason for his happiness was not because he had so many pleasures, but because he was kind and generous to everyone round about him. It seemed as if there was a little singing bird in the golden cage of his heart, a bird that was always singing happy songs, and its name was Unselfishness.

Now, as soon as the boy grew old enough, he was sent away to Rome as his parents had planned, for they wished him to learn many things which he could never be taught in the little island of Britain. It seemed to Alban as if he had come to a different world when first he entered the city of Rome. Accustomed as he was to the little town with its few well-built houses, the rude huts and wild marsh wastes, the rolling mists and grey skies, he had never dreamed of such a city as this. Palaces of white marble triumphantly rearing their columns up to heaven; temples of the gods more beautiful than a dream; baths as luxurious as those of a king's dwelling; and above all the blue sky, such a blue as he had never even dreamed of, and sunshine which kept him even warmer than his fur coat had ever done.

There was much to learn and much to do in this new world of wonder and magnificence, but as Alban grew into a man, he found that there was something he loved better than all this splendor and luxury. Far away on the banks of the little river, on the island of the mist and grey skies, there was something which bound his heart with a golden thread of love and memory which nothing could snap. Although the house at Verulam was no grand palace; although the country was rough and wild and often cold and bleak, it was home. The great forests, the green flowery hills, the rolling mists seemed to be calling him. It meant home to him, and he loved it better than all the glory of Rome.

So, Alban returned to the island of the mists, and lived once more in the house where he was born, on the banks of the little river. He was rich and powerful and had everything that heart could desire, and he was as happy as ever, for he was so kind and generous that everyone loved him. Rich and poor alike were welcome at his house, and no one who needed help asked for it in vain. Travelers always stopped at his gate, and he never refused hospitality to any guest.

It was late one night when doors were barred and everyone had gone to rest, that a knocking was heard at the outer gate. It was an urgent knocking, although not very loud, and the servants, at last, went to see who it was that sought shelter at that unseemly hour. A weary-looking man dressed in a long cloak was standing there, and he begged that he might be taken in secret and hidden from his pursuers, who were even now close at hand.

The servants, knowing their master's will, brought him quickly in, and one went to his lord to tell him of the new arrival. "He has a strange cloak and seems to be a teacher, and one of those whom men call Christians," said the servant, as he told his tale. "He says that even now he is pursued and has endured great persecutions."

"See that he is made welcome," said Alban, "and that he is hidden secretly, and let no man gossip of his presence here."

The poor hunted man, who was indeed a Christian priest, was brought in and secretly hidden, as Alban had commanded, and for a while, his pursuers sought for him in vain. Alban knew well how cruel were the tortures and punishments which these Christians endured, and he expected to find his guest stricken with terror and fear, but to his surprise, the priest's face was calm and even happy.

"Are you not afraid that your persecutors may track you here?" asked Alban curiously.

"My Master is stronger than they," answered the priest calmly. "He will protect me."

"Who is your master?" asked Alban wonderingly.

"The Lord Christ," answered the priest.

"That poor man who died the death of a criminal?" said Alban, in a mocking voice.

"The King of Heaven, who deigned to come to earth as a helpless child," answered the priest, "and who became Man that He might teach us to be men."

"And what reward do you receive for your service to this King?" asked Alban, looking at the worn clothes and weary, thin face of the man before him.

"Those who serve Christ have no thought of reward," answered the priest. "Their only thought is how much service they may offer their Master. Stripes, persecutions, tortures, death, these are the rewards which His faithful soldiers gladly suffer, that they may be fit to call Him 'Lord.' Will you listen to the story of my King?"

"These sayings of yours are strange," said Alban, "I will hear no more. Your words sound almost like a call to battle in my ears, and yet I know it is all foolishness. Be silent; I will have no more of your idle talk."

Disturbed and angry, Alban turned to go, but all that day the words he had heard rang in his ears. How royally was this King served by His followers! Who was He that could command such splendid service? He had heard of this God of the Christians but had never troubled himself to learn of His life.

Then when night came and he lay sleeping, a dream was sent to him which told him the story of the King, which he had refused to hear that day. He saw the Man, crowned with the wreath of thorns; he saw the face of majesty and power gazing so pitifully at the cruel crowd who seized Him and nailed Him to the cross. He saw the body laid in the tomb, and then the figure of the living Christ ascending with great glory into heaven. And sweeping upwards, there followed a great multitude in white robes, following Him who had conquered death, for whom they too had laid down their lives.

Early next morning Alban went to the secret chamber to seek the priest and ask what that dream could mean.

"God has been very gracious to you, my son," answered the priest solemnly. "He has taught you Himself what you refused to hear from me."

"Tell me more," said Alban humbly; "I will listen to every word that you can tell me."

With a glad heart, the priest told again the story of his Master's life, and Alban listened eagerly. Again, the battle call sounded in his ears, and he longed to serve a Master such as this.

"But have you indeed counted the cost of such a service?" asked the teacher. "It is no pleasant service which He offers."

"I seek no pleasant service," answered Alban.

"A cruel death may be your only reward," said the priest again. "Do you not repent the kindness which made you harbor a Christian? '

"No," replied Alban; "you have brought me life instead of death. I have never yet repented of one kind or merciful act which I have done to any man."

Then the priest could no longer refuse to baptize the new soldier into the service of the king; but as they knelt in prayer together the servants came hurriedly to the door telling of a band of soldiers who had entered the courtyard and demanded to search the house for the hidden fugitive.

Alban sprang to his feet and caught up the heavy cloak and cowl of the priest. "Quick! quick!" he cried, "escape in my mantle, and I will stay here in your place. They will not discover who I am until you have escaped far away out of their reach."

"How can I do this?" said the priest. "You will die in my place."

"This is my first call to arms," said Alban gladly. "Let me thus begin to serve the King."

There was no time for words; the soldiers were at the door. But, when they entered there was but one cloaked figure there, who showed no resistance, but quietly gave himself into their hands.

The judge was in the temple, sacrificing to his gods when they brought the fugitive Christian to receive his sentence. And when the cloak was thrown back and he saw the young Roman noble, he was doubly furious because he had been deceived.

"You have hidden a traitor in your house, and well do you deserve to bear his punishment," he cried angrily. "Perhaps you too are a Christian. Sacrifice at once to the gods and beg for mercy."

"It is as you say; I am a Christian," answered Alban calmly. "I serve the King of Heaven and will offer no sacrifice to your false gods."

There was a note of triumph in the voice of the young Roman, and the people wondered when they saw him standing there so fearless and triumphant. Did he not know what it meant to call himself a Christian? He was young and rich and powerful; all the tempting pleasures of life lay spread out before him; all the great and alluring things which men strive after lay within his grasp; and yet he was choosing torture, dishonor, and death. The wondering 'why?' was echoed in every heart.

But there was little time for wonder. The soldiers, by order of the judge, seized Alban and dragged him away to be tortured, and then he was led out to be executed in the arena on the opposite side of the river.

All the inhabitants of the town came out to see the sight, and some looked on with pity, remembering the kindness they had received at the hands of the young Roman noble. Others came out to mock. How gallant and happy he had always looked. There would surely be no smile on his face now! But when they pressed forward and caught sight of that pale young face, their mocking words were silenced, and a feeling of awe fell upon the crowd. Yes, the old happy look was there still, but there was something higher and purer added to it.

A light of wondrous happiness seemed to shine forth, and the people as they looked felt as did those men who gazed upon St. Stephen. "They saw his face, as it had been the face of an angel."

Down to the little river, they led him; but when they came to the bridge there was no room to pass, for the crowd was so great. The order was given to ford the river, but the legend tells us that before St. Alban could step down, the stream dried up, and he crossed over, without so much as wetting his feet.

Then the old legend goes on to tell how the executioner, who watched this miracle from the opposite bank, was struck with fear and remorse. How could he put to death a man whom heaven itself so carefully guarded? He would not fight against the God of Alban, so he threw down his sword and refused to touch him.

But Alban walked steadfastly on to the place of execution. Up the grassy slopes of the green hill, he went, along the flowery path of scented thyme and golden-eyed daisies, where he had loved to play as a little lad. On this bright June day, the hill was starred with flowers, and they seemed indeed a fitting carpet to spread beneath the feet of the first English martyr.

There were other executioners ready to do the bidding of the governor, and there, on the green hillside, the first faithful English soldier in the noble army of martyrs laid down his life.

A clear spring of water, it is said, sprang up to mark the spot where St. Alban was put to death, near the little town of Verulam which now bears his name; but the miracle was scarcely needed. The memory that sprang from the life laid down in merciful kindness for another, in the service of the King, is a spring of living water that can never fail or be cut off.

Saint Cecilia

by Amy Steedman

It was in the days when cruel men killed and tortured those who loved our Blessed Lord that, in the city of Rome, a little maid was born. Her father and mother were among the richest and noblest of the Roman people, and their little daughter, whom they called Cecilia, had everything she could possibly want. She lived in a splendid palace, with everything most beautiful around her, and she had a garden to play in, where the loveliest flowers grew. Her little white dress was embroidered with the finest gold, and her face was as fair as the flowers she loved.

But it was not only the outside that was beautiful, for the little maiden's heart was fairer than the fairest flowers and whiter than her spotless robe.

There were not many people who loved our Lord in those dark days. Anyone who was known to be a Christian was made to suffer terrible tortures and was even put to death.

But though Cecilia's father and mother knew this, they still taught their little daughter to be a servant of Christ and to love Him above all things. For they knew that the love of Christ was better than life, and worth all the suffering that might come.

And as Cecilia grew into a stately maiden everyone wondered at the grace and beauty that shone out of her face. And everyone loved her because she loved everyone. She was always ready and willing to help others, and she was especially careful to be kind to the poor. The more she heard of Christ, the more she longed to grow like Him. She could not bear to think that she wore fine dresses, while He had been so poor and suffered so much.

Some say the meaning of her name Cecilia is 'Heaven's Lily.' And that name certainly suited this little Roman maiden. For as God plants the lilies in the dark earth, and presently they grow up and lift their pure white cups to heaven, so Cecilia seemed to lift her heart above the sins and sorrows of this world where God had planted her and to turn her face ever heavenwards.

And the poor people whom she helped and cheered with her kind sympathy loved to look at her, for the peace of paradise shone in her eyes, seeming to bring heaven nearer to the poor souls.

As soon as Cecilia was old enough, it was arranged that she should marry a young Roman noble called Valerian, and this made her very unhappy. She had so hoped to belong only to Christ, and this Valerian was a pagan who knew nothing of the Lord whom she served. But she knew that her guardian angel would watch over her and keep her from all harm, and so she obeyed her father's and mother's wishes and was married to the young Roman noble.

When Valerian had taken Cecilia home and all the guests had gone, they were left alone together. She told him that, though she was married, she belonged first of all to Christ, and that her guardian angel, who never left her, would guard and protect her from all danger.

"Will you show me this angel, so that I may know that what you say is true?" asked Valerian.

"You cannot see the heavenly messenger until you learn to know my Lord," answered Cecilia.

And as Valerian eagerly asked how he should learn to know this Christ, Cecilia told him to go along the great Appian Way, outside the walls of Rome, until he should meet some poor people who lived in the Campagna. And to them, he should say, "Cecilia bids you show me the way that I may find the old man, Urban the Good."

So, Valerian started off and went the way Cecilia directed. And the people guided him as she had promised, until they came to a curious opening in the ground, down which they told him he must go if he wished to find Pope Urban. This opening was the entrance to a strange underground place called the Catacombs.

There were miles and miles of dark passages cut out of the rock, with here and there a little dark room, and curious shelves hollowed out of the walls. It was here that many poor Christians lived, hiding from those who would have put them to death. And the little shelves were where they buried the bodies of poor Christians who had died for Christ.

It was here that the old Pope, Urban the Good, lived, and he welcomed Valerian most gladly, knowing why he had come. He began at once to teach him all that he should know—how God was our Father, and Jesus Christ His Son, our Savior. And as Valerian listened to the strange, wonderful words, the love of God shone into his heart, so that when the old man asked, "Do you believe this?" he answered with all his heart, "All this I steadfastly believe."

Then Urban baptized Valerian, and by that sign, the young Roman knew that he was indeed a Christian, a servant of Christ.

All the world looked different to Valerian as he walked back along the Appian Way to Rome. The flat, low fields of the Campagna, fading away into the ridges of the purple Apennines, seemed almost like the fields of paradise, and the song of the birds was like the voice of angels. He scarcely thought of the dangers and difficulties that were before him, or if he did it, was only to feel glad that he might have anything to bear for his new Master.

When he reached home and went back to the room where he had left Cecilia, he found her waiting for him, with glad welcome in her eyes. As they knelt together, they heard a rustle of wings, and looking up they saw an angel bending over them, with a crown of lilies and roses in each hand. These he placed upon their heads, and to Valerian, he said, "You have done well in allowing Cecilia to serve her Master; therefore, ask what you will, and your request shall be granted."

Then Valerian asked that his brother, whom he dearly loved, might also learn to know Christ. And just then the door opened, and the brother whom Valerian loved so much came in. He, of course, only saw Valerian and Cecilia, and could not see the angel, or even the wreaths of heavenly roses. But he looked round in astonishment and said, "I see no flowers here, and yet the fragrance of roses and lilies is so sweet and strange, that it makes my very heart glad."

Then Valerian answered, "We have two crowns here, which you cannot see because you do not know the Lord who sent them to us. But if you will listen and learn to know Him, then you will see the heavenly flowers, whose fragrance has filled your heart."

So, Valerian and Cecilia told their brother what it meant to be a Christian. And after the good Urban had taught him also, he was baptized and became God's knight. Then he, too, saw the heavenly crowns and the face of the angel who guarded Heaven's Lily.

The home of Valerian and Cecilia was now like a paradise on earth, filled with happiness. Cecilia loved music above everything. Her voice was like a bird's, and she sang her hymns of praise and played so exquisitely that they say even the angels came down to listen.

But before long, it began to be known that Valerian and his brother helped the poor Christians, and the wicked governor of the city ordered them both to be seized and brought before him. He told them that there were but two ways before them: either they must deny that they were Christians, or they must be put to death.

But God's knights did not fear death, and they went out to meet it as if they were on their way to a great victory. And when the soldiers wondered, and asked them if it was not sad that they should lose their lives while they were still so young, they answered that what looked like loss on earth was gain in heaven—that they were but laying down their bodies as one puts off one's clothes to sleep at night. For the immortal soul could never die but would live forever.

So, they knelt down, and the cruel blows were struck. But, looking up, the soldiers saw a great pathway of light shining down from heaven. And the souls of Valerian and his brother were led up by angel hands to the throne of God, there to receive the crowns of everlasting glory which they had won on earth.

And so, Cecilia was left alone. But she did not spend her time grieving. Gathering the people and soldiers around her, she taught them about the Lord of Heaven, for whose sake Valerian and his brother had so gladly suffered death. And it was not long before she also trod the shining pathway up to heaven and met the ones she loved.

For the governor was not satisfied with the death of Valerian and his brother but ordered Cecilia to be brought before him.

"What sort of a woman are you, and what is your name?" he asked.

"I am a Roman lady," she answered with grave dignity, "and among men, I am known by the name of Cecilia. But"—and her voice rang out proudly as she looked fearlessly into those angry eyes— "my noblest name is Christian."

This made the governor more furious than ever, and he ordered that she should be beheaded. But even after she had received three strokes from the sword, she did not die but lived for three days, ever singing in her sweet voice the praises of God.

And so at the end of three days, God's angel came and led Cecilia home, and all that was left of her on earth was her fair body, lying like a tired child asleep, with hands clasped, gently resting now that her work on earth was done.

In Rome today there is a splendid church built over the place where Cecilia's house stood.

Someday if you go there, you will see her little room and a beautiful marble figure lying under the altar, and you will know exactly how Cecilia looked when she left her tired body lying there and went up the shining path to God.

Rulers and Puppets

by Charlotte Mary Yonge

Septimus Severus. Septimus Severus was an able emperor and reigned for a long time. He was stern and harsh, as was needed by the wickedness of the time; and he was very active, seldom at Rome, but flashing as it were from one end of the empire to the other, wherever he was needed, and keeping excellent order. There was no regular persecution of the Christians in his time; but in Lyons, where many of the townspeople were Christians. The country-folk by some sudden impulse broke into the town and made a horrible massacre of the Christians. It was in this attack that the bishop, St. Irenaeus, was killed. So few country people were converts, that the Roman word for a peasant - *paganus* - came to be used as a term for a heathen (pagan.)

Severus was, like Trajan and Hadrian, a great builder and roadmaker. The whole empire was connected by a network of paved roads, cutting through hills, bridging valleys, straight, smooth, and so solid that they remain to this day. These roads, constructed by the empire's soldiers, made communication so rapid that Severus could actively rule throughout his empire. When he was an old man, he came to Britain and marched far north, but he saw it was impossible to guard Antonius's wall on the border of Scotland, and only strengthened the rampart of Hadrian. He died at York, in Britain, in A.D. 211, while he was returning, and his last watchword was "Labor!"

Alexander Severus. Alexander Severus was a good and just prince, whose mother is believed to have been a Christian, and he had certainly learned enough of the Divine Law to love virtue and be firm while he was forbearing. He loved virtue, but he did not accept the faith, and would only look upon our Blessed Lord as a sort of great philosopher, placing His statue with that of Abraham, Orpheus, and all whom he thought great teachers of mankind, in a private temple of his own, as if they were all on a level. He never came any nearer to the faith, and after thirteen years of good and firm government, he was killed in a mutiny of the Praetorians in A.D. 235.

The Praetorians. The Praetorian Guard, the private guards of the emperor, had become so powerful by this time that they, not the emperor, had all the real power. They set up and put down emperors so rapidly that there are hardly any names worth remembering. In this unsettled state of the empire, no one had time to persecute the Christians, and their numbers grew and prospered. In many places, they had churches, with worship going on openly, and their bishops were known and respected. Emperor Philip, called the Arabian, was actually a Christian, although he would not admit it openly. When he was at Antioch, he joined in the service at Easter, and presented himself to receive the Holy Communion. Bishop Babylas refused him until he would do open penance for the crimes which he had committed in order to become emperor and renounce all of his heathenism. The emperor turned away rebuked but put off his repentance. The next year he celebrated the games called the Seculae, because they took place every Seculum or hundredth year, with all their heathen ceremonies, and with great splendor, in honor of this being Rome's thousandth birthday.

Soon after, another general named Decius was chosen by the army on the German frontier. Decius wanted to be an old-fashioned Roman; he believed in the gods and thought the troubles of the empire was caused because of ignoring them. As the Parthians attacked from the East, and the Goths and Germans from the North, the Roman soldiers seemed more ready to kill their emperors than the enemy. Decius decided to win back prosperity for the empire by forcing all citizens to return to the old worship. He began the worst persecution the Church had yet known. Rome, Antioch, Carthage, Alexandria, and all the major cities were searched for Christians. If they would not throw a handful of incense on the idol's altar or disown Christ, they were cruelly punished in the hope that they would renounce their faith. Some did fall, but the greater number stood firm and gave a glorious witness of their faith.

Diocletian Divides the Empire

by Charlotte M. Yonge

Diocletian began a dominion unlike that of any who had gone before. Emperors had often been simply overgrown generals, but Diocletian made his reign as Emperor like that of the kings of the East. He never visited Rome, avoiding any obligation to acknowledge the authority of the Senate. In fact, he contrived to entirely take away the Senate's power, and "Senator" became only a title of which to boast, with no real authority.

He divided the empire into two parts, feeling that it was beyond the management of any one man. He chose an able soldier of low birth but much courage, named Maximian, to rule the West, while he himself ruled the East. Each of the two Emperors chose a future successor, who was to rule in part of his dominion under the title of Caesar, and to reign after him. Diocletian chose his son-in-law Galerius; and Maximian chose, as Caesar, Constantius, who commanded in Britain, Gaul, and Spain. Thus, everything was done to ensure that a strong hand was ready everywhere to keep the legions from setting up emperors at their own whims.

Diocletian was the most just and kind of the Emperors, while Maximian was the fiercest and most savage. Maximian had a bitter hatred of the Christian name, as did Galerius. They were determined to put down the faith. Maximian is said to have commanded a whole legion of Christians in his army, to sacrifice to the Roman gods, and when they refused, had them decimated – that is, every tenth man was slain. They were called on again to sacrifice, but still were staunch, and after a last summons were, every man of them, slain as they stood with their tribune Maurice, whose name is still held in high honor.

On the other hand, the wife of Diocletian was believed to be a Christian, and the wife of Constantius, St. Helena, was certainly one. Diocletian was slow to become a persecutor until a fire broke out in his palace. It damaged much of the city but spared the chief Christian church. The enemies of the Christians accused them of having caused it, and Diocletian required everyone in his household to clear themselves by offering sacrifice to Jupiter. His wife and daughter yielded, but most of his officers and slaves held out and died. The Christians were hunted down from one end of the empire to the other, everywhere except Britain, where, under Constantius, only one martyrdom is reported to have taken place, that of the soldier St. Alban. It was the worst of all the persecutions and lasted the longest.

Rivals for the Throne

Constantius and Galerius. The two emperors, Diocletian and Maximian, were good soldiers and kept their enemies back, but just after a great triumph, Diocletian had an illness, and he decided that it would be better to resign the empire while he was still in his full strength. He persuaded Maximian to do the same, in A.D. 305, making Constantius and Galerius emperors instead. Constantius stopped the persecutions of Christians in the West, but it raged as much as ever in the East under Galerius.

Constantius fought bravely, both in Britain and Gaul, with the enemies who tried to break into the empire on the eastern frontier of Gaul, and the on the northern border of the settlements in Britain. He opposed them gallantly and was much loved, but he died in Britain in A.D. 306.

Constantine and Maximian. Constantius's son, Constantine, was so beloved by the army and people of Gaul that they proclaimed him Emperor. He held the province of Britain and Gaul securely against all enemies.

Old Maximian then came out from his retreat and called on Diocletian to do the same, but Diocletian was far too happy on his little farm to leave it. When a messenger urged him to again take up his purple robes and be emperor, he answered with, "Come and look at the cabbages I have planted."

Maximian was accepted as the true Emperor by the Senate, but his son soon turned out to be a rebel, driving his own father away to Gaul. There, Constantine kindly gave Maximian a home, on the condition that he did not interfere with government. But old Maximian could not rest and he raised troops against Constantine. Constantine's army marched eagerly against him and made him prisoner, but even then, he was pardoned; yet he still plotted, and finally, Constantine was obliged to have him put to death.

Galerius fell ill with a horrible disease and was filled with remorse for his cruelties to the Christians; before he died, he requested their prayers and ordered a stop to the persecutions.

Saint Sebastian of Rome

Adapted from the work of Allen Hinds, M.A., John Gilmary Shea, LL.D, and Rev. D Chisholm

Sebastian was born at Narbonne, France, and lived in Milan, Italy. When he came to Rome, he became a great favorite of the Emperors Diocletian and Maximian, who made him captain of their private guards. He was charged with command of about 420 soldiers, and he surpassed them all in wisdom and virtue. Because he wore the Roman military uniform, he was allowed to visit the imprisoned Christians. He secretly used these visits to comfort them before they were taken away to be martyred.

There lived at Rome twin brothers named were Marcus and Marcellianus. They were Christians, but their father and mother were pagans. When Diocletian was putting to death all those who were faithful to God, these two brothers were also arrested and brought before the Judge. They were asked to deny the true God and to worship idols, but they firmly refused, and for this, they were condemned to death.

But their father, who was a man of a high position, obtained from the Judge a delay of thirty days to see if he could make them give up their faith. He tried every way to shake their courage, for he was fond of his two boys, and was determined to save their lives.

Friends came to visit the brothers, and begged them, "Why are you so foolish, to throw away your lives? You who are so young and have so many chances of enjoying yourselves?" The parents, also, continued to implore them to renounce their faith, and the brothers nearly gave up. But Sebastian broke into the midst of them and urged them to turn away from the world and to win the crown of martyrdom.

"O brave and faithful soldiers of the King of Kings," he said, "stand firm! Do not allow yourselves to be overcome in this terrible conflict! You have already confessed Jesus Christ; you have already suffered much for Him and are even under sentence of death for Him. Is it possible, then, that a few tears shall overcome you?"

With these and other stirring words, the holy Sebastian spoke to them to encourage them to persevere and be faithful.

Then, turning to the bystanders, he said, "Do not let these two young men lose Heaven for the short comforts of this life. Do not grieve for their departure from you, for they are going to a kingdom of joy and happiness to pray for you that you may come to know God here and go to possess Him with them in Heaven hereafter."

Then Marcus said, "My most loving parents, the worst thing a man can do in this world is to love it more than God. We must take more care of our souls, which can never die, than our bodies, which must die so soon. Let us lose this wretched life, then, that we may gain an eternal one in Heaven."

Then, turning to his brother, he continued, "Brother, let us fight bravely like soldiers of Jesus Christ; let us die for Our Heavenly Master and let us strive to see which of us will first reach our home above."

These words made such an impression on those who heard them that they also wished to join a Faith that made men such heroes. Everyone present became a Christian, and many of them laid down their lives for their Faith, as those two brothers did.

This took place in the house of Nicostratus where the young men were in custody. The wife of Nicostratus had lost the ability to speak for six years, and kneeling on the floor she asked forgiveness of Sebastian by nodding. At his prayer, she received the gift of speech. She immediately declared that she had seen an angel near Sebastian who held an open book in his hand containing all the words which Sebastian had said. Near him stood seven other angels of shining white. At this miracle, both Nicostratus and his wife were baptized, together with the parents of the two young men. The brothers chose to suffer martyrdom although Nicostratus offered to release them.

After the martyrdom of Marcus and Marcellianus, the Roman prefect Chromatius, who was healed by Sebastian, was baptized, together with his son Tiburtius. After his conversion, the prefect escaped to his estates in Campania and took a great number of his fellow-converts with him to this place of safety. It was a question whether Polycarp the priest or St. Sebastian should accompany the new Christians. Each was eager to stay and face the danger at Rome, and at last, the Pope decided that the Roman church could not spare the services of Sebastian. He continued to work, always in danger, until he was betrayed by a false disciple.

Sebastian could not remain hidden, so when Emperor Diocletian heard of all that he had done, he accused him of ingratitude to the Roman gods. When Sebastian said that he was a Christian and would always pray for the empire, Diocletian commanded that he should be tied up and that the archers should use him as a target. When they had covered him with arrows, they left him. They believed that Sebastian was dead.

However, a widow named Irene came by night to take the body away. She found Sebastian still alive, so she carried him to her house and cared for him. In a few days he was completely recovered and standing on the steps of the palace he scolded the emperors for their unjust persecution of the Christians and begged him to stop. Diocletian was astonished, asking if he was Sebastian who had been shot to death by arrows. To this, the saint replied that he had been revived by Christ that he could rebuke them for the evil which they did. Then the emperor ordered that Sebastian was to be taken into the Hippodrome of the palace and killed.

The Church honors Sebastian for his bravery and double martyrdom.

Reflections

- Your ordinary daily work will give you opportunities for laboring for the faith. Ask help from St. Sebastian. He was not a priest nor a religious, he was a soldier.
- Remember daily the fact that when you receive the Sacrament of Confirmation you will be made, really and truly, a soldier of Christ.

Cosmas and Damian, Saints of the Eastern Empire

by Amy Steedman

It is difficult sometimes to learn a great deal about the saints who lived a very long time ago. Few people knew how to read or write in those old days, and the only way they had of remembering and handing on what was interesting was to tell it to their children; then these little ones, when they were grown up, would repeat it to other little children, and so the stories were not forgotten.

But sometimes one thing would be left out and sometimes another, or different people would add stories of their own, which would become part of the true story. And so, when at last these histories come to us, we find we have lost a great deal, and perhaps not gained very much.

The two saints, to whose story we are going to listen today, are of this long-ago time, and the history of their lives has almost faded from men's memories. But whoever happens to go to Florence, that city of flowers, will see the portraits of our two saints wherever they go. For the old painters loved to tell the saint stories in their own beautiful way, and today the little dark-eyed Italian children can read them without books, for they are told more plainly and far more beautifully than in any written story.

Cosmas and Damian were brothers and were born in Arabia three hundred years after Christ. When they were quite little boys their father died, and they were left alone with their mother. She was a Christian, and taught her boys, as soon as they were old enough to understand, that though they had no earthly father, God was their Father in heaven. She told them that the great King of Heaven and Earth called them His children, and he who could do a mean or cruel act, or stain his honor by an untruthful word, was not worthy to be called a King's son. And because they were noble, she taught them that they must do noble deeds, bravely defend and protect the weak, and help those who could not help themselves.

So, the boys grew up straight and strong in mind and body. Their bitterest punishment was to feel that they had done anything unworthy of their King, and although they often made mistakes and did wrong thoughtlessly, they never went far astray since God's honor was their own.

Their mother was rich, for their father had had great possessions, but there were so many poor and suffering people around their home that it was almost impossible to help them all. So the boys learned early to deny themselves in many ways and often gave up their dinner to the starving poor. In that land, there was a great deal of sickness and suffering, and this was greatly troubling to Cosmas and Damian. They could not bear to see people in pain and be unable to help them. They often thought about this, and at last determined to learn all about medicine and become doctors, so that they might at least soften suffering when they could not cure it.

After years of patient study, they became very clever doctors, and their kind hearts and gentle hands soothed and comforted those who were in pain, even when skill could do nothing for them.

They visited rich and poor alike and would take no money for their services, for they said it was payment enough to know they had been able to make the world's suffering a little less.

And it was not only people they cared for but animals, too. If any animal was in pain, they would treat it as gently and carefully as if it had been a human being. Indeed, they were perhaps even more pitiful towards animals, for they said, "People who can speak and complain of their ills are greatly to be pitied, but these creatures, made by our King, can only suffer in silence, and surely their suffering will be required at our hands."

It always seemed strange to these great men that boys who would never mistreat a younger child, or take mean advantage of a weak one, would still think nothing of staining their honor by mistreating an animal, infinitely weaker and smaller, and less able to protect itself. It was one of the few things that raised the wrath of these gentle doctor saints.

Now it happened that a poor woman who had been ill for many years heard of the fame of the two young doctors and sent to implore them to come to help her. She believed that although her illness seemed incurable these good men might heal her.

Cosmas and Damian were touched by her faith, and they went at once and did for her all that their skill could devise, and, moreover, prayed that God would bless their efforts.

To the wonder of all, the woman began to grow better, and very soon was completely cured. In her great gratitude, she offered all that she had in payment to the two doctors, but they told her that they could take nothing. Then she humbly offered them a little bag in which were three eggs, praying them not to go away from her empty-handed. But Cosmas turned and walked away and would not so much as even look at what she offered, for it was a very strict rule with the brothers that they should accept no payment or reward of any kind. Then the woman caught at a fold of Damian's cloak as he also turned to go and begged him, for the love of Christ, to take her little gift.

When Damian heard the name of his Master, he paused, and then took the present and courteously thanked the poor woman.

But when Cosmas saw what Damian had done, he was very angry, and that night he refused to remain in the same house with him, saying that from then on they would no longer be brothers.

But in the stillness of the night, God came to Cosmas and said, "My son, why are you so angry with your brother?"

"Because he has taken reward for our services," said Cosmas, "and You know, Lord, that we receive no payment but from You"'

"But was it not in My name that he took the offering?" asked the voice. "Because that poor woman gave it for love of Me, your brother did well to accept it."

Then Cosmas awoke in great joy and hurried to the bedside of his brother, and there begged his forgiveness for having misjudged him so sorely. And so, they were happy together once more and ate the eggs merrily.

In those days there were many pilgrims passing through Arabia, and because the journey was hard and most of them were poor, they often fell ill and required the care of Cosmas and Damian. One night, a poor man was brought in, fainting and fever-stricken. He lay on the bed with his thin, grey face pinched and worn with suffering, and the kind doctors feared that he would die.

All night they sat by his bedside doing everything within their skill to ease his pain, and they only smiled when the poor man said in his faint, low voice, "Why do you take all this trouble for a poor pilgrim, who has nothing to repay you?"

"We would not take your payment if you had all the riches in the world," answered the doctors, "for we receive payment only from our King."

Then, when the first pale light of dawn began to steal through the little window, and the doctors anxiously watched the still form lying there, they started with surprise. For the face seemed to change in an instant, and instead of a bed of suffering they saw a cloud of glory; out of the midst of which Christ's face, infinitely tender, looked upon them; and His hands touched their heads in blessing as He said, "All the riches of the world are indeed mine though I seemed but a poor pilgrim. I was sick and you visited me, and surely you shall receive payment from your King."

Then Cosmas and Damian knelt in worship and thanked their Lord that they had been counted worthy to minister to His need.

But soon the fame of Cosmas and Damian spread abroad, and the Proconsul of Arabia heard about their good deeds. When he discovered that they were Christians, and helped the poor and suffering, he was filled with rage and ordered that the two brothers should be cast into the sea.

Immediately Cosmas and Damian were seized and led up to the steep cliffs, and the guards bound them hand and foot. Not a complaint escaped their lips, not a sign of fear, as the soldiers raised them on high and flung them over into the cruel sea, far below. But as the crowd above watched to see them sink, great fear and amazement seized the soldiers, for from the calm blue sea they saw the brothers rise slowly and walk towards the shore, led by an angel who guided them with loving care until they were safe on land.

In a greater rage than ever, the Proconsul ordered that a great fire should be made and that the brothers should be cast into the midst of it. But though the fire roared and blazed before Cosmas and Damian were cast in; as soon as it touched them it died down and nothing could make it burn again. It seemed as if God's good gifts refused to injure His servants.

After that, they were bound to two crosses and the soldiers were ordered to stone them. But the stones did no harm to those two patient figures, but instead fell backward and injured the men who threw them.

Then everyone cried out that they were enchanters, and it was ordered that to make sure of their death they should be beheaded.

So, the work of the two saint doctors was finished on earth, but for many years afterward, those who were ill would pray to these saints for their protection.

Many wonderful stories have grown up around the names of Saint Cosmas and Saint Damian. While we cannot tell if many of these legends really happened, this we do surely know to be true, that these two brothers, who lived in an age when men were cruel and selfish, spent their whole lives in trying to help those who suffered pain and then went bravely to death in the service of their King. And though we know little about them, they have left us an example of patient kindness and helpfulness; and they teach us that as servants of their King we also are bound in honor to protect the weak and help those who suffer, whether they are people like ourselves or any of God's creatures.

Unit Five:
Rise of Christendom, Fall of the Empire

THEME: PERSEVERANCE

FREEDOM FOR THE CHURCH

Adapted from the work of Rev. Monsignor Edmund J. Goebel Ph. D. and Charlotte M. Yonge

Constantine's claim to the empire was disputed by several rivals; but the strongest among them was Maxentius, who ruled Italy and had a large army. A terrible struggle for power began. Constantine was friendly to the Christians; his mother, St. Helena, was a Christian who would become famous for her discovery of the True Cross of Christ. But until now, Constantine had remained undecided in his belief between Christianity and paganism.

He marched from Gaul to Italy to wage war with his rival for the throne. In the year A.D. 312, just before the Battle of Milvian Bridge near Rome, a bright cross appeared in the sky to Constantine and his whole army. On this cross of light was written, "*In hoc signo vinces*" –"In this sign conquer." This wonderous sight decided his mind; Constantine immediately placed a cross on each standard of his legions.

Although outnumbered three to one, Constantine won the battle. Maxentius was defeated. Constantine entered Rome and was declared by the Senate as Emperor of the West.

He did not immediately become a Christian. But the next year, A.D. 313, Constantine issued an edict, or law, which promised the Christians his favor and protection and permitted them to practice their religion freely. This was called the Edict of Milan. Only two years before, the worst persecution of the Church had raged under Diocletian's rule. Now, under Constantine, the Christians were free to come out of the catacombs.

In the year A.D. 305, Christianity was a religion despised and persecuted by the Roman emperors. By A.D. 395, the Roman emperors had made Christianity the religion of the state. The pagan temples were closed or were taken over by the Christians. Pagan gods were no longer worshipped in Rome or any city of the empire. All the festivals in honor of the pagan gods, including the Olympic Games, were abolished. The pagan civilizations of Greece and Rome had nothing more to contribute.

Constantinople

by Rev. Monsignor Edmund J. Goebel Ph. D.

For about three hundred years after the time of Augustus, the Roman Empire remained strong and powerful. But it was hard for the emperor living in Rome to keep in close touch with the eastern part of the Mediterranean world. Large armies had to be kept in this area to hold back the enemies who tried to invade the empire.

When Constantine became emperor, he wanted to strengthen his hold over this eastern territory. He decided to build a new capital and to locate it in the East. The new capital was named Constantinople, that is, the city of Constantine. In 1929 the Turks changed its name to Istanbul.

Constantinople became an important city because it is located on the narrow strip of water which forms the only passage for ships going from the Black Sea into the Mediterranean. And, also, it is on one of the leading land routes between Asia and Europe. Naturally, the city became very important as a trading center.

During his lifetime, Constantine ruled the entire Roman Empire from his new capital. But after his death, the empire was divided into two parts. The part which had its capital as Constantinople became known as the Eastern Roman Empire. The other part was known as the Western Roman Empire; it was ruled from Rome.

Saint Helena and the Finding of the True Cross

adapted from the work of Eleanor C. Donnelly, James Joseph Baxter, and the Rev. Francis Spirago

The Emperor Constantine's mother, St. Helena, although eighty years old, undertook a pilgrimage in A.D. 326 to the Holy Land, determined to find, if possible, the True Cross.

The sacred wood upon which our Lord Jesus Christ was crucified was hidden for centuries. When Helena arrived in Jerusalem, she ordered the Roman buildings that had been erected on Calvary to be removed and put a band of men to work excavating near the summit of Mount Calvary.

Presently, they came upon three crosses. The difficulty now was to distinguish the cross of Our Lord from the other two. Accordingly, all three were carried in solemn procession to the home of a lady who was dangerously ill. The first and second crosses were touched to the invalid without effect, but when the third was applied to her sick body, she was miraculously restored to health. The authenticity of the sacred relic was instantly proven.

The Feast of the Exaltation of the Cross was established in the Church, and in Palestine, Helena continued to assist in public services and provide a fervent example to all the faithful. She erected monuments worthy of God and the empire. She founded churches, monasteries, and hospitals, and lent aid to every enterprise which built up the Church. Yet this powerful princess still mingled humbly with the crowds of poor faithful.

The Last Fight in the Colosseum

By Charlotte M. Yonge.

From the pits of the Colosseum, Christianity worked its way upwards, and at last, was professed by the emperor on his throne. Persecution came to an end, and no more martyrs fed the beasts in the Colosseum. The Christian emperors endeavored to prevent any more shows where cruelty and death formed the chief attraction, and no truly religious person could endure the spectacle, but custom and love of excitement prevailed even against the emperor. They went on for fully a hundred years after Rome had, in name, become a Christian city.

After one glorious conquest, the Senate invited one of Rome's victorious generals to enter the city in triumph, at the opening of the new year, with the white horses, purple robes, and vermillion-painted cheeks with which triumphant generals of old were welcomed at Rome. The churches were visited instead of the Temple of Jupiter, and there was no murder of the captives; but Roman bloodthirstiness was not yet quenched, and, after the procession had been completed, the Colosseum shows began, innocently at first, with races on foot, on horseback, and in chariots; then followed by a grand hunt of beasts turned loose in the arena; and next a sword dance. But after the sword dance came the arraying of swordsmen, not with blunted weapons, but with sharp spears and swords—a gladiator combat in full earnest. The people, enchanted by this gratification of their savage tastes, applauded with shouts of ecstasy.

Suddenly, however, there was an interruption. A roughly robed man, bareheaded and barefooted, had sprung into the arena and begun waving back the gladiators He called upon the people to stop this shedding of innocent blood and not to scorn God, Whose mercy had just turned away the sword of their enemy, by encouraging murder. Shouts, howls, cries, broke in upon his words; this was no place for preaching, – the old customs of Rome should be observed, –"Back, old man!" "On, gladiators!"

The gladiators thrust aside the meddler and rushed to the attack. He still stood between, holding them apart, striving in vain to be heard. "Sedition! sedition!" – "Down with him!" – was the cry, and the prefect in authority himself added his voice. The gladiators, enraged at interference, cut him down. Stones, or whatever came to hand, rained upon him from the furious people, and he perished in the midst of the arena! He lay dead; then the people began to reflect upon what had been done.

His clothes showed that he was one of the hermits who had vowed themselves to a life of prayer and self-denial, and who were greatly reverenced, even by the most thoughtless. The few who had previously seen him, told that he had come from the wilds of Asia on a pilgrimage, to visit the shrines and keep his Christmas at Rome. They knew that he was a holy man – no more. But his spirit had been stirred by the sight of thousands flocking to see men slaughter one another, and in his simple-hearted zeal, he had resolved to stop the cruelty or die.

He had died, but not in vain. His work was done. The shock of such a death before their eyes turned the hearts of the people; they saw the wickedness and cruelty to which they had blindly surrendered themselves; and since the day when the hermit died in the Colosseum, there has never been another fight of gladiators. The custom was utterly abolished; and one habitual crime was wiped from the earth by the devotion of one humble, obscure man, St. Telemachus.

The Organization of the Church

by Rev. Monsignor Edmund J. Goebel Ph. D.

Even during the persecutions, the Church had grown to such an extent that it needed organization and order. By the time it became free under Constantine, its government was well established.

Christ Himself began the organization of the Church when He chose twelve apostles and seventy-two disciples. To the apostles, He gave full powers to perform all the sacraments. They became the first bishops of the Church. They, in turn, ordained other bishops and left them as overseers in the chief cities of the empire. Later, each diocese was put in the charge of a bishop.

As the Church grew, each province was placed under the charge of an archbishop. The bishops of Jerusalem, Antioch, Constantinople, and Alexandria were known as patriarchs, a title which they have even today.

Christ made St. Peter the visible head of the Church. Throughout the New Testament, the apostles recognized St. Peter's authority. St. Peter was the first Bishop of Rome. Since then, each Pope, St. Peter's successor as Bishop of Rome, has likewise been the visible head of the Church.

Assisting the bishops were the priests and deacons. Priests were ordained by the bishops and had the power to say Mass and to perform most of the sacraments. The deacons had charge of the charitable duties of the Church. They visited the sick and gave food and clothing to the poor.

The Church borrowed several good ideas from the Roman Empire. For instance, a diocese was a division of the empire. The Christians also began to build their churches like the basilicas, or law courts, of the Romans. Furthermore, the vestments which the priest wears at Mass are developments of two Roman garments – the toga and the tunic.

The Council of Nicaea

by Rev. Monsignor Edmund J. Goebel Ph. D.

After Constantine freed the Church from persecution, the Church began the practice of holding councils of bishops to discuss problems. These were held under the leadership of the Pope. The first of these was held in 325 A.D. at Nicaea in Asia Minor. Some people had denied that Christ was God. The council decided that Christ was divine and equal with God the Father.

The council also wrote a profession of faith for all true Christians. This is known as the Nicene Creed. It is said at every Mass every Sunday and on great feasts. We say a shorter and older creed – the Apostles' Creed – when we pray the Rosary.

Saint Nicholas

by Amy Steedman

Of all the saints that little children love, is there any to compare with Santa Claus? The very sound of his name has magic in it, and calls up visions of well-filled stockings, with the presents we particularly want peeping over the top or hanging out at the side, too big to go into the largest sock. Besides, there is something so mysterious and exciting about Santa Claus, for no one seems to have ever seen him. But we picture him to ourselves as an old man with a white beard, whose favorite way of coming into our rooms is down the chimney, bringing gifts for the good children and punishments for the bad.

Yet this Santa Claus, in whose name the presents come to us at Christmas time, is a very real saint, and we can learn a great deal about him, only we must remember that his true name is Saint Nicholas and that he is a real person who lived long years ago, far away in the East.

The father and mother of Nicholas were noble and very rich, but what they wanted most of all was to have a son. They were Christians, so they prayed to God for many years that he would give them their heart's desire; and when at last Nicholas was born, they were the happiest people in the world.

They thought there was no one like their boy; and indeed, he was wiser and better than most children, and never gave them a moment's trouble. But alas, while he was still a child, a terrible plague swept over the country, and his father and mother died, leaving him quite alone.

All the great riches which his father had possessed were left to Nicholas, and among other things, he inherited three bars of gold. These golden bars were his greatest treasure, and he thought more of them than all the other riches he possessed.

Now in the town where Nicholas lived there dwelt a nobleman with three daughters. They had once been very rich, but great misfortunes had overtaken the father, and now they were all so poor they had scarcely enough to live upon.

At last, a day came when there was not even enough bread to eat, and the daughters said to their father, "'Let us go out into the streets and beg, or do anything to get a little money, that we may not starve."

But the father answered, "Not tonight. I cannot bear to think of it. Wait at least until to-morrow. Something may happen to save my daughters from such disgrace."

Now, just as they were talking together, Nicholas happened to be passing, and as the window was open, he heard all that the poor father said. It seemed terrible to think that a noble family should be so poor and actually in want of bread, and Nicholas tried to plan how it would be possible to help them. He knew they would be much too proud to take money from him, so he had to think of some other way. Then he remembered his golden bars, and that very night he took one of them and went secretly to the nobleman's house, hoping to give the treasure without letting the father or daughters know who brought it.

To his joy, Nicholas discovered that a little window had been left open, and by standing on tiptoes, he could just reach it. So, he lifted the golden bar and slipped it through the window, not waiting to hear what became of it, in case anyone should see him. (And now do you see the reason why the visits of Santa Claus are so mysterious?)

Inside the house, the poor father sat sorrowfully watching, while his children slept. He wondered if there was any hope for them anywhere, and he prayed earnestly that heaven would send help. Suddenly something fell at his feet, and to his amazement and joy, he found it was a bar of pure gold.

"My child," he cried, as he showed his eldest daughter the shining gold, "God has heard my prayer and has sent this from heaven. Now we shall have enough and to spare. Call your sisters that we may rejoice together, and I will go instantly and trade this treasure."

The precious golden bar was soon sold to a moneychanger, who gave so much for it that the family was able to live in comfort and have all that they needed. And not only was there enough to live upon, but so much was left over that the father gave his eldest daughter a large dowry, and very soon she was happily married.

When Nicholas saw how much happiness his golden bar had brought to the poor nobleman, he determined that the second daughter should have a dowry too. So, he went as before and, finding the little window again open, he was able to throw in the second golden bar as he had done the first. This time the father was dreaming happily and did not find the treasure until he awoke in the morning. Soon afterward the second daughter had her dowry and was married too.

The father now began to think that, after all, it was not usual for golden bars to fall from heaven, and he wondered if by any chance human hands had placed them in his room. The more he thought of it the stranger it seemed, and he made up his mind to keep watch every night, in case another golden bar should be sent as a portion for his youngest daughter.

And so, when Nicholas went the third time and dropped the last bar through the little window, the father came quickly out, and before Nicholas had time to hide, caught him by his cloak.

"O Nicholas," he cried, "is it you who has helped us in our need? Why did you hide yourself?" And then he fell on his knees and began to kiss the hands that had helped him so graciously.

But Nicholas begged him to stand up and give thanks to God instead; warning him to tell no one the story of the golden bars.

This was only one of the many kind acts Nicholas loved to do, and it was no wonder that he was beloved by all who knew him.

Soon afterward Nicholas made up his mind to enter God's service as a priest. He longed above all things to leave the world and live as a hermit in the desert, but God came to him in a vision and told him he must stay in the crowded cities and do his work among the people. Still, his desire to see the deserts and the hermits who lived there was so great that he went off on a journey to Egypt and the Holy Land. But, remembering what God had told him to do, he did not stay there but returned to his own country.

On the way home, a terrific storm arose, and it seemed as if the ship he was in would be lost. The sailors could do nothing, and great waves dashed over the deck, filling the ship with water. But just as all had given up hope, Nicholas knelt and prayed to God to save them, and immediately a calm fell upon the angry sea. The winds stilled and the waves ceased to lash the sides of the ship so that they sailed smoothly on, and all danger was past.

Thus, Nicholas returned home in safety and went to live in the city of Myra, in what is now the country of Turkey. His ways were so quiet and humble that no one knew much about him until it came to pass one day that the Archbishop of Myra died. Then all the priests met to choose another archbishop, and it was made known to them by a sign from heaven that the first man who should enter the church next morning should be the bishop whom God had chosen.

Now Nicholas used to spend most of his nights in prayer and always went very early to church, so next morning just as the sun was rising and the bells began to ring for the early mass, he was seen coming up to the church door and was the first to enter. As he knelt down quietly to say his prayers as usual, what was his surprise to meet a company of priests who hailed him as their new archbishop, chosen by God to be their leader and guide. So, Nicholas was made Archbishop of Myra to the joy of all in the city who knew and loved him.

Not long after this there was great trouble in the town of Myra, for the harvests of that country had failed and a terrible famine swept over the land. Nicholas, as a good bishop should, felt the suffering of his people as if it were his own, and did all he could to help them.

He knew that they must have food, or they would die, so he went to the harbor where two ships lay filled with grain and asked the captains if they would sell him their cargo. They told the bishop they would willingly do so, but it was already sold to merchants of another country and they dared not sell it over again.

"Do not think of that," said Nicholas, "only sell me some of your grain for my starving people, and I promise you that there shall be nothing wanting when you arrive at your journey's end."

The captains believed in the bishop's promise and gave him as much grain as he asked. And behold! when they came to deliver their cargo to the owners, there was not a bag missing.

It is said, too that two men in Myra had been unjustly condemned to death, and the bishop was told how greatly in need they were of his help. No one ever appealed to Nicholas in vain, and he went off at once to the place of execution. The executioner was just about to raise his sword when Nicholas seized his arm and wrenched the sword away. Then he set the poor prisoners free and told the judge that, if he dared to deal so unjustly again, the wrath of heaven and of the Bishop of Myra would descend upon him.

There are many other stories told about the good bishop. Like his Master, he ever went about doing good; and when he died, there were a great many legends told about him, for the people loved to believe that their bishop still cared for them and would come to their aid. We do not know if all these legends are true, but they show how much Saint Nicholas was loved and honored even after his death, and how everyone believed in his power to help them. It ever helped and comforted his people to think that, though they could no longer see him, he would love and protect them still.

Young maidens in need of help remembered the story of the golden bars and felt sure the good saint would not let them want. Sailors tossing on the stormy waves thought of that storm which had calmed at the prayer of Saint Nicholas. Poor prisoners with no one to take their part were comforted by the thought of those other prisoners whom he had saved. And little children perhaps have remembered him most of all, for when the happy Christmas time draws near, who is so much in their thoughts as Saint Nicholas, or Santa Claus, as they call him? Perhaps they are a little inclined to think of him as some good magician who comes to fill their stockings with gifts, but they should never forget that he was the kind bishop who, in olden days, loved to make the little ones happy. There are some who think that even now he watches over and protects little children, and for that reason, he is called their patron saint.

Saint Augustine of Hippo

By Amy Steedman

The story of the life of Saint Augustine is different from almost every other saint story because it is taken from his own words and not from what has been said about him. He wrote a wonderful book called *The Confessions of Saint Augustine*, and in it, we find all that he thought and did from the time he was a little child.

Augustine was born in 354 in the northern part of Africa, which then belonged to Rome, and was one of the richest countries in the world. His mother, Monica, was a Christian, but all her prayers and loving care could not keep her son from evil ways. He is often called the prodigal saint because he wandered very far astray for many years like the youngest son in the parable, living in the midst of the sins and evil pleasures of the world until he learned to say, "I will arise and go to my father."

And so, Augustine's story comforts and helps us when we feel how easy it is to do wrong, and how we fail every day to do the good things we meant to do. There are so few days we can mark off as really having tried our best to be good, and so many days we are glad to forget because of our failings. And yet, if we fight on to the end, we too may be saints as Augustine was, for he won his crown through many failures.

The story, in Augustine's own words, begins from the time when he was a very little baby, not from what he remembers, but from what he had learned as he watched other babies in whom he saw a picture of himself.

First of all, Augustine tells of the tiny baby, who does nothing but sleep and eat and cry. Then the baby begins to laugh a little when he is awake, and very soon shows clearly his likes and dislikes, and kicks and beats with his little hands when he does not get exactly what he wants. Then comes the time of learning to speak and walk.

After that Augustine begins really to remember things about himself. For who could ever forget the trial of first going to school? Oh, how Augustine hated it, and how hard it seemed to him! The lessons were so difficult, and the masters were so strict, and he loved play so much better than work. When he went back to school with lessons unlearned and work undone, the result was that he was punished. It did seem so unjust to him, for he could not see the use of lessons, and the punishments were so painful. And in his book, he tells us how they made him say his first prayer to God—"I used to ask Thee, though a very little boy, yet with no little earnestness, that I might not be punished at school."

Augustine could not see the reason why he should be forced to stay indoors and learn dull, wearisome lessons when he might be playing in the sunshine and learning new games, which seemed so much more worth knowing. How those games delighted him! He was always eager to be first, to win the victory, and to be ahead of everyone else.

He did not understand how it could all be meant for his good. We never quite understand that until we have left school far behind.

I wonder if we all wrote down just exactly what we felt and did when we were little children, whether we would have as many things to confess as Augustine had? There are some little faults that no one is very ashamed to confess. But who would like to confess to being greedy and stealing sweet things from the table when no one was looking? Who would care to admit that he cheated at games, caring only to come out first whether he had played fairly or not? Yet this great saint tells us that he remembers doing all these mean things and looks back on them with great sorrow. He warns other little children to stop these faults at the very beginning, for he knows how strong they grow and how difficult to conquer they become when the mean child grows into a man whom no one can trust.

As time went on and he grew to be a big boy, he went further and further astray. When he was little, he stole things to eat because he was greedy or because he wanted to bribe other little boys to sell him their toys. But now that he was older it was out of mere pride and boastfulness that he took what did not belong to him. He thought it was grand and manly to show off to other boys how little he cared about doing wrong.

Augustine tells us that in a garden near his house there was a pear tree covered with pears that were neither sweet nor large. But just because it belonged to someone else, and he thought it fun to steal, he and his companions went out one dark night and robbed the tree of all its fruit. They did not care to eat the pears, and after tasting one or two threw all the rest to the pigs. There was no particular pleasure in this he admitted, and he would never have done it alone, but he wanted the other boys to admire him and to think he was afraid of nothing.

And so, years went on and Augustine grew up into manhood, and it seemed as if his evil ways would break his mother's heart. Through all his sin and foolishness, she loved him and prayed for him; but he paid no heed to her, and wandered further away into that far country, wasting all he had in living wildly and forgetting the God he had prayed to when he was a child.

One day when his mother, Monica, was weeping over this wandering son of hers and praying for him with all her heart, God sent a comforting dream to her which she never forgot. She thought she saw herself standing on a narrow wooden plank, and towards her there came a shining angel who smiled upon her as she stood there, worn out with sorrow and weeping.

"Why are you so sad, and why do you weep these tears every day?" asked the angel.

"I weep over the ruin of my son," answered the poor mother.

Then the angel told her to stop grieving and be at rest, telling her to look more closely. For on the same narrow plank of salvation where she was standing, Augustine stood beside her.

His mother told Augustine of this dream, and though he only laughed at it, it seemed to sink into his heart, and he remembered it many years after. And to Monica, it came as a breath of hope and comforted her through many dark days. For she was sure that God had sent this dream to tell her that in the end she and her son would stand together in His presence.

But though Monica believed this, she never ceased to do all that was in her power to help Augustine. And once she went to a learned bishop and begged him to talk to Augustine and try what he could do. But the bishop was a wise man and knew that by speaking he would do more harm than good, for Augustine was proud of his unbelief and had no longing in himself for better things. But Monica did not see this and could only implore the bishop to try, until the good man grew frustrated with her and said at last, "I cannot help you in this matter, but go on your way in peace. It cannot be that a son of such tears should perish."

And these words comforted Monica, as the dream had done, and made her sure that in the end, all would be right.

The good bishop spoke truly, for after many years had passed, Augustine began to be weary of his own way and to look for a higher, better life. He longed to turn his face homeward, but now he had lost the way, and for a long time he sought it with bitter tears.

At last, one day, he felt he could bear the burden of his evil life no longer. His sins felt like a heavy chain dragging him down into darkness, with no light to show him which way to turn. Taking a roll of the scriptures he wandered out into the garden and there, as he wept, he heard a voice close by chanting over and over again, "Take, read." He thought it must be some game that children were playing, but he could remember no game that had those words in it. And then he thought perhaps this was a voice from heaven in answer to his prayer, telling him what to do.

Eagerly he took the holy writings in his hand and opened them to read, and there he found words telling him what sort of life he should lead. In a moment it all seemed clear to him. His Father was waiting to receive and pardon him; so, he arose and left the far country and all his evil habits and turned his face to God.

And then he tells how he went straight to his mother – the mother who had loved and believed in him through all those evil days and told her like a little child how sorry he was at last.

Then, indeed, Monica's mourning was turned into joy. And so, at her life's end, she and her son sat hand in hand, both looking up towards the dawning heaven, he with eyes ashamed but full of hope, and she with tears all washed away, and eyes that shone with more than earthly joy.

When his mother at last died and left him alone, Augustine did not grieve, for he knew the parting was not for long. All that was left for him to do now was to strive to make good those years he had wasted and be more fit to meet her when God should call him home.

And so, it came to pass that this great sinner became one of God's saints and did wonderful works for Him in the world. He was made Bishop of Hippo, a city in Africa, and was one of the most famous bishops the world has ever known.

There is one legend told of Augustine which has comforted many hearts when puzzling questions have arisen, and it has seemed so difficult to understand all the Bible teaches us about our Father in heaven.

They say that once when this great father of the Church was walking along by the seashore, troubled and perplexed because he could not understand many things about God, he came upon a little child playing there alone. The child had dug a hole in the sand and was carefully filling it with water which he brought from the sea in a spoon. The bishop stopped and watched him for a while and then he asked:

"What are you doing, my child?"

"I mean to empty the sea into my hole," answered the child, busily going backward and forwards with his spoon.

"But that is impossible," said the bishop.

"Not more impossible than that your human mind should understand the mind of God," said the child, gazing upwards at him with grave, sweet eyes.

And before the bishop could answer the child had vanished, and the saint knew that God had sent him as an answer to his troubled thoughts, and as a rebuke for his trying to understand the things that only God could know.

The Weakened Empire

by Rev. Monsignor Edmund J. Goebel Ph. D.

Many weaknesses had developed within the Roman Empire, although it appeared to be strong and powerful. Some of the emperors were weak leaders. Many of the Romans had lost the virtues which made their country great. They had become greedy and lazy. They were too lazy either to work or to fight. Those who were wealthy preferred to live in extreme luxury. They looked upon work as something which only slaves should do. The poor were also unwilling to work.

The fields of Italy became idle. Italy did not produce enough grain for the people of the cities. The emperors had to bring grain from distant parts of the empire. This was given to the people free. It was an expensive method of feeding the idle mob of Rome. It meant that taxes increased and became a great burden.

The old Roman line declined in numbers. The emperors had difficulty finding enough soldiers for their armies. Gradually, they had to depend on the Teuton tribes who lived outside the empire. They brought thousands of these outsiders, who they called "barbarians," to Rome as slaves to do the work in the city and on the farms. Later they permitted several of the tribes to come into the empire and settle down. Very soon the Roman legions were made up almost entirely of the barbarians. Some of the Teuton leaders became Roman generals, and some became the chief advisers of the emperors. Without realizing what they were doing, the Romans had permitted the outsiders to take over the empire.

The Teutonic Tribes

by Rev. Monsignor Edmund J. Goebel Ph. D.

All along the northern boundary of the Roman Empire, there lived tribes whom the more civilized Greeks and Romans called barbarians. The tribes living in Gaul and Britain at the time Julius Caesar conquered those regions belonged to the Celts.

Near the river Rhine, Caesar found tribes of the Teutons. The Rhine and the Danube rivers formed a natural boundary between the Teutons, or Germans, and the Roman Empire. A great wall and a series of forts were erected between the two rivers by the Romans to keep the tribes from entering the empire.

Yet the warm climate, the fertile lands, and the wealthy cities of the Roman Empire continued to attract these tribes from the colder areas of Europe. The Teutonic tribes lived among rough mountains, dense forests, and swamplands in what are now Germany and Austria. The peoples who lived farther to the east – the Slavs and the Huns – were pushing the Teutons westward and southward.

The Romans have left us some vivid descriptions of the Teutons. They were very tall and seemed like giants to the shorter Romans. They had fair skin, blond hair, and fierce blue eyes. Living outdoors most of the time in a cold climate made them very hardy and strong.

They lived in small villages. Their houses were like thatched huts. Their food was simple. They ate fish, meat, fruit, vegetables, grains, milk, and cheese. The clothing of these barbaric tribesmen was coarse and simple. Usually, it was made from the skins of animals or rough woolen or linen cloth.

These people were very warlike. They enjoyed fighting much more than working. In fact, the warriors left most of the work to the old men or the women.

They had many good qualities. They were brave and courageous. They were always true to their word. They treated women with great respect, and their family life was superior to that of the Romans at the time of the empire.

Before the Christian missionaries taught the German tribes about the true God, their religion was pagan. They worshipped many gods and goddesses. The chief of the gods was Woden. His wife was Frigg. Thor, the son of Woden, was the god of thunder. Another son was Tiu, the god of war. The days of our week have come from the names of these four gods. Wednesday is Woden's day; Friday, Frigg's day; Thursday, Thor's day; and Tuesday, Tiu's day.

There was very little government among the Teutonic tribesmen. They had no written laws. But they had a great respect for the customs and rules of their tribes. At the head of each tribe was a chief, who was chosen by warriors. When the tribe was at peace, the chief acted as judge and settled the less important disputes that arose. In matters of more importance, he discussed affairs with the people in their assemblies. Then a vote of the warriors was taken. If the warriors agreed to his suggestions, they clashed their spears or swords against their shields. This was their method of voting.

Alaric the Visigoth

by Eva March Tappan, Ph. D.

The time had come when Rome needed to be defended. In the early days, it had been only a tiny settlement, but it had grown in power till the Romans ruled all Europe south of the Rhine and the Danube, also Asia Minor, Northern Africa, and Britain. Nearly all the people of Europe are thought to have come from Central Asia. One tribe after another moved to the westward from their early home into Europe, and when the hunting and fishing became poor in their new settlements, they went on still farther west. The Celts came first, pushing their way through Central Europe, and finally into France, Spain, and the British Isles. Later, the Latins and Greeks took possession of Southern Europe. Meanwhile, the Celts had to move faster than they wished into France, Spain, and Britain, because following close behind them and taking possession of Central Europe came the Teutons. These Teutons, a group of men who lived a wild, restless, half-savage life, roamed back and forth between the Danube and the shores of the Baltic Sea. They consisted of many different tribes, but the Romans called them all Germans. For many years the Germans had tried to cross the Danube and the Rhine, and break into the Roman Empire, but the Roman armies had driven them back and had destroyed their rude villages again and again. Sometimes, however, the Germans were so stubborn in their efforts to get into the empire that the Roman emperors found it convenient to admit certain tribes as allies.

As time went on, a tribe of Teutons called Goths became the most troublesome of all to the Romans. Part of them lived on the shores of the Black Sea, and were called Ostrogoths, or Eastern Goths; while those who lived near the shores of the Danube were called Visigoths, or Western Goths. Toward the end of the fourth century, the Visigoths found themselves between two fires, for another people, the Huns were driving them into the Roman Empire, and the Romans were driving them back. The Visigoths could not fight both nations, and in despair, they sent ambassadors to the Romans. "Let us live on your side of the river," they pleaded. "Give us food, and we will defend the frontier for you." The bargain was made, but it was broken by both parties. It had been agreed that the Goths should give up their arms, but they bribed the Roman officers and kept them. The Romans had promised to furnish food, but they did not keep their word. Hungry warriors with weapons in their hands make fierce enemies. The Goths revolted, and the Roman emperor was slain.

As the years passed, the Goths grew stronger and the Romans weaker. By and by, a man named Alaric became the leader of the Visigoths. He and his followers had fought under Roman commanders. He had been in Italy twice, and he began to wonder whether it would not be possible for him and his brave warriors to fight their way into the heart of the Roman Empire. One night he dreamed that he was driving a golden chariot through the streets of Rome and that the Roman citizens were thronging about him and shouting, "Hail, O Emperor, hail!" Another time, when he was passing by a sacred grove, he heard, or thought he heard, a voice cry, "You will make your way to the city." "The city" meant Rome, of course; and now Alaric called his chief men together and laid his plans before them. First, they would go to Greece, he said. The warlike Goths shouted for joy, for in the cities of Greece were treasures of gold and silver, and these would fall into the hands of the victors. They went on boldly, and before long Alaric and his followers were feasting in Athens, while great masses of treasure were waiting to be distributed among the soldiers. The Greeks had forgotten how brave their ancestors had been, and Alaric had no trouble in sweeping the country. At last, however, the general Stilicho was sent with troops from Rome; and now Alaric would have been captured or slain if he had not succeeded in slipping away. Before this, the Roman Empire had been divided into two parts, the western and the eastern. The capital of the western part was Rome; that of the eastern was Constantinople.

The young man of eighteen who was emperor in the eastern part of the empire became jealous of Stilicho. "If he wins more victories, he will surely try to make himself emperor," thought the foolish boy; and he concluded that it would be an exceedingly wise move to make Alaric governor of Eastern Illyricum. This was like setting a hungry cat to watch a particularly tempting little mouse; for Illyricum stretched along the Adriatic Sea, and just across the narrow water lay Italy. Of course, after a few years, Alaric set out for Italy. The boy emperor in the western part of the empire ran away as fast as he could go. He would have been captured had not Stilicho appeared. Then Alaric and his warriors held a council. "Shall we withdraw and make sure of the treasure that we have taken, or shall we push on to Rome?" questioned the warriors. "I will find in Italy either a kingdom or a grave," declared the chief; but Stilicho was upon them, and they were obliged to retreat. Then the boy emperor returned to Rome to celebrate the victory and declare that he had never thought of such a thing as being afraid. Nevertheless, he hurried away to a safe fortress again and left Rome to take care of itself.

Alaric waited for six years, but meanwhile, he watched everything that went on in Italy. The boy emperor had become a man of twenty-five, but he was as foolish as ever; and now, like the emperor in the East, he concluded that Stilicho meant to become ruler of the empire, and he murdered the only man who could have protected it.

This was Alaric's opportunity, and he marched straight up to the walls of Rome, shut off food from the city, and commanded it to surrender. The luxurious Romans were indignant that a mere barbarian should think of conquering their city. Even after they were weakened by famine and pestilence, they told Alaric that if he would give them generous terms of surrender, they might yield; "but if not," they said, "sound your trumpets and make ready to meet a countless multitude." Alaric laughed and retorted, "The thicker the hay, the easier it is mowed." He would leave Rome, he declared, they would bring him all the gold and silver of the city. Finally, however, he agreed to accept 5000 pounds of gold, 30,000 pounds of silver, 4000 robes of silk, 3000 pieces of scarlet cloth, and 3000 pounds of pepper.

Only two years later Alaric came again, and the proud Romans were ready to do whatever he commanded. This time he put the prefect of the city upon the throne, but a little later he came a third time and encamped before the walls of Rome. The trumpets blew blast after blast, and the invaders poured into the city. Alaric bade his men spare both churches and people, but the Goths killed all who opposed them, or whom they suspected of concealing their wealth. Then they went away, loaded with gold and silver and silk and jewels. They were in no haste to leave Italy with its wine and oil and cattle and corn; moreover, Alaric was not satisfied with sacking Rome; he meant to get possession of Sicily and then make an expedition to Africa. Suddenly all these plans came to an end, for he was taken ill and died. His followers turned aside a little river from its channel, wrapped the body of their dead leader in the richest of the Roman robes, and made his grave in the riverbed. They heaped around it the most splendid of their treasures and then turned back the waters of the stream to flow over it forever. Finally, lest the grave should become known and be robbed or dishonored, they put to death the multitude of captives whom they had forced to do this work.

The Romans Leave Britain

by Eva March Tappan, Ph. D.

If the Romans could have given all their attention to Britain, they would have been able to overcome the whole island, but there was trouble in Rome. The barbarous tribes that lived to the north and east were pressing nearer and nearer to the city, and the Romans must defend their own country. Every year fewer Romans came to Britain, and every year some of the conquerors had to return to Italy. At last, in A.D. 410, soldiers and commanders departed from the island, and never again did they set foot on British soil.

While the Romans had been in Britain, the conquered people had learned from them much that was good. They had learned how to make excellent roads and how to drain the swamps. They had seen that houses could be built that would be far more comfortable than huts of poles. They had found that it was not enough for soldiers to be brave and fearless; they must also be drilled and know how to obey their commander so that an army could be managed as if it were a great machine.

With this gain, there was also a loss, for many of them had begun to feel that the way to be happy was to live in luxurious houses and be waited upon by slaves instead of working for themselves. Then in their fighting, although they were just as brave as ever, they had become accustomed to thinking that their leaders must be Romans; and when, a few years later, the time came that they must both fight and lead, they felt helpless and wished that the Romans were with them again.

The Saxon Conquest. After the Romans had gone, matters grew worse and worse with the Britons, for the Scots and Picts were coming down upon them from the north and northwest, and the Saxons were coming from over the sea and landing on the eastern and southern shores. These marauders burned the houses and crops, stole the treasures, and wither killed the people or carried them away as slaves. At last, the sufferers sent a piteous letter to Rome. It was called "The Groans of the Britons," and it begged that the Roans would come and help them. "The barbarians," it said, "drive us to the sea, the sea drives us back to the barbarians; between them, we are either slain or drowned." There were other barbarians, however than those that distressed Britain, and now great hordes of them were coming down upon Rome so that the Romans had more than they could do to take care of themselves, and not one soldier could be spared to help the poor Britons. What should the distressed people do?

The chief men met together and talked it over. At last one of them said, "The Romans do not help us, and there is no one else to call upon. The Saxons are stronger than the Scots and Picts. Let us, then, as the Saxons to come over and fight for us. We can give them the island of Thanet for their home, and we shall be free from the robbers of the north."

The strangers were invited to come. They came, they drove away the Scots and Picts, and they settled on Thanet. Before long, they found Thanet too small, so they drive the Britons away from the southeastern corner of the land and took it for themselves. More and more of the Saxons came, and farther and farther to the west were the Britons driven. They were not cowards, and they resisted so valiantly that it was more than one hundred years before they were completely overcome. The end of it was, however, that most of the Britons were killed or else became slaves, while the few who escaped had to flee to the mountains of Wales to save their lives. Britain was in the hands of the Saxons.

The Saxons. These new conquerors had lived in Jutland, which is now a part of Denmark and Germany. They were called Saxons, Angles, and Jutes, but the Britons spoke of them all as Saxons, perhaps because the short, broad knife that they carried in battle was called a seax. Savage as they were with the Britons, the Saxons had many good traits. They were brave and warlike on land and sea. They had so much respect for women that when, in their earliest poem, a wicked woman is introduced, the author speaks of her as if he were greatly surprised that a woman should be evil. They cultivated the ground, lived on simple food, and were always ready to share whatever they had with anyone who came to be their guests. They were not willing to live in cities, but wished every family to have a house with some land around it. Their leaders never told them what they must do, but they all met in the open air and talked over what was best; then they decided the question by voting. They worshipped many gods, and among them were the seven from whom the days of the week are named: the sun, the moon, Tui, Woden, Thor, Freya, Seotre. Our word *Easter* comes from their *Eostre*, who was the goddess of spring.

Before the Saxons came to Britain, they composed an epic poem called *Beowulf.* This poem was not written until perhaps four hundred years after it was composed. One harper would sing it, and then another would sing it as he remembered it, putting in new lines whenever he forgot and adding to the story wherever he thought that he could improve it. Finally, the poem was written, and one of the manuscripts chanced to be saved.

The Struggle Against the Huns

by Rev. Monsignor Edmund J. Goebel Ph. D.

The Celtic tribes to the west and the Slavic tribes to the east were similar to the Teutons. All these people might have made a peaceful settlement with the Romans. The tribes who lived along the border of the empire had already become partly civilized. But now a new threat entered Europe from the east.

These were the fierce Huns, who came from somewhere in central Asia. Coming on horseback, the Huns appeared suddenly in great numbers. Wherever they went, they threw fear into all who saw them. According to writers of the time, they seemed fearful to look at, for the fair-haired Teutons found their dark eyes and long, dark hair strange.

The Huns struck terror into the Teutonic tribes. Directly in the path of the Huns were the Gothic tribes. The East Goths, or Ostrogoths, surrendered to the Huns, but the West Goths, or Visigoths, fled before them. The Visigoth chieftains begged the emperor Valens at

Constantinople to permit them to cross the Danube River into the empire.

Valens made an agreement with the Visigoths. They were to furnish him with warriors, and Rome was to supply food to the Visigoths. When the Romans failed to keep their promises, the Visigoths rose in rebellion. At Adrianople, in the year A.D. 378, they defeated Valens and his army.

Later, the entire Visigoth nation, under their leader Alaric, began to move again. They crossed through Greece and marched up around the Adriatic Sea into Italy. In A.D. 410 they captured and sacked the city of Rome. Many of the treasures of the city were destroyed or stolen. The Visigoths finally went into Spain, where they settled in a fertile, pleasant area.

Attila, the Hun. The Huns had moved into the territory abandoned by the Visigoths, north of the Danube. But they were restless and wanted to push into the Roman Empire. Under a terrible leader, Attila, they marched first into Gaul.

For three years Attila and his Huns burned and ravaged the towns in Gaul and Italy. Attila was called the "Scourge of God." As he advanced toward Rome, Pope St. Leo went out to meet him. Attila was impressed by the dignity of the Pope and agreed not to attack Rome.

Shortly thereafter, Attila died, and his followers were forced back to the east. They were no longer a threat to Europe and, in fact, disappeared from history.

Attila the Hun

by Eva March Tappan, Ph. D.

While Alaric was winning his victories, the Huns had built on the banks of the Danube what they looked upon as their capital. The homes of the poorer folk were huts of mud or straw; but the king, Attila, and his chief men lived in houses of wood with columns finely carved and polished. There was plenty of some kinds of luxury in this strange capital, for the tables of the chiefs were loaded with golden dishes; and swords, shoes, and even the trappings of the horses gleamed with gold and sparkled with jewels. King Attila, however, would have no such elegance. "I live as did my ancestors," he declared; and in his wooden palace, he wore only the plainest of clothes. He ate nothing but flesh, and he was served in rough wooden bowls and plates. Nevertheless, he was proud of his wealth because it had been taken from enemies, and so was proof of the bravery and daring of his people.

This king of a barbarous tribe meant to become the greatest of conquerors. Even in the early years of his reign, he had hoped to do this. It is said that one of his shepherds noticed one day that the foot of an ox was wet with blood. He searched for the cause and discovered a sharp point of steel sticking up from the ground. He began to dig around it and soon saw that it was a sword. "That must go to the king," he said to himself, and he set out for the palace. King Attila examined the weapon closely and declared, "This is the sword of Tyr. I will wear it as long as I live, for no one who wears the sword of the war-god can ever know defeat."

When Attila had made his preparations, he set out with his followers to conquer the world. Before long, Constantinople was in his power. The emperor in the East called himself the Invincible Augustus, but he could not meet Attila, and to save his city and his life he had to give the barbarians 6000 pounds of gold and a large tract of land on the Roman side of the Danube.

Wherever Attila went, he was successful. His ferocious warriors rode like the wind. They would dash down upon some village, kill the inhabitants, snatch up whatever there was of booty, and level the homes of the people so completely that it was said a horse could gallop over the ruins without danger of stumbling. In the far East, he was thought to be a magician. "The Huns have a wonder-stone," declared the folk of that region, "and whenever they choose they can raise storms of wind or rain." It is no wonder that men trembled at the sound of Attila's name and shuddered at the thought of the Scourge of God, as he called himself when they heard any strange sound in the night. "Attila and his Huns are the children of demons," they whispered; and those who had seen them were ready to believe that this was true. They were of a different family from the Goths and Celts and Romans. They were short and thick-set, with big heads and dark, swarthy complexions. Their eyes were small and bright, and so deep-set that they seemed to be far back in their skulls. Their turned-up noses were so short and broad that it was commonly said they had no noses, but only two holes in their faces.

Although Attila had made peace with the Emperor in the East, before long he found an excuse for invading his empire. With the sword of Tyr in his hand, he swept across what is now Germany and France, killing and burning wherever he went. When he came to Orleans, he expected that city to yield as the others had done; but the people had just made their fortifications stronger, and they had no idea of surrendering even to the terrible Huns. But before long, Attila had got possession of the suburbs, he had weakened the walls with his battering-rams, and the people of Orleans began to tremble with fear. Those who could not bear arms were at the altars praying, and their bishop was trying to encourage them by declaring that God would never abandon those who put their trust in Him. "Go to the rampart," he bade a faithful attendant, "and tell me if aid is not at hand." "What did you see?" he asked when the messenger returned. "Nothing," was the reply. A little later the man was sent again, but he had nothing of comfort to report. A third time he climbed the rampart, and now he ran back to the bishop, crying, "A cloud! there is a cloud on the horizon as if made by an army marching!" "It is the aid of God," the bishop exclaimed. "It is the aid of God," repeated the people, and they fought with fresh courage. The cloud grew larger and larger. Now and then there was a flash of steel or the gleam of a war banner. The bishop was right; it was the brave Roman general Aëtius with his army, and Orleans was saved.

Attila withdrew to the plain of Châlons. The Romans and their former foes, the Goths, had united against him, and on this plain was fought one of the most bloody battles ever known. It raged from the middle of the afternoon until night, and some of the people of the country believed that in the darkness the spirits of those who had fallen arose and kept up the fight in mid-air. Attila retreated across the Rhine. If he had won the day the heathen Huns instead of the Christian Germans would have become the most powerful people of Europe. That is why this conflict at Châlons is counted as one of the decisive battles of the world.

After a winter's rest, Attila started to invade Italy. He meant to go straight to Rome, but the strong city of Aquileia was in his way. After a long siege, however, it yielded. Some of the inhabitants of that and other conquered cities fled to a group of marshy islands, where Venice now stands. City after city he captured and burned.

The Romans were thoroughly frightened, for now, Attila was near their city. Aëtius was calm and brave, but he was without troops. Then Pope Leo I, courageous as the Bishop of Orleans, went forth to meet the Huns and begged Attila to spare the city. Attila yielded, but no one knows why. A legend arose, that the apostles Peter and Paul appeared to him and declared that he should die at once if he did not grant the prayers of Leo. It is certain that before he started for Rome his friends had said to him, "Beware! Remember that Alaric conquered Rome and died." He had no fear of a sword, but he may have been afraid of such warnings as this. Whatever was the reason, he agreed to spare Rome if the Romans would pay him a large ransom.

The gold was paid, and Attila returned to his wooden palace on the Danube. Soon after this he suddenly died. His followers cut off their hair and gashed their faces, so that blood rather than tears might flow for him. His body was enclosed in three coffins, one of gold, one of silver, and one of iron. It was buried at night with a vast amount of treasure. Then, as in the case of Alaric, the captives who had dug the grave were put to death. His followers belonged to different tribes. Several chieftains tried to become king, but no one of them was strong enough to hold the tribes together, and they were soon scattered, and the power of the Huns declined forever.

Genevieve, the Shepherd Girl of Nanterre

by Charlotte M. Yonge

Four hundred years of the Roman dominion had entirely tamed the once wild and independent Gauls. Everywhere, except in the moorlands of Brittany, they had become as much like Romans themselves as they could accomplish; they had Latin names, spoke the Latin tongue, all their citizens of higher rank were enrolled as Roman citizens, their chief cities were colonies where the laws were administered by magistrates in the Roman fashion, and the houses, dress, and amusements were the same as those of Italy. The greater part of the towns had been converted to Christianity, though some paganism still lurked in the more remote villages and mountainous districts.

It was upon these civilized Gauls that the terrible attacks came from the wild nations who poured out of the center and east of Europe. The Franks came over the Rhine and its dependent rivers and made furious attacks upon the peaceful plains, where the Gauls had long lived in security, and reports were heard everywhere of villages attacked by wild horsemen, with short double-headed battleaxes, and a horrible short pike, covered with iron. Walled cities usually stopped them, but every farm or villa outside was stripped of its valuables, set on fire, the cattle driven off, and the more healthy inhabitants seized for slaves.

It was during this state of things that a girl was born to a wealthy peasant at the village now called Nanterre, about two miles from the city of Paris. She was christened by an old Gallic name, probably Gwenfrewi, or White Stream, but she is best known by the French name of Genevieve. When she was about seven years old, two celebrated bishops passed through the village, Germanus, and Lupus, on their way to Britain. All the inhabitants flocked into the church to see them, pray with them, and receive their blessing; and here the sweet childish devotion of Genevieve so struck Germanus, that he called her to him, talked to her, made her sit beside him at the feast, gave her his special blessing, and presented her with a copper medal with a cross engraved upon it. From that time the little maiden always considered herself especially consecrated to the service of Heaven, but she still remained at home, daily keeping her father's sheep, and spinning their wool as she sat under the trees watching them, always with a heart full of prayer.

After this St. Germanus proceeded to Britain. He never forgot Genevieve, the little maid whom he had so early recognized for her devotion to God.

After she lost her parents she went to live with her godmother, and continued the same simple habits, leading a life of sincere devotion and strict self-denial, constant prayer, and much charity to her poorer neighbors.

In the year 451, the whole of Gaul was in the most dreadful state of terror at the advance of Attila, the savage chief of the Huns, who came from the banks of the Danube with a host of savages of hideous features, scarred and disfigured to render them more frightful. The old enemies, the Goths, and the Franks seemed like friends compared with these formidable beings whose cruelties were said to be intolerable, and of whom every exaggerated story was told that could add to the horrors of the miserable people who lay in their path. Tidings came that this 'Scourge of God', as Attila called himself, had passed the Rhine, and was in full march for Paris. The whole country was in the utmost terror. Everyone seized their most valuable possessions, and would have fled; but Genevieve placed herself on the only bridge across the Seine River, and argued with them, assuring them in a voice that was afterward thought of as prophetic, that, if they would pray, repent, and defend instead of abandoning their homes, God would protect them. They were at first almost ready to stone her for thus withstanding their panic, but just then a priest arrived with a present for Genevieve from St. Germanus. This reminded the people of the high estimation in which he held her; they became ashamed of their violence, and she held them back to pray and to arm themselves. In a few days, they heard that Attila had paused to besiege the city of Orleans and that the Roman general, hurrying from Italy, had united his troops with those of the Goths and Franks, and given Attila so terrible a defeat that the Huns were fairly driven out of Gaul.

Here it must be mentioned that when the next year, 452, Attila with his murderous host came down into Italy, and after horrible devastation of all the northern provinces, came to the gates of Rome, no one dared to meet him but the holy Bishop, Leo, the pope, who, when his flock were in despair, went forth to meet the invader, and endeavor to turn his wrath side. The savage Huns were struck with awe by the fearless majesty of the unarmed old man. They conducted him safely to Attila, who listened to him with respect, and promised not to lead his people into Rome, provided a tribute should be paid to him. He then retreated, and, to the joy of all Europe, died on his way back to his native dominions.

But with the Huns the danger and suffering of Europe did not end. Peace was utterly unknown in Europe throughout the long breakup of the Roman Empire, and in a few more years the Franks were overrunning the banks of the Seine and actually venturing to lay siege to the Roman walls of Paris itself. The fortifications were strong enough, but hunger began to do the work of the besiegers, and the garrison, unwarlike and untrained, began to despair. But Genevieve's courage and trust never failed. Finding no warriors willing to run the risk of going beyond the walls to obtain food for the women and children who were perishing around them, this brave shepherdess embarked alone in a little boat. Guiding it down the stream, she landed beyond the Frankish camp, and traveling to the different Gallic cities, she begged them to send food to the famished citizens of Paris. She obtained complete success. The Franks probably had no means of obstructing the passage of the river, so that a convoy of boats could easily penetrate into the town, and at any rate, they looked upon Genevieve as something sacred and inspired whom they dare not touch; probably as one of the battle maids in whom their own myths taught them to believe.

But a city where all the valor resided in one woman could not long hold out, and in another inroad, when Genevieve was absent, Paris was seized by the Franks. Their leader, Hilperik, was absolutely afraid of what the mysteriously brave maiden might do to him, and commanded the gates of the city to be carefully guarded lest she should enter; but Genevieve learned that some of the chief citizens were imprisoned and that Hilperik intended their death, and nothing could withhold her from making an effort in their behalf. The Franks had made up their minds to settle, and not to destroy. They were not burning and slaying indiscriminately, but while despising the Romans, as they called the Gauls, for their cowardice, they were in awe of the superior civilization and the knowledge of arts. The country people had free access to the city, and Genevieve in her homely gown and veil passed by Hilperik's guards without being suspected of being more than an ordinary Gaulish village maid; and thus she fearlessly made her way, even to the old Roman halls, where the long-haired Hilperik was holding his wild carousal. Would that we knew more of that meeting—one of the most striking that ever took place! We can only picture to ourselves the Roman tiled floors littered with wine, bones, and fragments of the barbarous revelry. There were untamed Franks, their sun-burnt hair tied up in a knot at the top of their heads, and falling down like a horse's tail, their faces close-shaven, except two mustaches, and dressed in tight leather garments, with swords at their wide belts. Some slept, some feasted, some shouted out their favorite war songs around the table which was covered with the spoils of churches. At their head sat the wild, long-haired chieftain, Hilperik. Yet, there, in her strength, stood the peasant maiden, her heart full of trust and pity, her looks full of the power that is given by fearlessness of them that can kill the body. What she said we do not know—we only know that the barbarous Hilperik was awed; he trembled before the protests of the brave woman, and he granted all she asked—the safety of his prisoners, and mercy to the terrified inhabitants. No wonder that the people of Paris have ever since looked back to Genevieve as their protectress, and that she has become the patron saint of the city.

She lived to see Clovis, the son of Hilperik, marry a Christian wife, Clotilda, and after a time became a Christian. She saw the foundation of the Cathedral of Notre-Dame and gave her full share to the first efforts for bringing the rude and bloodthirsty conquerors to some knowledge of Christian faith, mercy, and purity. After a life of constant prayer and charity she died, three months after King Clovis, in the year 512.

Genseric the Vandal

by Eva March Tappan, Ph. D.

A few years after the death of Attila, Rome was once more in the hands of an invader, Genseric the Vandal. The Vandals were great wanderers. They slowly made their way from the shores of the Baltic Sea to the Danube, passed through what is now France, and went south into Spain. Only eight or nine miles from Spain, just across what is now the Strait of Gibraltar, lay Africa.

Northern Africa belonged to Rome. It was one of her most valued provinces because, while Italy could not raise enough grain to feed her people, Africa could supply all that was needed. Genseric longed to add Africa to his domain, and he was more fortunate than most men who wish to invade a country, for after a little while he received a cordial invitation to come to Africa and bring his soldiers with him. The invitation was given by no less a man than the brave-general Boniface, who had been appointed governor of the province. This is the way it came about. Aëtius was jealous of the success of Boniface, and he persuaded the mother of the child emperor to send the governor a letter recalling him. Then he wrote a letter to his "friend" Boniface with the warning that the empress was angry with him, and he would lose his head if he risked it in Rome. Boniface was in a hard position. He concluded that the safest thing for him to do was to remain where he was and ask Genseric to help him to hold Africa.

Genseric did not wait to be urged. He hurried across the Strait of Gibraltar and began his career of violence. A Vandal conquest was more severe than that of any other tribe, for the Vandals seemed to delight in ruining everything that came into their power. They killed men, women, and children; they burned houses and churches; they destroyed whatever treasures they could not carry away with them. Some said that whenever they conquered a country, they cut down every fruit tree within its limits. This is why people who seem to enjoy spoiling things are sometimes called *vandals*.

After a while, Boniface discovered that he had been tricked by Aëtius, and he begged Genseric to leave the country; but the barbarian refused, and Boniface could not drive him away. Genseric and his followers settled in Africa, making the city of Carthage the capital of their kingdom, and they became a nation of pirates. They built light swift vessels and ravaged the shore of any country where they expected to find plunder.

All this time Genseric had his eyes fixed upon Italy, and again he was fortunate enough to be invited to a land which he was longing to invade. This time the widow of a murdered emperor begged him to come and avenge her wrongs. He wasted no time, but crossed the narrow sea and marched up to the walls of Rome. Behold, the gates were flung open, and once more Leo, now a gray-haired old man, came forth with his clergy, all in their priestly robes, to beg the Vandals to have mercy. Genseric made some promises, but they were soon broken. For fourteen days the Vandals did what they would. They were in no hurry; they had plenty of ships to carry away whatever they chose; and after they had chosen, there was little but the walls remaining. They snatched at gold and silver and jewels, of course, but they took also brass, copper, and bronze, silken robes, and even furniture. Works of art were nothing to them unless they were of precious metal and could be melted; and what they did not care to take with them, they broke or burned. The widowed empress had expected to be treated with the greatest honor, but the Vandals stripped off her jewels and threw her and her two daughters onboard their ships to be carried to Africa as prisoners.

Genseric kept his people together as long as he lived; and indeed, though the Romans made many expeditions against the Vandals, it was nearly eighty years before they were conquered.

The Power of Rome is Broken

by Rev. Monsignor Edmund J. Goebel Ph. D.

Fall of the Western Roman Empire. Other Teutonic tribes were seizing great sections of the Roman Empire. The power of Rome over her western empire was broken. The emperor at Rome had to rely almost entirely on Teutonic soldiers to defend Rome. Finally, in the year A.D. 476, the legions at Rome deposed the last of the Roman emperors, Augustulus. They then proclaimed one of their generals, a Teuton named Odoacer, as king. A barbarian now ruled from the throne of the Caesars.

Results of the Invasions. During the invasions of the barbarians, and for many years afterward, Europe was in a sad state of disorder. Great numbers of people were turned out of their homes to wander aimlessly here and there. Instead of working for a living, many became robbers and took by force what they wanted. There was very little business and trade. Travel became difficult and dangerous because roads and bridges were no longer kept in repair.

Instead of being ruled by Roman law and judges in Roman courts, both the conquered and conquerors usually followed the tribal customs of the barbarians. For a long time, almost everything the Romans had achieved seemed to be lost.

Over time, however, the different peoples began to mingle, and throughout the empire, the barbarian Teutons and the civilized Romans gradually settled down to peaceful living. They traded with one another. They intermarried. In France, Spain, Portugal, and Italy, the barbarians adopted the dress, the language, the customs, and the laws of the Romans.

This mixture of the Romans and the Teutons had many good results. The invaders brought new strength and new life into Europe. They taught the world to love liberty, and they revived the virtue of courage. In fact, these two peoples finally became the founders of many of the present-day nations of Europe. This, of course, means that they are also the ancestors of many of the people in America.

The Church Survives. The mighty empire of the Romans had been destroyed. But the Catholic Church, which also had its capital at Rome, continued to survive. Goths, Huns, and Vandals had attacked or threatened Rome, but the Church continued to elect successors to St. Peter as Bishops of Rome.

Not only did the Church survive; it set out to convert and to civilize the barbarian tribes. This was a slow task at first, but it makes a thrilling story.

Conversion of the Franks

by Rev. Monsignor Edmund J. Goebel Ph. D.

The kingdom of the Franks was the most important of all the nations established by the Teutonic tribes. It became the strongest of the new nations. In fact, for a while, the Franks were to become masters of most of the other Teutonic peoples.

The Franks did not break off connections with their homeland when they invaded the Roman Empire. Instead, they kept what territory they had and slowly extended it until they controlled the Roman province of Gaul. In this way, the Franks gained a firmer hold on the territory which they conquered than the tribes who wandered far from their homeland.

Just five years after the barbarians had driven the last Roman emperor of the West from his throne, a fifteen-year-old boy became king of the Franks. This was Clovis, who became the greatest of their early kings. Despite his youth, he was a good leader and a strong ruler. He defeated the Roman governor of Gaul and all the other Teutonic tribes in that region.

Clovis was the first Teutonic king to become a Catholic, and his people became the first of the barbarian nations to accept Christianity. Clovis had married Clotilde, a Burgundian princess who was a devout Catholic. Because of her good example and prayers, Clovis became interested in Christianity. On Christmas Day, in the year 496, Clovis and three thousand of his warriors were baptized by St. Remigius, the Bishop of Reims. Gradually, the entire nation of the Franks became converted and was a strong support to the Church.

Clovis was able to unite the various Frankish tribes into one strong nation. He provided law and order for a large section of Western Europe when it was so badly needed after the fall of the Roman Empire of the West. Clovis appointed many Romans to important positions in his kingdom. In this way, he helped to unite his Frankish people with the Romans of Gaul. The language of the Franks became more and more like Latin. The people of the Frankish kingdom adopted Roman customs and manners.

When Clovis died, his kingdom was divided among his four sons. These sons and the rulers who followed them quarreled among themselves. The hundred years after the death of Clovis were years of rivalry and bloodshed. Much of the good civilizing work of Clovis was lost.

Clovis

by Eva March Tappan, Ph. D.

Of all the Teutons who came to live on Roman territory, the most important were the Franks or free men. They had no wish to wander over the world when they had once found a country that pleased them, and so, since they liked the land about the mouth of the Rhine, they settled there and held on to it, adding more and more wherever a little fighting would win it for them. Each tribe had its chief; but Clovis, one of these chiefs, came at last to rule them all. The country west of the Rhine, then called Gaul, was still partly held by the Romans, but Clovis meant to drive them away and keep the land for the Franks.

When he was only twenty-one, he led his men against the Roman governor at Soissons and took the place. From here he sent out expeditions to conquer one bit of land after another and to bring back rich booty. The most valuable treasures were usually kept in the churches, and the heathen Franks took great delight in seizing these. Among the church treasures captured at Rheims was a marvelously beautiful vase. Now the bishop of Rheims was on good terms with Clovis, and he sent a messenger to the young chief to beg that, even if the soldiers would not return all the holy vessels of the church, this one at least might be given back. Clovis bade the messenger follow on to Soissons, where the booty would be divided. At Soissons, when all the warriors were assembled, the king pointed to the vase and said, "I ask you, O most valiant warriors, not to refuse to me the vase in addition to my rightful part." Most of the soldiers were wise enough not to object to the wishes of so powerful a chief; but one foolish, envious man swung his battle-ax and crushed the vase, crying, "Thou shalt receive nothing of this unless a just lot gives it to thee." It is no wonder that the whole army was amazed at such audacity. Clovis said nothing but quietly handed the crushed vase to the bishop's messenger. He did not forget the insult, however, and a year later, when he was reviewing his troops, he declared that this man's weapons were not in fit condition, and with one blow of his ax he struck the soldier dead, saying, "Thus thou didst to the vase at Soissons."

Clovis showed himself so much stronger than the other chiefs of the Franks that at length they all accepted him as their king. Soon after this, he began to think about taking a wife. The story of his wooing is almost like a fairy tale. In the land of Burgundy lived a fair young girl named Clotilda, whose wicked uncle had slain her father, mother, and brothers that he might get the kingdom. Clovis had heard how beautiful and good she was, and he sent an envoy to ask for her hand in marriage. The wicked uncle was afraid to have her marry so powerful a ruler, lest she should avenge the slaughter of her family; but he did not dare to refuse Clovis or to murder the girl after Clovis had asked that she might become his queen. There was nothing to do but to send her to the king of the Franks. Clovis was delighted with her, and they were married with all festivities.

Clotilda was a Christian, and she was much grieved that her husband should remain a heathen. She told him many times about her God, but nothing moved him. When their first child was born, Clotilda had the baby baptized. Not long afterward, the little boy grew ill and died. "That is because he was baptized in the name of your God," declared Clovis bitterly. "If he had been consecrated in the name of my gods, he would be alive still." Nevertheless, when a second son was born, Clotilda had him baptized. He, too, fell ill, and the king said, "He was baptized in the name of Christ, and he will soon die." But the mother prayed to God, and by God's will, the boy recovered. Still, Clovis would not give up the gods of his fathers. It came to pass, however, that he was engaged in a fierce battle near where Cologne now stands. His enemies were fast getting the better of him, and he was almost in despair when suddenly he thought of the God of his queen, and he cried, "Jesus Christ, whom Clotilda declares to be the Son of the living God if Thou wilt grant me victory over these enemies, I will believe in Thee and be baptized in Thy name." Soon the enemy fled, and Clovis did not doubt that his prayer had been answered.

When he told Clotilda of this, she was delighted. She sent for the bishop and asked him to teach her husband the true religion. After a little, Clovis said to him, "I am glad to listen to you, but my people will not leave their gods." He thought a while and then he declared, "I will go forth and tell them what you have told me." He went out among his people, and, as the legend says, even before he had spoken a word, the people cried out all together, "We are ready to follow the immortal God." Then the bishop ordered the font to be prepared for the baptism of the king. The procession set out from the palace and passed through streets made gorgeous with embroidered hangings. First came the clergy, chanting hymns as they marched, and bearing the Gospels and a golden cross. After them walked the bishop, leading the king by the hand. Behind them came the queen, and after her the people. They passed through the door and into the church. The candles gleamed, the house was hung with tapestries of the purest white and was fragrant with incense; and there the king of the Franks, his sisters, and more than three thousand of his warriors, besides a throng of women and children, were baptized and marked with the sign of the cross.

Clovis died in 511, but before that time all the lands between the lower Rhine and the

Pyrenees had been obliged to acknowledge his rule. He made Paris his capital and went there to live. This was the beginning of France. The descendants of Clovis held the throne for nearly two centuries and a half. They were called Merovingians after Merovaeus, the grandfather of Clovis.

Conversion of Ireland

by Rev. Monsignor Edmund J. Goebel Ph. D.

At the time the barbarians captured control of most of the continent, two outposts of Europe remained untouched. There were Ireland in the West and Constantinople in the East. Constantinople had been a center of Christianity since its founding in 326. About a century later, Ireland was converted to the Faith and became completely Catholic before the barbarians destroyed the Roman Empire. From these two points, as well as from Rome, the center of European life, went the first missionaries that were to win Europe for Christianity.

The man who accomplished the conversion of Ireland was St. Patrick. Patrick was born in Britain about the year 389. His family were Roman nobles and devout Christians. The name "Patrick" means "noble" and comes from the same Latin word as "patrician." As a young boy, Patrick was captured by pirates and sold into slavery in Ireland. For six years he tended the flocks of his master in the northeast of Ireland. Here he learned to love the Irish people and to speak their Celtic language.

He was able to escape from Ireland and to return to his own people. But Patrick longed to return to Ireland and to convert the pagan Irish to Christianity. For nearly twenty years Patrick prepared himself for his missionary work.

St. Patrick secured the permission of the pope for his mission, and he was consecrated a bishop before he left for Ireland. In the year 432, he landed on the east coast of Ireland at Wicklow, where there were a few Christians. But knowing the Irish language and the Irish customs, he went to the court of the Ardri, or high king of Ireland, at Tara.

At Tara, he baptized Conall, the brother of the Ardri. Conall gave Patrick land for the building of a church, which he made his headquarters. St. Patrick visited most of Ireland, preaching, converting, and baptizing.

Before his death, St. Patrick had converted nearly all the Irish people. He had established a clergy of native Irish educated in the monasteries of France just before that area was overrun by the barbarians.

The Irish Monasteries. St. Patrick founded many monasteries in Ireland. Many of these were still small at the death of St. Patrick, but they continued to grow and prosper. Other great Irish saints in the next century founded many other monasteries, which became famous throughout Europe.

These monasteries became important for the future of Europe and the Church. For two centuries the most important schools and colleges in all Europe were in the Irish monasteries. Scholars came from all parts of Europe to these monastic schools. Ireland became known as "the Isle of Saints and Scholars."

As the barbarian nations began to settle down, it was from these same monastery schools that the Irish monks went as missionaries. They journeyed to all parts of Europe in the important work of converting a civilizing the pagans.

Saint Patrick

by Amy Steedman

It was a dark night of storm and wind, but the people in the little farm on the western coast of Scotland were accustomed to stormy winds and the sound of breakers dashing upon the rocky shore, and they paid little heed to the wintry weather. They were all tired out from their day's work, and thankful, when the darkness closed in, to bar the doors and shut out the wild night as they gathered around the fire within. They were a rough-looking set of people in the light of the great peat fire that burned on the hearth. Only one, a boy of sixteen, seemed different to the rest, and had a gentler, more civilized look, while he held himself as if accustomed to command.

This boy was Patrick, son of the master Calponius, who belonged to the Roman colony at Dumbarton, and he had been brought up with care and taught all that a young Roman citizen should know. His gentle mother, a niece of the holy Saint Martin of Tours, had brought with her many a cherished memory of courtly manners from the sunny land of her birth, and she had taught the boy to be courteous and knightly in his bearing. So it was that Patrick learned many things which were unknown in the uncivilized northern land where he lived, but the most important thing among all was the faith of Christ, taught to him by his father and mother, who were both Christians.

But all these lessons seemed very dull and uninteresting to the restless boy. It was such a waste of the golden hours to sit indoors and learn those endless psalms. Prayers, too, took such a weary time, when he might be out on the hillside, as free as the happy birds and all the wild creatures that lived under the open sky. Sometimes in his heart, he almost wondered whether it might not be pleasanter to be a pagan rather than a Christian. The pagans had no psalms to learn and could do just as they pleased.

"Someday you will grow wiser," said his mother, "and what is a dull lesson to you now will be like apples of gold in pictures of silver."

But Patrick could not understand what she meant, and he was only too glad when lesson time was over and he was allowed to go off to the little farm close to the sea, where he could work with his hands and not with his head. How he loved the free life there; the days spent in the fields and woods, the evenings when the peat was heaped high on the glowing hearth, and he listened to the stories of brave deeds and wild adventures which were told or sung in the flickering firelight! What did he care for shrieking winds and the roar of the waves outside? It was fitting music to echo around the splendid tales that made his heart beat like a drum and his eyes glow like the fire.

"It is a wild night," said one of the men, "and black as the pit. We must have a wild song to match the night and chase away the blackness."

So, the simple chant of wild adventures was taken up one by one, until the roar of the storm was drowned in their ears and the wail of the wind became part of the mournful music.

But outside in the blackness, the wind had sterner work to do than to act as chorus to idle tales. What were those mysterious long black boats that fought their way so stubbornly through the angry waves? They seemed like phantoms of the night, so silently they moved, never showing a glimmer of light from stem to stern. In vain the icy wind swept down upon them and strove to beat them back. Slowly but surely, they crept on until they reached a sheltered bay where the sand was smooth, and it was safe to land.

Black and silent as their boats the pirate crew landed one by one and crawled stealthily over the rocks and up the hill towards the farm that nestled in a hollow there. The light from the peat fire shone through the little window; a burst of song came floating out into the dark night: there was no thought of lurking danger or surprise.

Closer and closer crept the black figures until they too could listen to the story that was chanted by the fireside, and they laughed aloud to hear such brave words coming from the lips of men who sat safe and warm inside, little dreaming of the real danger that approached them outside.

"Listen!" cried one of the singers suddenly, "surely the wind has a strange voice tonight."

All together the men jumped to their feet, for the sound they heard was not the voice of the storm. The door burst inwards with a tremendous crash. The men fought fearlessly and bravely, but one by one they were overpowered. The pirate captain stood and looked at the row of sullen captives.

"Away with them to the boats," he cried. Then, pointing to Patrick, he added, "See that you handle that one carefully, he is a strong lad and will fetch a good price when we land on the other side."

There was nothing to be done, no rescue to hope for, and resistance only made matters worse. Patrick lay stunned and despairing in the bottom of the boat which was to carry him away from his home and his friends. It was all like a bad dream, the tossing of that stormy sea, the long dark night, the landing in a strange country, and the knowledge that he was now a slave to be sold to the highest bidder.

So, Patrick came to Ireland and was sold to a man whom they called Michu and sent out into the fields to feed his master's swine.

Strong and hardy as the boy was, the life which he had to lead now stretched his endurance to the uttermost. There was little rest or leisure, for a slave's work is never finished, and he was often so hungry and so bitterly cold that he felt half stunned with misery. Even when the snow was on the ground, he had to drive out his herd of pigs to find food for them, and often he was out all night upon the hillside, sheltering in some rocky corner as best he could from the biting wind that swept over the mountains.

In those long dark nights, there was plenty of time for thinking, and the boy's thoughts were always of the far-off home and all that he had lost. Strangely enough, it was not of the happy careless hours that he dreamed, but rather of the times that had once seemed so tiresome and so long. He loved to think of his mother and those dull lessons which had once made him so impatient. Little by little all that he had learned came back to him, but instead of being only tiresome lessons, the psalms and prayers held a comforting message, as if a friend were speaking to him. Then their meaning became clearer and clearer until he realized that they were indeed a message from a real Friend. Though he was alone, homeless, and utterly friendless, God was still there.

"Our Father," said the boy to himself, and the very words seemed to change everything around. God was here in this terrible unknown country, and God was his Father. To be a slave lost half its bitterness when he could stand upright and know himself to be God's servant as well.

For six long years, Patrick served his master, Michu, diligently and well, for all this time he was also learning to serve God. With that love in his heart, he learned to care for all helpless things, and to see what was beautiful in common things around. Years afterward, when he was a great teacher and the pagan priests scoffed at his teaching and asked how he could explain the Trinity. "Three Persons in One God," Patrick stooped down and plucked a leaf of the little green shamrock, which had taught him one of his lessons on the lonely hillside. Showing its three leaves in one, he gave a simple illustration of the great Mystery.

It was at the end of his sixth year of slavery that one night Patrick drove his pigs to a distant hill overlooking his master's farm, and there, under the stars, in the shelter of a rock, he lay down to rest. It was not long before he fell asleep, but in his sleep, he heard a voice close at hand speaking to him.

"Your fasting is good," said the voice. "You shall soon return to your country. Behold a ship is ready for you, but you must journey many miles."

Patrick started up, never doubting for a moment but that this was the message of an angel. He had lived so close to God that he was ever ready to receive His commands. In the story of his life, which he has written himself, he says, "I went in the power of the Lord, who directed my way for good, and I feared nothing until I arrived at that ship."

Weary, footsore, and worn after the long journey on foot, Patrick presented himself before the ship's captain and begged that he might be taken aboard and carried over to Britain. It was perhaps a small wonder that the captain looked with suspicion at the wild figure of the runaway slave and told him angrily to be gone.

It was a bitter ending to Patrick's hopes, and he turned very sorrowfully away. The journey had been so long, and he had felt so sure that all would be well at the end. Then, as ever, his first thought was to turn to his One Friend, and so he knelt on the shore and prayed for help and guidance. The answer came even as he prayed, and he heard a shout from one of the sailors, who had followed him.

"Come along," he cried, "they are asking for you."

Patrick hurried back and found that meanwhile, the captain had changed his mind.

"Come, we will take you on trust," he said, meaning that Patrick should work out his own passage, or repay him when they landed. "We are about to sail and hope to reach land in three days."

Those were three days of great happiness to Patrick, as he saw Ireland growing fainter and fainter in the distance, and knew that before him lay freedom and home, and all that he had lost.

But although the ship reached land in three days, it was not the land he knew, and he was still far off from home. The crew of the ship landed somewhere on the coast of Brittany and tried to find their way to some town, having to travel across a strange, desolate country where there were no inhabitants and nothing to guide them. Day by day their store of food grew less, until they had nothing left to eat, and it seemed as if they must die of starvation.

Now the captain had found that Patrick was to be trusted, and had watched him often at his prayers, and came to think there must be some truth in a religion that made a man so honest and ready to do his duty. So now he called Patrick to him to ask for his advice.

"Christian," he said, "your God is powerful; pray for us, for we are starving." "I will pray," answered Patrick, "but you too must have faith in the Lord."

So just as a hungry child turns to his father and asks for bread, Patrick knelt and prayed aloud to God, and suddenly there was a sound of rushing and tearing through the wood, and a herd of wild boars came sweeping along. The men chased them, and soon captured and killed enough to provide food for many days.

After many adventures Patrick, at last, reached home, and for a while forgot all the hardships he had endured in the joy and happiness of that wonderful homecoming. But the careless happy days of boyhood were over now, and a man's work was waiting for him.

"Only let the work be here," said his mother. "O my son, promise that you will never leave us again, now that we have so wonderfully found you." For a while that too was Patrick's only wish, never to leave his dear home and those he loved so well.

But, as he lay asleep one night, the heavenly messenger came once more to him and pointed out the path which God would have him tread. It seemed to Patrick that the angel held in his hand a bundle of letters, and on one was written "the voice of the Irish." He gave this to Patrick, who, as he read, seemed to hear the call of many voices echoing from the land where he had been a slave. Even the voices of little children rang in his ears, and all of them were calling to him and saying, "We beg you, come and walk in the midst of us."

The thought of those poor untaught people who had never heard of God had often made him long to help them, and this call decided him. He would enter God's service as a priest, and then go back to the country of his captivity to carry the torch of God's love in his hand and spread abroad the glorious light in every corner of the dark land.

After a long time of preparation and study, Patrick was at last consecrated bishop and then set out at once to return to the country where he had suffered so much.

It was a very different coming this time than the arrival of the boy slave many years before. With his group of clergy and helpers, the bishop, pastoral staff in hand, landed on the sandy shore of Strangford Lough, and he bore himself as a conqueror marching to victory.

Strangely enough, the first person to greet the band of strangers was a swineherd guarding his pigs, just as Patrick had done in those long years of slavery. The lad was terrified when he saw these strange men, and although Patrick spoke kindly to him in his own tongue, the swineherd fled away to the woods. He immediately returned to his master, Dichu, and told his news.

"Pirates are landing at the bay," he cried, "strange men who come to rob and kill."

Dichu in alarm immediately armed himself and his followers and set out to meet the enemy. But instead of the savage pirates he expected, he found a band of peaceful unarmed men, with one at their head whom it was easy to see was no robber.

Patrick came forward then to meet the chief, and the two men talked a while earnestly together. "Put down your weapons," cried Dichu, turning to his followers, "these men are friends and not enemies."

As friends, then, Dichu led them to his house and made them welcome. The fearless bravery of Patrick and his strong kind face had won the chieftain's heart, and he prepared to entertain him royally. But Patrick could neither rest nor eat until his message was delivered, and as Dichu listened to his words, they seemed to seize him with a strange power and made him long to hear more. He would have gladly kept Patrick with him, but there was much work to be done, and the bishop wished, first of all, to seek out his old master Michu and pay the money due to him as the price of the runaway slave.

How well he knew every step of the way to the old farm! It seemed as if he must be walking in a dream, that he must be still the barefooted, hungry, ill-clad boy of long ago. There were the woods through which he had so often driven his pigs, the banks where he had found the first spring flowers, the rocks which had so often sheltered him, the little green friendly shamrock which he had loved so dearly. Up the steep hillside he climbed, and at the top he paused and knelt in prayer, remembering the vision he had seen there and the message of the angel. Then, rising, he looked eagerly towards the spot where his master's farm nestled in the hollow beneath.

Alas! he had come too late; nothing but a thin grey curl of smoke marked the place where the smoldering ashes of the farm lay, and, saddest of all, his master too had perished in the fire.

So, there was nothing to do but turn back and carry the message to others. But Patrick's heart was sad for his old master.

The glad season of Easter was close at hand, but it held no meaning for the people of this dark land. True, they had their own religion, a strange worship of the sun, and their priests, who were called Druids, were said to possess magical powers and great wisdom. They had great festivals too in which all the people joined, and one of these was just about to be held at Tara. The Druids were all assembled to do honor to the sun, which was becoming powerful enough to put winter to flight and warm the spring buds into summer blossoms. For some days before the feast, every fire was put out, and not a light could be kindled, on pain of death, until the great festival light would be lighted on the Hill of Tara.

Now Patrick was brave as a lion, and his heart was set on delivering his message and spreading the True Light in this heathen darkness, so there was no room for fear. The gathering of the priests and the presence of the powerful King Laoghaire seemed to him a splendid opportunity of righting the powers of evil.

He traveled swiftly, across hill and dale, with his little band of followers until he reached the Hill of Slane, close to Tara. There, on Easter Eve, when the land was wrapped in darkness, when not the faintest glimmer of light could be seen in the solemn blackness that brooded over Tara's Hill, he lit his Easter fire and watched the tongues of flame as they shot up and lighted the whole country round.

The King and his councilors, the Druids, came together quickly in anger and astonishment when they saw the glowing light.

"Who has dared to do this thing?" asked the King in a fury.

"It is none of our people," said the priest. "It is the challenge of an enemy."

The wise men were troubled and talked together in half-fearful tones. There was an ancient prophecy which rung in their ears and made them wonder if the man they had seen wending his way at the head of his little company that day to the Hill of Slane had some magic power.

"Whoever he is, he shall not come to challenge our power," said the King. "We will go forth and punish this bold stranger."

Down the dark silent hillside, the King and his councilors rode furiously and did not stop until they reached the Hill of Slane. But there the Druids called a halt.

"Let a messenger be sent to fetch forth the man," they said. "We will not venture within the line of his magic fire."

"We will receive him here," said the King, "and let no man rise when he approaches in case he thinks that in any way we seek to honor him."

So, the men sat down silently to wait until the messenger should return, and soon Patrick was seen coming swiftly down the hill towards them. That was the man, there was no doubt about it. As he came nearer, they could see the shaven crown, the robe pierced at the neck, and in his hand the crook-like staff, while from the hilltop could be heard the music of the Easter hymn and the chanting of the loud "Amen."

The company sat silent and unmoved as Patrick approached. Only one little lad, watching with intent eyes the face of the stranger, rose to his feet in reverent greeting, forgetting the King's command.

A gentle look came into Patrick's eyes as he noticed the eager greeting and, raising his hand, he blessed the little lad.

"Who are you, and what is your errand here?" thundered the King.

"I am a torchbearer," answered Patrick. "I bring the True Light to lighten this dark land, to spread around peace and goodwill. All I ask is that you will hear my message."

Alone and unarmed but quite fearless, Patrick stood up before the angry men the next day and spoke such words as they had never heard before. It was a new and wonderful teaching, and many of the wise men and nobles listened eagerly; and when he was done, they came and asked to be baptized and enrolled under the banner of Patrick's God.

That was a glad Eastertide for the bishop, and as time went on the light spread far and wide. Many shut their eyes and loved the darkness rather than the light, but Patrick was wise in his dealings with them all. He was never harsh or scornful of their beliefs but always tried to lead them through what was good and beautiful in their own religion, using old customs and feasts to do honor to Christ, giving them a new meaning that linked them to His service.

Then, too, he wisely tried to win over the chief men of the land to become Christians, knowing that their followers would more readily follow their masters. Young boys were also his special care, remembering as he always did his bitter years of lonely slavery, and these lads were like sons to him. The boy he had blessed on that Easter Eve on the hillside of Slane was now one of his followers, and years afterward we hear of him as Bishop of Slane. It was one of these lads whom Patrick loved so well, whose bravery and loyal devotion once saved the good bishop's life.

Coming one day to the spot where a great stone marked the place of the Druids' worship, Patrick rolled over the stone that he so that he could set up an altar instead. This was considered a terrible insult, and one of the pagan chiefs vowed that come what might, he would kill Patrick wherever he found him.

Now the young man who drove Patrick's chariot heard this threat, and so he guarded his master with increased watchfulness. At last, however, his enemy's opportunity came, for Patrick's travels took him past the chief's home. The young man, whose name was Oran, knew that his master had no fear and would never turn aside to escape danger, so, as they neared the place, he thought of a plan to save him.

"I grow so weary with this long day of driving, my master," he said. "My hands can scarcely hold the reins. If you would drive for a little while and let me rest, all would be well."

"You should have asked sooner, my son," said the bishop kindly. "I am but a hard master to overtask your strength."

Saying this, Patrick changed seats, and gathering up the reins, drove on, while Oran sat behind his master's seat, and prayed that the gathering darkness might close in swiftly so that no one could notice the change.

Very soon they reached the outskirts of a dense wood, and from the sheltering trees a dark figure sprang out. The frightened horse reared for a moment, there was a singing sound of some weapon whizzing through the air, and when Patrick turned to see what it meant, Oran lay dead with a javelin in his heart, the murderer's weapon which had been meant for Patrick. As he knelt there in his bitter grief, Patrick heard in his heart the echo of his Master's words, "Greater love has no man than this, that a man lay down his life for his friends."

The years went by, and each day was filled by Patrick with service for his Master until the useful life drew to a close. Then, in the spring of the year, when the March winds were blowing, when the shamrocks he loved were decking the land in dainty green, came the King's command, "Come up higher." It was only a gentle call, for he had lived so close to the Master that it was only a step from the Seen to the Unseen, and he needed no loud summons, for his feet were on the threshold of home.

"Christ with me, Christ before me, Christ behind me, Christ within me, Christ beneath me, Christ above me, Christ at my right, Christ at my left, Christ in the fort, Christ in the chariot-seat, Christ in the ship."

So runs part of the beautiful old hymn of St. Patrick, and we do not wonder that he who was so truly a follower of Christ came to be called a saint.

A helpless captive, a hard-worked slave, a lonely swineherd! Who would have dreamed that to him would have belonged the honor of leading into freedom and light the land of his captivity? Who would have thought that the lowly slave would be the torchbearer of the King, the patron saint of the green isle of Ireland?

Unit Six:
Light Shines in the Darkness

THEME: HOPE AND LIGHT

Irish Missionaries

by Rev. Monsignor Edmund J. Goebel Ph. D.

St. Columba, Apostle to Scotland. One of the first of the missionaries to leave Ireland was Columba. He was a descendant of the famous Niall of the Nine Hostages. As a young man, he became a monk. He founded many churches and monasteries.

When he was about forty-five years old, he decided to leave Ireland and cross over into Scotland to convert the people. He took with him twelve companions, in imitation of Our Lord and His twelve apostles. St. Columba made his headquarters on the island of Iona, off the west coast of Scotland. Iona became one of the most important monastic schools in Europe in the next century.

St. Columba was never idle. He was always preaching, studying, writing, or praying. Before his death in 597, he had won all Scotland for Christ.

St. Columban. St. Columban was about twenty years younger than his namesake, St. Columba. He became a monk in the monastery of Bangor, in county Down. But he was filled with the missionary spirit and longed to preach the gospel of Christ in foreign lands.

Finally, he made his preparations. Like St. Columba, he took twelve companions with him. His journey took him to the kingdom of the Franks. His preaching was so eloquent that he attracted a large number of followers. The king of Burgundy invited him to make his headquarters in that region.

St. Columban and his disciples founded over one hundred monasteries. These were located in the Rhineland, in Switzerland, and northern Italy. The most famous of St. Columban's monastic schools was at Bobbio, in Italy.

St. Gall, Apostle of Switzerland. One of the Irish companions of St. Columban, St. Gall, became fond of the people in what is now Switzerland. In the mighty Alps, he established a monastery. The town which grew up around the monastery came to be known as St. Gall.

The monastery at St. Gall became of the most famous in all Europe. It became a center of great learning. Its monks were so active in making copies of books that its library is still one of the best in Europe.

Saint Columba

by Amy Steedman

The Princess Eithne lay asleep, dreaming of summer days and happy hours spent in flowery meadows. Outside the stormy wintry winds swept the snowdrifts high among the mountain passes, and the howls of hungry wolves mingled with the shriek of the wind. It was cold and bleak at the castle of Gartan among the wild hills of Donegal when winter held sway, and then the Princess would watch the swirling snowflakes and the grey mists that wrapped the hills in solemn majesty. But in the springtime, it was a different world, and Eithne could see from her window the length and height of the valley and count the little mountain lakes that shone like diamonds in their emerald setting. She thought it was the fairest spot in all the world.

There were so many beautiful things in the life of the Princess, so much to make her happy with the Prince her husband, that there seemed scarcely room for more joy; and yet, as she lay dreaming, she knew that the greatest happiness of all was yet to come.

It seemed to her that, as she dreamed of those flowery meadows, an angel stood beside her and placed in her hands a wonderful robe, more beautiful than anything she had ever seen. It was sewn all over with dainty flowers the mountain flowers that are fairer and finer than any others because they grow closer to heaven. It was as if a rainbow had fallen into a shower of flowers upon this wondrous mantle and set it thick with buds and blossoms, crimson, white, and blue.

For a while the angel waited while the Princess held the robe and gazed upon its beauty, then very gently it was taken from her, and Eithne found her hands were empty.

"Why do you take away my beautiful robe so soon?" asked the Princess, stretching out her hands towards the angel and weeping bitterly.

"It is too dearly prized for you to keep it," was the answer. And as Eithne looked with longing eyes, she saw the angel spread out the robe, and its beautiful folds floated further and further until it covered all that land.

Then in her ears there sounded the comforting voice of the angel bidding her grieve no more but prepare to receive the little son whom God was sending to her. And Eithne knew that the vision of the robe was sent as a lesson to teach her that her son would belong not only to her but to the world, where God needed him.

Soon after this, the little Prince was born, and, as his mother held him in her arms, her heart was filled with the same great joy as when she had clasped the angel's robe.

More than fifty years had passed since the good Saint Patrick had brought Christ's light to Ireland, and now most of the people there were Christians. The father and mother of the little Prince took early care that the baby should be baptized, and in the little chapel of the clan O'Donnel, they gave him two names Crimthann, which means a wolf, and Colum, which means a dove.

Perhaps it was the chief, his father, thinking of his wild brave ancestors living free among those mountains, who gave his little son the name of the wolf, and surely it was the mother, thinking of the angel vision, who wished him to be called by the gentler name.

There was no doubt from the first which name suited the child the best. Strong and fearless, and showing in a hundred ways that he came of a kingly lineage, there was nothing of the wild wolf nature about Columba. It was always Colum, the dove, that gladdened his mother's heart. Like a flower turning to the light, his heart seemed to always turn naturally to all that was beautiful and pure and good. He was eager to learn and loved to listen to the stories of those soldiers of Christ who fought against the Evil One and brought light and peace into the wild dark places of the earth. When he grew up, he too would become one of those soldiers, and meanwhile, there was nothing he loved so much as to steal away into the little chapel to join in the service of the Master he meant to serve someday.

The people wondered as they watched the boy leave his games and turn with a happy eager face towards the church whenever the bell called the monks to prayer.

At the monastery school, the boy was quick to learn, and the monks told one another that he had the gift of genius. But the schoolmaster wondered even more at the goodness than the cleverness of his pupil. Watching him one day, he was heard to say that he saw an angel walking by the side of Columba, guiding and guarding him as he went. And, indeed, the boy's face always had the look of one who walked close to his guardian angel.

So, Columba grew to be a man, and learned all the wisdom of the great monasteries, and then, strong and purposeful, he began his work for God, going throughout the land teaching, and founding monasteries and building churches.

But although he worked well and with all his heart, still his great desire had always been to carry God's message of peace and goodwill to the heathen lands outside Ireland, and many a time he gazed across the sea to the faint blue line of distant hills, thinking of those poor souls in Scotland who knew nothing of God's love and mercy.

Still, the years went by, and there always seemed more than enough work for him to do in his own land until, when he was more than forty years old, something happened which changed his life, and sent him forth to begin the new great work.

Now you must know that Columba loved books and delighted in making copies of them, for in those days all books were written by hand. He was very skillful in this work of copying. He laid the colors on most carefully for the capital letters and made the printing black and firm and even. Nothing gave him more pleasure than to have a new book to copy, and he was greatly pleased when one day he heard that his old schoolmaster had a wonderful copy of the gospels that he might allow Columba to see.

"My father," he said to the old abbot, "may I see the fair copy of the gospels of which I have heard so much? Men say there is no other copy like it in Ireland."

"Ay, my son," answered the abbot proudly, "It is, as you say, a very fair copy. But you have a careful hand and know the value of such a book, so I will trust the treasure to you for a while."

Overjoyed at the permission, Columba carried the book carefully home, and the more he looked at it, the more he longed to have one like it. At last, he began to secretly and swiftly make a copy, and he did not return the precious book until it was done.

Before long, however, the matter came to the ears of the abbot, and he was very angry. He demanded at once that the copy should be given to him, and he told Columba to deliver it immediately.

"The copy is mine," said Columba calmly, "but if you think it is yours, we will let the King decide."

So, the matter was taken to the King of Meath, and he decided that Columba must give up the book.

"It is written in the ancient law of our land," said the King, "that to every cow belongs its calf, therefore it must be that to every book belongs its copy."

There was a great outcry against this decision, and the clansmen of Columba went out to do battle with the men of Meath, and by the time Columba's anger had cooled, many thousand men had been killed.

Bitterly repentant, Columba went to the old priest Molaise and asked him what he should do to show his sorrow. Then Molaise bade him leave the land he so dearly loved, cross the sea to Scotland, and win for God from among the heathen as many souls as those whom his hasty quarrel had brought to death.

The long waves of the Atlantic rolled in and broke upon the beach, grey and cold in the light of early morning when twelve sorrowful-looking men pushed off their frail boats from the Irish shore and set sail for distant Scotland.

The boats were light, made only of wickerwork with skins stretched tightly over, and they rose gaily on the long waves which came sweeping in as if eager to overwhelm them. But there were heavy hearts in those light boats, and the men looked back with sad eyes at the dear green home they were leaving, seeing it but dimly through a mist of tears. They loved their home, but they loved their master Columba better, and so they were setting sail with him for the land of exile. Through storm and tempest the frail boats held their way, and the hearts, if sad, were brave and hopeful too, for their faith in God and their leader was strong.

The first landing-place was on the island of Colonsay, and there the little company waited on the shore while Columba climbed the hill, that he might view the land and see if it was a fit place to make their home.

With long strides, he climbed up over rocks and heather until he reached the top at last and then he stood quite still and looked around him. Yes, the island was just the kind of resting-place he was seeking since he must no longer live in his own dear land. Lifting his eyes then, he gazed longingly across the blue sea in the direction of home, and his heart leaped when he saw in the distance the faint blue hills of Ireland. Then he sighed and went slowly back to his waiting companions.

"We must push on," he said. "If we stay here our hearts will be filled with a sore home-longing whenever we gaze across the sea. We must go further, where we cannot see the hills of home."

So, the boats were pushed off once more, and the men rowed on until they reached the little island of Iona. Not the faintest trace of the blue Irish hills could be seen from here, so it was decided that this was to be the place where they would make their new home.

The warm May sunshine was flooding the island as the boats were pulled high on the shore. Sunbeams sparkled on the deep blue waves, and the shining sand of the little bay was dazzling in its whiteness. The seabirds, disturbed in their loneliness, swooped and screamed over the heads of the newcomers, but there was nobody else to dispute their possession.

Very soon the building of the new home was begun. Columba, tall and strong, with clever hands and clever brain, planned and worked himself, and directed the others. One by one the huts were finished, and the little chapel built, and then the monastery was complete. The King of that part of the country, knowing Columba, gave him the island for his own, and so there was no fear that the monks would be disturbed. There were other sounds now besides the screaming of seabirds to be heard on Iona. There was the chapel bell calling the brothers to prayer; there was the music of the morning and evening hymns, and the cheerful busy sounds of daily work.

Then when all was set in order, fields prepared for harvest, cows brought over to give milk, and everything arranged for the daily life Columba set out to begin the great work he had planned.

Far in the north lived the pagan King Brude, in a country where no Christian foot had ever trod. He was a strong and powerful King, and he sat in his grey northern castle fearing no man, for there was no army strong enough to march against him, and no one dared to withstand his power.

Who then were these strangers who came so boldly up to the gates and demanded an entrance? They were not soldiers, for they carried no weapons; they wore only robes of coarse homespun cloth, and their shaven heads were uncovered. Yet they bore themselves with a fearless air, and their leader spoke in a voice that seemed accustomed to command. Like a trumpet-call, the words rang out, "Open the gates in the name of Christ.

"The gates shall not be opened," swore the King. "These men are workers of magic and of evil. Keep the gates barred."

Then the leader, who was Columba, lifted his head still higher, and those who saw him wondered at the look that shone on his face, while the brothers, seeing that look, were cheered and encouraged as if they too could see the angel who stood near and guided him.

There was a breathless silence as the people waited to see what the strange man would do next, and they saw him slowly lift his hand on high and make the sign of the cross. At that sign, as if opened by unseen hands, the gates swung back, the guards fled to right and left, and the way was clear for Columba to enter. Not as an enemy or the worker of evil magic, as the King had feared, did the great man come, but rather as a dove bearing the olive-branch of God's peace.

And as the gates of iron had opened to God's servant, so the gates of the King's heart were unlocked as he listened to the words of Columba's message. The victory which no earthly force and weapons could win was won by God's unarmed messenger alone. The King and many of his people were baptized, and the banner of Christ floated over the citadel.

But although the King had become a Christian, there were still many people who hated Columba and his religion. The Druids, priests of the heathen religion, were very angry and tried in every way to harm this man who had brought a new religion into their country. They could not bear to see the people listening to his teaching, and when it was time for evensong and the brethren were singing their evening hymn of praise, these Druids strove to drown the sound by making hideous noises and raising a terrible din. Little did they know the strength of that voice against which they were striving. Loud and clear rose the hymn of Columba, swelling into a great burst of praise which throbbed through the air and could be heard a mile away. Each word sounded distinctly and it drowned the evil sounds of those pagan priests. It rose to heaven as clear and pure as the song of a lark.

Wherever Columba preached and taught he also built a little church and left behind some of the brethren to go on with the work of spreading God's light. So, through all the land there was a chain of churches and the light grew ever brighter and brighter.

But it was always to Iona that Columba returned, and which he made his home. There he worked and prayed and gathered fresh strength to fight the good fight. There in his cell, he made fair copies of the books he loved and was ready to help anyone who came to him for advice and counsel. He was so kind and patient, this great saint, that he never lost his temper, even when the visitors came and interrupted his work with unnecessary questions, and in their eagerness to embrace him knocked over his inkhorn and spilled his ink.

There was much work to be done by the brothers of the monastery besides their life of prayer and praise. There was the corn to be sown, the harvest to be reaped, cows to be tended, and there was also a seal farm to be cared for on one of the islands close by, where young seals were raised.

As time went on, Columba returned once or twice to Ireland; but he never stayed there long, for his heart was in his work and the 'Island Soldier' was always at the forefront of the battle.

Like his Master, too, Columba loved to seek some lonely quiet place where he could spend the time in prayer, and the place he loved best was the little hill behind the convent. The brothers sometimes wondered why he stayed there so long, and once it happened that one of them, filled with curiosity, climbed up secretly to see what their abbot was doing. But the sight that he saw there put his prying eyes to shame, for it was a vision of angels that met his gaze. There, around the praying form of Columba, God's white-robed messengers hovered, waiting to carry his prayers up to the throne of God. So it is that the place is called the "Angels' Hill" to this day.

The years passed by and Columba, growing old and frail, knew that his work was nearly done and the end drawing near. He had half hoped that at Easter time God would call him home but knowing that the Easter joy of the others would then be turned into sadness, he waited patiently for God's good time.

Saint Brendan

by the Franciscan Sisters of Perpetual Adoration

Would you like to hear a story as it was told at the firesides of the Northmen about a thousand years ago? If so, find St. Brendon's Bay on the map of Ireland.

Let us imagine ourselves living fifteen hundred years ago on this famous bay. It is a beautiful summer morning. A boat is anchored in the bay. On the shore we see a man clad in the garb of a monk. His bearing is noble. His kindly face expresses wisdom, prudence, and manly courage. This man is the holy abbot, St. Brendan the Voyager. About him are gathered groups of monks. All are silent and thoughtful, awaiting the signal to embark.

"Let us," says St. Brendan, "set out on our long voyage in the name of the Holy Trinity."

And where are these voyagers going? They are setting out in search of an unknown western country in which they expect to find strange people whom they will teach to know and love God by the wonderful stories of Bethlehem, of Nazareth, of Jerusalem, and of Calvary.

A favorable wind spreads and fills the sail, and the brave little company speeds smoothly on. Before long every trace of land is lost. The lonely bark seems but a tiny speck upon the mighty, boundless ocean.

"Tell us," says one of the monks to St. Brendan, "do you really believe that there is another country far away to the westward?"

"I do," answers St. Brendan. "We are told that long, long ago, even before Christ came upon this earth, the pagan people of our nation discovered a wonderfully beautiful western island in which lived a happy people." "May we hope to be as fortunate as were these first western navigators?" asks another monk thoughtfully.

As if to say "no" to the good monk's inquiry, the wind suddenly ceases to blow, and the boat comes to a standstill. The monks eagerly reach for the oars and take turns at propelling the bark along. But alas, their strength is soon spent, and on beholding the seemingly endless expanse of water, they begin to lose courage.

But the holy Brendan knows no fear. "Be not afraid, my good Brothers," he answers. "Trim the sail and let the vessel float where Providence will guide it."

The boat now drifts steadily and safely westward. But our brave voyagers are weary and hungry. Their store of food and drink is fast giving out. They have already been forty days upon the water, and all this while have not seen even a sign of land.

"Look!" exclaims one of the monks in sudden joyous surprise. "Do you see that vast stretch of land and those towering hills shaded in the mists?"

With joyful hearts, the brave navigators steer towards the land. They moor their boats and hasten to step ashore, where they fall on their knees and raise their hearts and voices to God in fervent thanksgiving. They find the new land covered with rocky cliffs and fertile plains and see sparkling streams flowing into the sea. Heavy forests bound the horizon. Who can describe the joy and delight of St. Brendan and his brave companions! For seven long years, they wander about, exploring the country, and enjoying the newness of its scenes and products. Then they return to their native land.

Where Brendan's voyage really led him we do not know. The story of his strange adventures, however, spread throughout Europe. The bold, sea-roving Northmen told and retold the tale at their firesides and recorded it with their own bold adventures in their sagas.

Monasticism

by Rev. Monsignor Edmund J. Goebel Ph. D.

The Mission of the Church. The peace and order which Rome had established throughout the Mediterranean world helped the Christian missionaries to spread the gospel in the early days of the Church. The migrations of the barbarian tribes destroyed that peace and order in Europe for several centuries. The barbarians also killed thousands of Christians and destroyed many of their churches. The very life of the Church was threatened by the barbarism of the wandering tribes. But just as the Church had survived the Roman persecutions, so the Church survived the invasions.

The Church now had the opportunity to create a civilization founded on Christian ideas. It was a slow process that took several centuries. In this great work, the monks of the Church played an important part.

The Monks of the East. Many young Christians thought that the best way to save his soul was to withdraw from the world and its temptations. Many were like St. Anthony of Egypt. He was a wealthy young noble who decided to carry out the directions that Christ gave to the rich young many in the Gospel: "Sell all that though hast, and give to the poor, and thou shalt have treasures in heaven; and come follow Me."

St. Anthony retired to the desert, where he spent many years in prayer and in trying to make himself perfect according to the teachings of Christ. For many years he did not see any other person. But the fame of his holiness spread. Many others followed him into this solitary life. Each lived alone in his own hut, but they all met together daily for prayers, sermons, and readings from the Bible. These holy men were called hermits or monks. "Monk" is a Greek word that means "living alone." When a group of monks lived in one place, it was called a monastery.

The Establishing of Monasteries

The Rule of St. Basil. This type of holy life spread throughout the Church in the East. A great scholar and bishop named St. Basil visited all the monasteries in Egypt, Palestine, and Syria. Then he wrote a set of rules for the monks in his monastery. This "Rule" of St. Basil was adopted by all the monks in the East, and it is still in use in that area.

St. Benedict. A few years after the barbarians drove the last Roman emperor from Rome, a son was born to a noble family in Italy. This boy, whose name was Benedict, attended school in Rome. But he did not like the teachings of the pagans in the schools, and he did not like the wickedness and warfare in the world about him.

Benedict decided to become a hermit. So, in the mountains not far from Rome, he lived by himself in a cave. There he denied himself bodily comforts and pleasures. He ate only enough food to keep himself alive. He wore only the plainest and coarsest of clothing. At night he slept on a bed of thistles. In his lonely cave, he devoted himself to prayer and quiet thought.

The monks of a nearby monastery learned of Benedict's great piety. They asked him to come and be their leader. Benedict agreed. In the years that followed, Benedict founded a number of monasteries. The most important of his monasteries was at Monte Cassino, halfway between Rome and Naples.

The Rule of St. Benedict. St. Benedict saw that there was a need for rules to govern the monks. Like St. Basil, he thought that monks should live useful lives. He thought that they should eat enough food, wear enough clothing, and get enough sleep so that they could do useful work. He believed that idleness was a great source of wickedness. He thought monks should always be busy reading, working, or praying. So he wrote his famous "Rule." The Rule of St. Benedict became the pattern for the management of most monasteries in the West.

St. Benedict took as a motto for his monks the expression, "To labor and to pray." One of the reasons for the decline of the Roman Empire had been the growing laziness of its citizens. They thought that work should be done only by slaves. Christ, however, by His own example in the carpenter shop at Nazareth, showed the dignity of work.

St. Benedict expected his monks to follow the example of Christ. He believed that the monks could raise all the food they needed on the monastery land, make their own clothes, and copy manuscripts for their studies. According to the Rule, each monk had regular hours for work, for church services, and for prayer.

The monks of each monastery elected a leader called an abbot. The word "abbot" is from an Aramaic word meaning father. Aramaic is the language that Jesus spoke while on earth. The entire monastery was like a family. The abbot was to rule the monastery as a father ruled a household.

The Vows of the Monks. The young men who wished to become monks took special vows. They promised to practice poverty, chastity, and obedience. Every monk gave up his wealth, which was used to feed the poor. The monastery could own land and property, but the individual monks had no personal possessions at all. The monks all wore the same kind of plain robes so that no one could be proud of his clothes.

The Monastery Schools. Each monastery educated the boys who wished to become monks. Gradually, Roman families, as well as barbarian chiefs, sent their sons to the monasteries to be educated. In most places, there were no schools except those in the monasteries. In this way, the monasteries became the chief centers of civilization in the lands where the barbarians settled.

Education for Girls. St. Benedict had a sister who was called St. Scholastica. She founded a convent for nuns not far from Monte Cassino. The nuns adopted the Rule of St. Benedict also. Gradually, this convent became a great school for the education of girls. Other convent schools were founded throughout Europe. For the first time in history, the education of girls became important.

First Monk to Become Pope. One of the most remarkable monks in this period, which we call the Middle Ages, was St. Gregory the Great. His family, which had been Christian for a long time, was one of the most important in Rome. But Gregory became a monk. He founded a monastery in his own mansion on one of the hills of Rome. He adopted the Rule of St. Benedict for this monastery and others that he founded. From time to time, the Pope called on Gregory to leave the monastery for a while to perform some important duty.

On the death of the Pope in the year 590, the clergy and people of Rome elected Gregory as the next Pope. He was the first monk to become a Pope. In his new position, he encouraged all the monasteries in the West to adopt the Benedictine Rule.

Saint Benedict

by Amy Steedman

It was in the year of our Lord 540 that Saint Benedict was born at Spoleto in Italy and he was a boy of sixteen on the night when our story begins.

It was a cold night. Piercing wind swept over the mountains, whistling through the pine trees and hurrying on to the great city of Rome that lay in the plains below. It was cold enough in the city where the people could take shelter in their house and sit warming their hands over their little pots of fire, but out on the bare hillside, it was even worse. For the icy breath of the winter wind, which had come far over the snow, swept into every nook and corner as if determined to search out any summer warmth that might be lingering in a sheltered corner.

In a cave high up among the rocks, a boy sat listening to the wind, and thinking of many things, as he tried to wrap his worn old cloak closer round him.

He was a tall thin lad, with sad dreaming eyes and a face already sharpened by want and suffering. The cave in which he sat had little in it, except a heap of dried leaves which served him for a bed, and it was difficult to imagine how anyone could live in so dreary and comfortless a place, so far from any other human being.

But he was thinking of a very different home, as he sat shivering in the cold that night. Only a year ago he had lived in a beautiful palace, where everything was pleasant and warm and bright. His father was the lord of the country around, and he, the only son of the house, had everything that he could want. They were all proud of him, he was so clever and brilliant, and as soon as he was old enough, he was sent to study in Rome, so that he might become a great lawyer.

There the boy's eyes saw a different scene—the great city of Rome, where all was a pleasure, where everything pleased the eye, the ear, and the taste, but where, alas, so much wickedness dwelt as well. He had tried to shut his eyes to things he did not wish to see, but day by day the sights and sounds around him, the talk of his companions, and the things they thought were so pleasant had become hateful to him. And one day he had run secretly away from Rome, leaving everything behind, determined to go away into a deserted place and live alone. This it seemed to him was the only way of truly serving God, to learn to deny himself in everything, and to keep himself unspotted from the world.

Here he was indeed alone, and the only food he had was a little bread which a kind old hermit gave him daily, and his only drink the clear water of the mountain streams.

He seemed to live with God alone, seeing no one but the kind old hermit who brought him his daily bread. He was happy and peaceful, never ceasing to pray for those who in the busy world might forget to pray for themselves.

So, Benedict began his life of self-denial and solitary prayer. Years passed by and despite the loneliness of the place and the few people who ever passed by that way, it began to be known that one of God's saints lived in the mountain cave. The shepherds who fed their flocks on the lower hills would bring him little offerings of milk or cheese and ask his blessing, or perhaps a prayer for one who was sick. And gradually people began to call him their saint of the mountain and to come to him for help in all their troubles.

One by one man came and built huts close to his cave, that they might be near so great a saint, and before long there was a great company living around him.

Benedict's fame had spread even to Rome, and two of the Roman nobles sent their sons to be taught by him. One was only five years old and the other twelve, and it seemed a hard life for such children. But Benedict cared for them and watched over them, and they loved him as if he had been their own father.

And after all, life was very pleasant on the mountainside, when the sun shone, and lessons and prayers were over. They could play among the pine trees and chase the goats over the rocks, and when the sun grew too hot creep back into the cave to rest. In spring there were the first flowers to hunt for, and they would come back with eager hands filled with violets and mountain anemones. And in autumn there were nuts and berries to be gathered, which they laid up like young squirrels for their winter store.

And among the daily duties, there was nothing they liked so well as to go down to the lake to fetch water when the mountain springs had run dry. One day it was the little one's turn to do this, and as he was leaning over, his foot slipped, and he fell into the lake, and before he could utter a cry the water closed over his head.

At that very moment Benedict, who was kneeling in prayer on the hill above, saw a vision of the boy's danger, and hastily sent the older boy down to the lake to help the child.

He never stayed to question why he was sent but sped down the mountainside, and without a moment's delay threw himself into the lake, hoping to be able to reach the little dark head that had risen above the water for the last time. And lo! he found that the water grew firm beneath his feet, and he walked as if he was on dry land, and lifting the child, carried him safely ashore.

When Benedict saw that so many other hermits had begun living on the mountain, he decided to form them into a company of brothers, and give them a Rule to live by, and by and by they built a little chapel where they could meet for daily service.

It troubled Benedict greatly about this time to hear that not very far off on Monte Cassino there was a heathen temple where the people worshipped false gods and were living in darkness and sin.

It seemed terrible that such a thing should be suffered in a Christian land, so Benedict made up his mind to go himself and force the people to listen to him.

It was a strange contrast to see him in his coarse, poor robe and thin wan face standing preaching among the crowd of pleasure-seekers, who cared for nothing but eating and drinking and making merry. They could not understand why anyone should choose to be poor and suffer pain and hunger for the sake of any god.

But as Benedict taught them day by day, the majesty of his face and the solemn notes in his voice forced them to listen half unwillingly. Then, as they began to learn about the true God, they saw that the gods they had worshipped were false, and they pulled down their temple and built two chapels on the place where it had stood.

Here, too, Benedict built the first great monastery which was named after him; and after this, the brothers began to be known by his name, and were called Benedictines.

But the Evil One saw with great rage that Benedict was taking away his servants, and destroying his temples, and he tried in every way to hinder the work. Once when the workmen were trying to raise a stone, they found it impossible to move it, though they worked hard all day. At last, in despair, they begged Benedict to come to help them.

As soon as he came, he saw at once what was the matter, for on the stone sat a little black demon laughing at the efforts of the workmen; knowing they could never move the stone while he chose to sit there.

"Get you gone, messenger of Satan," cried Benedict.

And with a howl of rage, the demon fled, and the stone was lifted easily into its place.

One day, not long after the monastery was built, as Benedict was praying in the chapel of the convent, one of the brothers came to tell him that a great company of soldiers was coming up the hill, and at their head was Totila, king of the Goths, who had sent a messenger to ask the saint to receive him.

Benedict, who cared little for earthly kings, was yet too courteous to refuse any such request, so he went out to where the company was gathered on the mountainside.

The rough soldiers stood with heads uncovered, and from their midst came one who wore a crown and sandals of gold and a kingly robe. He knelt before the saint, and said in a loud, clear voice:

"I, Totila, king of the Goths, have come to ask your blessing, father, for your fame has spread even to the wild north country where I reign"

The brothers, crowding behind Benedict, eager to see these curious strangers, were surprised to hear no answering words of welcome fall from the lips of the saint. And still more surprised were they when Benedict pointed an accusing finger at the glittering crown that shone on the king's head and said:

"Why do you wear upon your head the sign of royalty which does not belong to you? And why have you lied? Go to your master, and tell him to come to me in truth, and do not think that I could mistake a servant for a king."

And to the amazement of all, the real king, who had disguised his armor-bearer to test the power of the saint, came forward quickly, and with no royal robe or golden crown, knelt low before the saint, confessing all, and praying to be forgiven. He was sure now that this was indeed a servant of God, and he listened humbly while Benedict reproved him for his many sins and warned him of the fate that awaited him.

So the years passed on, bringing much honor and earthly renown to him who had once lived a lonely boy upon the wild mountainside.

Things had changed since those early days. He could no longer live quite alone as he had once loved to do, for the world had followed him even into the wilderness. But his heart was as pure and his purpose as strong as when he was a lonely boy seeking only to serve God.

Perhaps the one great pleasure of his earthly life was the yearly visit he paid to his sister Scholastica, who had for many years come to live near him. She had formed a little company of nuns, who strove to live as the brothers were living, working and praying and denying themselves all earthly pleasures.

And as it was a great delight to Benedict to visit his sister, so to Scholastica the day of his coming was the happiest day of all the year. The only thing that grieved her was that the golden hours of that bright day seemed to fly faster than any other, while she listened to his words of counsel and advice and told him all her troubles.

As it drew near the time for one of these yearly visits, Scholastica began to long for her brother as she had never longed before. Something told her that these bright summer days were to be the last she should spend on earth, and the longing to see and talk to her brother grew almost more than she could bear.

When he came the hours slipped past even faster than usual, and before she could realize it the time had come for him to go. There was so much still to say, and she needed his help so much, that she begged him to wait a few hours longer. But Benedict was persuaded that it was his duty to set off, and duty to him ever came before all else. He gently told her it could not be; that he must return to the brothers that night.

But while he spoke, Scholastica was not listening to his words, nor heeding what he said. With her whole heart, she was praying to God that He would grant her this one request, and prevent her brother from leaving her so soon.

And as she prayed the light suddenly died out of the sky, great clouds arose, and, before Benedict could set out, a terrible storm began to rage. The thunder pealed overhead, the hail came down in a blinding shower, and it was impossible for anyone to leave the shelter of the house.

Thus, God answered the prayer of Scholastica, filling her heart with thankfulness. And afterward, the heart of Benedict was also filled with gratitude, for not many days later he saw in a vision the soul of his sister flying like a white dove up to heaven's gate, and he knew he would see her on earth no more.

Benedict had lived a long, hard life, eating little, suffering cold, and denying himself in all things. But though his spirit only grew stronger and brighter as time went on, his body was worn out, and at last, he prepared to lay it aside, as men lay aside the worn-out robe which has grown threadbare.

And as he had longed to live alone, so, when death came, he asked to be carried to the little chapel, and there to be left before the altar alone with God. So, Benedict, the Blessed went home, at last, leaving his tired body in God's house, while his spirit returned to God who gave it.

The Conversion of England

by Rev. Monsignor Edmund J. Goebel Ph. D.

The Anglo-Saxons. After the Teutonic tribes gained possession of Britain, the country received the new name of Angleland, or England, after the tribes of Angles. Since the Angles and the Saxons were more numerous than the Jutes, the term Anglo-Saxon is usually used to refer to all the Teutons of Britain.

West-Saxon Supremacy. The Teutonic tribes did not unite for a long time. Instead, they formed seven small kingdoms. The Jutes settled in Kent, in the southeastern part of the island. The Angles took over the northern section of England, where they had the three kingdoms of Northumbria, Mercia, and East Anglia. The Saxons also established three kingdoms, which covered nearly all the southern part of the Island. These were the kingdoms of Wessex, Essex, and Sussex.

There was constant rivalry and warfare among these seven kingdoms. For a time, Kent was the leading kingdom. Its capital was Canterbury. It was to Kent and Canterbury that St. Augustine came when he brought Christianity to the Teutonic people of England.

St. Augustine of Canterbury, Apostle of England. When Pope Gregory decided to send missionaries to England, he selected a band of forty monks from his own monastery in Rome, placing them in the charge of Augustine.

The Angles, Saxons, and Jutes who invaded England had settled down into seven small kingdoms. Augustine and his companions arrived in the kingdom of Kent early in the year 597. Ethelbert, the king of Kent, had married a Frankish princess, Bertha, who was a devout Catholic. Ethelbert met Augustine and his monks at Canterbury, the capital of Kent. Ethelbert gave Augustine permission to preach in his kingdom and became one of the first converts. At Canterbury, Augustine established his headquarters. He became the first Archbishop of Canterbury.

Saint Augustine of Canterbury

by Amy Steedman

It was market day in the great city of Rome, and the people were busy buying and selling and shouting, just as they do today with us when market day comes around. But there was a great difference between this Roman market and ours, a difference which would have seemed to us strange and cruel. For instead of sheep and oxen, or green vegetables from the country, they were selling men and boys, and even little girls. There in the great marketplace, with the sun beating down on their bare heads, they stood, looking with dull, despairing eyes, or with frightened glances at the crowds of buyers and sellers who were bargaining around.

Suddenly a hush fell on the crowd, and a stately figure was seen crossing the square. People stood aside and bent their heads in reverence as Gregory passed by, for he was Abbot of a great monastery in Rome and was much beloved even by the rough Roman soldiers. He walked swiftly as if he did not care to linger in the marketplace, for it grieved his gentle heart to see the suffering of the slaves when he could do nothing to help them.

But suddenly the crowd seemed to divide in front of him, and he stopped in wonder at the sight which met his eyes. It was a group of little fair-haired English boys who had been captured in the wars and carried off to be sold as slaves in the Roman market. But Gregory had never seen anything like them before. These boys with their sunny, golden hair, fair faces, and eyes blue as the sky overhead, seemed to him creatures from a different world.

"Where did these children come from, and what is the name of their people?" the bishop asked a man who stood beside him."

"'From an island far over the sea,' he answered, 'and men call them Angles.'

Then the kind bishop looked with pitying eyes upon the beautiful children, and said to himself, as he turned to go: 'They should be called not Angles, but angels.'

The sight of those boys, so strong and fearless and beautiful, made Gregory think a great deal about the little island of Britain, far away across the sea, where they had come from. He knew the people who lived there were fierce, warlike, with a strange religion of their own, and that very few of them were Christians. But he knew, too, that though they were hard to conquer and difficult to teach, still they were a people worth teaching, and he longed to win them to the side of Christ and to show them how to serve the true God.

In those days people in Italy knew very little about that far-away island, and it seemed to them as difficult and dangerous to go to England as it would seem to us if we were asked to go to the wildest part of a jungle. True there were no lions nor tigers in England, but the tall, fair-haired giants who lived there were as savage as they were brave and might be even worse to deal with than the wild beasts of other lands.

So, it may well be believed that when Saint Gregory, who was now Pope of Rome, chose forty monks and sent them on a mission to this distant island, they were not very anxious to go, and set out in fear and trembling.

But at their head was one who knew no fear and who was willing to face any danger in the service of his Master. This man was Augustine, a monk of Rome, whom Gregory had chosen to lead the mission, knowing that his courage would strengthen the others, and his wisdom would guide them aright.

It took many long days and nights of travel to reach the coast where they were to find a ship to carry them across to Britain, and before they had gone very far, the forty monks were inclined to turn back in despair. From every side they heard such terrible tales of the savage islanders they were going to meet, that their hearts, never very courageous, were filled with terror, and they refused to go further. Nothing that Augustine could say would persuade them to go on, and they would only agree that he should go back to Rome and bear their prayers to Pope Gregory, imploring him not to force them to face such horrible danger. If Augustine would do this, they promised to wait for his return and to do then whatever the Pope ordered.

They had not to wait many days, for Augustine speedily brought back the Pope's answer to their request. His face glowed and his eyes shone with the light of victory, as he read to them the letter which Gregory had sent. There was to be no thought of going back. Pope Gregory's words were few but decisive. 'It is better not to begin a work than to turn back as soon as danger threatens; therefore, my beloved sons, go forward by the help of our Lord.'

So, they obeyed, and with Augustine at their head once more set out, hardly hoping to escape the perils of the journey, and expecting, if they did arrive, to be speedily put to death by the islanders.

Perhaps the worst trial of all was when they set sail from France and saw the land fading away in the distance. In front, there was nothing to be seen but angry waves and a cold, grey sky, and they seemed to be drifting away from the country of sunshine and safety into the dark region of uncertainty and danger. The island of Britain, whose very name was terrible to them, was nowhere to be seen and seemed all the more horrible because it was wrapped in that mysterious grey mist.

But though they did not know it, they had really nothing to fear from the island people, for the queen of that part of England where they landed was a Christian and had taught King Ethelbert to show mercy and kindness. So, when the company of cold, shivering monks came ashore they were met with a kind and courteous welcome, and instead of enemies, they found friends.

The king himself came to meet them, and he ordered the little group of foreigners to be brought before him, that he might learn their errand. He did not receive them in any hall or palace, but out in the open air, for it seemed safer there, in case these strangers should be workers of magic or witchcraft.

It must have been a strange scene when the forty monks, with Augustine at their head, walked in procession up from the beach to the broad green meadow where the king and his soldiers waited for them. The tall, fair-haired warriors who stood around, sword in hand, ready to defend their king, must have looked with surprise at these black-robed men with shaven heads and empty hands. They carried no weapons of any sort, and they seemed to bear no banner to tell men where they came from. Only the foremost monks carried on high a silver cross and the picture of a crucified man, and instead of shouts and war-cries, there was the sound of a melodious chant sung by many voices yet seeming as if sung by one.

Then Augustine stood out from among the company of monks and waited for the king to speak.

"Who are you, and from where have come these men who are with you?" asked the king. "I think you come in peace, or else you would have carried more deadly weapons than a silver charm and a painted sign. I want to know the reason for your visit to our island."

Slowly Augustine began to tell the story of their pilgrimage and the message they had brought. He spoke so long that the sun began to sink, and the twilight fell over the silent sea that lay stretched out beyond the meadow where they sat before his story was done.

The king bent forward, thoughtfully weighing the words he had heard, and looking into the faces of these strange messengers of peace. At length, he spoke, and the weary monks and stalwart warriors listened eagerly to his words.

"You have spoken well," he said to Augustine, "and it may be there is truth in what you say. But a man does not change his religion in an hour. I will hear more of this. But meanwhile, you shall be well cared for, and all who choose may listen to your message."

Those were indeed welcome words to the company of poor tired monks, and when the kindly islanders, following their king's example, made them welcome and gave them food and shelter, they could well echo the words of Gregory in the Roman market, "These are not Angles but angels."

And soon King Ethelbert gave the little company a house of their own and allowed them to build up the ancient church at Canterbury, which had fallen into ruins. There they lived as simply and quietly as they had done in their convent in Italy, praying day and night for the souls of these heathen people, and teaching them, as much by their lives as their words, that it was good to serve the Lord Christ.

And before very long the people began to listen eagerly to their teaching, and the king himself was baptized with many others. The chant which the monks had sung that first day of their landing no longer sounded strange and mysterious in the ears of the islanders, for they too learned to sing the 'Alleluia' and to praise God beneath the sign of the silver cross.

Now Augustine was very anxious that the Ancient British Church should join his party and that they should work together under the direction of Pope Gregory. But the British Christians were not sure if they might trust these strangers, and it was arranged that they should meet first, before making any plans.

The ancient British Church had almost been driven out of the land, and there were but few of her priests left. They did not know whether they ought to join Augustine and his foreign monks or strive to work on alone. In their perplexity, they went to a holy hermit and asked him what they should do.

"If this man comes from God, then follow him," said the hermit.

"But how can we know if he is of God?" asked the people.

The hermit thought a while and then said:

"The true servant of God is ever humble and lowly of heart. Go to meet this man. If he rises and bids you welcome, then will you know that he bears Christ's yoke, and will lead you aright. But if he is proud and haughty, and treats you with scorn, never rising to welcome you, then see to it that you have nothing to do with him."

So, the priests and bishops of the British Church arranged to meet Augustine under a great oak-tree, which was called ever afterward "Augustine's oak." They carefully planned that the foreign monks should arrive there first, in time to be seated, so that the hermit's test might be tried when they themselves should arrive.

Unhappily, Augustine did not think of rising to greet the British bishops, and they were very angry and would agree to nothing that he proposed, though he warned them solemnly that if they would not join their forces with his, they would sooner or later fall by the hand of their enemies.

Greatly disappointed Augustine returned to Canterbury and worked there for many years without help until all who lived in that part of England learned to be Christians.

And Pope Gregory hearing of his labors was pleased with the work his missionary had done and thought it fit that the humble monk should be rewarded with a post of honor. So, he made Augustine Archbishop of Canterbury, the first archbishop that England had known. It was a simple ceremony then, with only a few faithful monks kneeling around the chair on which the archbishop was enthroned, but Augustine's keen, dark face shone with the light of victory and humble thankfulness, for it seemed a seal upon his work, a pledge that the island should never again turn back from the faith of Christ.

And could those dark eyes have looked forward and pierced the screen of many years, Augustine would have seen a goodly succession of archbishops following in his footsteps, each in his turn sitting in that same simple old chair, placed now in Westminster Abbey and guarded as one of England's treasures.

And he would have seen, too, what would have cheered his heart more than all—a Christian England venerating the spot where his monastery once stood and building upon it a college to his memory. And there he would have seen England's sons trained to become missionaries and to go out into all the world to preach the gospel, just as that little band of monks, with Augustine at their head, came to the island in those dark, far-off days.

But though Augustine could not know all this, his heart was filled with great hope and a great love for the islanders who now seemed like his own children, and he was more than content to spend his life among them.

And when his work was ended, and the faithful soul gave up his charge, they buried him on the island which had once seemed to him a land of exile, but which at last had come to mean even more to him than his own sunny land of Italy.

The Cowherd Who Became a Poet

by James Baldwin

In England, there was once a famous abbey, called Whitby. It was so close to the sea that those who lived in it could hear the waves forever beating against the shore. The land around it was rugged, with only a few fields in the midst of a vast forest.

In those far-off days, an abbey was half church, half castle. It was a place where good people and timid, helpless people could find shelter in time of war. There they might live in peace and safety while all the country round was overrun by rude and barbarous men.

One cold night in winter the serving men of the abbey were gathered in the great kitchen. They were sitting around the fire and trying to keep themselves warm.

Out of doors, the wind was blowing. The men heard it as it whistled through the trees and rattled the doors of the abbey. They drew up closer to the fire and felt thankful that they were safe from the raging storm. "Who will sing us a song?" said the master woodman as he threw a fresh log upon the fire.

"Yes, a song! a song!" shouted some of the others. "Let us have a good old song that will help to keep us warm."

"We can all be minstrels to-night," said the chief cook. "Suppose we each sing a song in turn. What say you?"

"Agreed! agreed!" cried the others. "And the cook shall begin."

The woodman stirred the fire until the flames leaped high and the sparks flew out of the roof hole. Then the chief cook began his song. He sang of war, and of bold rough deeds, and of love and sorrow.

After him the other men were called, one by one; and each, in turn, sang his favorite song. The woodman sang of the wild forest; the plowman sang of the fields; the shepherd sang of his sheep, and those who listened forgot about the storm and the cold weather

But in the corner, almost hidden from his fellows, one poor man was sitting who did not enjoy the singing. It was Caedmon, the cowherd. "What shall I do when it comes my turn?" he said to himself. "I do not know any song. My voice is harsh and I cannot sing."

So he sat there trembling and afraid; for he was a timid, bashful man and did not like to be noticed.

At last, just as the blacksmith was in the midst of a stirring song, he rose quietly and went out into the darkness. He went across the narrow yard to the sheds where the cattle were kept in stormy weather.

"The gentle cows will not ask a song of me," said the poor man. He soon found a warm corner, and there he lay down, covering himself with the straw.

Inside of the great kitchen, beside the fire, the men were shouting and laughing; for the blacksmith had finished his song, and it was very pleasing.

"Who is next?" asked the woodman.

"Caedmon, the keeper of the cows," answered the chief cook.

"Yes, Caedmon! Caedmon!" all shouted together. "A song from Caedmon!" But when they looked, they saw that his seat was vacant.

"The poor, timid fellow!" said the blacksmith. "He was afraid and has slipped away from us."

In his safe, warm place in the straw, Caedmon soon fell asleep. All around him were the cows of the abbey, some chewing their cuds, and others like their master quietly sleeping. The singing in the kitchen was ended, the fire had burned low, and each man had gone to his place.

Then Caedmon had a strange dream. He thought that a wonderful light was shining around him. His eyes were dazzled by it. He rubbed them with his hands, and when they were quite open he thought that he saw a beautiful face looking down upon him and that a gentle voice said,

"Caedmon, sing for me."

At first, he was so bewildered that he could not answer. Then he heard the voice again.

"Caedmon, sing something."

"Oh, I cannot sing," answered the poor man." I do not know any song, and my voice is harsh and unpleasant. It was for this reason that I left my fellows in the abbey kitchen and came here to be alone."

"But you *must* sing," said the voice. "You *must* sing."

"What shall I sing?" he asked.

"Sing of the creation," was the answer.

Then Caedmon, with only the cows as his hearers, opened his mouth and began to sing. He sang of the beginning of things; how the world was made; how the sun and moon came into being; how the land rose from the water; how the birds and the beasts were given life.

All through the night he sat among the abbey cows and sang his wonderful song. When the stable boys and shepherds came out in the morning, they heard him singing; and they were so amazed that they stood still in the drifted snow and listened with open mouths.

At length, others of the servants heard him and were entranced by his wonderful song. And one ran quickly and told the good abbess, or mistress of the abbey, what strange thing had happened.

"Bring the cowherd hither, that I and those who are with me may hear him," said she.

So Caedmon was led into the great hall of the abbey. And all of the sweet-faced sisters and other women of the place listened while he sang again the wonderful song of the creation.

"Surely," said the abbess, "this is a poem, most sweet, most true, most beautiful. It must be written down so that people in other places and in other times may hear it read and sung."

So she called her clerk, who was a scholar, and bade him write the song, word for word, as it came from Caedmon's lips. And this he did.

Such was the way in which the first true English poem was written. And Caedmon, the poor cowherd of the abbey, was the first great poet of England.

Emperor Justinian

by Rev. Monsignor Edmund J. Goebel Ph. D.

Law and Government. The Romans made their greatest contribution to civilization through their ideas on law and government. There were many different tribes and nations within the Roman Empire. The Romans gave the empire a good government for several centuries. They showed the world that many nations could be united under a single government. And the world has never lost the hope that once again nations might unite and live in peace under one government.

The Roman people had great respect for law. They also believed that the laws should be just. One of the ideas which the Romans developed in their laws was that a man is considered innocent until he has been proven guilty.

One of the Christian emperors who ruled the empire long after the time of Augustus was called Justinian. He performed a very important service for the world. He thought that the Roman laws were confusing to the people. So, he had a group of well-educated men collect all the Roman laws. They studied the laws and then arranged them in good order. This new collection of Roman laws was called the Justinian Code. It became the law for the entire empire. It was so good that many of the European nations which were later formed out of the Roman Empire kept the Justinian Code. Even today, laws in Europe and the Americas are based on Justinian's code of laws.

Muhammed and His New Religion

by Rev. Monsignor Edmund J. Goebel Ph. D.

Muhammed. The barbarian tribes were just beginning to settle down and live peacefully when a new danger threatened Europe. It came from the Near East. A new religion, Islam, appeared in Arabia. Its followers began with fire and sword to force this religion on all the peoples of the East. Their methods were very different from the quiet and beautiful sermons with which St. Peter and St. Paul and their successors spread the gospel of Christ.

Muhammed was born in Mecca, a city of Arabia. He became a camel driver and led caravans across the desert. On his journeys, he met many shepherds and traders. Some of these were Christians and Jews. From them, he learned many things about the Christian and Jewish religions.

Muhammed came to believe that there was only one God. His name for God was Allah. He claimed that the angel Gabriel appeared to him and revealed many new ideas to him. Muhammed became convinced that he was the chosen prophet of God. He denied that Christ was God. He said that Moses and Christ were prophets of the true God, but Muhammed was the greatest of the prophets.

The Hegira. When Muhammed began to preach his new religion at Mecca, he gained very few converts. The people of Mecca were still pagans and worshipped many idols. Muhammed and his small band of followers were driven from Mecca in the year A.D. 622. They fled to Medina, another Arabian city. This flight is now known as the hegira. The Muslims count the years in their calendar from the hegira.

Muhammed had more success in Medina. He attracted many followers, and after about eight years, he captured control of the city. Then, with his followers, he returned to Mecca and captured that city too. He made Mecca the holy city of Islam, which is the name he gave his new religion.

The Koran. After the death of Muhammed, his sayings were collected in a book called the Koran. It is the holy book of the followers of Muhammed, whom he called Muslims. It contained the laws for a good Muslim and encourages prayer, fasting, and the giving of alms to the poor. A good Muslim was also required to make, if possible, at least one journey to Mecca during his lifetime.

The Muslim faith is summed up in a very short creed: "There is no God but Allah, and Muhammed is His prophet." This is sung five times every day from the high tower of every Muslim mosque, which is the name they gave to their churches.

The Spread of Islam

Muslim Conquests. The Muslims believed that any man who died battling to extend his religion would go to paradise. For this reason, the followers of Muhammed were eager to fight for their religion. In the name of Allah, they set out to conquer the world. They conquered all of Arabia and then all the countries of western Asia. They attempted to cross over into Europe, but the emperor at Constantinople prevented them from advancing in that direction.

They then turned around and captured Egypt. By this time, they had captured the three great Christian centers of Jerusalem, Antioch, and Alexandria. They then began a path of conquest across northern Africa. Soon, they had conquered all the Christian communities as far as the Atlantic Ocean.

At Gibraltar, they crossed over into Spain and destroyed the kingdom of the Visigoths. When they crossed the Pyrenees into France, it seemed as if all Europe would be conquered by the Muslims.

However, on the northern side of the Pyrenees were the Franks. They had become Christians and rose up to defend Europe against this new invader. Near the city of Tours, in the year A.D. 732, the Franks defeated the Muslims. This battle is often considered one of the most important battles in history. It stopped the Muslim advance into Europe. As a result, Europe remained Christian.

Muslim Civilization. The Muslims brought about many changes in the lands that they conquered. They introduced Arabian ideas and customs. For instance, they introduced Arabic numerals. The Europeans found that these were easier to use than the Roman numbers. Today in your arithmetic, you use Arabic numbers, which are 1, 2, 3, 4, 5, 6, 7, 8, 9, and 0.

They also brought to Europe many new products from the East. Among these were fine steel weapons, tapestries, muslin, silk, carpets, and a heavy cloth for use in making tents. They also taught the people of Europe to raise and to use many new foodstuffs – rice, sugar cane, peaches, melons, apricots, oranges, and lemons. They introduced into Europe several kinds of fine sheep and the swift Arabian horse.

A new city that became the center of the Muslim civilization was built in Bagdad, on the Tigris River, near the ruins of Babylon. Most of the caravan routes of the East went through this city, which became very wealthy and powerful. Perhaps you have read some stories of Bagdad in the book which is called *The Arabian Nights' Entertainment.* Among the best known of these tales are "Ali Baba and the Forty Thieves," "Aladdin and His Wonderful Lamp," and "Sinbad the Sailor."

The Conversion of Europe

by Rev. Monsignor Edmund J. Goebel Ph. D.

St. Boniface, Apostle of Germany. A young Saxon noble named Winfried became one of the great missionaries of the Church. He entered the Benedictine school at Exeter as a young boy and later became a monk. His great ambition was to bring the Faith to the pagan Saxons who had remained in central Germany.

He left England and went to Rome to receive the blessing of Pope Gregory the Second. The Pope changed his name to Boniface, which means "one who does good." His work was so successful during his first three years in central Germany that the Pope asked him to return to Rome for a visit. While there, Boniface was consecrated a bishop.

On his return to Germany, he gave a deathblow to paganism in that region. The pagan Germans held a gigantic oak tree in great veneration. It was dedicated to Thor, the god of thunder. St. Boniface with his own hands chopped down this oak while throngs of pagans watched. They expected that Thor would strike down St. Boniface with a thunderbolt. When the monk remained unharmed, the pagans realized that their belief in many gods was false. Many of them immediately asked to be baptized.

His Work Successful. The missionary work of St. Boniface was so successful that he needed more priests. He sent back to England, and a large group of monks responded to his call. A group of English nuns, some of them cousins of St. Boniface, also came to Germany to found convent schools. The Pope rewarded the missionary work of St. Boniface by making him an archbishop.

The most famous of the monasteries founded by St. Boniface was at Fulda, in central Germany. This was the largest monastery in Germany, as St. Boniface intended that it should be a training school for other missionaries and priests. It became the center of the Catholic Faith in Germany.

The reputation of St. Boniface continued to grow. Great leaders sought his advice. It was

St. Boniface who crowned Pepin, king of France, at the request of the Pope.

His Martyrdom. Yet, when he was almost eighty years of age, he resigned as archbishop in order to become a plain missionary again. He had always wanted to convert the people of Friesland. This territory forms that part of Germany and the Netherlands which is close to the North Sea. Despite his advanced age, his preaching brought many of the Frisians into the Faith. He was so successful that he aroused the enmity of the pagan leaders. As he was preparing a group of converts for the sacrament of Confirmation, a band of pagans attacked him. The Apostle of Germany suffered the death of a martyr, along with fifty-two of his followers.

Other Fervent Missionaries

St. Ansgar, Apostle to Scandinavia. St. Ansgar preached the Faith to the people of Denmark and Sweden. He became Archbishop of Hamburg, where he made his headquarters for the missionary trips to the countries of the North. He became famous for his works of mercy. He built hospitals ransomed captives and helped to reduce the slave trade in the northern areas.'

St. Virgil, Apostle to the Southern Slavs. An Irish monk named Fergal crossed over to the Continent. He took the Latin version of his name and became known as St. Virgil. Later, he became Bishop of Salzburg, which is in Austria. His diocese bordered the lands of the southern Slavic tribes.

The Two St. Adalberts. The first St. Adalbert was a German monk who was made Bishop of Magdeburg for the purpose of bringing the Faith to the Slavic people of the North.

A young Bohemian monk who studied under St. Adalbert took the same name as his great teacher. This second St. Adalbert became the Bishop of Prague. He worked successfully among his own countrymen and in Poland. He also baptized St. Stephen, the king of Hungary. St. Adalbert was martyred in the year 1000.

St. Stephen of Hungary. St. Stephen was the son of Duke Geza, the ruler of Hungary. The duke and all his family were baptized Christians, but it was not until Stephen succeeded his father that the people of Hungary adopted the Catholic Faith.

The conversion of Hungary was due to the zeal of St. Stephen. He founded monasteries, established dioceses, and helped the priests spread the gospel of Christ. St. Stephen became the first king of Hungary. In the year 1001, Pope Sylvester the Second sent him a consecrated crown, which all the kings of Hungary wore thereafter.

By this time, many pious Christians of Europe made journeys or pilgrimages to the Holy Land. With the conversion of Hungary to Christianity, a direct land route was possible across Europe to the Eastern Roman Empire. St. Stephen gave the pilgrims protection throughout his kingdom. In addition, he established hospices at Rome, Ravenna, and Constantinople. A hospice was an inn where a tired pilgrim might find rest and refreshment. St. Stephen also established a monastery in Jerusalem to care for the pilgrims when they reached the birthplace of Christianity.

Saints Cyril and Methodius. Missionaries came also from the East to aid in the conversion of the Slavic peoples. The eastern emperors at Constantinople and the patricians of that city were also interested in the spread of Christianity. Two of the chief missionaries from Constantinople were Saints Cyril and Methodius.

Cyril and Methodius were brothers. They worked as missionaries among the Bulgarians for several years. The Duke of Moravia invited them to preach in his land. They were well prepared for this work. They had studied the Slavic language, and St. Cyril had invented an alphabet that is still used in Slavic countries. The two brothers had also translated the Gospels and other books into the Slavic language. They were able to preach to the people in their own language. After a visit to Rome, the Pope even permitted them to say Mass in the native tongue of the Slavic people.

St. Olga and Vladimir of Russia. Russia also received the Faith from Constantinople. Vladimir the Great, ruler of Russia, was intrigued by Christianity. His grandmother, St. Olga, had become a Catholic and encouraged many of the people to accept the Faith of Christ.

When Vladimir decided to become a Christian, he asked the emperor at Constantinople to send a special mission to give him instructions and baptism. The people of Russia must have been eager for Christianity, for they joined the Church in large numbers after the conversion of Vladimir.

After his conversion, Vladimir gave up his warlike career. He tried earnestly to give his people a good government. He built churches, established schools, and did all he could to spread the work of conversion and civilization.

A Christian Continent. We have traced the work of the missionaries across Europe, from Ireland to Russia, and from Sweden to Italy. The task took about six hundred years, but by the year A.D. 1000 it was almost complete: practically all Europe was Christian.

Charles Martel

Adapted from the work of Eva March Tappan, Ph. D. and Henrietta E. Marshall

For more than a century following the death of Clovis, a king was always on the Frankish throne, but he never ruled; and these sovereigns have been nicknamed the "do-nothing kings." The real rulers were officers called mayors of the palace. The "mayor" was at first only a sort of royal attendant, but several of the kings were children when they came to the throne, and the mayors acted as their guardians with all but regal powers.

Some of the kings were stupid, and some cared only for amusement, and hardly any of them were strong and manly enough to govern. The mayors of the palace were rulers in peace, and as the "do-nothing kings" were, of course, unable to lead armies, the mayors became also commanders in war. This arrangement suited the Frankish nobles. They were always afraid that their kings would get too much power over them; but as a mayor was chosen from among themselves, they were not jealous of his power.

One of these mayors was named Pepin. He treated the king with the utmost respect, permitted him to live on one of the royal estates, and sent servants to wait on him. When some national festival was to be held, the king was brought to court dressed in most elegant robes and with his long hair floating over his shoulders. He rode in a heavy wagon drawn by oxen and driven by a cowherd. This was according to the ancient custom, and the people would have been displeased to have it altered. He was escorted into the palace and seated upon the throne, and the nobles came to do him honor. He recited a little speech, composed for him beforehand, urging the army to be valiant and to be always ready for service. If ambassadors were to be received, he met them graciously and said what Mayor Pepin told him to say. Then with all deference, he was led to the cart and driven back to the estate upon which he lived. He was free to go on hunting or raising doves or combing his long hair until a figurehead was needed again.

When Pepin died, his son Charles became mayor. It was fortunate that he was a good fighter, for there was a great deal of fighting to be done. There were hostile tribes on the north and east to be subdued. Then, too, there were rumors of trouble coming from another people, the Muslims.

It was against this vast horde that Charles now gathered all the strength of his army. From the farthest corners of his dominion, he called men to fight for their faith. And they came from such distant countries that the mighty host which gathered together formed a European rather than a Frankish army.

It was near the town of Poitiers that the two armies met. There for seven days, they lay opposite each other. On the one side were the men of the North. They were clad in coats of steel, shining helmets covered their heads, and they carried long swords and heavy battle-axes. On the other side were the men of the South, wearing white turbans and robes, mounted upon swift horses, and carrying small round shields and light spears and bows.

One by one the October days slid by. The Muslim horsemen dashed over the plain upon their prancing horses, raising clouds of dust, but never attacking the steel-clad warriors who watched in silent waiting. At length one Sunday, toward the end of October, In the gray of morning, the Muslim call to prayer was heard. Soon the plain was covered with white-robed warriors praying for victory. When the prayer was over, the battle signal was given.

"God Is great! God Is great!" they shouted as they dashed upon the enemy. But under the fearful onslaught, the Franks stood unmoved. Again and again, from the glittering wall of steel, the white-robed warriors were thrown back like the foam of waves which beat upon a rocky shore. In vain the javelins and arrows of the Muslims rained upon the Christian host. "The Franks stood like a wall of Iron as If frozen to blocks of Ice," said a writer of the time. "They stood locked to one another like men of marble."

Twenty times the Muslims returned to the attack. Twenty times their furious charge was broken against the Immovable wall until hundreds lay dead upon the field, and riderless horses rushed madly over the plain.

Hour after hour the battle lasted. The sun had begun to sink toward the west when a great cry of distress arose from behind the Muslims. Part of the Frankish army had quietly crept around the enemy and was now attacking the camp. Then Charles ordered the body of his troops, which had stood until now Immovable as the wall of steel, to advance. And thus, taken on both sides, the Muslim army broke and fled in unutterable confusion. Night, at last, put an end to the slaughter and pursuit, and silence fell upon the field which, from dawn till dark, had rung with battle cries and the clash of steel on steel.

When day dawned once more the Franks again made ready for battle. But all was still and silent in the gleaming white tents of the enemy. In vain the Franks listened and watched for any sign of life. None came. Then Charles sent a company of soldiers to discover what this might mean. Across the plain, strewn with thousands of dead, they rode, and at length reached the camp of the Muslims. Once after another, they entered the tents. Each one was empty. Not a living man was left in all the vast camp. In the night, the Muslims had fled, taking only their horse and arms and leaving all their rich spoils and booty behind.

This battle of Poitiers, which was fought in 732, Is one of the great battles of ancient times for on It hung the fate of the Christian world. Between the Infidel Muslims and the wild heathen people of the North, there was only the empire of the Franks. Had Christianity been crushed out there, the fate of Europe would have been changed.

It was after this battle that Charles received the surname of Martel or Hammer, "for as a hammer breaks Iron and steel and all metals so he broke by his blows in battle all his enemies and all strange nations." The power of the Muslims was broken, but they were not utterly crushed. Charles fought them again and yet again, and in time they were driven out of France altogether.

Toward the end of his life, Charles was greatly honored by Pope Gregory III, who sent him many great presents such as he had never before sent to any king. Among these were said to be the "Keys of the Holy Sepulcher," and the chains with which St. Peter was bound. The Pope called Charles the Illustrious Viceroy of France and begged his help to drive the Lombards, who were attacking him, out of Italy. "Our tears flow day and night from our eyes," he said, "when we see the Church forsaken on all sides by those of her children, from whom she most hoped for defense and protection. I Implore your goodwill before God that you may hasten to soothe our sorrows, or, at the least, to send us an answer in which we may rejoice." He offered, also, to make Charles Consul of Rome. This was, in fact, to make him Emperor of the West In place of the old, long-dead Caesars.

Charles the Hammer received the Pope's messengers with great honor and sent them back to Rome laden with presents. But he never went to Italy to be made Emperor, and never fought the Lombards. For soon after this he fell Ill and died. He was buried In the Church of St. Denis In Paris. Charles the Hammer had ruled for twenty-five years. He had vastly enlarged the borders of France and left the kingdom in great peace and prosperity. A few years before he died the King Do-nothing had died. But he had become so much of a pretense that Charles did not think It worthwhile to crown another. So, in 741, when Charles the Hammer died, the throne was empty.

The Kingdom of the Franks

by Rev. Monsignor Edmund J. Goebel Ph. D.

Pepin, King of the Franks. Charles Martel did not take the title of king, even though he was the actual ruler. After his death, one of his sons, Karlmann, entered the monastery which St. Benedict had founded at Monte Cassino. This left the other son, Pepin, as ruler of all the Franks.

After he had ruled as mayor of the palace for ten years, Pepin sent a bishop and an abbot to Rome. They were to see Pope Zachary and to ask him who should be king – a weakling who had only the title of king or the man who actually ruled the kingdom. The Pope replied that the man who actually ruled the kingdom should be called king.

Pepin then set aside the last of the "do-nothing" kings. With the consent of the bishops and nobles, Pepin became king. St. Boniface anointed the new king in the manner in which the prophet Samuel anointed King Saul in the Old Testament. This was a new idea to the Franks and made a great impression on them.

The Papal States. The eastern emperor at Constantinople still claimed to be the ruler of Italy. But he did very little to prevent a Germanic tribe called the Lombards from conquering all of Italy. In order to provide some defense for Rome and central Italy, the Pope was obliged to raise an army and to try to stop the Lombards.

Finally, the Pope appealed to Pepin for help against the continual threats of the Lombards. Pepin led his army against the Lombards and defeated them. Then he gave the land of central Italy to the Pope. This made the Pope a civil ruler as well as the spiritual head of the Church. The civil power of the Pope prevents another ruler from interfering with the spiritual work of the head of the Church. At the present time, the Pope is the ruler of a small section of the city of Rome, which is called Vatican City.

Charlemagne and a New Empire

by Rev. Monsignor Edmund J. Goebel Ph. D.

Charlemagne. After Pepin's death, his son Charles became king. So great a king was Charles that he is to this day known as Charlemagne, a name which means "Charles the Great." Charlemagne was the greatest king of the Middle Ages and ruled for forty-six years.

Charlemagne had a secretary who wrote down many things about him. This secretary tells us that Charlemagne was a big man, more than six feet tall. He had fair hair, blue eyes, and a prominent nose. He was a man of such dignified bearing that he would have been noticed in any crowd.

Charlemagne was very energetic and liked to take part in active sports. He enjoyed riding and hunting and was an expert swimmer. He never ate or drank too much. His frequent exercise and good habits in eating and drinking made his body strong and his mind bright.

His Conquests. Charlemagne wanted to bring all the Teutonic peoples together into one great Christian empire. He did much toward accomplishing this.

This Saxons who lived in northern Germany were one of the fiercest of all the Teutonic tribes. Charlemagne was determined to subdue them. However, it took Charlemagne thirty years to bring them under his rule. Then he encourages the missionaries in their work of converting and civilizing the Saxons. A hundred years later, the Saxons were the most important Germanic tribes.

This conquest of the Saxons brought Charlemagne in contact with the Slavic tribes farther east. In a single campaign, Charlemagne forced the Slavic tribes to accept him as their overlord. Then he established several marches along the eastern boundary of his dominions. A "marc" was a military district set up to protect the rest of the country from invasion. The Easter March – later the country of Austria – became one of the most important.

Charlemagne in Spain. When Charles Martel defeated the Muslims at Tours, in southern France, he pushed them back across the Pyrenees Mountains. From time to time, however, the Muslims attempted to invade the southern part of Charlemagne's kingdom. For twenty years Charlemagne waged war against the Muslims in Spain. He succeeded in conquering a part of northern Spain.

One of the men who accompanied Charlemagne in his battles against the Muslims was a very brave knight named Roland. Many famous stories have been told about him in the *Song of Roland.*

King of the Lombards. Like his father, Charlemagne wanted to protect the Pope against the Lombards. He made several expeditions against them. Finally, he deposed the Lombard king. Then he took the famous Iron Crown of Lombardy and placed it upon his own head. Thus he became king of the Lombards as well as the king of the Franks.

Emperor of the Romans

Charlemagne as Emperor. By his vast conquests, Charlemagne had made himself ruler of all the land from the Atlantic Ocean to the Danube River, and from the Pyrenees to the North Sea. He ruled either in whole or in part, Spain, France, Belgium, Holland, Germany, Austria, Hungary, Italy, and Switzerland. Western Europe had once against been united. This time a German, and not a Roman, had established law and order in the western half of Europe. A German empire had really taken the place of the Western Roman Empire. The Anglo-Saxons in England and the Scandinavians were the only Teutonic groups not included in this empire.

On Christmas Day, in the year 800, an important event happened in Rome. As Charlemagne was kneeling before the altar of St. Peter's Church at Rome, the Pope placed a golden crown on his head and called him "Emperor of the Romans."

The coronation of Charlemagne made a great impression on all the people of Europe. It gave him no additional power and no new territory. But Charlemagne was now considered to be the successor of the Western Roman Emperors. But his empire was very different from that of the Roman emperors. The ruling people were not Romans but Teutons. Charlemagne's capital city was not Rome but the German town of Aachen, which is generally known by its French name of Aix-la-Chapelle.

Governing the Empire. Governing this vast territory was a great task. Charlemagne did not revive the old Roman methods. Instead, he worked out a new plan and proved that he was a capable governor as well as an able warrior.

There was in Charlemagne's empire no system of general taxation for the support of the government. Instead, Charlemagne had to depend on the income of his royal estates. Therefore, he took great care to see that his estates were well cultivated and that the accounts of their produce were accurately kept.

Charlemagne divided his empire into smaller divisions called counties. In order to manage local affairs, he appointed a noble, with the title of count, over each of these divisions. It was a duty of the counts to act as judges when disputes arose among the landowners. It was also their duty to keep order and to raise troops for Charlemagne. Sometimes, several counties were combined into a duchy, and the governor held the title of duke.

Charlemagne also invented a system of keeping a check on the counts. Each year, two inspectors were sent out to every county. One was a bishop and the other a noble from the royal court. They were instructed, "to do justice to churches, widows, orphans, the poor, and all the people." They called the people together to find out whether there were any complaints. The inspectors gave Charlemagne a complete report of the affairs in each county. In this way, he could know what was happening in each section of his large empire.

Each spring at Aix-la-Chapelle or some other center in his empire, Charlemagne held a great outdoor meeting called a May-field. At this meeting, Charlemagne discussed the laws with his people and explained to them the purposes of new laws. Sometimes he even let the people vote on some question. Having this meeting was very wise because it made it impossible for unfair judges to change the laws to please themselves.

Charlemagne Revives Education. Charlemagne was much interested in school and in learning. He wished to educate his people and to develop great schools. He himself was a grown man before he learned to read and write. He learned to speak Latin as fluently as his native German. He also learned to understand Greek. Thus, he was able to listen to the great scholars when they lectured.

At Aix-la-Chapelle, he founded a great Palace School. Here his children and the children of the nobles were educated. He wanted to train these children for their future duties in helping to govern the empire. He brought to his Palace School the best scholars in Europe. From Germany, Italy, Spain, England, and Ireland came learned men to teach at the school of Charlemagne. Charlemagne himself often visited the school. He was always eager to learn. In spite of his duties as emperor, he studied religion, grammar, astronomy, and history.

The greatest of the scholars at the Palace School was a Saxon from England. This was Alcuin, who had been educated at the Cathedral School of York in England. Charlemagne made him director of the Palace School. He also helped Charlemagne plan the other schools of the kingdom.

Charlemagne ordered that every monastery and cathedral should open a school. These schools were open to all boys, no matter how poor their parents might be. If a boy wanted a good education and was willing to study hard, he might attend free one of these great schools. Charlemagne also tried to have a school in every village, under the direction of a parish priest, to teach elementary subjects.

Even during Charlemagne's lifetime, his plan of schools was never completely carried out. In fact, it would have taken several lifetimes to put all his plans into effect. Unfortunately, his successors showed little interest in promoting learning. But Charlemagne's efforts were not all in vain, for never again was ignorance so widespread in Western Europe as it had been before his time. Documents, letters, and writings of the period after Charlemagne's rule showed a great improvement in spelling, handwriting, and grammatical accuracy. In some monasteries and cathedrals, the schools which Charlemagne encourages and supported continued to exist and grew into universities.

Charlemagne and the Church. Charlemagne was devoted to the Christian religion. He was especially eager that all church ceremonies and services be conducted in the proper manner. He established schools for church music.

He attended Mass and other services regularly at the cathedral of Aix-la-Chapelle. To this church, Charlemagne gave many gifts – fine vestments for the clergy and candlesticks of silver and gold for the altar. The church of Aix-la-Chapelle was not the only one that knew his generosity. He gave rich gifts to other churches in his empire, especially to St. Peter's in Rome. He was very generous in giving to the poor. He event sent gifts to needy Christians in Jerusalem, Alexandria, and Carthage.

In his zeal to extend Christianity, Charlemagne required the people whom he conquered, especially the Saxons, to be baptized. He believed that they could be more easily civilized by converting them to Christianity. However, Alcuin and some of the bishops warned Charlemagne that if people were forced to accept Christianity, they may become Christians in name only. But gradually, the monks and missionaries changed this compulsory Christianity to more genuine faith. In a very few generations, the very people upon whom Charlemagne had forced Christianity spoke of him as their friend and as a great teacher of Christianity.

The Emperor and the Abbot

Retold by Lilian Gask

Emperor Charlemagne was a splendid horseman, and there was nothing he enjoyed more than a long ride through field and forest. He galloped just where his fancy led him, only stopping his flying steed when he wished to gaze with pride over his vast dominions.

On one of these occasions, he saw before him the Abbey of St Gall and noticed with much amusement the sleek and contented air of the good Abbot, who was just then strolling through the lovely gardens. His brow was smooth and open; his eyes were bright and placid as a child's, and from his well-nourished appearance it was plain that care sat lightly upon him. As the Emperor surveyed him, himself unseen, he felt a pang of envy.

"My good Abbot takes life too easily," he thought; "I must give him something to think of." And leaving his horse with a startled servant, he entered the gardens and greeted the Abbot with kindly dignity. So pleasant was he in his inquiries as to his mode of life, the way he employed his time, and so on, that the Abbot was ill-prepared for his concluding speech.

"I have three more questions to ask you," said the Emperor. "If you can answer them correctly, you shall continue to be the Abbot of St Gall. If you fail, however, I shall command you to ride around the city on a donkey, with your back towards his head, and holding his tail in your hand instead of a bridle."

The Abbot turned pale and trembled, and his voice shook as he inquired what his Majesty's will might be. He knew, poor man, that he was far from clever, and the thought of riding upon the donkey in the way described disturbed him as nothing had done for years. The Emperor, well satisfied to have ruffled his calm content, smiled to himself as he continued.

"Listen," he cried, "and listen well! For the peace of your future depends upon this. I will ask you my questions now, but I will give you three months in which to answer them so that you cannot complain I have taken you unaware. The first one is, how long to a minute will it take me to go around the world?"

The Abbot gasped, and the Emperor smiled grimly as he put the second question.

"How much am I worth to a penny, when my crown is on my head, my scepter in my hand, and I am dressed in my royal robes?"

He paused a moment to let the meaning of his words sink into the Abbot's mind; then struck his final blow.

"Lastly," he said, "you must not only tell me what I am thinking of at the moment when I next put the question, but you must prove that I am mistaken, and quite in the wrong."

The Abbot was beyond speech now, and, laughing heartily at his discomfort, and reminding him of the humiliating penance that awaited him if he failed, the Emperor mounted his horse and rode away.

Gone was the good Abbot's peace of mind. Night and day, he was haunted by those terrible questions; he could not sleep, and he could not eat. His plight indeed was pitiable. In vain he consulted the learned men throughout the Emperor's dominions. The wisest professors in the great universities shook their heads when the questions were put to them, and the answers they gave were so unsatisfactory that even the Abbot could see they would not do. A month flew by; a second followed it swiftly, and when the third drew to its close the Abbot was in despair. None of his friends could comfort him, and, sad at heart, he wandered over the country, envying the humblest creature that made its home in the fields.

He was in this mood when he was suddenly approached by a shepherd, to whom he was well known by sight.

"Good morning, Lord Abbot," said the man. "You seem distressed. I would gladly serve you if I could, for many a sip of good red wine did you send my wife when she was ill, and food for the children when times were hard. Tell me, I pray you, what troubles you so much? A mouse before now has been known to help a lion."

The Abbot was touched by the poor man's sympathy, which he accepted as simply as it was offered.

Be thankful," he said, "that you are only a shepherd, for many are the troubles that your position spares you." And he told him of the penance he must perform if he failed to answer the Emperor's terrible questions.

"The time that his Majesty gave me has nearly expired," he added mournfully, "and I am no nearer to solving them than I was at first."

Too dispirited to try and hide the tears that filled his eyes, the Abbot sadly resumed his walk. The shepherd laid a hand on his flowing mantle.

"My lord," he said, "I am only a humble shepherd, but I believe I can answer those questions for you. If you will lend me your cloak, your miter, and your cross, I will appear before the Emperor in your place, and you will be spared this trial."

The Abbot shook his head at this suggestion, but after a moment or two, it did not appear to him so wild as it had done at first. Strange to tell, the shepherd was much the same build as himself, and had the rosy cheeks and unwrinkled brow that had been his own before the Emperor's visit. His eyes also were similar in color to the good Abbot's, and when he spoke gently, as he did now, his voice was not too rough.

"You are a good fellow," said the Abbot gratefully, suddenly realizing that if the shepherd took his place before the Emperor, he would also have to carry out the penance if he failed to answer the questions. After a little more urging on the poor man's part, he consented to his request. It was a forlorn hope, but a drowning man catches at a straw, and the Abbot's dreams were still haunted by a giant donkey that had the head of the Emperor and a thousand tongues.

When the last day of the three months' grace had expired, his Majesty, who had by this time forgotten the whole occurrence, was told that the Abbot of St Gall awaited his royal pleasure. Laughing, he contemplated for some moments the man whom he believed to be the victim of his ingenious questions, noting with satisfaction that his figure appeared less bulky than before.

"Oho!" he cried, "it strikes me, my Lord Abbot, that you are somewhat thinner than you used to be! less sleek of hair too, and your face is oval instead of round.... Have you found the answers to my questions? If not, remember, you must pay the penalty!"

To his amazement, the Abbot looked him bravely in the face instead of cringing.

"I quite understand, your Majesty," he replied, "and am prepared to carry out your conditions."

"Well, then," said the Emperor, rather taken aback, "tell me, in the first place, the exact time, to the very minute, in which I could go around the world on horseback. Do not hurry–I want an accurate reply."

"If your Majesty will set out the instant the sun flames his banners above the horizon and travel as quickly around the world as he does, you will have completed the tour in just twenty-four hours."

This answer so amazed the Emperor that he remained silent for a while. As he could find no fault with it, he passed on to the second question.

"Well, then, how much am I worth, to the very penny, when dressed in my royal robes, with my crown on my head, and my scepter in my hand?"

Without showing the least sign of fear or hesitation, the pretend Abbot still looked him steadily in the face, and reverently lowered his voice.

"The Savior of the World," he said, "was sold for thirty pieces of silver, and, since your Majesty would not claim to be so great as He, I, therefore, estimate your value at one piece less."

This answer did not please the Emperor, but he could not openly find fault with it.

"Well," he said haughtily "you have certainly answered two of my questions, but the third is yet to come, and if you fail with this, you must still ride through the city on a donkey. Tell me what I think at this present moment!"

"You think that I am the Abbot of St Gall," was the quick reply.

"I do," returned the Emperor, "and I am curious to know how you are going to prove that I am wrong!"

The shepherd took off his cloak and miter, displaying his peasant's garb.

"Then I am not," he said with emphasis, "as you may see." The contrast between the Abbot's robes and the shepherd's clothing so tickled the Emperor's fancy that he burst out laughing.

"You are a daring fellow," he exclaimed, "and a witty one also. Since you have afforded me so much amusement, I will give you any reward that you may ask–even to making you the Abbot of St Gall in the place of your master."

"As your Majesty has so graciously promised to give me what I ask," returned the honest shepherd, "let my good master remain the Abbot for the rest of his life, without further anxiety."

"Would that my courtiers were as true to me as you are to him!" replied the Emperor, greatly struck by this poor man's loyalty and devotion. He did as he wished, and promised that the Abbot should be left in peace for the rest of his life, but he made it a condition that the shepherd himself should be well paid so that in future he and his children need fear neither cold nor hunger. To do him justice, the Abbot was in no danger of forgetting his services, and as a further token of gratitude for his timely help, no one in need was ever allowed to leave the Abbey in want or misery.

Unit Seven: Invasions and Conversion

THEME: UNITY

Division of Charlemagne's Empire

by Rev. Monsignor Edmund J. Goebel Ph. D.

Charlemagne died in 814 at the age of seventy. He was buried in the cathedral of Aix-la-Chapelle, where his tomb may still be seen. Charlemagne was succeeded by his son, Louis the Pious. Louis was not so strong a ruler as his father. He decided to divide his empire among his three sons. Through the Treaty of Verdun, Charles the Bald took as his kingdom the western part of the empire, which later became known as France. Louis the German took the eastern part, and this section became Germany.

Lothaire, the oldest son, received as his kingdom northern Italy and the land between the kingdoms of his brothers. This territory, which is now known as Lorraine, became a battleground between Charles and Louis. And it has remained even in modern times a battleground between France and Germany. Thus, the unity which Charlemagne had given to Western Europe was again broken. But the idea remained in the thoughts of the people of Europe.

Henry the Fowler

by Eva March Tappan, Ph. D.

About one hundred years after the death of Charlemagne, one of his descendants, a little boy only six years old, succeeded to a part of his kingdom. Although the child had guardians, they did not seem to be able to defend the crown. There was trouble from without the kingdom and more trouble from within. The trouble from without was because the Hungarians, or Magyars, were making fierce and bloody invasions of the country. The trouble from within came from the five dukes, each of whom was afraid that the others would become more powerful than he. The child-king died when he was only eighteen, and then there was quarreling indeed, for every duke wanted to be sovereign. At length Conrad, Duke of Franconia was set upon the throne; but that did not quiet matters, for some of the dukes had not agreed to his election.

Conrad was a gentle, thoughtful man. He defended his people as well as he could, but perhaps the best thing he did for them was to give them a piece of good advice when he was dying. He had sent for the nobles to come to him, and when they stood around his bed, he talked to them as if they were his children and begged them to live peaceably together. "I do now command you." he said, "to choose Henry, Duke of Saxony, for your king. He is a man of energy in battle, and yet he is a strong friend of peace. I can find no one else so well fitted to rule the kingdom, and therefore I send to him the crown and the scepter and bid him shield and protect the realm."

The nobles were amazed, for this Henry of Saxony had opposed most strongly of them all the election of Conrad; but the more they thought of their king's advice, the more they saw that it was good; and after Conrad was dead they carried the crown and the scepter to Henry's castle. He was not there. "Where is he?" the nobles demanded, and the attendants replied, "He is in the forest hunting with his falcons."

Then the nobles and their followers set out into the forest to search for a king. It was several days before they found him; and when they did discover him, he was standing in his hunting suit, and on his wrist was a falcon waiting patiently until its master should give it the signal to fly after a wild duck or whatever other bird he was pursuing. The falcon and the Duke were both surprised when the company of nobles and their attendants appeared, and Henry was still more amazed when they showed him the crown and the scepter and told him that they had followed the will of Conrad and had chosen him for their king. This is the way that Duke Henry of Saxony became King Henry I of Germany and won his nickname of "The Fowler.

The Magyars came upon the land in swarms. Henry met them bravely; but in every battle the invaders had one great advantage—they fought on horseback, while the Germans were skilled only in fighting on foot. Something happened very soon, however, that changed the whole face of matters. Henry captured a Magyar chief, said to have been the king's son. The Magyars were ready to do almost anything to secure his release; and at length, Henry said to them, "If you will leave my country and promise to make no attacks upon it for nine years, I will give back your chief and pay you five thousand pieces of gold every year." The Magyars were glad to accept this offer, and soon they were rejoicing over the return of their chief.

Henry, however, did not spend time in rejoicing. He had much business to attend to in the nine years, and he set about it at once. First, he brought his people together in cities which could be fortified, instead of allowing them to live in scattered villages. Next, he trained his men to fight on horseback. To test their ability, he tried his new cavalry in battles with the Danes and some tribes around him. Then he waited.

The Magyars were in no haste to give up the tribute of gold, and when the tenth year had come, they demanded that the king should send it as usual. But now he was ready to fight them, and he refused. Their great army started out to make this defiant ruler yield; but to their surprise he drove them out of his kingdom. They never succeeded in entering the northern duchies again, and it was many years before they were seen in any part of Germany.

The wisdom and courage of Henry the Fowler brought peace to his country; and when he died, he left to his son Otho a quiet and prosperous kingdom. Otho was quite as energetic as his father. He took the title of Emperor of the Romans as if his rule were a continuation of the ancient Roman Empire, and for nine hundred years after him every German king claimed the same title.

Hugh Capet

by Eva March Tappan, Ph. D.

It has already been said that Charlemagne was a German. He, of course, spoke German, but even in his day the people in the western part of his kingdom, in what is now the land of France, used a language that was beginning to approach somewhat to what is now known as French. This change had begun long before, in the days when the country fell into the hands of the Romans, who introduced their own language, Latin.

Now, if a new language were introduced into any country today, few people would speak it correctly, and it was so in France. The people mixed the new language with their own. For instance, when a Roman wished to say *of* or *to*, he usually added a letter or two to the noun following. The people of France used the prepositions *de* or *à* and did not trouble themselves to change the noun. Other words or expressions were made simpler or altered in much the same way, and before the end of the tenth century the people of France were speaking a language that was composed of a little Celtic, a little German, and a great deal of Latin; but the Latin had become quite different from that used in Rome. This mixture was rapidly turning into French as it is spoken today.

The French people, then, differed in language from the Germans, and many of the nobles were feeling more and more strongly that they did not wish to be ruled by a German, but by one of themselves, who would talk French and feel and think like a Frenchman, one who would be satisfied with ruling France and would not be ever thinking of forming an empire and becoming emperor.

In A.D. 987 there was an excellent opportunity to put a new family upon the throne, for the last of Charlemagne's direct descendants, Louis the Child, had just died. The great barons met together to choose a ruler. They decided upon Duke Hugh Capet, and he became king. He had little more power, however than some of his counts and dukes; and it may be that he sometimes wished he was still a duke, for some of the nobles refused to accept him as their ruler. There is a story that one of his vassals, that is, one who held land from him by feudal tenure, overran the district of Touraine, and forthwith began to call himself Count of Tours and Poitiers. "Who made you count?" demanded Hugh; and the independent vassal retorted, "Who made you king?" Indeed, if the brave men of Normandy had not stood by him, Hugh would have had a hard struggle to keep his throne. He meant not only to keep it, but to hand it down in his family, and only a few months after his election he asked his nobles to elect his son Robert king also. Then, while he lived, he reasoned shrewdly, Robert would help him govern the kingdom, and at his death, there would be no question as to who should rule and no division of the kingdom. At first the nobles hesitated a little. "We cannot elect two kings in one year," they gave as an excuse; but at length, they yielded, and Robert was crowned.

This was the beginning of the rule of the powerful Capetian family, which was to hold the throne of France for more than three centuries. Gaul, or France, had been ruled for many years by Romans and by Germans, but Hugh Capet was a Frenchman, ruling French people, the first king of France.

The Danish Invasions

by Rev. Monsignor Edmund J. Goebel Ph. D.

Invasions of the Northmen. The last great invasion of Europe by Teutonic tribes came from the northern countries. A bold and daring Teutonic people had settled in Norway, Sweden, and Denmark, the region which we call Scandinavia. These countries are situated on peninsulas, and the inhabitants were as much at home on the sea as they were on land. Sometimes they were called Northmen, sometimes they were called Danes, and sometimes the name of Vikings was given to these hardy sea rovers.

Some of these Northmen had invaded the land of the Franks after the death of Charlemagne. Others plundered the coasts of England and Ireland. Some invaded Russia and became the rulers of that vast land. Others found their way to southern Italy, where they established a kingdom.

The Vikings Sail the Northern Seas

by Margaret Bertha Synge

We turn to the frozen north, to the wild region at the back of the north wind, for new activity and discovery. Out of this land of fable and myth, legend, and poetry, the fierce inhabitants of Scandinavia begin to take shape. The Roman historian, Tacitus, speaks of them as "mighty in fame," the Greek geographer, Ptolemy, as "savage and clothed in the skins of wild beasts."

From time to time we have glimpses of these folk sailing about in the Baltic Sea. They were known to the Finns of the north as "sea-rovers." "The sea is their school of war and the storm their friend; they are sea-wolves that live on the pillage of the world," sang an old Roman long years ago. The daring spirit of their people had already attracted the attention of Britons across the seas. The careless glee with which they seized either sword or oar and waged war with the stormy seas for a scanty livelihood, raiding all the neighboring coasts, had earned them the name of Vikings or creek men. Their black-sailed ships stood high out of the water, prow and stern ending in the head and tail of some strange animal, while their long beards, their loose shirts, and battle-ax made them conspicuous. "From the fury of the Northmen save us, Lord," prayed those who had come in contact with these Vikings.

Rollo the Viking

by Henrietta E. Marshall

Some of the Northmen became tired of their pirate's life and settled in the northern part of France. From land, Rollo, their leader, could now lead even fiercer attacks. The French king, Charles, saw that he could not bribe them away nor banish them by force. But might he win them as subjects for the right price?

In return for the lands which we now call Normandy, Charles asked that Rollo become a Christian, be baptized, and declare himself a vassal of the king. The two rulers agreed, but Rollo had yet to perform his part of the bargain and pay homage to King Charles as his overlord.

Upon the appointed day, the king seated himself upon his throne with his priests and courtiers about him. In came the rough old Northman and his warriors. The ceremony began, but when Rollo was told that he must kneel before the king and kiss his feet he started back in wrath.

"I will kiss no man's feet!" he cried.

"You must! There is no other way to claim your land." replied the priests.

"Then let one of my followers do it for me," replied the proud sea king.

Nothing would move Rollo. So, Charles had to be content with that. One of Rollo's followers was ordered to perform the act of homage for his master. But the proud Viking warrior had as little liking as Rollo for the plan. He had never bent his knee to any man, and he did not mean to do it now.

Striding, therefore, up to the throne, without even bending, he seized the king's foot and raised it to his mouth, so roughly and suddenly that poor King Charles fell backward to the ground. The strange ceremony ended amid the loud laughter not only of the rude Northmen but of the Frankish courtiers as well.

After this, Rollo was baptized and received the Christian name of Robert, and many of his warriors followed his example and were baptized also. Strangely, Normandy became the best-governed part of France. The cruel exploits of Rollo the Viking were forgotten in the fame of righteous Robert, Duke of Normandy.

Eric the Red and Leif Ericsson

by the Franciscan Sisters of Perpetual Adoration

The rugged island of Iceland is located between Scandinavia and Greenland, close to the Arctic circle. The inhabitants of Iceland possess a wealth of handwritten history stories, or sagas, as they are called.

These famous Icelandic sagas tell us of a great prince, Eric the Red, so named because he had red hair. Eric was born in Norway, where he lived, not in a castle, but in a large, rudely-built wooden house with an open roof. Norway is a land of snow-capped mountains and woodland plains, of thousands of lakes and numerous mountain torrents. Its high-walled coast is deeply cut by numberless bays and is fringed by countless islands that are rich in meat and eggs and birds and fish. In this rugged country, Eric led a wild, free life. He fearlessly followed the sharp bark of the wolf and tracked the shaggy bear into its favorite haunts. Above all, the boy Eric loved to sit before a roaring fire and listen to the stories of the chiefs or Vikings, as they were called, from the Norwegian word viks, meaning "bay."

These Vikings were tall, strong, and fine-looking men with blue eyes, long, light hair, and shaggy beards. They were clad in rich clothing and glittering armor with curious iron helmets. The proudest possession of the Viking was his ship. The prow, or front, was high, and usually had a savage-looking dragon's head upon it. Its stern looked like a huge dragon's tail. Both head and tail were covered with gold and seemed all on fire when the sun shone upon them. The long oars resting in the oar-locks of the swelling sides looked like so many legs. The single brightly-colored sail, set into a huge block of wood, resembled the wings of the dragon. From the masthead of this strange ship fluttered a square yellow flag with the picture of a raven upon it.

Hardy, vigorous, and daring were the pagan Northmen. But they were sometimes also fierce and cruel. They made their way far around Cape North to the White Sea and even sailed as far south as Algiers and Constantinople. They enjoyed nothing more than a raid upon European market towns, many of which they left in ashes.

Eric the Red became the proud captain of a large Viking ship, representing a dragon. In this ship he roved the seas in every direction, robbing and plundering as he went. He finally got into a quarrel with some of his countrymen and had to flee to Iceland for his life. Here he became as lawless as ever and was again obliged to seek safety in flight.

But in which direction did he this time turn his dragon's head? Hear him shouting in tune with the lashing waves as he pushed out from the shore: "West, west, on to the westward, my trusty dragon, steer me on!" And on, on, ever westward, dashed the fearless Viking.

He was already far out at sea. Dense clouds hid the sun by day and the stars by night. Fogs and mists surrounded him. But the sea king knew no fear. Setting a screeching raven free, the Viking watched its flight with intense, straining eyes. But the raven soon returned, and Eric knew that no land was near. So on, on, through the fog, against storm and wind, he again pushed his trusty dragon. Once more he set his feathered pilot free. This time the bird did not return; so the sea king rowed with all speed in his power in the direction of its flight, and soon came upon a large island all covered with ice and snow, excepting one spot on the low, southwestern coast which was overgrown with green grass and shrubs. The sea king swung his dragon around what is now Cape Farewell and leaped upon the largest island on the globe.

Eric the Red named this gray and white country of rocks and ice and polar bears Greenland, thinking that his friends would be more anxious to come and settle in this new land if he gave it this inviting name. After whiling away three years on the coast of Greenland, Eric ventured back to Iceland. He soon returned with several friends and kinsmen. Other Icelanders followed, and by and by a small colony grew up on the southwestern coast of Greenland.

A certain young Icelander named Bjarni wished to join his father in Greenland. On his way there, he was driven out of its course by a storm. When the storm was over, he caught sight of land to the southward. This land being so far out of his way, he paid but little attention to it, and steered northward, finally reaching Greenland. He later returned to Norway, and the news of his having seen land to the south greatly interested Eric's son, named Leif. Leif's home was in Iceland, but he happened to be in Norway at the court of King Olaf at the time. The young Northman at once resolved to see the new land. So, he bought Bjarni's ship and with some thirty hardy sailors prepared for his long ocean voyage. Meanwhile, the missionaries of the Catholic Church had been preaching the Gospel throughout the land of Norway. King Olaf had become a zealous Catholic. Leif Ericsson, too, with his whole crew of sailors, had become a convert, and his chief motive in sailing westward was to take missionaries to Greenland.

Let us picture to ourselves the noble captain and his brave crew setting out from Norway in the year 1000, fourteen years after Eric the Red had discovered Greenland. This famous Norse leader was thirty years of age, a stately, prudent, and wise man. His ship was a real Viking boat except that, above its fluttering yellow banner with the raven, rose the cross. The voyagers reached Greenland in safety, and from there Leif turned his course southward and presently sighted the coast seen by Bjarni. He touched upon what may have been the peninsulas of Labrador and Nova Scotia.

With shouts of joy, the hardy Northmen leaped upon our American continent. In some places, they found the land barren and bleak. Rocky tracts stretched back to snow-capped western mountains. In other places were great forests in which the deer roamed, beautiful flowers bloomed, and many kinds of birds sang. The waters of the bays and rivers were alive with fish. The sagas tell us that one of Leif's party, a German, hailed some clusters of berries with intense joy. "It is grapes we have found!" he exclaimed, "such as abound in my native land. This is truly a land of the vine."

"So it is," said Leif, "and therefore we shall call it Vinland. It is a far better country than Greenland, and the Northmen will gladly come to live in it. Let us erect log huts and spend the winter here."

The party passed a very comfortable winter. They found the weather mild compared with the extreme cold of their native country. When springtime came, they all returned to Greenland.

Leif now became chief of the Greenland colony in the place of his father who had died. He never again visited the country he had discovered, but his brother, Thorvald, and some other people from Greenland came at different times to Vinland. Some came only to visit, while others remained and built homes. Before long a little Norse village sprang up. Soon the settlers found, to their great surprise, that strange, broad-faced, copper-colored people lived in the new country. Who were these people? The Northmen, considering these men inferior, called them "Skraelings." They were probably Native Americans. The Skraelings came to trade with the newcomers, and the Vikings noted that they used bows and arrows and stone hatchets and that their boats were made of skins.

These Skraelings did not long remain friendly. One day while they were very busy exchanging their furs for strips of red cloth, a bellowing steer, belonging to the new settlers, burst from the woods. The furious creature scattered the sand in showers as it made directly for the crowd of traders on the beach. The Skraelings were so frightened that they fled headlong in every direction. Some weeks later, a great many of the Skraelings came up the river in their skin-boats, all yelling and howling at the top of their voices. An attack followed, in which Thorvald was killed by a poisoned arrow. The brave young leader was buried on a pleasant cape, the very spot from which he had joyfully cried out when landing: "On this beautiful spot I should like to fix my home." A cross was set at his head and one at his feet and the place called Cape of the Cross.

There was great joy among the people in the little Norse village when one day a blue-eyed baby boy came to them. He was the first Norse child born on the continent and was named Snorri. Snorri and his mother later went on a pilgrimage to Rome, where they told the Holy Father all about Vinland, the good new country in the far West.

Trading voyages between Greenland and Vinland became common and continued for many years. The last record of a Norse ship going from Greenland to Vinland for timber is in 1347. Then an awful plague, called the "Black Death," ravaged the countries of the Northmen, sweeping off about one-third of the people. After this, we hear no more of the hardy Viking in North American waters. The people of Europe did not, at that early date, know enough about geography to understand the importance of Leif Ericsson's discovery. And gradually even the story of the Norse voyages to a distant western country was quite forgotten, except that the people had a vague sense of something done somewhere. This something, however, is clearly and truly stated in the Icelandic sagas, which tell us that the Catholic Norwegian, Leif Ericsson, with his Catholic Norse crew, were the first Europeans to set foot on the American continent.

Rurik the Norseman

by Eva March Tappan, Ph. D.

The people who lived in the central part of Russia in the ninth century did not all belong to any one nation. Many tribes had come from Asia and passed through the land, and some members of the tribes went no farther. These people were tall and strong. They could climb cliffs which one would think only goats could scale, and they could swim across the swiftest rivers. They taught their children that every injury must be avenged and that it was a disgrace to forgive a wrong.

They had no idea of what it meant to be afraid, and when they went to battle, it was the same to them whether they were fighting with some tribe as wild as themselves or with the well-trained Roman soldiers, and they had but one style of attack; when the enemy drew near, the whole tribe flung themselves furiously upon their foes. If they had once taken any stolen goods from those they conquered, they would die rather than give it up, no matter how useless it might be to them.

There are two good things to say about these people. The first is that they were kind to one another. The second is that they were very hospitable. They had a custom of putting some food in sight when they left their huts so that no random traveler would go away hungry. Indeed, their hospitality went so far that if a stranger came to them and they had no food for him, it was regarded as entirely proper to steal whatever was needed.

They believed in a great god, whom they called the thunder-maker, and in a vast number of less powerful gods. They never thought of their gods as kind and gentle, but always as fierce and savage, and they carved hideous images, into which they believed the spirits of the gods would enter so that they could be worshipped.

In time, the wisest and bravest among them became chiefs. Still, they were a savage folk.

Around the Baltic Sea, in northern Russia, lived people who were fiercer still than those in central Russia. They were always ready to leap into their boats and go as fast as wind and oars would carry them wherever they thought they could find plunder. These were the people whom the English called Danes. They were also called Northmen or Norsemen because they came from the north, and Vikings, which meant pirates.

Some of them entered the service of the emperors at Constantinople. They were most loyal bodyguards and they could be trusted freely with the keys of both the palace and treasury. In battle, they were valuable friends, but sometimes the officers must have been a little puzzled to know how to manage them. Once, the odds were so much against them that the Greek commander, whose allies they were, sent a herald to them to ask, "Will you fight, or will you retreat?" "We will fight," the Northmen shouted; and one of them was so enraged at the suggestion of retreat that he gave the herald's horse such a blow with his fist as to strike it dead.

The Northmen usually went to Constantinople by launching their boats in the headwaters of the Dnieper River and floating down to the Black Sea. They had seen a good deal of the world and were bright and keen. They succeeded in making the people of central Russia pay them tribute. According to the old story, there came a time when the people decided not to pay it any longer. They united and drove the Northmen away. But they did not stay united. They quarreled among themselves, for each man did whatever he chose, and no one cared for the rights of his neighbor. It is said that one man among them who was wiser than the rest saw that they needed some power to govern them. He knew how much more civilized the Northmen were, and he persuaded several of the tribes about him to send envoys to the Russ, a tribe of Northmen, to say, "Our country is large and rich, but we have no order. Come and rule over us."

A Northman named Rurik and his two brothers said, "We will come," and the three set out with their followers, all well-armed, as were those who had come as envoys. Rurik built his stronghold at Novgorod; one brother went farther south, and the other farther northeast. After a year or two, the younger brothers died, and Rurik was left to rule alone. He chose men whom he could trust and gave them land. In return, they built fortresses and helped him to keep peace in the land, to govern the unruly tribes, and to teach them to obey. As soon as he had them well in hand, he conquered neighboring tribes; and so, his little kingdom grew rapidly until it became a large kingdom, which took the name of Russia from the Russ tribe. Rurik himself was now called veliki knias, or *grand-prince.*

After Rurik had reigned for seventeen years, he died, leaving his throne to his little son. So it was that the first ruler of Russia was a bold and daring warrior and the second a boy only four years old.

Egbert, King of Wessex

by Rev. Monsignor Edmund J. Goebel Ph. D.

The man who brought unity to the separate kingdoms of England and brought the West Saxons to leadership was a young prince named Egbert. Before he became king of Wessex, he had been in exile for some time at the court of Charlemagne. He had seen how Charlemagne had united the Franks and had established a great kingdom on the continent. He had noticed that the policies of Charlemagne brought greater opportunities for the spread of religion, education, and civilization because there were fewer wars.

No sooner had Egbert become king of the West Saxons than he began the work of increasing his power. One after another, the other kingdoms of England, and the Celtic kingdoms of Wales recognized Egbert as overlord.

Shortly after Egbert succeeded in making all England recognize his supremacy, the Danish raids became more frequent and more destructive. As a result, Egbert had no time for organizing the parts of his kingdom and for setting himself up as a real ruler over all England. He had to give his attention to defending his home kingdom of Wessex from the invaders.

It was not until Alfred, a grandson of Egbert, came to the throne of Wessex that the Danes were stopped. This young man, who was only twenty-two years old when he became king, was to be known as one of the great kings of the Middle Ages. For many reasons, he deserved the title of Alfred the Great.

Alfred the Great

by Rev. Monsignor Edmund J. Goebel Ph. D.

The Danes who made raids on the coasts of England and Ireland were not civilized. They were still pagan and worshipped Woden and Thor and the other old Teutonic gods. Coming in their swift, long boats, these tall, fair-haired, blue-eyed men from northern Europe attacked the coast towns, plundered monasteries and churches, burned whole villages, and were gone before the unfortunate settlement could summon aid.

When Alfred became king of the West Saxons, the Danes were already in possession of northern and eastern England, and they were still making frequent attacks upon the West Saxons. For a time, it seemed they would succeed in taking Wessex, too. But Alfred rallied his people to resist them.

At length, after many encounters with the Danes, Alfred made them agree to a line separating Saxon and Danish lands. By this agreement almost all England was divided into two parts, with Alfred as king of them both. The southern and western part was to be governed by Saxon laws. The northern and eastern section became known as the Danelaw, for in that region all matters were settled according to Danish law. By this agreement, Alfred gave up half of his kingdom to the Danes to save the rest from their attacks.

Alfred's military reforms. King Alfred realized that his country needed an army always prepared to fight. In this way, the Saxons would be prepared to withstand the attacks of invaders. So, Alfred divided the men of his kingdom into three groups. One group was always to be armed and ready for battle. Another group was to be stationed in forts which Alfred built along the Danish border. The third group was to till the fields to maintain the supply of food.

By these defensive measures, Alfred succeeded in checking the advance of the Danes. He allowed them to manage their local affairs according to Danish laws, but he made them recognize him as overlord and king. Thus, Alfred became king of all England.

Alfred's interest in learning and religion. Alfred did more than prevent the Danes from destroying all civilization in England. He did everything he could to encourage literature and learning. He is known as the Father of English Literature. He became a student of Latin and translated several important books from Latin into the language of his Saxon people. He also began the Anglo-Saxon Chronicle, which was the first history of England written in the English language. Alfred wished that all his people should be able to read and write their native tongue.

When he became king, he founded a palace school at Winchester. He encouraged the founding of schools in all the monasteries.

Alfred was a devoted Catholic. He did much for the churches and monasteries in England, and he contributed regularly to the support of the Holy Father in Rome. He built two new monasteries, and he gave generously to the churches and monasteries throughout England. He also devoted much attention to the conversion of the Danes.

Alfred's government. Alfred ruled his people wisely. His kingdom was divided into several districts, called shires. These were like our counties. The shires were governed by officers directly responsible to the king. The shire reeve, or sheriff, collected the taxes and enforced the law. The ealdorman was the chief agent of the king in a shire. The bishops had a very prominent part in the government of the shires because they were the best-educated men of the time. In each of the districts, the people had a share in the local government. In this way, Alfred combined a strong central rule with local self-government.

How a Prince Learned to Read

By James Baldwin

A thousand years ago boys and girls did not learn to read. Books were very scarce and very precious, and only a few men could read them. Each book was written with a pen or a brush. The pictures were painted by hand, and some of them were very beautiful. A good book would sometimes cost as much as a good house. In those times there were even some kings who could not read. They thought more of hunting and fighting than of learning.

There was one such king who had four sons, Ethelbald, Ethelbert, Ethelred, and Alfred. The three older boys were sturdy, half-grown lads; the youngest, Alfred, was a slender, fair-haired child. One day when they were with their mother, she showed them a wonderful book that some rich friends had given her. She turned the leaves and showed them the strange letters. She showed them the beautiful pictures and told them how they had been drawn and painted.

They admired the book very much, for they had never seen anything like it. "But the best part of it is the story which it tells," said their mother. "If you could only read, you might learn that story and enjoy it. Now I have a mind to give this book to one of you"

"Will you give it to me, mother?" asked little Alfred.

"I will give it to the one who first learns to read in it", she answered.

"I am sure I would rather have a good bow with arrows," said Ethelred.

"And I would rather have a young hawk that has been trained to hunt," said Ethelbert.

"If I were a priest or a monk," said Ethelbald, "I would learn to read. But I am a prince, and it is foolish for princes to waste their time with such things."

"But I should like to know the story which this book tells," said Alfred.

A few weeks passed by. Then, one morning, Alfred went into his mother's room with a smiling, joyous face. "Mother," he said, "will you let me see that beautiful book again?"

His mother unlocked her cabinet and took the precious volume from its place of safe-keeping. Alfred opened it with careful fingers. Then he began with the first word on the first page and read the first story aloud without making one mistake.

"O my child, how did you learn to do that?" cried his mother.

"I asked the monk, Brother Felix, to teach me," said Alfred. "And every day since you showed me the book, he has given me a lesson. It was no easy thing to learn these letters and how they are put together to make words. Now, Brother Felix says I can read almost as well as he."

"How wonderful!" said his mother.

"How foolish!" said Ethelbald.

"You will be a good monk when you grow up," said Ethelred, with a sneer.

But his mother kissed him and gave him the beautiful book. "The prize is yours, Alfred. I am sure that whether you grow up to be a monk or a king, you will be a wise and noble man." And Alfred did grow up to become the wisest and noblest king that England ever had. In history, he is called Alfred the Great.

King Alfred and the Cakes

By James Baldwin

Many years ago, there lived in England a wise and good king whose name was Alfred. No other man ever did so much for his country as he did; and people now, all over the world, speak of him as Alfred the Great. In those days a king did not have a very easy life. There was war almost all the time, and no one else could lead his army into battle so well as he. And so, between ruling and fighting, he had a busy time of it indeed.

A fierce, rude people, called the Danes, had come from over the sea and were fighting the English. There were so many of them, and they were so bold and strong, that for a long time they gained every battle. If they kept on, they would soon be the masters of the whole country. At last, after a great battle, the English army was broken up and scattered. Every man had to save himself in the best way he could. King Alfred fled alone, in great haste, through the woods and swamps.

Late in the day, the king came to the hut of a woodcutter. He was very tired and hungry, and he begged the woodcutter's wife to give him something to eat and a place to sleep in her hut. The woman was baking some cakes upon the hearth, and she looked with pity upon the poor, ragged fellow who seemed so hungry. She had no thought that he was the king.

"Yes," she said, "I will give you some supper if you will watch these cakes. I want to go out and milk the cow, and you must see that they do not burn while I am gone."

King Alfred was very willing to watch the cakes, but he had far greater things to think about. How was he going to get his army together again? And how was he going to drive the fierce Danes out of the land? He forgot his hunger; he forgot the cakes; he forgot that he was in the woodcutter's hut. His mind was busy making plans for tomorrow.

In a little while, the woman came back. The cakes were smoking on the hearth. They were burned to a crisp. Ah, how angry she was! "You lazy fellow!" she cried. "See what you have done! You want something to eat, but you do not want to work!" I have been told that she even struck the king with a stick, but I can hardly believe that she was so ill-natured.

The king must have laughed to himself at the thought of being scolded in this way, and he was so hungry that he did not mind the woman's angry words half so much as the loss of the cakes. I do not know whether he had anything to eat that night, or whether he had to go to bed without his supper. But it was not many days until he had gathered his men together again and had beaten the Danes in a great battle.

Alfred and the Beggar

By James Baldwin

At one time the Danes drove King Alfred from his kingdom, and he had to lie hidden for a long time on a little island in a river. One day, all who were on the island, except the king and queen and one servant, went out to fish. It was a very lonely place, and no one could get to it except by a boat. About noon a ragged beggar came to the king's door and asked for food.

The king called the servant, and asked, "How much food have we in the house?"

"My lord," said the servant, "we have only one loaf and a little wine."

Then the king gave thanks to God, and said, "Give half of the loaf and half of the wine to this poor man." The servant did as he was bidden. The beggar thanked the king for his kindness and went on his way.

In the afternoon the men who had gone out to fish came back. They had three boats full of fish, and they said, "We have caught more fish today than in all the other days that we have been on this island." The king was glad, and he and his people were more hopeful than they had ever been before.

When night came, the king lay awake for a long time and thought about the things that had happened that day. At last, he fancied that he saw a great light like the sun; and in the midst of the light there stood an old man with black hair, holding an open book in his hand. It may all have been a dream, and yet to the king, it seemed very real indeed. He looked and wondered but was not afraid.

"Who are you?" he asked of the old man.

"Alfred, my son, be brave," said the man; "for I am the one to whom you gave this day the half of all the food that you had. Be strong and joyful of heart and listen to what I say. Rise early in the morning and blow your horn three times, so loudly that the Danes may hear it. By nine o'clock, five hundred men will be around you ready to be led into battle. Go forth bravely, and within seven days your enemies shall be beaten, and you shall go back to your kingdom to reign in peace."

Then the light went out, and the man was seen no more.

In the morning the king arose early and crossed over to the mainland. Then he blew his horn three times very loudly; and when his friends heard it, they were glad, but the Danes were filled with fear. At nine o'clock, five hundred of his bravest soldiers stood around him ready for battle. He spoke and told them what he had seen and heard in his dream; and when he had finished, they all cheered loudly, and said that they would follow him and fight for him so long as they had strength.

So, they went out bravely to battle; and they beat the Danes and drove them back into their own place. And King Alfred ruled wisely and well over all his people for the rest of his days.

Beginnings of the English Nation

by Rev. Monsignor Edmund J. Goebel Ph. D.

Alfred died in the year 900. His son and grandson devoted themselves to making England one united nation. Little by little, they brought the Danelaw under the rule of Anglo-Saxon laws. Gradually, the Danes became absorbed by the Anglo-Saxons, and the differences between the two peoples began to disappear. When Edgar, Alfred's great-grandson, became king just a little more than half a century after Alfred's death, all England was ruled as one kingdom. A common language and common law and customs were uniting the inhabitants of England.

The Catholic Church provided another bond of unity for the people of England since all now belonged to one religion. When Edgar became king of England, he was crowned in a very solemn ceremony by the archbishop of Canterbury. This became the pattern for all later coronations of English kings. Edgar's solemn oath to rule with justice and mercy was also taken by all later kings.

Confusion and disorder in England. For more than a hundred years after Edgar's time, there was much disorder and confusion in England. Quarrels among the landowners caused many civil wars. To add to her troubles, England was threatened by attacks from without. From Denmark and Norway came a new horde of invaders. This Danish invasion differed from that of Alfred's time. The invaders of Alfred's time had been separate tribes without one central leader and unity of purpose.

Canute—a Danish King. The new invasions were led by Danish kings supported by large armies. So successful were these invaders that for a time, England was ruled by Danish kings.

Canute, who ruled in England from 1016 to 1035, was the greatest of these Danish kings. He gave up his pagan religion and became a fervent Catholic, founding monasteries and making many gifts to the cathedrals of England. He even made a pilgrimage to Rome.

Canute was a very important man in Europe because he ruled Denmark, Norway, and Sweden as well as England. Although he was an invader, the English people admired him because he was a wise and just ruler. He kept the best of the English laws of Alfred and Edgar. He was crowned by the archbishop of Canterbury and took the same oath as the earlier English kings. He appointed Englishmen to most of the important positions in the kingdom. He permitted the people to keep their local self-government. He kept the taxes low and tried always to rule for the benefit of the people.

King Canute on the Seashore

By James Baldwin

A hundred years or more after the time of Alfred the Great there was a king of England named Canute. King Canute was a Dane, but the Danes were not so fierce and cruel then as they had been when they were at war with King Alfred.

The great men and officers who were around King Canute were always praising him.

"You are the greatest man that ever lived," one would say. Then another would say, "O king! there can never be another man so mighty as you." And another would say, "Great Canute, there is nothing in the world that dares to disobey you."

The king was a man of sense, and he grew very tired of hearing such foolish speeches.

One day he was by the seashore, and his officers were with him. They were praising him, as they were in the habit of doing. He thought that now he would teach them a lesson, and so he bade them set his chair on the beach close by the edge of the water.

"Am I the greatest man in the world?" he asked.

"O king!" they cried, "there is no one so mighty as you."

"Do all things obey me?" he asked.

"There is nothing that dares to disobey you, O king!" they said. "The world bows before you, and gives you honor."

"Will the sea obey me?" he asked, and he looked down at the little waves which were lapping the sand at his feet. The foolish officers were puzzled, but they did not dare to say "No."

"Command it, O king! and it will obey," said one.

"Sea," cried Canute, "I command you to come no farther! Waves, stop your rolling, and do not dare to touch my feet!" But the tide came in, just as it always did. The water rose higher and higher. It came up around the king's chair, and wet not only his feet but also his robe. His officers stood about him, alarmed, and wondering whether he was not mad.

Then Canute took off his crown and threw it down upon the sand.

"I shall never wear it again," he said. "And do you, my men, learn a lesson from what you have seen. There is only one King who is all-powerful, and it is he who rules the sea and holds the ocean in the hollow of his hand. It is he whom you ought to praise and serve above all others."

The Coming of the Normans

by Rev. Monsignor Edmund J. Goebel Ph. D.

St. Edward the Confessor. Canute's sons were harsh and cruel. Fortunately for the people of England, they ruled only a few years. Then the English nobles elected as king Edward, the grandson of Edgar and a descendant of Alfred the Great. Edward was a very religious man. So pious was he that he is known as St. Edward the Confessor.

Edward had spent most of his life in Normandy in northern France, just across the channel from England. His mother was a Norman; so Edward was more Norman than English.

Normandy was a region that had been overrun by Northmen. During the time of Charlemagne, invaders from the northern part of Europe made attacks upon northern France. Gradually these invaders made permanent settlements in the land of the Franks. At about the same time that the early Danes or Northmen were taking possession of northern England and setting up the Danelaw, the Northmen in northern France subdued the Franks and made themselves rulers.

We have seen how the Danes in England gradually adopted the language and customs of the Anglo-Saxons. The Northmen who settled in northern France also were influenced by the people whose land they invaded. Gradually the language and the customs of the Franks were adopted by the invaders. So many of these Northmen poured into that part of France that the land itself was called Normandy, or the land of the Northmen, and the people became known as Normans. But their language and customs were French.

Brought up among the Normans, Edward the Confessor was Norman in speech and manner. When he became king of England, he brought with him some of his Norman nobles and gave them high positions in his kingdom.

Saint Edward the Confessor

by Amy Steedman

King Edward of England, the last of the Saxon kings, sat in his chamber deep in thought and troubled beyond all measure. It was but a short while ago that he had been living in exile at the Norman Court, with little hope of returning to his native land, and now kind fortune had not only called him home but set him there as king upon the throne. One would have thought he had been granted more than his heart's desire and should have been content, but there were troubled lines on the King's forehead as he sat and thought of those days of exile.

Amidst all the gaiety and wild revels of the Norman Court, the exiled prince had seemed to live in a world apart from the pleasure-loving courtiers, with whom he had but little in common. He was a strange, dreamy boy, and even his appearance had something dreamlike about it. His soft shining hair was almost milky white in its fairness, and the rose pink of his cheeks made that curious whiteness seem truly dazzling by contrast. While others talked of warlike deeds and boasted of wild adventures, he dreamed his dreams of the saints of old and the good fight which they had fought. Of all those saints the one he loved the best was brave, headstrong St. Peter, so weak at first, so firm and faithful at last. And next, he loved the kind St. John with his great loving heart and gentle kindly ways. These two dream friends were far more real to him than any of the fun-loving companions among whom he lived, and it is little wonder that the boy prince with such friends kept himself pure and unspotted from the world and earned the title of "Confessor."

The only thing outside his dream life in which Prince Edward delighted was in the chase. After long hours spent in church he would gallop off for days into the forest, hunting, and hawking, no longer a dreamy youth with downcast eyes, but a keen alert sportsman whose eyes shone with daring and excitement.

It was while hunting one day that his horse stumbled on the edge of a dangerous cliff, and, with a swift appeal to his unseen friend, the Prince called upon St. Peter to save him.

"St. Peter," he cried, "save me, and I vow that I will make a pilgrimage to thy shrine in Rome to mark my gratitude."

The stumbling horse recovered its foothold and Edward rode safely home. Going straight to church, he knelt there giving thanks for his safety, and while he was still on his knees there came a messenger from England bidding him return and rule over the people as their rightful King.

This good fortune made him more anxious than ever to keep the vow he had made that day. The saint had been his friend and helper in the time of exile, and now, when fortune smiled upon him, he longed to show his gratitude the more.

But Edward had soon to learn that a king belongs to his people and not to himself.

As soon as it was known that the new king desired to make a pilgrimage to Rome, the people were dismayed and horrified.

"We cannot allow it," they cried. "A king can only leave his kingdom with the consent of the Commons, and that consent we will not give."

The wise councilors and advisers also shook their heads.

"'The risks are too great,' they said. 'There are perils by road and sea, by mountain pass and river, dangers from robbers and armed foes. Who would venture among those Romans who are such villains, caring only for the red gold and the white silver?"

So it was that the King was sorely troubled that day as he sat and thought of all these things. He had sent messengers to Rome to beg that he might be pardoned for breaking his vow, and now he was awaiting their return, wondering what answer the pope would send.

Before long the answer came, and the pope's message cheered Edward's heart. Instead of making a pilgrimage to Rome to do honor to St. Peter, the king was to show his gratitude by building or restoring some monastery belonging to St. Peter, which should be forever after under the special protection of the Kings of England.

It was a happy way out of the difficulty, and the king began at once to consider where the abbey should be built. He was deep in thought one day, sitting with his head resting on his hand, his dreamy eyes already seeing visions of a wonderful minster pointing its spires heavenward when a servant entered and told him that a holy man, a hermit, begged to be allowed speech with the King.

"Bring him here at once," said Edward, "it is not fit that a holy man should be kept waiting."

It was very trying to be interrupted when his whole heart was filled with thoughts of the great plan, but he put them aside and turned to give a kindly greeting to the old man, who had perhaps come to ask a favor of his King. He little guessed that this very interruption was to bring him the help which he sought.

Very slowly and with trembling steps the old hermit came into the royal presence. King's palaces were strange abodes to one who lived in the caves and rocks of the earth. The green boughs of the trees were the only canopy which the old man knew; the daisied grass was his carpet, and for companions, he had the squirrels and the birds, with whom he shared his meal of fruit and roots. But God had sent His servant with a message and he was here to deliver it to the King. The strange city, the bewildering noise, and the wonderful palace were things which had nothing to do with him. His one desire was to tell his tale. The King listened with earnest attention, for the message was a strange one.

"Three nights ago," said the hermit, "as I knelt at prayer, behold there appeared to me in a vision an old man, bright and beautiful, whom I knew to be St. Peter. He told me to tell you that you would even now be released from your vow and commanded instead to build an abbey. The place where you should build the abbey, said he, should be on the Isle of Thorns, two leagues from the city. A little chapel of St. Peter already stands there, and there the great abbey shall be built, which shall be indeed the Gate of Heaven and the Ladder of Prayer. As soon as the vision was ended I wrote all the words down upon this parchment, sealed it with wax, and now have brought it to your Majesty."

So the spot was chosen on which the fair abbey should be built, and King Edward gave his whole heart and attention to the great work.

The little Isle of Thorns of which the hermit spoke had taken its name from the wild forest and thickets with which it was overgrown. It was also called the 'Terrible Place' in the days when it was the refuge for the wild animals which came down from the hills around. In those days it was said that a heathen temple had been built on the island and that later, in the time of King Sebert, it had been turned into a Christian chapel and dedicated to St. Peter.

Now there was a strange old legend about the dedication of that little chapel amid the wild thicket of thorns, and perhaps it helped the dreamy king to decide to build his abbey there.

The legend tells that in the days of King Sebert, when the monastery was finished, it was arranged that on a certain day Mellitus, the first Bishop of London, should consecrate the chapel. It so happened that, the night before the consecration, a fisherman named Edric was casting his nets into the Thames River from the Isle of Thorns when, on the opposite shore, he saw an old man, who hailed him and asked that he might be rowed across to the little island. The old man was dressed in a strange foreign robe and seemed to be a stranger, but he had a beautiful kindly face, and Edric willingly did his bidding. Across the dark stream, they rowed, and when the old man landed on the island, Edric stood watching to see where he would go.

The stranger walked straight to the chapel door, and as he entered, the whole chapel was flooded with a blaze of light, so that it stood out fair and shining without darkness or shadow. Then a host of angels, swinging their golden censers, began to descend from above and to ascend, linking earth with heaven, and the sweet blue breath of the incense trailed in thin clouds around the brightness of the heavenly torches. Slowly and solemnly the service of consecration was performed, while the awe-struck fisherman, forgetting his nets and his fishing, gazed in wonder at the heavenly vision.

Presently the lights faded, the angels vanished, and the little chapel was left in darkness once more. Then the old man came out of the chapel and greeted the wondering fisherman.

"How many fish have you caught?" asked the stranger.

Edric stammered out that he had caught no fish, and the old man smiled kindly upon him, seeing his confusion.

"Tomorrow you shall tell the Bishop Mellitus all you have seen," he said. "I am Peter, Keeper of the Keys of Heaven, and I have consecrated my own church of St. Peter, Westminster. For yourself, go on with your fishing, and you shall catch a plentiful supply. This I promise you on two conditions. First, that you shall no longer fish on Sundays; and secondly, that you shall pay a tithe of your salmon to the abbey of Westminster."

Early next day the Bishop Mellitus came to consecrate the chapel, as he had arranged, and the first to meet him was the fisherman Edric, who stood waiting there with a salmon in his hand. He told his tale and presented his salmon from St. Peter, and then showed the Bishop where the holy water had been sprinkled and all the signs of the heavenly consecration.

The Bishop bowed his head in reverence as he listened, and prepared to return home.

"My services are not needed,' he said,' the chapel has indeed been consecrated in a better and more saintly fashion than a hundred such as I could have consecrated it."

In the days of King Edward the Isle of Thorns was no longer the Terrible Place, for the forest had been cleared and St. Peter's chapel stood in the midst of flowery meadows; but still, the fishermen cast their nets in the river and caught many a silver salmon, and once a year St. Peter's fish was carried to the monastery in payment of the tithe which Edric had promised.

There were two other legends told of the little chapel which seem to have made King Edward love the place with a special love.

One story tells how a poor crippled Irishman named Michael sat one day by the side of the path which led to the chapel, watching for the king to pass. The kindly king at once noticed the lame man and stopped to talk to him. Michael with piteous earnestness told his tale and begged for help. There seemed no cure for his lameness, although he had made six pilgrimages to Rome, but at last St. Peter had promised that he would be cured if only the king would carry him up to the chapel upon his royal shoulders.

The courtiers mocked and turned their backs on the ragged beggar, but King Edward, with kind compassionate words, bent down and lifted the cripple, and carried him up to the chapel, where he laid him before the altar. Immediately strength returned to the poor crippled limbs; the man stood upright, then knelt and thanked God and his King, and blessed the little chapel of St. Peter.

The other legend tells of a wonderful vision sent to bless the eyes of King Edward the Confessor in the same chapel, as he knelt before the altar. Perhaps it was because his heart was pure and innocent and his faith so strong that his earthly eyes were opened to see the Christ-Child Himself standing there 'pure and bright like a spirit,' while a glory shone around.

It was small wonder, then, that the king was glad to choose this spot on which to build a great abbey to the glory of God and St. Peter. The work was begun at once, and the king came to live in the Palace of Westminster so that he could be near at hand and watch the building. A tenth part of all the wealth of the kingdom was spent upon the abbey, and it took fifteen years to build; but the king grudged neither time nor money in carrying out this, his heart's desire. Indeed the king had little idea of the value of money and was sometimes rather a trial to his steward Hugolin, who had charge of the chest where the royal gold was kept. Sometimes Hugolin lost all patience with his royal master and shook his head over his dreamy ways.

There had been one day when Edward had actually encouraged a thief to steal his gold! The money-chest had been left open in the King's room, and a worker from the kitchen had come creeping in thinking the King was asleep. Edward had watched the thief help himself three times to the gold and then had warned him to hurry and get away beforeHugolin returned.

"He will not leave you even a halfpenny," cried the King,' so be quick!

The words only added to the thief's terror, as he gazed upon the white-haired king who was watching him so intently. He fled from the room, glad to take the king's advice, and to escape before the steward's return.

"Your Majesty has allowed yourself to be robbed," said Hugolin reproachfully, when he saw the empty chest and heard the King's story.

"The thief has more need of it than we," said his master, "King Edward has enough treasure."

The king's treasure was indeed spent lavishly upon the building of the great abbey, and soon it began to rise from its foundations like a flower, growing in beauty and stateliness year by year, while the dreamy King watched over it, and added every beauty that his fancy could devise. Rough grey stone was cut and sculptured into exquisite shapes and designs; the daylight, as it streamed through the rich stained glass of the windows, was turned as if by magic into shafts of purest color: purple, crimson, and blue. Fair as a dream the abbey stood finished, at last, built by a dweller in dreamland, but solid and firm as a rock upon its foundations, and as firmly it is fixed in the hearts of the English people, while they weave around it their dreams of all that is great and good of the honor and glory of England.

The king's life was drawing to a close just as the great abbey was completed, and Edward knew that this was so. All his life he had relied greatly on warnings and visions, and now strange tales were told of how the end had been foretold.

It was said that as the king was on his way to the dedication of a chapel to St. John, he was met by a beggar who asked for alms from him.

"I beg that you help me, for the love of St. John," cried the beggar.

Now the King could not refuse such a request, for he loved St. John greatly. But he had no money with him and Hugolin was not at hand, so he took off from his finger a large ring, royal and beautiful, and gave it with a kindly smile to the poor beggar.

Not very long afterward, the legend tells us, two English pilgrims far away in Syria lost their way, and wandered about in darkness and amidst great dangers, not knowing which road led to safety. They were almost in despair when suddenly a light shone across their path, and in the light, they saw an old man with a bowed white head and a face of wonderful beauty.

"Where do you come from? ' asked the old man, 'and what is the name of your country and your king?"

"We are pilgrims from England," replied the wanderers, "and our King is the saintly Edward, whom men call the Confessor."

Then the old man smiled joyously and led them on their way until they came to an inn.

"Do you know who I am?" he asked. "I am St. John, the friend of Edward your king. This ring which he gave for love of me, you shall bring back to him, and tell him that in six months we will meet together in Paradise."

So the pilgrims took the ring and carried it safely over land and sea until they reached the King's palace, where they gave it back into the royal hand and delivered the message from St. John.

It was midwinter when the abbey was ready for consecration. The river ran dark and silent as on that long-ago night when the fisherman rowed St. Peter across to the little chapel and the angels came to sing the service. Now all that earthly hands could do was done, and the greatest people in the land were gathered there to be present at the consecration of St. Peter's abbey. Only the king was absent. He who had dreamed the fair dream and had it built in solid stone and fairest ornament, was lying sick and dying while the seal was set upon his work.

For a few days, he lingered on, and then from the land of dreams he passed to the great Reality, and the old chronicles add the comforting words, "St. Peter, his friend, opened the gate of Paradise, and St. John, his own dear one, led him before the Divine Majesty."

They laid the king to rest in the center of his beautiful abbey, and, ever since, England has held no greater honor for her heroes than to let them sleep by the resting-place of the saintly King.

All honor to those who, through the might of sword or pen, by courage or learning, have won a place within St. Peter's Abbey of Westminster! But for the simple of the earth, it is good to remember, that he who was first laid there won his place not by great deeds of courage or gifts of wondrous learning, but by the simple faith that was in him, the kindly thought for those who were poor and needed his help, the loving-kindness which even a child may win, though he may not have a hero's grave in the King's abbey.

Rivals for the Throne

by Rev. Monsignor Edmund J. Goebel Ph. D.

Edward had been a weak king. It was not he who was the real ruler of England, nor was it his Norman nobles. The real rulers of England were a man named Godwin and his son, Harold, who were powerful West Saxon nobles and advisors to the king.

In January of the year 1066, Edward the Confessor died, leaving no son to succeed him. According to custom, it was the duty of the dead king's advisers to choose a new king. Although Harold was not a descendant of Alfred, he was chosen as king.

Harold's right to the throne was not to go unchallenged. No sooner was he declared king than a powerful rival set out to take the kingdom from him. This rival was William, Duke of Normandy, who later was known as William the Conqueror.

William was a strong and powerful leader. By the age of twenty-four, William had established himself as ruler over Normandy and made himself the strongest lord in all of France.

William was Edward the Confessor's cousin, and William's wife was a descendant of the line of Alfred the Great. At the death of Edward the Confessor, William claimed the kingship of England. He said, too, that Edward had promised him the English throne. Besides, Harold himself had once made a promise to support William as Edward's successor.

The Battle of Hastings. No sooner had Harold been named king than William began preparations to take the English throne. He made public announcements of his intended conquest. To his banner came many adventurers from nearby regions. He gained the support of many Norman nobles by promising to give them lands in England. In a short time, he had gathered about him a large band of followers. In the fall of 1066, he crossed the English Channel. At Hastings, about fifty miles south of London, William and Harold met in battle. This battle was to be a turning point in English history.

Harold and his English soldiers took their stand on a little hill and waited for the Normans to attack. The English were armed with their lances and battle-axes. Their weapons were useful only when the enemy was at close range.

The Normans had an array of skilled archers. From a safe distance, they were able to send great showers of arrows against the English. Many of the Norman knights were on horseback. This permitted them to make sudden charges against the soldiers of Harold.

Although the English fought bravely and valiantly, by the close of the day, Harold had been killed, and William, Duke of Normandy had defeated the English.

William the Conqueror. After his victory at Hastings, William marched toward London. In the meantime, a group of influential nobles and churchmen decided that it was useless to oppose William. They agreed to accept him as king. When William reached London, the city opened its gates to him. In Westminster Abbey on Christmas Day, 1066, William was crowned king of England.

William the Conqueror

by Eva March Tappan, Ph. D.

The young Duke William of Normandy, a bold, ambitious man, was Edward the Confessor's friend and kinsman, and Edward had promised to bequeath to him the English throne. After Edward had been in England a while, however, he learned that he could not give away the throne as if it were a bag of gold, but that the English people had something to say about who should rule them. When Edward died, therefore, they asked a brave Englishman named Harold to become their king. Duke William of Normandy was indignant. He was a descendant of Rollo and was as energetic as the Viking himself. He set out with a great force of men and ships to seize the kingdom that he believed was justly his own. He sailed straight for the English coast, and not a ship came out to fight him. He landed at Pevensey, near Hastings, and not a man cast a spear at him. He began to pillage the country, and no one opposed him. There were good reasons why the English were so quiet. One was that their fleet was made up of fishing vessels, which were now scattered here and there, for, according to custom, their owners were allowed at stated times to take them away in order to attend to their fishing. Secondly, the army was made up chiefly of farmers, and they had been permitted to go home to attend to their harvesting. Harold, meanwhile, was in the north with a few followers, repelling an invasion of the Danes, led by his brother Tostig and Harald Hardrada. These he conquered at Stamford Bridge; then, making a rapid march to the south, he brought together what troops he could, and with no time to train them, he fought a fierce battle with the Normans and was defeated. It is possible that the invaders might not have won the day if they had not used a favorite trick of their pirate ancestors of pretending to run away. The English forgot their orders to keep in their places, and dashed forward in pursuit. Then, when they were unprotected and scattered, the Normans suddenly turned upon them and overcame them, and Harold was slain. This was the famous Battle of Hastings, or Senlac, one of the most important battles in all English history, because it decided that England should be ruled by the Normans. In France there are some very interesting pictures of this invasion embroidered upon a strip of linen seventy yards long called the Bayeux Tapestry. These pictures look as if a little child had drawn them, but there is a good deal of life in them, and they do tell the story. It is possible that they were worked by

William's wife, Matilda, and her ladies in waiting.

After the Battle of Senlac, William marched to London. No one dared to oppose him, and the chief men of the nation went to his camp and asked him to become their ruler. So on Christmas Day, 1066, William the Conqueror, as he is known in history, was crowned king in Westminster Abbey by the Archbishop of York.

The English watched anxiously to see how their new sovereign would treat them. Those who wished to keep their land had to go to him and swear to be faithful. The land of those who would not take the oath, and of those who had fought at Hastings, came into his hands, and he gave it to his Norman followers. He also gave the highest offices in Church and State to Normans. That was natural; but it was hard for the English to bear, especially as the Normans looked upon them as rude, ignorant folk, much their inferiors. The English rose against William again and again. Four years after the Battle of Hastings, a valiant leader named Hereward, with a large number of men encamped on the Isle of Ely,[1] and resisted him for more than a year. William built a causeway through the marsh that surrounded the island, but for a long time his efforts to break up the Camp of Refuge, as it was called, were unsuccessful. Finally, through treachery some believe, the English were overcome. Hereward escaped, but this was the last rising of the English against their conqueror.[2]

William was severe, and those who broke his laws rarely escaped punishment, but even the English admitted that he was just. On one occasion he threw one of his own brothers into prison for wronging his English subjects. Three of his acts, however, they never forgave. One was his driving away the tenants from many thousand acres of land near his palace in Winchester. He may have done this to prevent any sudden attack upon him; but the people believed it was in order to provide him with a convenient hunting ground, the New Forest, as it was called; and they were angry. Again, they were indignant because he ordered that a curfew, or *cover fire*, bell should be rung every evening, and that at its sound all fires should be covered and all lights put out. William may have felt that this was necessary to prevent people from coming together at night to plot against him. Moreover, it was an old French custom to prevent the burning of houses; but the English objected stoutly to being told when they were to go to bed. On the whole, however, nothing else made them quite so angry as William's Doomsday Book (so-called because its records were supposed to be final). In order to assess the taxes fairly, he sent men throughout the kingdom to find out just how much property each person owned. The men went into every house, barnyard, and sheepfold, and wrote in their accounts not only who held the land, but even how many animals there were. Then the English were enraged. They were afraid their taxes would be made larger; but, worse than that, they felt that it was a great insolence for strange men to come into their homes and write down the value of their property. They had to yield, however, to this and whatever else William thought best to do.

---

1 A marshy plain in Cambridgeshire, north of the River Ouse.

2 The Story of Hereward, by Douglas C. Stedman, B.A.

Altogether, the English people were not very happy, but to have such a king was really what they needed. They were a little slow and grave, while William was quick and liked a jest. They were good followers and steady fighters; while William was a bold leader, and could change his plans on the battlefield in a moment if those that he had made failed.

William still ruled Normandy, and he had to go back and forth between the two countries. Normandy was a fief of France, that is, it was held by feudal tenure, but it was a most independent duchy, and was not at all afraid to resist the French king, William's overlord. In one of their struggles the city of Mantes was burned. When riding over the ruins, William was thrown from his horse, and afterward died of his injuries. The English royal family is descended from William the Conqueror and Matilda his wife, and Matilda was descended from Alfred the Great; therefore the present king of England represents both Alfred the Great and William the Conqueror.

Effects of the Norman Conquest

by Rev. Monsignor Edmund J. Goebel Ph. D.

Political and social changes. The conquest of England by the Norman duke, William, was one of the most important events in the history of England. A great many changes took place – some of them immediately, and some of them only very gradually.

William declared that he would keep the laws, customs, and government as they had been under Edward the Confessor. The people continued to settle their disputes in the local courts according to Anglo-Saxon laws. The local officials who governed the people kept their Anglo-Saxon titles and duties. William even kept the Witan, which was a council of bishops and nobles. This council advised the king and assisted him in governing the kingdom. In many ways, it seemed as if no changes had been made by the conqueror.

However, William began to appoint Normans to all the high positions in England and distribute great areas of land to his Norman followers. Soon mighty Norman castles began to appear all over England. William ordered that a great castle fortress be built for himself in London. This castle, which is known as the Tower of London, is still in use after nearly nine hundred years.

When William gave land to a Norman noble, he was careful to never give too large an estate in any one area. Instead, he gave the noble several small estates scattered in various parts of England. This prevented the noble from becoming too powerful. He could not collect a large army in any one place. In this way, no noble would be strong enough to revolt against the king.

In addition, William required every landowner, from the lords of the great estates to the men who held only a few acres, to take an oath of loyalty and service to him. By taking this oath, all English landholders became vassals to the king. This was a change in the customs of feudalism, according to which a man owed allegiance to the lord above him. From now on, in England, a man's first allegiance was to the king.

The Domesday Book. William wanted to know all about the land and the people that he had conquered in England. So, he ordered a census to be taken. Today in the United States, a census is taken every ten years, but in William's day, a census was taken very rarely.

William's remarkable census was recorded in a book of two volumes. Partial copies of this book are still in existence. The record was used for levying and collecting taxes.

To get the information for the *Domesday Book*, William sent commissioners into every shire and town. They called the people together and asked them questions about their families and their property. In this way, they found out how much farmland there was in England and who were the owners. Every single piece of property, including the cattle in the barns and the crops in the fields was recorded.

The language changes. Perhaps the greatest influence of the Normans in England was their influence upon the language which we speak, read, and write. As you know, the Normans had adopted the language of the Franks, a language so mixed with that of the Romans that it was more Latin than Teutonic. Naturally, the Normans carried this language to England with them.

For some time after the Norman conquests, three languages were used in England. The rulers, who were small in numbers, spoke Norman-French. The mass of the people continued to speak Anglo-Saxon. At the same time, the ceremonies of the Church and the official documents of the government were in Latin.

However, a common language gradually appeared between the conquerors and conquered. The Normans and Anglo-Saxons needed to understand each other, and both began to learn and to use words of the other language. At length, their languages were mixed to form one language. Usually, the Anglo-Saxon words for common everyday things remained in use. But in many cases, the Norman-French words took the place of the Anglo-Saxon words. Thus, a large part of our present-day English language is of Latin origin. Some words, like "Mass" and "Benediction," entered the English language directly from the Latin. Many words came from the Norman-French, which was a Latin or Romance language.

The mingling of the Anglo-Saxon languages with that of the Normans gave England a richer language than ever before. Now we often have the choice of two words that refer to the same thing. The Anglo- Saxons spoke of "hues," while the Normans used the word "color." An Anglo-Saxon would say "storm," while his Norman master would use the word "tempest."

The Sons of William the Conqueror

By James Baldwin

William the Conqueror had three sons. One day King William seemed to be thinking of something that made him feel very sad. The wise men who were about him asked him what the matter was.

"I am thinking," he said, "of what my sons may do after I am dead. For, unless they are wise and strong, they cannot keep the kingdom that I have won for them. Indeed, I am at a loss to know which one of the three ought to be the king when I am gone."

"O king!" said the wise men, "if we only knew what things your sons admire the most, we might then be able to tell what kind of men they will be. Perhaps, by asking each one of them a few questions, we can find out which one of them will be best fitted to rule in your place."

"The plan is well worth trying, at least," said the king. "Have the boys come before you, and then ask them what you please." The wise men talked with one another for a little while and then agreed that the young princes should be brought in, one at a time and that the same questions should be put to each.

The first who came into the room was Robert. He was a tall, willful lad, and was nicknamed Short Stocking. "Fair sir," said one of the men, "answer me this question: If, instead of being a boy, it had pleased God that you should be a bird, what kind of bird would you rather be?"

"A hawk," answered Robert. "I would rather be a hawk, for no other bird reminds one so much of a bold and gallant knight."

The next who came was young William, his father's namesake. His face was jolly and round, and because he had red hair, he was nicknamed Rufus or the Red. "Fair sir," said the wise man, "answer me this question: If, instead of being a boy, it had pleased God that you should be a bird, what kind of bird would you rather be?"

"An eagle," answered William. "I would rather be an eagle because it is strong and brave. It is feared by all other birds and is, therefore, the king of them all."

Lastly came the youngest brother, Henry, with quiet steps and a sober, thoughtful look. He had been taught to read and write, and for that reason, he was nicknamed Beauclerc which means the Handsome Scholar. "Fair sir," said the wise man, "answer me this question: If, instead of being a boy, it had pleased God that you should be a bird, what kind of bird would you rather be?"

"A starling," said Henry. "I would rather be a starling because it is good-mannered and kind and a joy to everyone who sees it, and it never tries to rob or abuse its neighbor."

Then the wise men talked with one another for a little while, and when they had agreed among themselves, they spoke to the king. "We find," said they, "that your eldest son, Robert, will be bold and gallant. He will do some great deeds and make a name for himself, but in the end, he will be overcome by his foes and will die in prison.

"The second son, William, will be as brave and strong as the eagle; but he will be feared and hated for his cruel deeds. He will lead a wicked life and will die a shameful death.

"The youngest son, Henry, will be wise and prudent and peaceful. He will go to war only when he is forced to do so by his enemies. He will be loved at home and respected abroad, and he will die in peace after having gained great possessions."

Years passed by, and the three boys had grown up to be men. King William lay upon his deathbed, and again he thought of what would become of his sons when he was gone. Then he remembered what the wise men had told him; and so he declared that Robert should have the lands which he held in France, that William should be the King of England, and that Henry should have no land at all, but only a chest of gold.

So, it happened in the end very much as the wise men had foretold. Robert, the Short Stocking, was bold and reckless, like the hawk which he so much admired. He lost all the lands that his father had left him and was at last shut up in prison, where he was kept until he died.

William Rufus was so overbearing and cruel that he was feared and hated by all his people. He led a wicked life and was killed by one of his own men while hunting in the forest.

And Henry, the Handsome Scholar, had not only the chest of gold for his own, but he became by and by the King of England and the ruler of all the lands his father had had in France.

Section Two:

Logic Level

Unit One: Preparation for the King, End of the Roman Republic

THEME: PREPARE THE WAY

The Birth of the Roman Republic

Adapted from the work of Hendrik van Loon

When the Roman armies returned from many victorious campaigns, they were received with great jubilation. But this sudden glory did not make the country any happier. On the contrary. The endless campaigns had ruined the farmers who had been obliged to do the hard work of Empire making. It had placed too much power in the hands of the successful generals (and their private friends) who had used the war as an excuse for wholesale robbery.

The old Roman Republic had been proud of the simplicity which had characterized the lives of her famous men. The new Republic felt ashamed of the shabby coats and the high principles which had been fashionable in the days of its grandfathers. It became a land of rich people ruled by rich people for the benefit of rich people. As such it was doomed to disastrous failure.

Within less than a century and a half, Rome had become the mistress of practically all the land around the Mediterranean. In those early days of history, prisoners of war lost their freedom and became slaves. The Roman regarded war as a very serious business and he showed no mercy to a conquered foe. After the fall of Carthage, the Carthaginian women and children were sold into bondage together with their own slaves. And a similar fate awaited the obstinate inhabitants of Greece and Macedonia and Spain and Syria when they dared to revolt against the Roman power.

Two thousand years ago a slave was merely a piece of machinery. Nowadays a rich man invests his money in factories. The rich people of Rome (senators, generals, and war-profiteers) invested theirs in land and slaves. They bought or took the land in acquired provinces. They bought slaves in open market wherever they happened to be cheapest. During most of the third and second centuries before Christ, there was a plentiful supply, and as a result, the landowners worked their slaves until they dropped dead in their tracks, when they bought new ones at the nearest bargain-counter of Corinthian or Carthaginian captives.

And now behold the fate of the freeborn farmer!

He had done his duty toward Rome and he had fought her battles without complaint. But when he came home after ten, fifteen or twenty years, his lands were covered with weeds and his family had been ruined. But he was a strong man and willing to begin life anew. He sowed and planted and waited for the harvest. He carried his grain to the market together with his cattle and his poultry, to find that the large landowners who worked their estates with slaves could underbid him all along the line. For a couple of years, he tried to hold his own. Then he gave up in despair. He left the country and he went to the nearest city. In the city, he was as hungry as he had been before on the land. But he shared his misery with thousands of other disinherited beings. They crouched together in filthy hovels in the suburbs of the large cities. They were apt to get sick and die from terrible epidemics. They were all profoundly discontented. They had fought for their country and this was their reward. They were always willing to listen to those plausible spellbinders who gather around a public grievance like so many hungry vultures, and soon they became a grave menace to the safety of the state.

But the class of the newly rich shrugged its shoulders. "We have our army and our policemen," they argued, "they will keep the mob in order." And they hid themselves behind the high walls of their pleasant villas and cultivated their gardens and read the poems of Homer which a Greek slave had just translated into very pleasing Latin hexameters.

In a few families however, the old tradition of unselfish service to the Commonwealth continued. Cornelia, the daughter of Scipio Africanus, had been married to a Roman by the name of Gracchus. She had two sons, Tiberius and Gaius. When the boys grew up, they entered politics and tried to bring about certain much-needed reforms. A census had shown that most of the land of the Italian peninsula was owned by two thousand noble families. Tiberius Gracchus, having been elected a Tribune[3], tried to help the freemen. He revived two ancient laws that restricted the number of acres that a single owner might possess. In this way, he hoped to revive the valuable old class of small and independent freeholders. The newly rich called him a robber and an enemy of the state. There were street riots. A party of thugs was hired to kill the popular Tribune. Tiberius Gracchus was attacked when he entered the assembly and was beaten to death. Ten years later his brother Gaius tried the experiment of reforming a nation against the expressed wishes of a strong privileged class. He passed a "poor law" which was meant to help the destitute farmers. Eventually, it made the greater part of the Roman citizens into professional beggars.

He established colonies of destitute people in distant parts of the empire, but these settlements failed to attract the right sort of people. Before Gaius Gracchus could do more harm he too was murdered, and his followers were either killed or exiled. The first two reformers

3 Tribune of the people or plebeian tribune, was the first office of the Roman state that was open to the plebeians (common people), and throughout the history of the Republic, the most important check on the power of the Roman Senate and magistrates.

had been gentlemen. The two who came after were of a very different stamp. They were professional soldiers. One was called Marius. The name of the other was Sulla. Both enjoyed a large personal following.

Sulla was the leader of the landowners. Marius, the victor in a great battle at the foot of the Alps when the Teutons and the Cimbri[4] had been annihilated, was the popular hero of the disinherited freemen.

Now it happened in the year 88 B.C. that the Senate of Rome was greatly disturbed by rumors that came from Asia. Mithridates of Pontus, king of a country along the shores of the Black Sea [Persia, now Iran], and a Greek on his mother's side had seen the possibility of establishing a second Alexandrian Empire. He began his campaign for world domination with the murder of all Roman citizens who happened to be in Asia Minor: men, women, and children. Such an act, of course, meant war. The Senate equipped an army to march against the King of Pontus and punish him for his crime. But who was to be commander-in-chief? "Sulla," said the Senate, "because he is Consul, which was the highest office in the Republic." "Marius," said the mob, "because he has been Consul five times and because he is the champion of our rights."

Possession is nine points of the law. Sulla happened to be in actual command of the army. He went west to defeat Mithridates and Marius fled to Africa. There he waited until he heard that Sulla had crossed into Asia. He then returned to Italy, gathered a motley crew of malcontents, marched on Rome and entered the city with his professional highwaymen, spent five days and five nights, slaughtering the enemies of the Senatorial party, got himself elected Consul and promptly died from the excitement of the last fortnight.

There followed four years of disorder. Then Sulla, having defeated Mithridates, announced that he was ready to return to Rome and settle a few old scores of his own. He was as good as his word. For weeks his soldiers were busy executing those of their fellow citizens who were suspected of democratic sympathies. One day they got hold of a young fellow who had been often seen in the company of Marius. They were going to hang him when someone interfered. "The boy is too young," he said, and they let him go. His name was Julius Caesar.

As for Sulla, he became "Dictator," which meant sole and supreme ruler of all the Roman possessions. He ruled Rome for four years, and he died quietly in his bed, having spent the last year of his life tenderly raising his cabbages, as was the custom of so many Romans who had spent a lifetime killing their fellowmen.

But conditions did not grow better. On the contrary, they grew worse. Another general,

---

4 The Cimbri were an ancient tribe. They are generally believed to have been a Germanic tribe originating in Jutland, but Celtic influences have also been suggested. Together with the Teutones and the Ambrones, they fought the Roman Republic between 113 and 101 BC. The Cimbri were initially successful, particularly at the Battle of Arausio, in which a large Roman army was routed, after which they raided large areas in Gaul and Hispania. In 101 BC, during an attempted invasion of Italy, the Cimbri were decisively defeated by Gaius Marius, and their king, Boiorix, was killed.
Cimbri From Wikipedia, the free encyclopedia. 29 April 2019, [Creative Commons Attribution-ShareAlike 3.0]

Pompey, a close friend of Sulla, went east to renew the war against the ever troublesome Mithridates. He drove that energetic potentate into the mountains where Mithridates took poison and killed himself, well knowing what fate awaited him as a Roman captive. Next, he re-established the authority of Rome over Syria, destroyed Jerusalem, roamed through western Asia, trying to revive the myth of Alexander the Great, and at last (in the year 62) returned to Rome with a dozen shiploads of defeated Kings and Princes and Generals, all of whom were forced to march in the triumphal procession of this enormously popular Roman who presented his city with the sum equivalent of forty million dollars in plunder.

The government of Rome needed to be placed in the hands of a strong man. Only a few months before, the town had almost fallen into the hands of a good-for-nothing young aristocrat by the name of Catiline, who had gambled away his money and hoped to reimburse himself for his losses by a little plundering. Cicero, a public-spirited lawyer, had discovered the plot, had warned the Senate and had forced Catiline to flee. But there were other young men with similar ambitions, and it was no time for idle talk.

Pompey organized a triumvirate (rule by three men) which was to take charge of affairs. He became the leader of this Vigilante Committee. Gaius Julius Caesar, who had made a reputation for himself as governor of Spain, was the second in command. The third was an indifferent sort of person by the name of Crassus. He had been elected because he was incredibly rich, having been a successful contractor of war supplies. He soon went upon an expedition against the Parthians and was killed.

As for Caesar, who was by far the ablest of the three, he decided that he needed a little more military glory to become a popular hero. He crossed the Alps and conquered that part of the world which is now called France. Then he hammered a solid wooden bridge across the Rhine River and invaded the land of the wild Teutons. Finally, he took a ship and visited England. Heaven knows where he might have ended if he had not been forced to return to Italy. Pompey, so he was informed, had been appointed dictator for life. This, of course, meant that Caesar was to be placed on the list of the "retired officers," and the idea did not appeal to him. He remembered that he had begun life as a follower of Marius. He decided to teach the Senators and their "dictator" another lesson. He crossed the Rubicon River which separated the province of Cisalpine Gaul from Italy. Everywhere he was received as the "friend of the people." Without difficulty, Caesar entered Rome, and Pompey fled to Greece. Caesar followed him and defeated his followers near Pharsalus. Pompey sailed across the Mediterranean and escaped to Egypt. When he landed, he was murdered by the order of young king Ptolemy. A few days later Caesar arrived. He found himself caught in a trap. Both the Egyptians and the Roman garrison which had remained faithful to Pompey attacked his camp.

Fortune was with Caesar. He succeeded in setting fire to the Egyptian fleet. Incidentally, the sparks of the burning vessels fell on the roof of the famous library of Alexandria (which was just off the waterfront,) and destroyed it. Next, he attacked the Egyptian army, drove the soldiers into the Nile, drowned Ptolemy, and established a new government under

Cleopatra, the sister of the late king. Just then word reached him that Pharnaces, the son and heir of Mithridates, had gone on the warpath. Caesar marched northward, defeated Pharnaces in a war which lasted five days, sent word of his victory to Rome in the famous sentence "veni, vidi, vici," which is Latin for "I came, I saw, I conquered," and returned to Egypt where he fell desperately in love with Cleopatra, who followed him to Rome when he returned to take charge of the government, in the year 46. He marched at the head of not less than four different victory-parades, having won four different campaigns.

Then Caesar appeared in the Senate to report upon his adventures, and the grateful Senate made him "dictator" for ten years. It was a fatal step.

The new dictator made serious attempts to reform the Roman state. He made it possible for freemen to become members of the Senate. He conferred the rights of citizenship upon distant communities as had been done in the early days of Roman history. He permitted "foreigners" to exercise influence upon the government. He reformed the administration of the distant provinces which certain aristocratic families had come to regard as their private possessions. In short, he did many things for the good of the majority of the people, but which made him thoroughly unpopular with the most powerful men in the state. Half a hundred young aristocrats formed a plot "to save the Republic." On the Ides of March (the fifteenth of March according to that new calendar which Caesar had brought with him from Egypt) Caesar was murdered when he entered the Senate. Once more Rome was without a master.

Social Classes in the Ancient World

by Charles A. Beard and William C. Bagley

The Antiquity of Classes. Humanity had not gone very far on the path from savagery before it was divided into many classes. Tribes, kingdoms, empires, city-states, and republics all had classes. First were the priests, who had charge of the religious ceremonies. Next were the nobles, whose pride of birth united the ownership of cattle and land in large amounts. Then there were the merchants, who traded far and wide, carrying goods from one section of a country to another and even from nation to nation. Below the merchants were the small farmers and the skilled artisans — the metal workers, stone cutters, and other wielders of tools. At the bottom of the scale were the serfs and slaves, bound fast to the soil they tilled or to the master who owned them.

Sometimes these classes were united in defense against a foreign invader. Sometimes they engaged in struggles among themselves over the division of land and cattle. Many a time did the slaves rise in terrible rebellion against their masters, only to meet, usually, with equally terrible punishment.

The Nobles. Whether we turn to ancient Egypt, Greece, or Rome we find a class of wealthy and powerful landowners — men who held great estates tilled by slaves or bondmen of some kind. The fields of the Nile Valley were laid out into immense farms, each owned by a noble. Today, historians dig up the ruins of their fine houses, visit their tombs, and read such of their books as have escaped the ravages of time.

From the earliest days, there existed in Athens and Rome a class in most respects similar to the nobles of Egypt. In Rome, for instance, the most influential men were the nobles, owners of estates, and members of distinguished families. The nobles were proud of their rank and looked upon themselves and their ancestors as superior beings. They were entitled to wear the purple stripe on their garments to distinguish them from the common people and slaves. In the latter days of the republic, when Rome had become rich, the nobles by birth found themselves rudely elbowed by men who had made great fortunes in trade and politics — men who "broke into" the nobility by one method or another.

All Italy was dotted with the fine houses and estates of Roman nobles. The house of one of them, we are told, had more "rooms than many cities embrace within their walls." These palaces were decorated with beautiful marbles and statues brought from Greece, Asia, and Egypt. The families that dwelt in them were waited on by slaves and their lands were tilled by slaves. They scorned trading and all kinds of manual labor and would do nothing except hold a government office or a command in the army. Eager to enlarge their holdings, the nobles bought up or seized the lands of the small farmers. In the later days of the empire, all Italy was a collection of huge estates worked by slave labor.

The Farmers. In several of the Greek states and in early Rome many farmers owned small farms and tilled them with their own hands. The plebeians, as these commoners were called at Rome, were citizens, but for many years their rights were limited. They could vote in the assembly, but they could not hold high office. Though the king might transform a plebeian into a noble, marriage between the nobles and the plebeians was forbidden.

Many and long were the conflicts between these two classes in Rome, until in the later days the distinctions between the two were nearly all abolished. Plebeians were permitted to marry nobles, and most of the offices were opened to them.

For a long time, the Roman farmers were able to hold their own. It was believed that the stalwart farmer, who left the plow to fight the battles of Rome, was the best kind of citizen. "Farmers furnish the bravest men and ablest soldiers," wrote the Roman Cato, "No other calling is so honorable, safe, and pleasant as this is." Efforts were sometimes made to multiply the number of farmers by breaking up great estates into small plots. It was a common practice to grant farms to returning soldiers — a kind of reward or bonus. As in the early days of the United States, it was said that Rome was rich enough to give every man a farm.

Over time, however, the number of free farmers became smaller and smaller. Their lands were often bought or seized by the nobles and changed into estates tilled by slaves. Many of them perished in battle. Thousands, unable to compete with slaves, drifted to the city of Rome or sank into the position of bondmen on the vast estates. As the republic gained new territories, it became the practice to grant the lands in huge plots to generals and politicians. A Roman writer tells us, for example, that six Romans owned half the province of Carthage and that the peasants of Africa were a wretched lot.

The Artisans or Skilled Workmen. In Athens and Rome, as indeed in all the cities of the ancient world, there were hosts of skilled workmen who were free in the sense that the small farmers were free. Along with them were found also, numerous day laborers. When the city of Rome became the center of a great empire, there were perhaps 500,000 people within its gates, probably half of whom were free. They usually lived in huge apartment houses, each family having a few dark rooms in a great building.

As the number of slaves who could do skilled work increased, the free artisan found it difficult to make a living. Often, he sank to the level of a beggar, haunting the streets of the city. In both Athens and Rome, the free workman was regarded with contempt by the upper classes. Aristotle, the Greek philosopher, declared that "no man can practice virtue who is living the life of a mechanic or laborer." Cicero, the Roman orator, looked upon workmen as belonging of an inferior order, saying with scorn, "A workshop can have nothing respectable about it."

Merchants and Professional Classes. Athens and Rome, like Egypt and Phoenicia before them, developed advanced trading systems. Their ships plowed all the waters of the Mediterranean and in their markets were found traders from every clime. In addition to commerce, there were other ways of making money. Tax-gathering was a very profitable business, for the publicans or tax-gatherers were permitted by law to gather about all they could wring from the people. Moneylending was also profitable. So was office-holding in Rome and her provinces. Though merchants and bankers grew rich, the aristocracy continued to look upon them with scorn. Cicero thought all retail merchants contemptible "because they can make no profit except by a certain amount of falsehood." Aristotle exclaimed that in the life of a merchant "there is no room for moral excellence." Nevertheless, impoverished noblemen were often glad to marry their daughters to the sons of rich traders or moneylenders.

Somewhat above the trading classes in the eyes of the Roman aristocracy were the professional classes, but they too varied in their degree of esteem. First among them, in the heyday of the Roman empire, were the architects and engineers, the men who planned and built the amphitheaters, palaces, and bridges. Musicians were in great demand for entertainments, public and private. Doctors, owing to the number of fraudulent fellows, or "quacks," had a hard time to win the regard of the people. Some of them, however, rose to eminence. Such, for example, was Galen, who lived at the end of the second century after Christ. He was so famous that people from the ends of the empire wrote to him for advice and he told them by letter what medicine to take. Poets, historians, and teachers were frequently honored for their talents.

In many cases, however, in the later days of Rome, the teacher was a slave in the house of the rich aristocrat. Roman noblemen took pride in importing from Greece educated slaves as tutors for their children, or as reciters to amuse their guests. Some of the distinguished writers of Rome were of this servile origin.

The Slaves. The masses of people among all the great nations of antiquity were slaves. Slaves built the pyramids of Egypt, rowed the warships of Athens, and tilled the fields of Italy. The history of labor in antiquity is largely a history of bondage. As Rome grew, slavery multiplied. When the Romans conquered Italy, Greece, Africa, Gaul, Spain, Britain, and parts of Germany, they brought the captives into Rome by the thousands as slaves. It is estimated that Caesar in his conquest of Gaul took a million prisoners who were sold into bondage. In the slave markets of Rome could be found Greeks, Germans, and Africans penned up together.

Those who were sold as domestic servants usually had a fairly easy life, but most of them passed into a servitude on the great estates that was truly horrible. They were worked in the fields in chain gangs and thrown into dungeons at night. The owner had the power of life and death over his slaves. Those who resisted their masters or ran away were frequently crucified along the highways as terrible examples to their fellows. Toward the latter days of the empire, Italy was crowded with slaves and the descendants of slaves. Thousands of them had been freed by their masters. Some of them rose to positions of wealth and influence. Others swarmed into the cities, where they helped to swell the mobs that would become so famous in Roman history.

Roman Amusements

by Helene A. Guerber

The Romans, by this time, had entirely forgotten their old simple ways. As their lands increased with each new victory, so did their wealth and pride. Instead of comprising only the city on the seven hills and a few neighboring villages, the Roman republic now extended over most of Italy. The Romans' provinces, moreover, which were governed by officers sent out from Rome, included large territories in Spain, Africa, Asia Minor, Greece, Macedonia, and northern Italy.

From these conquered countries the Romans had brought home all the spoil they had been able to gather. They thus had vessels of gold and silver, jewels of all kinds, fine cloths, beautiful furniture, and gems of painting and sculpture. They began to rival each other in the magnificence of their houses and dress, and their delicately spread tables.

There were more than three times as many slaves as freeborn citizens, owing to the many prisoners that were taken during these wars; so, all the rich Romans had plenty of servants, and soon learned to be idle and hard to please.

Some of these slaves were far better educated than their masters; for, with the conquest of Greece, many teachers and philosophers were brought to Rome to instruct the Roman children. These men taught their pupils how to read Greek so that they could enjoy all the fine and interesting things which had been written in that language; for the Romans had been so busy fighting until now, they had had no time to write histories, stories, poems, and plays of their own.

The Greek slaves, moreover, translated many of the masterpieces of their own literature into Latin, the language spoken by all the Romans. Thus, the Romans soon learned all about the heroes of Greece, read the teachings of their philosophers, and listened to their tragedies and comedies, which were played in the Roman theaters.

From the countries they had conquered, the Romans also brought back statues of the gods, and priests to serve them. These statues were later placed in a fine building, call the Pantheon, or home for all the gods, where the Romans worshiped them as well as their divinities.

You have already heard that the Romans delighted in processions and shows, so you will easily understand that they encouraged their priests to celebrate the festivals of these foreign gods, too. Then the Romans themselves took part in all these processions with as much zest as if they had been in honor of their own gods.

Caesar and the Britons

By Mary E. Doyle. Story rewritten and abridged from John Lingard and others.

The most famous of all the Roman generals was Julius Caesar. He was not only a great warrior and statesman, but he wrote books in which he told what he had done and described the things he had seen. It is in one of his books that we find the very earliest account of the people who at that time lived in the country which we call England.

Julius Caesar had conquered France, which was then called Gaul. From the north shore of France, on very clear days, he could look across the water and see, very far away, a line of white cliffs sparkling in the sun and seeming to rise from the waves. He was told that this was the shore of a large island called Britain – a wild, uncultivated land inhabited by a rude people called Britons.

Caesar had already heard of that land, which for ages had lain there silent and almost unknown to the rest of the world. Long before his time, it had been visited by traders on ships from Tyre, a city on the Mediterranean Sea; and these traders had bought great quantities of tin from the Britons and had carried it back to their own country and made much profit from it. Other people also had learned about the tin mines on the island of Britain, and they had been much talked of in Rome.

So, as Caesar looked across at the dim distant shores of Britain, he thought that perhaps there might be something in that land that would be valuable to the Roman people, and he decided to cross over and see. He, therefore, chose from his army about twelve thousand of his bravest soldiers, and before daybreak on a pleasant autumn morning, they set sail across the Channel. The water was smooth, and a south wind made the rowing easy; and not long after sunrise, the fleet was very close to the white cliffs of Britain.

But now Caesar and his soldiers beheld a sight which caused them to pause in astonishment. The cliffs, as well as the shore, were swarming with armed Britons. They were rushing back and forth, waving their spears and other weapons, and daring the Romans to land.

The Romans had not expected to be received in this way, and they hesitated while the rowers rested upon their oars and looked for a safer landing place. But Caesar's soldiers were accustomed to facing all sorts of dangers, and their hesitation was not long. One of the standard-bearers, seeing a place on the shore that was but feebly guarded, leaped boldly into the water. "Follow me!" he shouted to his comrades.

This was quite enough for brave men such as they, and with loud shouts, they sprang overboard, rushed to the shore, and engaged in battle with the Britons. The men in the other ships quickly followed the example of their fellows, and soon there was a battle all along the shore.

The Britons fought bravely; but with their half-naked bodies and clumsy weapons, they were poorly matched against the well-trained Roman soldiers, clad in strong armor. They were slowly driven back, and in the evening, Caesar's men pitched their tents on the white cliffs and by the shore. Brave and well-armed as they were, they had had a hard fight, and we may think of them sitting around their watch-fires through the night and lamenting the fate of many a slain comrade who would never return with them in triumph to Rome.

Caesar was now surer than ever that this island of Britain would be a valuable Roman possession, but he saw that with so small an army it would be impossible to conquer a country which was so bravely defended.

The next day, and again the next, the Britons fiercely attacked his camp, and it was all that his soldiers could do to defend themselves. For three weeks his little army remained by the shore; then in the dead of night, all went on board the ships again and sailed back to Gaul.

The Britons were no doubt delighted at their success in driving their enemy from their shores. But they had heard enough of the dreaded Romans to know that they would probably soon return in greater force.

Julius Caesar was never discouraged by opposition; he never gave up. The next summer, therefore, fifty-four years before the birth of our Savior, he again undertook the conquest of Britain. This time he had so large an army that it required eight hundred ships to transport the men and supplies across the Channel.

When they came within sight of the cliffs and the landing-place, not a Briton was to be seen. Those brave defenders of their land had thought it wiser not to risk another battle near the shore. They would allow their enemies to land and to follow them into their own woods and strongholds, where they hoped to meet them with a better advantage.

For about three months, Caesar with his legions pursued the Britons from one place to another. Several battles were fought, and the Romans suffered many losses. At last, however, the Britons were driven across the river Thames; their chief camp, with all their horses and war material, were captured; and their leaders were obliged to admit they were beaten.

Caesar might now have conquered the whole country, but there were so many things happening in Rome that he was anxious to return as speedily as possible. So, he called all the British chiefs together, and agreed with them to leave their country in peace, provided they would send a certain amount of tribute to Rome every year. This matter being settled to his liking, he again gathered his soldiers and sailed back to Gaul.

Never, in all his campaigns, had Caesar met an enemy more determined than the Britons; and never had he fought so hard to gain so little. Valuable as the island of Britain was supposed to be, the Romans were quite willing to let it alone for nearly a hundred years after Caesar's time. The Britons did not even pay the tribute which they had been forced to promise, and they were as free as ever.

Now, who were those Britons who so stoutly withstood the invaders of their country? All that we know of them in those very early times is what we have learned from the writings of Caesar and other Roman authors. They were the ancestors of the modern Welsh, and doubtless of many of the Irish and Scotch. Compared with the civilized Romans, they were a wild, bold, half-savage people.

Most of them were clad in skins, and certain tribes or clans painted their bodies with strange figures. They dwelt in poor huts, which were made of clay and covered with the branches of trees or turf. They planted little or no grain, for the country was mostly covered with forests and wild swamps.

They, however, had herds of cattle and flocks of sheep; and their food was chiefly the flesh and milk of these animals. They also hunted deer and other wild animals; they caught fish in the streams and ponds. They made little canoes of willow twigs which they covered with skins. These canoes were so light that they could be easily carried from place to place, but they were not very safe in deep water.

In the southern part of the island, the people were more civilized. They built comfortable houses, had small fields of grain, and knew how to spin and weave. Perhaps they had learned a good many things from the traders of Tyre who used to come to that part of the island to get tin.

The Britons had no king or queen to rule over them, as the English people have now; but each tribe or clan had its own chief and was independent of all other tribes. They knew how to build strong fortresses in the woods or among the hills.

They made swords of copper mixed with tin. They fought with wooden spears, to each of which a long strip of leather was fastened for the purpose of jerking it back after it had been thrown at an enemy. They also had war chariots with sharp iron blades on each side, and with these, they drove furiously among the ranks of their enemies.

The Britons did not know anything about the true God, but they worshiped many false gods. Their priests were called Druids, from a word which means an oak, probably because they dwelt chiefly in groves of oak trees.

The Druids were the only persons among the Britons of that time who had any learning. They were supposed to know a great deal about the stars, and some of these stars were likely worshiped as gods.

Some of the Druids were bards. It was the duty of these to compose songs and sing them in praise of the chiefs who fought most bravely in battle.

We know but very little about the strange false religion of the Britons. But it is quite certain that the Druids built rude temples that were very large and open to the sky. At Stonehenge, in the south of England, there are a number of huge blocks of stone which are probably the fragments of one of these temples. How such heavy masses of rock could have been moved and put into their proper places without the aid of modern machinery is a puzzling question which nobody has yet been able to answer.

Just when this strange superstition of Druidism gave place to Christianity is not exactly known. But we do know that the Britons were among the first of the peoples in those remote lands to embrace the religion of our Lord and Savior, Jesus Christ. The Angles and Saxons, by whom they were conquered about five hundred years later, were pagans but were in time converted to Christianity by missionaries from Rome.

The Chief of the Arverni

by Charlotte M. Yonge

52 B.C. In this story, we will see the Gauls showing the last courage of despair, defending their native lands against the greatest of all the conquerors that Rome ever sent forth.

The Celtic people had lived in Gaul ever since history has spoken clearly, and had become, in Gaul especially, slightly more civilized, due to their interaction with the Greek colony at Massilia, or Marseilles. But their home soon became a borderland of the Roman dominions, and there was little chance that they would not be absorbed; the tribes of Provence, the first Roman province, were already conquered, others were in alliance with Rome, and some had called in the Romans to help them fight their battles.

It would be hard to describe the seven years' war by which Julius Caesar added Gaul to the provinces claimed by Rome, and when he visited Britain; such conquests were brutal and far from being Golden Deeds. But here, we will dwell upon the last brave stand made by the losing party, and the true patriotism of one young chieftain.

In the sixth year of the war, the conquest seemed to have been made, and the Roman legions were guarding the north and west, while Caesar himself had crossed the Alps. But the Gauls would not accept subjection so willingly; some of their chiefs had been put to death, and the high spirit of the nation was stirred. Meetings took place between the warriors of the various tribes, and an oath was taken by those who inhabited the center of the country that if they once revolted, they would stand by one another to the last.

These Gauls were probably not tall, bony giants, like the pillagers of Rome; their appearance and character would be more like that of the modern Welsh, or of their own French descendants, small, alert, and dark-eyed, full of fire; though they were fierce at the first onset of battle, they could soon be rebuffed, yet they persevered in the long run. Their worship was conducted by Druids, like that of the Britons, and their dress was of checked material, formed into a loose coat and wide trousers. The superior chiefs, who had had any dealings with Rome, would speak a little Latin and have a few Roman weapons – great improvements upon their own.

Their fortifications were wonderfully strong. Trunks of trees were laid on the ground at two feet apart so that the depth of the wall was their full length. Over these, another tier of beams was laid crosswise, and the space between was filled up with earth, and the outside faced with large stones; the building of earth and stone was carried up to some height, then came another tier of timbers, crossed as before, and this was repeated to a considerable height, the inner ends of the beams being fastened to a planking within the wall so that the whole was of immense compactness. Fire could not damage the mineral part of the construction, nor the battering ram hurt the wood, and the Romans had been often placed in great difficulties by these rude but admirable constructions, within which the Gauls placed their families and cattle, building huts for shelter.

Of late, some attempts had been made at copying the regular streets and houses built round courts that were in use among the Romans, and Roman colonies had been established in various places, where veteran soldiers had received grants of land on condition of keeping the natives in check. A growing taste for arts and civilization was leading to Romans of inferior classes settling themselves in other Gallic cities.

The first rising of the Gauls began by a quarrel at the city we now call Orleans, ending in a massacre of all the Romans there. The tidings were spread through all the country by loud shouts, repeated from one to the other by men stationed on every hill, and thus, what had been done at Orleans at sunrise was known by nine at night 160 miles off among the mountains, which were then the homes of a tribe called by the Romans the Arverni, who have left their name to the province of Auvergne.

Here dwelt a young chieftain, probably really called Fearcuincedorigh, or Man who is chief of a hundred heads, known to us by Caesar's version of his name, as Vercingetorix[5], a high-spirited youth, who keenly felt the servitude of his country. On receiving these tidings, he instantly called on his friends to endeavor to shake off the Roman yoke. His uncle, who feared to provoke Roman vengeance, expelled him from the chief city; but he collected all the younger and more high-spirited men, forced a way into the city, and was proclaimed chief of his tribe. All the neighboring tribes joined in league against their common enemy, and tidings were brought to Caesar that the whole country round the Loire was in a state of revolt.

In the heart of winter, he hurried back and took the Gauls by surprise by crossing the snows that lay thick on the wild waste of the Cebenna, which the Arverni had always considered as their impenetrable barrier throughout the winter. The towns quickly fell into his hands, and he was rapidly recovering all he had lost. Vercingetorix collected his chief supporters and represented to them that their best hope would be in burning all the inhabited

5 *vur-sin-jet-uh-riks*

places themselves and driving off all the cattle, then lying in wait to cut off all the convoys of provisions that should be sent to the enemy, and thus starving them into a retreat. He said that burning houses were indeed a grievous sight, but it would be more grievous to see their wives and children dragged into captivity. To this, all the allies agreed, and twenty towns in one district were burnt in a single day; but when they came to the city of Avaricum, now called Bourges, the tribe of Bituriges, to whom it belonged, entreated on their knees not to be obliged to destroy the most beautiful city in the country, noting that, as it had a river on one side, and a bog everywhere else, except at a very narrow entrance, it might be easily held out against the enemy; and to their entreaties, Vercingetorix yielded, though much against his own judgment.

Caesar laid siege to the place, but his army suffered severely from cold and hunger; they had no bread at all and lived only on the cattle driven in from distant villages, while Vercingetorix hovered round, cutting off their supplies. They however labored diligently to raise a mount against a wall of the town; but as fast as they worked, the higher the Gauls within raised the stages of their rampart, and for twenty-five days there was a most brave defense. But at last, the Romans made their entrance and slaughtered all they found there, except 800, who escaped to the camp of Vercingetorix. He was not disconcerted by this loss, which he had always expected, but sheltered and clothed the fugitives, and raised a great body of archers and horsemen, with whom he returned to his own territory in Auvergne. There was much fighting around the city of Gergovia; but at length, owing to the revolt of another Gallic tribe, Caesar was forced to retreat over the Loire; the wild peaks of volcanic Auvergne were free again.

But no gallant resolution could long prevail against the ever-advancing power of Rome, and at length, the Gauls were driven into their fortified camp at Alesia, now called Alise, a city standing on a high hill, with two rivers flowing around its base, and a plain in front about three miles wide. Everywhere else it was circled in by high hills, and here Caesar resolved to shut these brave men in and bring them to bay. He caused his men to begin that mighty system of earthworks by which the Romans carried on their attacks, compassing their victim round on every side with a deadly slowness and sureness, by those broad ditches and terraced ramparts that everywhere mark where their foot of iron was trodden. Eleven miles round did this huge rampart extend, strengthened by twenty-three defensive forts, where a watch was continually kept.

Before the lines were complete, Vercingetorix brought out his cavalry, and gave battle, at one time with a hope of success; but the enemy was too strong for him, and his horsemen were driven into the camp. He then resolved to send home all of these, since they could be of no use in the camp and had better escape before the ditches shut them in on every side. He charged them to go to their respective tribes and endeavor to assemble all the fighting men to come to his rescue; for, if he was not speedily assisted, he and 80,000 of the bravest of the Gauls must fall into the hands of the Romans, since he had only corn for thirty days, even with the utmost saving.

Having thus exhorted them, he took leave of them, and sent them away at night, so that they might escape in the dark where the Roman trench had not yet extended. Then he distributed the cattle among his men, but retained the corn himself, serving it out with the utmost caution. The Romans outside fortified their camp with a double ditch, one of them full of water, behind which was a bank twelve feet high, with stakes forked like the horns of a stag. The space between the ditches was filled with pits and scattered with iron caltrops or hooked spikes. All this was against the garrison, to prevent them from breaking out; and outside the camp, he made another line of ditches and ramparts against the Gauls who might be coming to the rescue.

The other tribes were not deaf to the summons of their friends but assembled in large numbers, and just as the besieged had exhausted their provisions, an army was seen on the hills beyond the camp. Their commander was Vergosillaunus (most probably Fearsaighan, the Man of the Standard), a near kinsman of Vercingetorix; and all that bravery could do, they did to break through the defenses of the camp from outside, while within, Vercingetorix and his 80,000 tried to fill up the ditches, and force their way out to meet their friends. But Caesar himself commanded the Romans, who were confident in his fortunes, and raised a shout of ecstasy wherever they beheld his thin, marked, eagle face and purple robe. They rushed on the enemy with a confidence of victory that did, in fact, render them invincible. The Gauls gave way, lost seventy-four of their standards, and Vergosillaunus himself was taken a prisoner; and as for the brave garrison within Alesia, they were caught like flies struggling in vain within the enormous web that had been woven around them. Hope was gone, but the chief of the Arverni could yet do one thing for his countrymen—he could offer up himself in order to obtain better terms for them.

The next day he assembled his companions in arms, and told them that he had only fought for the freedom of their country, not to secure his private interest; and that now, since yield they must, he freely offered himself to become a victim for their safety. He left it to their judgment whether they thought it best for themselves to appease the anger of the conqueror by putting him to death themselves, or whether they preferred giving him up alive.

It was a piteous necessity to have to sacrifice their noblest and bravest, who had led them so gallantly during the long war; but they had little choice and could only send messengers to the camp to offer to yield Vercingetorix as the price of their safety. Caesar made it known that he was willing to accept their submission, and drawing up his troops in battle array, with the Eagle standards around him, he watched the whole Gallic army march past him. First, Vercingetorix was placed as a prisoner in his hands, and then each man lay down sword, javelin, or bow and arrows, helmet, buckler, and breastplate, in one mournful heap, and proceeded on his way, scarcely thankful that the generosity of their chieftain had purchased for them subjection rather than death.

Vercingetorix himself had become the property of the great man from whom alone we know of his deeds; who could perceive his generous spirit and high qualities as a general, nay, who honored the self-devotion by which he endeavored to save his countrymen. He remained in captivity — six long years sped by — while Caesar passed the Rubicon, fought out his struggle for power at Rome, and subdued Egypt, Pontus, and Northern Africa – and all the time the brave Gaul remained closely watched and guarded, and with no hope of seeing the jagged peaks and wild valleys of his own beautiful Auvergne. For well did he know, like every other marked foe of Rome, for what he was reserved, and no doubt he yielded himself in the full expectation of that fate which many a man, as brave as he, had escaped by self-destruction.

The day came at last. In July, 45 B.C., the victorious Caesar had the leisure to celebrate his victories in four grand triumphs, all in one month, and that in honor of the conquest of Gaul came first. The triumphal gate of Rome was thrown wide open, every house was decked with hangings of silk and tapestry, the household images of every family, dressed with fresh flowers, were placed in their porches, those of the gods stood on the steps of the temples, and in marched the procession, the magistrates first in their robes of office, and then the trumpeters.

Next came the tokens of the victory – figures of the supposed gods of the two great rivers, Rhine and Rhone, and even of the captive Ocean, made in gold, were carried along, with pictures framed in citron wood, showing the scenes of victory – the wild waste of the Cevennes, the steep peaks of Auvergne, the mighty camp of Alesia; there too would be the white cliffs of Dover, and the struggle with the Britons on the beach. Models in wood and ivory showed the fortifications of Avaricum, and many another city; and here too were carried specimens of the olives and vines, and other curious plants of the newly won land; here was the breastplate of British pearls that Caesar dedicated to Venus. A band of flute players followed, and then came the white oxen that were to be sacrificed, their horns gilded and flowers hung around them, the sacrificing priests with wreathed heads marching with them. Specimens of bears and wolves from the woods and mountains came next in order, and after them waved for the last time the national ensigns of the many tribes of Gaul.

Once more Vercingetorix and Vergosillaunus saw their own Arvernian standard and marched behind it with the noblest of their clan; once more they wore their native dress and well-tried armor. But chains were on their hands and feet, and the men who had fought so long and well for freedom were the captive gazing-stock of Rome. Long, long was the line of chained Gauls of every tribe, before the four white horses appeared, all abreast, drawing the gilded car, in which stood a slight form in a purple robe, with the bald head and narrow temples encircled with a wreath of bay, the thin cheeks tinted with vermilion, the eager aquiline face and narrow lips gravely composed to Roman dignity, and the quick eye searching out what impression the display was making on the people. Over his head, a slave held a golden crown, but whispered, 'Remember that you too are a man.' And in following that old custom, how little did the victor know that bay-crowned like himself, there followed close behind, in one of the chariots of the officers, the man whose dagger-thrust would, two years later, be answered by his dying word of reproach! The horsemen of the army followed, and then the legions, every spear wreathed, every head crowned with bay so that an evergreen grove might have seemed to be marching through the Roman streets, but for the war songs, and the wild jests, and ribald ballads that custom allowed the soldiers to shout out, often in pretended mockery of their own victorious general, the Imperator.

The victor climbed the Capitol steps and laid his wreath of bay on Jupiter's knees, the white oxen were sacrificed, and the feast began by torchlight. Where was the vanquished? He was led to the dark prison vault in the side of Capitoline hill, and there one sharp sword-thrust ended the gallant life and long captivity.

It was no special cruelty in Julius Caesar. Every Roman triumph was stained by the slaughter of the most distinguished captives after the degradation of walking in chains had been undergone. He had the spirit to appreciate Vercingetorix but had not nobleness to spare him from the ordinary fate. Yet we may doubt which, in true moral greatness, was the superior in that hour of triumph, the conqueror who trod down all in his way, that he might minister to his own glory, or the conquered, who, when no resistance had availed, had voluntarily confronted shame and death in hopes to win pardon and safety for his comrades.

Saint Anne, Mother of the Blessed Virgin

By Eleanor C. Donnelly

In Palestine, at the time of Julius Caesar, lived St. Anne, the mother of the ever-immaculate Virgin Mary, and the spouse of St. Joachim. Anne and Joachim were already far advanced in years when God bestowed upon them that glorious daughter whom all generations were to call Blessed. From an early age, they dedicated this cherished child to the service of the altar of the Lord. Tradition tells that St. Joachim died soon after the Presentation of the infant Mary in the Temple, but that St. Anne lived until her wonderful daughter was eleven years old. The height of the Blessed Virgin's sanctity is given in those few words, "Mary, of whom was born Jesus"; so the holiness of the spouse of Joachim may be expressed in one brief but significant phrase, "Anne, of whom was born the Mother of God."

The Immaculate Conception of the Blessed Virgin Mary

By Eleanor C. Donnelly

The great festival of the Immaculate Conception commemorates the extraordinary privilege of the Blessed Virgin Mary in being conceived without the stain of original sin in the womb of her mother, St. Anne. It was ordained that Mary would be the Mother of God, and so it was befitting that she should not have been permitted to be, for a single instant of her existence, be under the power of the Devil, whose head she was destined to crush. Prophetic words of Holy Scripture describe her dignity, "Thou art all fair, my beloved, and there is no spot in thee!"

The Festival of the Immaculate Conception was first kept as a feast of devotion by St. Anselm, archbishop of Canterbury, in 1070; it was then instituted by Sixtus IV in 1476, to be generally observed throughout the Church. The dogma of the Immaculate Conception was defined by Pius IX, by whom the feast was made a holy day of obligation.

Augustus

Adapted from the work of Hendrik Van Loon

There were two men who tried to continue the tradition of Caesar's glory. One was Antony, his former secretary. The other was Octavian, Caesar's grand-nephew and heir to his estate. Octavian remained in Rome, but Antony went to Egypt to be near Cleopatra with whom he too had fallen in love, as seems to have been the habit of Roman generals.

A war broke out between the two. In the battle of Actium, Octavian defeated Antony. Antony killed himself and Cleopatra was left alone to face the enemy. She tried very hard to make Octavian her third Roman conquest. When she saw that she could make no impression upon this very proud aristocrat, she killed herself, and Egypt became a Roman province.

As for Octavian, he was a very wise young man and he did not repeat the mistake of his famous uncle. He knew how people will shy at words. He was very modest in his demands when he returned to Rome. He did not want to be a "dictator." He would be entirely satisfied with the title of "the Honorable." But when the Senate, a few years later, addressed him as Augustus—the Illustrious—he did not object and a few years later the man in the street called him Caesar, while the soldiers, accustomed to regard Octavian as their Commander-in-chief referred to him as the Chief, the Imperator or Emperor. The Republic had become an Empire, but the average Roman was hardly aware of the fact.

In A.D. 14 his position as the Absolute Ruler of the Roman people had become so well established that he was made an object of that divine worship which hitherto had been reserved for the gods. And his successors were true "Emperors"—the absolute rulers of the greatest empire the world had ever seen.

If the truth be told, the average citizen was sick and tired of anarchy and disorder. He did not care who ruled him provided the new master gave him a chance to live quietly and without the noise of eternal street riots. Octavian assured his subjects forty years of peace. He had no desire to extend the frontiers of his domains, In the year A.D. 9, he had contemplated an invasion of the northwestern wilderness which was inhabited by the Teutons. But Varrus, his general, had been killed with all his men in the Teutoburg Woods, and after that, the Romans made no further attempts to civilize these wild people.

They concentrated their efforts upon the gigantic problem of internal reform. But it was too late to do much good. Two centuries of revolution and foreign war had repeatedly killed the best men among the younger generations. It had ruined the class of the free farmers.

It had introduced slave labor, against which no freeman could hope to compete. It had turned the cities into beehives inhabited by pauperized and unhealthy mobs of runaway peasants. It had created a large bureaucracy—petty officials who were underpaid and who were forced to take graft in order to buy bread and clothing for their families. Worst of all, it had accustomed people to violence, to bloodshed, to a barbarous pleasure in the pain and suffering of others.

Outwardly, the Roman state during the first century of our era was a magnificent political structure, so large that Alexander's empire became one of its minor provinces. Underneath this glory there lived millions upon millions of poor and tired human beings, toiling like ants who have built a nest underneath a heavy stone. They worked for the benefit of someone else. They shared their food with the animals of the fields. They lived in stables. They died without hope.

It was the seven hundred and fifty-third year since the founding of Rome. Gaius Julius Caesar Octavianus Augustus was living in the palace of the Palatine Hill, busily engaged upon the task of ruling his empire.

In a little village of distant Syria, Mary, the wife of Joseph the Carpenter, was tending her little boy, born in a stable of Bethlehem.

This is a strange world. Before long, the palace and the stable were to meet in open combat. And the stable was to emerge victorious.

Unit Three: Spread of the Kingdom, Age of the Apostles

Theme: Sharing The Faith

Why the Church is the Pillar and Ground of Truth

by Lucius Caspar Businger and Richard Brennan

"The house of God, which is the Church of the living God, the pillar and ground of the truth."
–1 Timothy 3:15

It is beyond all doubt that our divine Founder entrusted to the Apostles and their successors the duty and the power of directing His holy Church in sanctity and truth, and of leading all men into her fold. They had a very difficult duty to perform. The work was far above human strength and wisdom, while the Apostles themselves, as well as their successors, the bishops and priests of the Church, were mere men, liable to death and sin, and exposed to error and changes. How could such incapable men accomplish this superhuman task? And granting that the Apostles had been confirmed by Jesus Christ himself, in their faith, in sanctity of life, in zeal for God's kingdom upon earth, and hence succeeded in preserving His sacred legacy of truth and holiness among the nations of their times, how could their successors over the course of centuries be expected to enjoy similar strength and holiness? From where were they to draw it? Alas! poor human nature is sadly prone to whims, to passion, to instability and change. And will not this corruption of human nature affect the leaders in God's Church, so that in a few years after the death of the Apostles the work of Christ will languish, die, and be forgotten?

How many societies have been established within two thousand years, many with the very best and most laudable intentions; founded, too, with the wisdom and experience of wise men, and carried on with prudence and wisdom! Yet over time, evil crept in, they changed, became corrupt, fell to pieces, and have long since been forgotten even in history. Will not the society of the Church encounter a similar fate?

Certainly not; for this society has not only been founded by Christ, but he has infused into it for all time a divine vital power. He has sent his own Holy Spirit, as is related in the Acts of the Apostles.

From all this, we can understand why the Catholic Church is the only one among all the institutions upon the earth that remains unchanged and unchangeable; why, with her, truth has never been adulterated or obscured, even in the ages of darkest ignorance in the world; why her saving graces, amid all the corruptions of men, have never been weakened nor diminished. She was made immortal for all time by the infusion of God's breath, the Holy Ghost, on the day of Pentecost. Yes, the Holy Ghost dwells really and truly within her; that Spirit which renews the face of the earth, as the Psalmist sings; that good and comforting Spirit mentioned in the book of Wisdom; that Spirit of wisdom and understanding, of counsel and fortitude, of knowledge and piety, foretold by Isaiah; that Spirit which comes to aid us in our weakness, as St. Paul writes to the Romans; that Spirit promised by Christ to his Apostles, who was to teach them all things and to lead them to all truth.

Since the Catholic Church has received this Holy Spirit as her own peculiar life and soul and strength, the personal faults and failures of her visible rulers and leaders can do her no real harm.

Although some weak, unhappy priests may have gone astray, although even some bishops themselves may have fallen into error and false opinions, although a few Popes have made lamentable mistakes individually, nevertheless no general Council of the Church has ever erred, never has any Pope when speaking officially contradicted any Council or any previous decision of his predecessors in the chair of Peter. The divine power, which dwells and acts in the Church with mysterious and miraculous force and wisdom, is able and knows how to overcome, at all times, decay, error, and vice.

No! Christ did not wish by any means to extinguish the human in the bosom of his Church.

By sending the Holy Ghost, He did not intend to free the Heads of the Church from the duty of employing human prudence and reflection, of studying and of worldly reason, in order to settle and fix and decide truth, and guide the Church; so, too, He did not see fit to make it impossible for any individual person to fall into sin and error. But the Church herself is always intact, pure, blameless, and immortal, even if some individual members perish because of error and wickedness. She remains the pillar and ground of truth, as St. Paul describes her; and the gates of hell shall not prevail against her.

"Behold, I am with you always, even to the end of the world." (Matthew 28:20)

What the Church is. When we read in the New Testament how our beloved Lord Jesus Christ "went about doing good" in the land of Judea, preaching heavenly truths, imparting saving grace to men of good will, and infusing peace into the hearts of all, we are likely to indulge in feelings of regret that we too did not live in those happy days, that we were not permitted to enjoy His sacred presence and to listen to His voice.

Although, by reading Holy Scripture, we may in spirit accompany the Redeemer all through His earthly life from Bethlehem to Calvary; although we may see Him confirming and sealing His words of truth and his works of power and mercy by his atoning death on the cross, we might ask ourselves, What is Christ to us, or to all the generations who have lived and died during the long lapse of time since He dwelt upon earth? No one in our generation has looked upon Him with our own eyes. No one of us has heard the words of wisdom uttered by His sacred tongue, or felt the touch of His blessed, grace-imparting hand. We have not been permitted to stand with Mary and John and Magdalen under the cross, nor to be sprinkled like them with His saving blood. He has ascended into heaven and now sits in unapproachable majesty at the right hand of His Father, while we are living in exile upon earth. How then can we have any share in the truth, blessings, and graces of this Christ?

Our question is a vain and foolish one. If we but look with the eye of faith, we shall soon and easily discover that this same Christ, with all the fullness of His wisdom, power, and mercy, is still living in our midst, as He promised to do. "Behold, I am with you always, even to the end of the world," is the consoling assurance that falls from His own divine lips.

Let us, therefore, examine and study carefully the plan adopted by our Savior whereby He stills dwells on earth, continuing the work of salvation in all lands and during all time.

What method has Christ followed in order to achieve this plan?

He delegated His threefold office and character—namely, His teaching office, His priesthood, and His kingly authority —to a number of chosen men, in union with whom He continues to act as Teacher, Priest, and King to the end of time.

It was in this threefold character that Christ effected our salvation. He redeemed us as Teacher, as Priest, and as King: as Teacher, by preaching heavenly wisdom; as Priest, by the atoning sacrifice offered upon the cross; and as King, by enacting and instilling laws or commandments. As Teacher, He rescued us from spiritual blindness by giving us the truth of heaven; as divine-human Priest, He redeemed us from the guilt of sin by offering Himself in sacrifice on Mount Calvary; as Godman-king, He saved us, by His teachings and commandments, from the folly and wickedness of life.

This triple office He committed solemnly to a body of chosen men, a short time before His departure from earth. This truth can be plainly proven from Holy Scripture. The divine Teacher sent forth His Apostles to preach to all nations, to teach all truth as He had imparted it to them, and to teach it with the same authority and infallible certainty as He Himself taught it: "He who hears you hears me."

Our divine High-priest, on the eve of His Passion, instituted and offered up, in a mysterious manner and by anticipation, the saving sacrifice of the cross, saying, "This is my body which shall be delivered for you, this is my blood which shall be shed for you." He committed to the hands of the Apostles for all time this holy sacrifice of His body and blood, saying, "Do this," as I have just done, "in commemoration of me." He gave to the Apostles power to baptize, to forgive sins, to bless; in a word, to dispense graces in His name, so that the Apostles were able to say of themselves later, "This, then, is how you ought to regard us: as servants of Christ and as those entrusted with the mysteries God has revealed." (1 Cor. iv. 1).

Finally, our divine King transmitted His spiritual privileges of royalty to the Apostles, with the words, "All power is given to me in heaven and on earth. As the Father sent me, so I send you." It was with this responsibility that the Apostles prescribed for all the nations to whom they preached all those laws and regulations, and established all those institutions, which they deemed necessary for the spiritual welfare, or conducive to the eternal salvation, of men.

Hence, we see clearly that although Christ has returned to heaven, He has not left us orphans, but has been pleased to remain mystically with us, carrying on, through His Apostles as His chosen instruments, His threefold office of Redeemer till the end of time. In union with St. Peter, their visible Head, the Apostles were to travel the earth, preaching, dispensing graces, ordaining, and becoming fishers of men, in order to bring all men to a share in the benefits of truth, grace, and salvation through Christ. They were to unite them to Jesus himself in oneness of life and to join them together in one large and glorious mystical body, of which Christ was to be the invisible Head.

Such was the duty imposed by Christ on His Apostles. But the Apostles were mortal, and died, one after the other, during the first century of Christianity, while the threefold office of teacher, priest, and ruler committed to them by Christ will endure until the end of time. Therefore, it is clear that when the divine Founder of our Church imparted this threefold power to His Apostles in order to perpetuate His Church, He meant not only the twelve men standing there and then in His presence. His divine gaze extended to all their lawful successors, the Popes, bishops, and priests to the end of the world, as if they all stood in His presence when He spoke. It was in this sense that He said to them all, "Behold, I am with you always, even to the end of the world." The Apostles, therefore, and their legitimate successors are the persons to whom Christ entrusted the duty of forming, in His name, among all nations and in all ages, a holy community or spiritual society; or, rather, of extending and strengthening the original society established by Himself.

This spiritual society, consisting originally of the Apostles, disciples, and a few devout believers, became like the mustard seed of the parable, a great tree whose branches were spread over all the earth. And this is the universal or Catholic Church, in which Christ, through His Apostles and their successors, perpetuates forever His work of salvation and applies it to each individual soul. His truth, His saving grace, His redeeming sacrifice, all His merits as God-man from His birth to His death—these are the glorious treasures of this society, the riches of that grand corporation in which each member, who has been properly admitted by baptism, has a right to participate. Therefore, when we speak of the Church, we understand that holy society in which Jesus Christ exercises throughout all ages, by the instrumentality of the Apostles and their successors, the bishops and priests, His threefold office of Teacher, Priest, and King.

If the Church were a mere association of persons holding the same tenets, differing in no way from any other human society, it would not be the "mysterium fidei," or the mystical body of Christians united to Christ. But the Church embraces, besides the visible—that is to say, the laity of all nations and their ecclesiastical authorities —also the Invisible, namely, the inheritance of Christ's merits and the merits of His Saints, the treasures of truth and goodness, as well as supernatural guidance. It thus becomes a sublime mystery of faith, and hence the Christian can truthfully say, and with meaning, "I believe in one Holy Catholic Church."

The Apostles

by the Sisters of Notre Dame

St. John. The beloved disciple, St. John, first labored in Palestine. When obliged to leave Jerusalem because of the persecutions of the Jews, he went to Parthia, where he stayed for many years. St. John was present at the Council of Jerusalem in A.D. 50, and afterward preached in Asia Minor, making Ephesus his cathedral city (probably about A.D. 63).

During the second persecution, St. John was taken prisoner and sent to Rome (about A.D. 95). There, outside the Latin Gate, he was thrown into a cauldron of burning oil, but being miraculously preserved was banished to the island of Patmos. Here he had those wonderful revelations which he has left us in the Apocalypse. On the death of Domitian, St. John returned to Ephesus in A.D. 97, where he remained until his death. He probably wrote his Gospel then, and also his two Epistles to refute the heresies of the Corinthians and Ebionites against the Divinity of Christ. During the last years of his life, St. John's constant sermon was, "Little children, love one another." When asked why it was always the same, he said that it was our Blessed Lord's own command to his disciples. It is a tradition that lived to be a hundred years old.

St. James the Greater. Little is known of St. James after the Ascension of the Lord. He was the first of the Apostles to receive the crown of martyrdom, being beheaded by King Agrippa in A.D. 44. He preached in Palestine and the surrounding countries. There is a tradition that St. James visited Spain, but this is not certain, though he is honored as the patron Saint of that country, and his body is still kept with veneration in the church at Compostella.

St. Andrew. St. Andrew preached in Scythia (modern Russia in Europe and Asia) and Greece. He was martyred by crucifixion at Patrae, in Greece. In A.D. 357 his body was brought to Constantinople but was removed in A.D. 1210 to Amalfi, where it still remains.

St. Matthew. After the dispersion of the Apostles, St. Matthew preached the Gospel in the East among the Persians, Ethiopians, and Parthians. He was martyred at Nandabar in Parthia. Before St. Matthew left Jerusalem, he wrote the first of the four Gospels for the Jewish converts.

St. James the Less. St. James the Less was a near relation of our Lord and was commonly known as "the Just." He was made Bishop of Jerusalem soon after the Ascension and continued to govern this See until his martyrdom in A.D. 63. He was put to death by stoning. St.

James wrote one Epistle, addressed to all the Jews scattered throughout the world.

St. Thomas. Little is known about the labors of the other Apostles. St. Thomas preached in Parthia, India, Media, and Persia. There is a tradition that he baptized the Three Kings. He was martyred near Madras, in India.

St. Philip. St. Philip labored in Phrygia and Scythia and was crucified at Hieropolis.

St. Bartholomew. St. Bartholomew spread the Gospel in India, Arabia, Assyria, and Armenia. He was crucified in Armenia.

St. Simon the Zealot. St. Simon the Zealot is said to have preached in North Africa. He afterward went to Persia, where he was martyred.

St. Jude. St. Jude, known by the name of Thaddeus, labored in Samaria, Idumea, and Syria. He traveled through Mesopotamia towards the end of his life and visited Persia, where he was martyred. He wrote an Epistle to the Churches of the East, which is often called the "Catholic Epistle."

St. Matthias. St. Matthias, who was elected to replace Judas, preached the Gospel in Ethiopia. The place of his martyrdom is not known.

Spread of the Faith Beyond Jerusalem

by the Sisters of Notre Dame

Caligula, who had succeeded Tiberius as Emperor of Rome, treated the Jews with great tyranny because they would not consent to put up a golden statue to him in the Temple of Jerusalem. The Jews were so engaged in resisting the Imperial will that they had no time to persecute the Christians. Hence, throughout Judea, Galilee, and Samaria, the Churches enjoyed peace (Acts 9:31).

This gave St. Peter an opportunity of making an apostolic visitation of the Churches and thus exercising his right of headship over the whole Church. Some incidents of this journey are recorded in the Acts of the Apostles.

At Lydda, the miraculous cure of a man sick of the palsy caused the conversion of all the people of that city and of Saron. At Joppa, St. Peter raised a widow named Dorcas to life. This converted many, and the Apostle stayed a few days instructing the newly-baptized Christians.

It was during this time that St. Peter had the vision of clean and unclean animals being let down in a sheet, while a voice was heard saying, "Kill and eat." By this, the Apostle understood from God that he was to receive the Gentiles into the Church.

The same evening three men arrived, sent by Cornelius, a Roman centurion, begging the Apostle to come and instruct him. Accordingly, St. Peter set out for Caesarea, where Cornelius and his companions were waiting to receive him. After he had instructed them, the Holy Spirit came down upon the Gentiles, and they praised God in various tongues. Seeing in this a proof that God willed the reception of Gentile converts into the Church, St.

Peter immediately baptized them and made them partakers of all the privileges of the Faith (Acts 10). Most ancient historians tell us that after this, St. Peter traveled through Syria, and visited Antioch, where he fixed his See. This fact is commemorated in the Church by the feast of "St. Peter's Chair at Antioch." He afterward returned to Jerusalem through Pontus and Galatia.

The Jews of Antioch had been converted to the Faith before St. Peter's visit. The Gospel was carried to them by the disciples who had been scattered throughout Syria and the East by persecutions in Samaria. When the Mother Church in Jerusalem heard of the number of converts at Antioch, St. Barnabas was sent to confirm them. He was joined by St. Paul, and they labored together for one year. It was at Antioch that the disciples were first called Christians (Acts 11).

From quite the earliest times, the greatest union and charity were kept up among the Christians. Thus, when a famine broke out in Palestine, and the faithful there were in great want, those in Antioch, where there was no distress at that time, made rich offerings, which St. Paul and St. Barnabas carried to their suffering brethren in Jerusalem.

Caligula was succeeded by Claudius in A.D. 40. One of the new Emperor's first acts was to make Herod Agrippa King of Judea. This prince stopped the persecution against the Jews and sought to find favor with them by turning against the Christians. St. James the Greater suffered martyrdom by the sword. His heroic example converted his jailor, who begged St. James to forgive him. The Apostle embraced him, saying, "Peace be to thee," and both were beheaded together. Agrippa also imprisoned St. Peter, meaning to execute him, but, in answer to the prayers of the Church, the Apostle was released by an angel (Acts 12).

This persecution caused the Apostles to disperse and was the means of their preaching the Gospel to "the uttermost part of the earth" (Acts 1:8), according to the last command of our Lord.

The Gospel in Greece

by Charlotte M. Yonge

Athens had not had a great statesman or soldier in her for many long years, but her philosophers and orators still went on discoursing in the schools, and for four hundred years at least Athens was a sort of university town, where the rich young men from Rome, Carthage, Alexandria, Asia Minor, and Syria came to see the grand old buildings and works of art and to finish their education. For though the great men of Greece were all dead, their works, both in stone and in writing, still remained, and were the models of all the world, and their language was spoken all over the East. The Romans' own tongue, Latin, was used at home, of course, but every gentleman knew Greek equally well, and all the Syrians, Jews, and Egyptians who had much interaction with them used Greek as the language sure to be known—much as French is now used all over Europe.

But there was an answer coming to all these philosophical strainings and yearnings after God and His truth, which had made those old Greek writings beautiful. There is a story that one night, a ship's crew passing near a lonely island in the Aegean Sea, sacred to the gods, heard a great wailing and crying aloud of spirit voices, exclaiming, "Great Pan is dead."

Pan was the heathen god of nature, to whom sacred places were dedicated, and this strange crying was at the very night after a day when, far away in Judaea, the sun had been darkened at noon, and the rocks were rent, and One who was dying on a cross had said, "It is finished." For the victory over Satan and all his spirits was won by death.

Some fifteen years later, as Paul, a Jew of Tarsus, in Asia Minor, with the right of Roman citizenship, and a Greek education, was spreading the knowledge of that victory over the East.

While at Athens, the multitude of altars and temples, and the devotion paid to them, stirred Paul's spirit, so that he could not help but speak out plainly and point to the truth. The scholars of Athens had talked to shreds the old arguments of Plato and Epicurus and longed for some fresh light or new interest. These stirring words of Paul seemed a new philosophy to the talkers and inquirers, and he was invited to Areopagus to set forth his doctrine.

There, in the face of the Parthenon and the Acropolis, with philosophers and students from all parts of the empire around, he made one of his greatest and noblest speeches—"You men of Athens, I perceive that in all things you are greatly religious. For as I passed through your city, and beheld how you worship, I found an altar with this inscription, 'To the unknown god.' Whom, therefore, you ignorantly worship; Him declare I unto you."

Then, looking on the temples crowded on the rocks, he tried to open their minds to the truth that the God of all dwells in no temples made with hands, that all men alike are His children, and that, since living, breathing, thinking man has sprung from Him, it is lowering His greatness to represent Him by cold, dead, senseless stone, metal, or ivory. "He bore with the times of ignorance," said Paul, "but now He called on all men to turn to Him to prepare for the day when all should be judged, by the Man whom He had ordained for the purpose, as had been shown by His rising from the dead."

The Greeks had listened to the proclamation of one great unseen God, higher than art could represent; but when Paul spoke of rising from the dead, they burst into mockery. They had believed in spirits living, but not in bodies rising again, and the philosophers would not listen. Very few converts were made in Athens, only Dionysius, and a woman named Damaris, and a few more. The city of learning closed her ears against those who would have taught her what Socrates and Plato had been feeling after like men in the dark. However, in time Christianity won its way, and the oracles became silent, as the demons which spoke in them fled from the Name of Jesus.

The Cruelty of Nero

by Helene A. Guerber

Nero's First Crimes. Emperor Claudius was dead, poisoned by his own wife, the Empress Agrippina. Agrippina arranged that the real heir of the empire, her stepson Britannicus, should be kept out of sight until her own son Nero could be set upon the vacant throne. The senate and people did not object to her choice, and everybody hoped that Nero would rule very wisely, as he was advised by very able and upright men.

Because they were honest, these men first of all told Nero that he had better send his mother away from court, where her influence could do no good. Nero followed this advice, and during the first months of his reign, he was generous, clement, and humane. We are told that when he was first asked to sign the death warrant of a criminal, he did so regretfully, and exclaimed, "Oh! I wish I did not know how to write!"

Nero was only about seventeen years of age when he began his reign. He was handsome, well educated, and pleasant-mannered, but unfortunately, he was also a hypocrite. Although he pretended to admire all that was good, he was in reality very wicked.

His mother, Agrippina, had set him on the throne only that she herself might reign; and she was very angry at being sent away from court. However, she did not give up all hopes of ruling but made several attempts to win her son's confidence once more and to get back her place at court. Seeing that coaxing had no effect, she soon tried bolder means. One day she entered the hall where Nero was talking with some ambassadors and tried to take a place by his side.

Nero saw her come in and guessed what she intended to do. He rushed forward with exaggerated politeness, took her gently by the hand, and solemnly led her, not to a seat of honor by his side, but to a quiet corner, where she could see all, but where she would hardly be seen.

Agrippina was so angry at being thus set aside that she began to plan to dethrone Nero and give the crown to Britannicus instead. This plot, however, was revealed to the young emperor. As soon as he heard it, he sent for a deadly poison to be prepared, which he tested upon animals to make sure of its effect.

When quite satisfied that the poison would kill anyone who took it, Nero invited his stepbrother to his own table, and cleverly poisoned him. Although Britannicus died there, before his eyes, the emperor showed no emotion whatever; but later on, he saw that the people mourned the young victim, and then he pretended to weep, too.

Nero's wife, Octavia, the gentle sister of Britannicus, was sent away soon after, and in her place, he chose Poppaea, a woman who was as wicked as his own mother, Agrippina. This woman gave him nothing but bad advice, which he was now only too glad to follow.

Having killed his brother, Nero next began to plan how he might kill his mother. He did not wish to poison Agrippina, so he had a galley built in such a way that it could suddenly be made to fall apart. As soon as this ship was ready, he asked his mother to come and visit him. Then, after treating her with pretended affection, he sent her home on the treacherous galley. As soon as it was far enough from the shore, the bolts were loosened, and the ship parted, hurling Agrippina and her attendants into the sea.

One of the queen's women swam ashore and cried out that she was Agrippina, in order to secure prompt aid from some men who stood there. Instead of helping her, the men thrust her back into the water to drown, for they had been sent there by Nero to make sure that no one escaped.

The real Agrippina, seeing this, pretended to be only a servant maid, and came ashore safely. The young emperor was at table when the news of his mother's escape was brought to him. He flew into a passion on hearing that his plans had failed, and at once sent a slave to finish the work that had been begun. In obedience to this cruel order, the slave forced his way into Agrippina's room. When she saw him coming with drawn sword, she bared her breast and cried, "Strike here where Nero's head once rested!" The slave obeyed, and Nero was soon told that his mother was dead.

The Christians Persecuted. At first, Nero was rather frightened at his own crimes. The Romans, however, did not resent the murder of Agrippina, but gave public thanks because the emperor's life had been spared; and when Nero heard of this, he was quite reassured. Shortly afterward, the gentle Octavia died too, and then Nero launched forth into a career of extravagance as wild as that of Caligula.

Always fond of gladiatorial combats and games of all kinds, Nero himself took part in the public chariot races. Then, too, although he had a very poor voice, he liked to go on the stage and perform and sing before his courtiers, who told him that he was a great actor and a very fine singer.

Encouraged by these flatterers, Nero grew more conceited and wild. To win his favor, many great people followed his example; and noble ladies soon appeared on the stage, where they sought the applause of the worst class in Rome.

The poor people were admitted free of charge at these games, provided that they loudly applauded Nero and his favorites. As they could not attend to their work, owing to the many festivities, the emperor ordered that they should be fed at the expense of the state; and he made lavish gifts of grain.

In A.D. 64 a great fire began in Rome which burned for six days. A large part of the city was thus destroyed, many lives were lost, and countless people were made poor; but the sufferings of others did not trouble the monster Nero, who delighted in seeing misery of every kind.

Ever since the crucifixion of our Lord, during the reign of Tiberius, the apostles had been busy preaching the gospel. Peter and Paul had even visited Rome, and talked to so many people that, there were by this time a large number of Roman Christians.

The Christians, who had been taught to love one another could not, of course, approve of the wicked Nero's conduct. They boldly reproved him for his vices, and Nero soon took his revenge by accusing them of having set fire to Rome and by having them seized and tortured in many ways.

Some of these Christians were beheaded, some were exposed to the wild beasts of the circus, and some were burned at the stake for the emperor's games. Others were plunged in kettles of boiling oil or water or hunted like wild beasts.

All of them, however, died with great courage, boldly confessing their faith in Christ; and because they suffered death for their religion, they have ever since been known as Martyrs. During this first Roman persecution, St. Paul was beheaded, and St. Peter was crucified. St. Peter was placed on the cross head downward, at his own request, because he did not consider himself worthy to die as his beloved Master had died.

A Cruel Reign. As Rome had been partly destroyed, Nero now began to rebuild it with great magnificence. He also built a palace for his own use, which was known as the Golden Palace, because it glittered without and within with this precious metal.

Nero was guilty of many follies, such as worshiping a favorite monkey, fishing with a golden net, and spending large sums in gifts to undeserving courtiers; and he is said never to have worn the same garment twice.

Of course, so cruel and capricious a ruler as Nero could not be loved, and you will not be surprised to hear that many Romans found his rule unbearable and formed a conspiracy to kill him. A woman named Epicharis took part in the plot, but one of the men whom she asked to help her proved to be a traitor.

As Nero could not discover the names of the conspirators, he condemned all the Romans whom he suspected of having been in the secret and forced them to kill themselves. Even his tutor Seneca obeyed when ordered, and he died while dictating some of his thoughts to his secretary.

As Nero's crimes were daily increasing in number, a new conspiracy was soon formed against him. This time, his soldiers revolted. The legions in Spain elected their general, Galba, as emperor, and marched toward Rome to rid the world of the tyrant Nero.

The emperor was feasting when the news of Galba's approach reached him. He was so frightened that he fled in haste, carrying with him a little box that contained poisonous drugs. He rushed from door to door, seeking an asylum, which was everywhere denied him; but finally one of his freedmen led him to a miserable little hut, where he was soon followed by his pursuers.

When Nero heard his enemies coming, he realized that he could not escape death, and sadly exclaimed, "What a pity that such a fine musician should perish!" He then took his own life rather than falling into Galba's hands.

Nero was only a little over thirty when he died; he had reigned about fourteen years. He was the last Roman emperor who was related to Augustus, the wise ruler who had done so much to further the prosperity of Rome.

The Early Martyrs

by the Sisters of Notre Dame

For about two and a half centuries the Church was exposed to outbursts of persecution, sometimes throughout the whole Empire, sometimes only locally. The years of actual persecution, when added together, come to one hundred and twenty, interspersed with periods of comparative peace and prosperity for the Christians.

Under Nero, A.D. 64-68. Nero had burned Rome, for the city did not satisfy him; he wanted finer palaces. As he was afraid to admit it, he accused the Christians of being the perpetrators of the crime. He ordered a persecution against them as enemies of the state.

The persecution seems to have been confined to the city of Rome itself. the martyrs endured horrible torments. The most illustrious martyrs were Saints Peter and Paul, who are said to have suffered on the same day. While confined in prison, they converted forty-seven of the guard and their two captains. God caused a miraculous spring to rise in the prison, in which the converts were baptized. St. Peter was condemned to be crucified. Feeling himself unworthy to die in the same way as his Divine Master, he asked to be placed with his head downwards. The great church of St. Peter on the Vatican Hill was built over the spot where the Apostle was buried. St. Paul, being a Roman citizen could not be crucified, so Nero ordered him to be beheaded. His martyrdom took place outside Rome, where the church of the Three Fountains now stands. St. Andrew also suffered martyrdom by crucifixion during this persecution.

Under Domitian, A.D. 95-96. During the reigns of Vespasian and Titus, the Christians enjoyed peace, but Domitian renewed the edicts against them in A.D. 95. Many belonging to the noblest families in Rome suffered death or banishment.

It was during this persecution that St. John was thrown into a cauldron of boiling oil outside the Latin Gate, but, being miraculously preserved, he was banished to the island of Patmos.

The Buried Cities

by Helene A. Guerber

Mount Vesuvius was covered with vegetation, and near its foot were the two rich and flourishing cities of Pompeii and Herculaneum. The people felt no fear of the mountain, because it was not then, as now, an active volcano.

But one day they began to feel earthquakes, the air grew hot and very sultry, smoke began to come out of the crater, and all at once, with an awful noise, a terrible eruption took place. Red-hot rocks were shot far up into the air with frightful force; great rivers of burning lava flowed like torrents down the mountainside; and, before the people could escape, Pompeii and Herculaneum were buried under many feet of ashes and lava.

Thousands of people died, countless homes were burned or buried, and much land which had formerly been very fertile was made barren. Pliny, the naturalist, had been told of the strange, rumbling sounds which were heard in Vesuvius, and had journeyed there from Rome to investigate the matter. He was on a ship at the time, but when he saw the smoke, he went ashore near the mountain, and before long suffocated in the foul air.

Sixteen hundred years after the two cities were buried, an Italian began to dig a well in the place where Pompeii had once stood. After digging down to a depth of forty feet, he came across one of the old houses in a remarkable state of preservation.

Since then, the ruins have been partly dug out, and many treasures have been found there buried under the soil. The ruins of Pompeii and Herculaneum are visited every year by many travelers from all parts of the world. They go there to see how people lived in the days of the Roman emperors, and to admire the fragments of beautiful paintings, the statues, pottery, etc., which have been found there.

When Pompeii was destroyed all Italy was saddened by the terrible catastrophe.

The Siege of Jerusalem

by the Sisters of Notre Dame

During the forty years after the death of our Lord, the leaders of the Jews continued their persecutions of the Christians. Thus they put St. Stephen to death; that, until God called him to be an apostle and a saint, Saul had treated them with great cruelty for nearly six years; that Herod Agrippa had caused St. James the Greater to be beheaded and St. Peter to be imprisoned; and lastly, that when there was no Roman Governor in Jerusalem, Ananias, the High Priest, took the opportunity of beginning a fierce persecution, during which St. James the Less, Bishop of Jerusalem, was martyred.

But the Jews themselves had not been in peace. The Roman Emperor, Caligula, was not satisfied with being honored as a ruler, he wanted to be worshipped as a god. He had statues of himself put up in the Pagan temples all over the Empire and wished to erect one in the Jewish Temple also. But the Jews would not have it, and all through his reign, they had so much to suffer in consequence, that they often left the Christians in peace. Great troubles also befell the Jews in other parts of the world. In Palestine, robbers wandered unpunished throughout the land. The Roman Governors treated all the people with the utmost cruelty.

Fall of Jerusalem. According to Josephus, the Jewish historian, this is how the end came about. The Jews in Jerusalem rose against their harsh Roman rulers and massacred great numbers of soldiers. A terrible revenge was taken by the Romans, and the whole country was filled with warfare and bloodshed. An army marched towards Jerusalem but was driven back. The Christians withdrew as our Lord had told them to do when He said that when they should see "the abomination of desolation" foretold by Daniel, they should "flee to the mountains." They took refuge in Pella, a little town beyond the Jordan. A still larger army commanded by Vespasian and his son Titus was sent against Palestine, and gradually advanced on Jerusalem, capturing all cities on their route. Instead of uniting against their enemy, the Jewish leaders fought against themselves. For two years three various parties struggled for mastery. They ravaged the country around Jerusalem, and inside the city pillaged and destroyed all they could lay hands on. Famine overtook the town just as the Romans, under Titus, arrived in great numbers to begin the siege.

Jerusalem stands on the summit of a plateau, separated by deep valleys from the hill country around. Titus pitched his tents on the slopes of the heights facing the city. The attack was made on three sides at once, and continued night and day. The Jews fought so desperately that the Romans were at first driven back. Titus offered terms of peace, which were rejected. He then drew his army so closely around the city that none could enter or leave it without being caught by the Romans. In doing this Titus unconsciously fulfilled exactly the words of our Lord, "And when you shall see Jerusalem compassed about with an army, then know that the desolation thereof is at hand" (Luke 21:20). To terrify them into submission, Titus ordered that all the Jews captured should be crucified outside the walls of the town. Hundreds at a time were thus put to death. Then he built a strong wall all around the place. Inside the city, the strife among the defenders went on. At the time when the siege began, the crowds who had assembled for the Passover were still within the walls. All this multitude had nothing to eat. Anything that could serve as food, however disgusting, was eagerly devoured.

But despite all, the daily sacrifices in the Temple went on, until the Romans, after nearly five months' siege succeeded in capturing the fort called Antonia, which overlooked the courts of the Temple. Thousands then took refuge in the Temple itself, and still fought bravely to defend it. Titus gave orders that this glorious building should be spared, but a soldier threw into the interior a flaming brand, which at once set the whole on fire. Nothing could save the Temple, which was thus destroyed. Jerusalem was now in the hands of the Romans. A terrible massacre followed. Men, women, and children were slain in thousands.

Josephus wrote that altogether nearly a million persons perished during the siege. Most who remained alive were sold as slaves. Gold and silver melted by the fierce heat of the flames were found in large quantities among the ruins. This, with all the spoil they could save, was carried off by the Romans.

The city was leveled to the ground as Jesus had foretold. The space occupied by the Temple was plowed up and then strewn with salt, that nothing might grow on it again. All that remained of the once splendid city was a small portion of a boundary wall with three fortresses. These were left to show what a mighty stronghold had been overthrown by Roman arms. The conqueror, Titus, went to Rome, and with his father, Vespasian, now Emperor, enjoyed a triumph. In the procession, the Jewish leaders walked in chains, and immediately after were put to death. An arch was erected in Rome to record the conquest of Palestine. On it may still be seen cut in the stone the altar of showbread and the seven-branched candlestick that Titus carried off.

From that day to this, the Jews have had no Temple. Thus we see how point by point our Lord's prophecy about the destruction and desertion of Jerusalem was fulfilled, when He wept over the city and said, "For the days shall come upon you: and your enemies shall cast a trench about you, and compass you round, and straiten you on every side; and beat you flat to the ground, and your children who are in you, and they shall not leave in you a stone upon a stone" (Luke 19:43-44).

The Romans Return to Britain

by Helene A. Guerber

After Julius Caesar made his two expeditions into Britain in the years 55 and 54 B.C., the Britons, instead of keeping the treaty they had made, proved for a while very rebellious subjects. During the next one hundred years, the Romans were too busy elsewhere to pay much attention to them; so, it was not till the time of the emperor Claudius that legions were again sent out to their island.

This time the Britons were led by Caractacus, who fought for nine years before he was conquered. The Roman general then took this Briton chief to Rome, where the captive was forced to march in chains in the victor's triumph. As the barbarian slowly passed along the streets of the Eternal City, amid the deafening shouts of the people, he gazed in awe at the beautiful buildings, and bitterly cried: "Alas! how is it possible that a people possessed of such magnificence at home could envy me my humble cottage in Britain?"

This remark was repeated to the emperor Claudius, and, although he was not noted for his kind-heartedness, he was so touched by the Briton chief's bravery and homesickness that he set him free, as well as the other captives of his tribe.

Queen Boadicea

by Helene A. Guerber

In defeating Caractacus, the Romans had become masters of the southern part of the island only. Many Britons were not subdued and helped by the Celts and Gaels, they often revolted. The Roman generals stationed in Britain put down one revolt after another; but finally, Suetonius, one of them, declared that he was sure the Druids advised the Britons to fight. He, therefore, made up his mind to go and attack the priests on their island of Anglesey and set out with his legions.

As Suetonius drew near the Druid stronghold, he saw that the priests had been warned of his coming, for they rushed forward to meet him, uttering strange cries and curses. They were armed, and fought fiercely, while the women, too, attacked the enemy with lighted torches, uttering shrill screams, and wildly tossing their long hair.

Despite the brave defense of the Druids, Suetonius landed on the island, killed the priests and bards, overthrew the altars and temples, and cut down the sacred oak trees beneath whose shade they had gathered. But while he was doing this, some other Roman soldiers cruelly ill-treated Boadicea, the queen of one of the Briton tribes, and insulted her two daughters.

Escaping from their hands with her unhappy daughters, Boadicea drove in her chariot all through the land, calling the people together, and telling them how shamefully the Romans had treated her and her poor children. As she spoke, the men's eyes gleamed with anger; and at her appeal, they all took up their arms and swore to avenge her. Led by this woman, the Britons went forth to fight the Romans, took their principal city, killed the seventy thousand strangers who dwelt there and set fire to the beautiful buildings which the Romans had put up. But their triumph did not last long, for they soon met Suetonius coming back from Anglesey. He attacked them, and although the Britons fought more fiercely than ever before, they were soon completely beaten.

We are told that eighty thousand Britons died on that field of battle and that Boadicea killed herself and her children, rather than fall into the enemy's hands and be taken to Rome to figure in the victor's triumph.

This victory left the Romans masters of the greater part of the island. All the Britons who were not willing to obey them fled to the mountains, to join the Picts and Scots, who were also Celtic tribes. Here the Romans did not dare venture, for fear they should lose their way and fall into an ambush. From time to time, parties of warriors would make sudden raids down into the country, killing, burning, and robbing wherever they went. Then, before the Roman soldiers could overtake them, they would carry their spoil back to the mountains, to hide until it was time for a new expedition.

To prevent these inroads into the country, which was rapidly becoming fertile and civilized, the Romans built large fortified camps at Exeter, Chester, and York, which last they made their capital. In these camps or cities, they built beautiful houses, temples, and public baths, such as they had in Rome. There are still some traces of these fine buildings, and the well-made Roman roads, which connected the different camps, are still good today.

Little by little, the Britons learned many of the Roman arts; and in the first century of our era, some of them heard Christian soldiers tell the story of Christ and became Christians. For many years Roman soldiers did all the fighting in Britain, while the young Britons who joined the army were sent to fight in other lands, under Roman generals.

Unit Four: Seeds of the Kingdom, Martyrs and Fathers of the Church

THEME: TRADITION AND SACRIFICE

THE SPREAD OF THE FAITH

by the Sisters of Notre Dame

Our Blessed Lord had warned His Apostles and their successors that they and those who would embrace His Divine teaching would have much to suffer for His name and that they would be persecuted by even their nearest and dearest. The first Christians had difficulties of every kind to meet – sufferings for their mind and heart, and sufferings for their body also.

The world was very wicked when the Apostles began their preaching. The pagans lived only for pleasure. The rich had magnificent palaces, splendid furniture, luxurious food, and garments. They spent their fortunes on great public games and shows, while nothing was done for the poor and the unfortunate. There were immense numbers of slaves in the wealthy households; the masters and mistresses could do just as they liked with them – beat, or starve, or even kill them if they willed – and no one had the right to contradict them.

The Christians did the opposite: they imitated Jesus, who became poor for us; they helped all those suffering from poverty and want; they lived simple lives, practicing fasting and abstinence, and busied themselves with all kinds of useful work. This brought down on them the mockery and insults of their former friends. Besides this, they were accused unjustly of shocking crimes.

The pagans worshipped numerous gods and goddesses, many of whom were only vices represented as people, and they did many evil acts in honor of their false gods.

Christians refused to go to the Roman temples, no longer offered sacrifices in honor of the emperors, and no longer joined in the pagan festivals. This brought down on them the anger of both rulers and pagan priests. The rulers accused the Christians of being traitors to the State – that is, of being unfaithful to their Roman leaders. The pagan priests accused them of attacking the national gods, and of introducing new worship. It was true that the

Christians would have nothing to do with the old heathen gods and their false worship, for they adored the one true living God with the purest and holiest of worship; but it is not true that they were bad subjects, for whenever the Empire was at war, Christians were found fighting bravely in every army, and more than one victory was gained by their prayers.

At last, when every other means had been tried, the pagan rulers began to put the Christians to death if they would not give up their faith. This persecution resulted in the testimony of thousands of martyrs to the truth of their religion.

But instead of putting an end to Christianity, the persecutions seemed to cause multitudes to imitate the glorious courage of those who preferred to give up land, home, and kindred, and even life itself, rather than be untrue to their God. The religion of the Christians was seen by the better kind of pagans to be a pure one. The holy lives of these noble followers of our Lord made them ashamed of their wickedness, so that, as Tertullian truthfully said, "The blood of the martyrs is the seed of the Church."

Moreover, God gave the Christians power to work great miracles. Often the pagans did all they could to hurt a brave martyr without causing him the least pain. They saw the dead raised to life, incurable diseases healed, and they knew man could not do such deeds. They felt that God must be with these men and women, and yielding to grace, many were converted. Thus, despite all that men and devils could do to stop it, God's Church spread all over the Roman Empire and beyond. When the first three hundred years were over, it was the persecutors who were bested, not the Christians, for Christ had said of His Church, "the gates of hell shall not prevail against it."

The Colosseum

by Charlotte M. Yonge.

The grandest and most renowned of all ancient amphitheaters is the Colosseum in Rome. It was built by Vespasian and his son Titus, the conquerors of Jerusalem, in a valley surrounded by the seven hills of Rome. After the siege of Jerusalem, the Romans used the treasures they stole from the city to pay for the building of the Colosseum. They also brought 12,000 Jews as prisoners. The captive Jews were forced to labor as slaves to build the Colosseum. The materials—granite outside, and a softer stone within—are so solid, and so well put together, that it still remains one of the greatest wonders of Rome. Five acres of ground were enclosed within the oval of its outer wall, which outside rises perpendicularly in tiers of arches one above another. Within, the galleries of seats projected forwards, each tier coming out far beyond the one above it; so that between the lowest and the outer wall there was room for a great variety of chambers, passages, and vaults around the central space, called the arena.

Altogether, when full, this huge building could hold 50,000 to 60,000 spectators! It had no roof; but when there was rain, or if the sun was too hot, the sailors in the porticoes unfurled awnings that ran upon ropes and formed a covering of silk and gold tissue over the whole. Purple was the favorite color for this veil, because, when the sun shone through it, it cast such beautiful rosy tints on the snowy arena and the white, purple-edged togas of the Roman citizens.

When the emperor had seated himself and given the signal, the sports began. Sometimes a rope dancing elephant would begin the entertainment, by mounting even to the summit of the building and descending by a cord. Or a lion came forth with a jeweled crown on his head, a diamond necklace around his neck, his mane plaited with gold, and his claws gilded, and played a hundred pretty gentle antics with a little hare that danced fearlessly within his grasp.

Sometimes water was let into the arena, a ship sailed in, and falling to pieces in the midst, sent a crowd of strange animals swimming in all directions. Sometimes the ground opened, and trees came growing up through it, bearing golden fruit. Or the beautiful old tale of Orpheus was acted: these trees would follow the harp and song of a musician; but—to make the whole part complete—it was no mere play, but in earnest, that the Orpheus of the piece fell prey to live bears.

The Colosseum had not been built for such harmless spectacles as those first described. The fierce Romans wanted to be excited and to feel themselves strongly stirred; and, presently, the doors of the pits and dens around the arena were thrown open, and savage beasts were let loose upon one another—rhinoceroses and tigers, bulls and lions, leopards and wild boars—while the people watched with ferocious curiosity to see the various kinds of attack and defense, their ears at the same time being delighted, instead of horror-struck, by the roars and howls of the noble creatures whose courage was thus misused.

Wild beasts tearing each other to pieces might, one would think, satisfy any taste for horror; but the spectators desired even more brutal games to be set before them: men were brought forward to confront their favorite monsters. Some of these men were, at first, in full armor, and fought hard, generally with success. Or hunters came, almost unarmed, and gained the victory by swiftness and dexterity, throwing a piece of cloth over a lion's head, or disconcerting him by putting their fist down his throat. But it was not only skill but death, that the Romans loved to see; and condemned criminals and deserters were reserved as feasts for the lions and to entertain the populace with their various kinds of death. Among those condemned was many a Christian martyr, who bravely witnessed before the savage-eyed multitude around the arena, and "met the lion's gory mane" with a calm resolution and a hopeful joy that the onlookers could not understand. To see a Christian die, with upward gaze and hymns of joy on his tongue, was the most strange and unaccountable sight the Colosseum could offer.

A procession came forward—tall, well-made men, in the prime of their strength. Some carried a sword and a lasso, others a trident and a net; some were in light armor, others in the full, heavy equipment of a soldier; some on horseback, some in chariots, some on foot. They marched in and paid their homage to the emperor; and with one voice their greeting sounded through the building: "Hail, Caesar; those about to die salute you!" They were the gladiators—the swordsmen trained to fight to the death to amuse the populace.

Fights of all sorts took place – the light-armed soldier and the netsman, the lasso and the javelin, the two heavy-armed warriors, all combinations of single combat, and sometimes a general melee. When a gladiator wounded his adversary, he shouted to the spectators, "He has it!" and looked up to see whether he should kill or spare. When the people held their thumbs down, the conquered was left to recover, if he could; if they turned them up, he was to die; and if he showed any reluctance to present his throat for the deathblow, there was a scornful shout, "Receive the steel!"

Trajan

Adapted from the work of Helene A. Guerber and the Sisters of Notre Dame

Trajan was the Roman general in command of the troops in Germany. He had recently become the adopted son of Emperor Nerva, but he had stayed at his post and was still in Germany when he heard that Nerva was dead and that he was now emperor in his turn.

The Romans were very eager to have Trajan return, that they might welcome him; but the new emperor knew that duty comes before pleasure, so he remained on the frontier until the barbarians were all reduced to obedience. Only then did he march southward. He entered Rome on foot, not as a conqueror, but as a father returning to his waiting children. The people cheered him wildly, and all approved when they heard him say, as he handed a sword to the chief of the praetorian guard, "Use this *for* me if I do my duty; *against* me if I do not."

Trajan was so gentle and affable that he won the hearts of all the people. This kindness never changed as long as he lived; and it won for him the title "Father of his Country," which has never been given to any except the very best of men.

Ever ready to make his people happy and comfortable, Trajan built large granaries in which wheat could be stored in great quantities. This grain was sold to the poor, in good honest measures, at the lowest possible rate; for the emperor had said that they should never again be at the mercy of the rich, who had sometimes starved the people in their eagerness to get more money for their grain. Trajan's wife, Plotina, was as good and charitable as he and seconded him in all his generous plans. She was dearly loved by all the Romans, and during the emperor's absence, she always looked after the welfare of his people.

During Domitian's reign, that cowardly emperor had bought peace from the Dacians, and then came back to Rome, saying that he had conquered them. Well, this peace did not last very long, and during the reign of Trajan, the Dacians again began to make raids into the Roman territory. To repulse them, the emperor himself led an army into their country and won so many victories that they begged for peace. Then, on his return to Rome, he received the honors of a triumph and the surname of "The Dacian."

In the very next year, however, the war broke out again. This time, Trajan kept on fighting until the Dacians were completely conquered, and their king had killed himself in despair. Then all Dacia became a Roman province, and the emperor received a second and much more magnificent triumph.

Shortly after this, Trajan was forced to fight the Parthians, descendants of the Persians. He won great victories over them also and added a large province called Mesopotamia to the Roman Empire. During this campaign, he visited Babylon, which was rapidly falling into ruins, and saw the palace where Alexander the Great had died more than four hundred years before.

To commemorate the victories of Trajan, a column was erected in Rome. It still stands there perfectly preserved, and still bears the name of the good emperor.

While Trajan was in Asia, he was taken ill, and he died before he could reach Rome, although his dearest wish had been to breathe his last among his own people. In memory of him, the city where he died was named Trajanopolis ("City of Trajan").

You will doubtless be surprised to hear that this emperor, who was so good and charitable as a rule, persecuted the Christians sorely. Many of them even suffered martyrdom by his order, but this was because he believed that they were wicked and perverse.

He left the Church in peace until the ninth year of his reign, but when returning triumphant from a military conquest, he ordered a public thanksgiving to the gods in which the Christians refused to take part. By this time, the Roman Emperor and governors were getting alarmed at the progress of Christianity. The old laws against Christians were revived, and new ones added against secret assemblies. This was to prevent the faithful from meeting for Holy Mass. Then it was that the Catacombs were first used as churches.

Yet even in his persecution, Trajan was not relentlessly cruel as some emperors were. Pliny the Younger, Proconsul of Pontus and Bithynia, uncertain about the laws against the Christians, wrote to the Emperor for instructions. Trajan gave the following inconsistent reply: That he was not to search for the Christians but to punish them if they persevered in the faith after being denounced and convicted. In this way, he conveyed that they should not be ruthlessly hunted out, but that justice, or so he thought it, should be carried out if publicly challenged.

The persecution raged most fiercely in Asia Minor. The most illustrious martyrs were St. Simeon and St. Ignatius of Antioch. The former was a cousin of our Lord, and brother to St. James the Less, whom he succeeded as Bishop of Jerusalem. He was denounced as a Christian and suffered martyrdom at the advanced age of a hundred and twenty years.

Trajan, it is said, had been taught by Plutarch, a well-known writer, who related the lives of prominent men in a very fascinating way. In his book of Lives, you will find many of the stories which you have read here, for Plutarch wrote about all the greatest men in Roman history. He also compared them with the great men of Greece, whose lives he told in the same volume.

During this reign, also, lived Tacitus, the great Roman historian, Juvenal, the poet, and Pliny the Younger, who wrote a famous oration in praise of the emperor, which has been preserved.

The Romans felt such respect for Trajan that during the next two hundred years the senators always addressed a new emperor by saying, "Reign fortunately as Augustus, virtuously as Trajan!" Thus, you see, the memory of a man's good deeds is very lasting; even now Trajan's name is honored, and people still praise him for the good he did while he was emperor of Rome.

SAINT IGNATIUS, BISHOP OF ANTIOCH

by James Joseph Baxter, selected and arranged by the Rev. Francis Spirago

We ought to call upon God's holy name, often and with reverence. We will now meet a saint who delighted in uttering the name of Jesus and teaches us that we must honor God's holy name.

Ignatius became a priest, and afterward, he was made bishop of the large and important see of Antioch, where St. Peter had previously labored. The town soon became Christian. When Trajan, the Roman emperor, was on a military expedition, entered the town, and found the Roman temples empty and deserted, he asked the governor whose fault it was. The governor informed him that the bishop of the Christians, Ignatius, was to blame for it. The emperor summoned the gray-haired bishop to his presence and asked him whether he was indeed the evil spirit who had this disobedience in the city.

Ignatius answered, "He cannot be called an evil spirit who bears God in his heart."

The emperor said, "I suppose you mean Jesus of Nazareth."

Ignatius replied yes and proceeded to teach the foolishness of worshiping pagan gods.

The angered the emperor, and, turning to his soldiers, he ordered that Ignatius be cast to the lions. Thus, the sentence of death was passed, and the soldiers seized him to bring him to Rome.

The Christians of that city wanted to rescue him and save his life, but Ignatius wrote a letter, asking them not to deprive him of the crown of martyrdom. On his arrival in Rome, he was taken to the arena before a huge crowd of spectators, to be attacked by two hungry lions.

Standing there, he prayed aloud, saying, "The name of Jesus shall never depart from my lips; and even if it were to do so, it cannot be erased from my heart." The Roman spectators were filled with admiration at the faith and courage of this old man, and the joy with which he met death.

The Christians went by night to the arena and carried away his relics; they were taken to Antioch, where they were placed under an altar with the utmost reverence and veneration. God caused this saint to be so highly privileged because of his love and veneration for the name of Jesus.

Hadrian

by Helene A. Guerber

Trajan was succeeded by his cousin Hadrian, a good and true man, who had received an excellent education, and was very talented. Hadrian had fought with Trajan in most of his campaigns, and gladly accepted the title of emperor, which the legions gave him, and which was confirmed by the Roman senate.

The first act of the new emperor was to reward his soldiers for their devotion, and his next, to pardon all who had ever injured him. Thus, we are told that on meeting an enemy he said, "My good friend, you have escaped, for I am made emperor."

Hadrian was very affable, and always ready to serve others. When asked why he, an emperor, troubled himself thus about others, he replied, "I have been made emperor for the benefit of mankind and not for my own good."

Instead of continuing to enlarge the Roman Empire, as Trajan had done, Hadrian now said that it was large enough; so, he did all that he could to have it governed properly. He did not always remain at Rome but made a grand journey through all his vast realm.

Accompanied by able men of every kind, he first visited Gaul, Germany, Holland, and Britain. Everywhere he went he inspected the buildings, ordered the construction of new aqueducts, temples, etc., and paid particular attention to the training of his armies. He shared the soldiers' fatigues, marched at their head twenty miles a day in the burning sun, and lived on their scanty fare of bread, lard, and sour wine; so none of his men ever dared complain.

Wherever he went, Hadrian planned great improvements; and in Britain he built a rampart, or wall, seventy-three miles long, to protect the Britons from the barbarians who at that time lived in Scotland. Then, passing through the western part of Gaul, Hadrian went up into Spain, and from there into Africa.

He also visited the East and made a long stay in Athens, where he took part for the first time in a religious ceremony called the Eleusinian Mysteries. During his stay there, he ordered that the Temple of Jupiter should be finished and heard much about the new religion of the Christians.

Although he had at first objected greatly to the Christians, Hadrian now began to like them, and even proposed to place Christ among the Roman gods, as Tiberius is said to have done many years before.

The emperor Hadrian's chief delight was in building. For instance, he gave orders for the rebuilding of Carthage, and when he visited Egypt, he had Pompey's tomb carefully repaired.

In Palestine, Hadrian would have liked to rebuild Jerusalem. The Jews were delighted when they heard this because the Christians had declared that the city would never rise again. Their joy, however, did not last long, for they and the Romans soon began a terrible quarrel which ended in a war. More than five hundred thousand Jews perished in the struggle, and countless Romans and Christians also were killed.

After making two journeys to visit all the different parts of his empire, Hadrian went back to Rome, where he hoped to end his life in peace among learned men, and in devising new laws and erecting new buildings. He built a palace at Tibur and a fine tomb on the banks of the Tiber. This tomb was long known as "Hadrian's Mole," but is now generally called the "Castle of St. Angelo," on account of the statue of the angel Michael which surmounts it.

Hadrian, as we have seen, had been gentle and forgiving during the first part of his reign; but he now began to suffer from a disease that soon made him cross and suspicious. He, therefore, became very cruel, and, forgetting that he had once quite approved of the Christians, he ordered a fourth persecution, in which many were put to death.

To make sure that the Romans would be governed well after his death, Hadrian selected as his successor a very good and wise man named Antoninus. Then, feeling that his sufferings were more than he could bear, he implored his servants to kill him. They all refused, so he sent for many doctors, and took all the medicines they prescribed.

This, of course, somewhat hastened his death. We are told that he spent the last moments of his life dictating verses addressed to his soul, which are now well known. Hadrian was buried in the tomb which he had built on the banks of the Tiber, which can still be visited in Rome today, although it is so old that many changes have been made in it since it was first finished.

Marcus Aurelius, the Model Pagan

Adapted from the work of Helene A. Guerber and the Sisters of Notre Dame

Marcus Aurelius was one of the most remarkable men that ever lived. He traced his descent from the second king of Rome, Numa Pompilius, and he himself said, "To the gods, I am indebted for having good grandfathers, good parents, a good sister, good teachers, good associates, good kinsmen and friends, nearly everything good."

The new emperor had been most carefully brought up and educated, and never did good teachers have so good a pupil. He was not a Christian, but a pagan who practiced all the virtues which the Christians taught. He belonged to a school of philosophers called the Stoics, who said that people ought to bear nobly all the ills of this life and to seek to be good rather than happy.

He delighted in reading and hearing of the lives of great and noble men and especially admired Epictetus the philosopher. Marcus Aurelius thus learned to be simple, true, temperate, and good; and through the influence of Epictetus, he became a model of pagan virtue.

During his life, this emperor wrote down many of the beautiful thoughts which occurred to him and many maxims for the education of his son. These writings have been preserved in a book called "Meditations of Marcus Aurelius."

Marcus Aurelius, although so fond of peace, did not enjoy much of it during his reign, for there was constant trouble with the barbarians in Germany and Britain. As soon as these disturbances began, the Parthians in the East revolted also; and Verus, whom Marcus Aurelius had made associate ruler of Rome, was sent out to fight them.

This Verus, unfortunately, was as bad as Aurelius was good. While he was in Rome he behaved very well, but when far away from his virtuous colleague, he began to live a very wicked life. Had not his generals fought bravely for him, the Parthians would never have been conquered, for he spent most of his time in idleness, or in eating and drinking to excess.

When Verus returned home, he claimed and received the honors of a triumph, although they belonged in reality to his generals. The joy of the Romans at his return, however, was soon changed to mourning, because the troops brought back from the East a horrible disease, which caused the death of hosts of people.

The Romans were almost wild with terror, owing to this disease and to the floods and famines which took place at about the same time; but Marcus Aurelius showed great courage, and went among them trying to relieve their sufferings and exhorting them to be patient.

Hoping to put an end to such scourges, the people made great offerings to the gods; and when these failed to bring any relief, the pagan priests accused the Christians of causing all their woes. On the strength of such accusations, the Christians were again persecuted. The only fault which can be found with Marcus Aurelius is that he allowed them to be tortured during his reign.

Many historians, however, say that the blame of the persecution does not really rest upon Aurelius, who knew nothing about the new religion, but upon the senators, who made him believe that the Christians were very wicked and that they should be put down at any price.

Fresh edicts were issued against the Christians, and they were followed by an outburst of fury against the faithful in Rome, Asia Minor, and Gaul. In Asia Minor, St. Polycarp, Bishop of Smyrna and a disciple of St. John, when called upon to deny Christ, said "Six and eighty years have I been His servant, and He has never done me wrong. How, then, can I blaspheme my King?" St. Polycarp was condemned to be burnt alive, but, when placed on the pyre, the flames encircling him would not touch him, so that he had to be killed by the spear of one of the soldiers.

St. Pothinus, the Bishop of Lyons, was so old and feeble that he had to be carried before his judges. His bold profession of faith enraged the people, who beat him so violently that he died in prison from his wounds. He was succeeded by the great St. Irenaeus. It was during this persecution that Lucius, King of one of the small British States, sent to the pope for missionaries. Thus, it was that Britain so early received the faith.

Verus having died, Marcus Aurelius now became sole ruler. Meanwhile, a great rebellion had broken out among the barbarians in the north, and the emperor himself took command of the army that marched against them. We are told that once during this campaign, the Roman legions were in great danger. Had it not been for a sudden thunderstorm, accompanied by much hail, which fell upon the enemy, the emperor and his troops would surely have perished.

This timely thunderstorm was considered a miracle. The pagan Romans said that it was worked by their gods, whom they had called upon in their distress; but the Christians believed that it was owing to the prayers of some of their brothers who were in the imperial army. However it may be, Aurelius put a stop to the persecutions of the Christians on his return to Rome.

He died not long after, at Vienna, during another campaign, leaving the empire to Commodus, his young son, and imploring the senators to give the new emperor good advice.

The victories and life of Marcus Aurelius were commemorated by a column, still standing in Rome, where the miracle related above is also represented. A better monument, however, is the book he wrote, which has been translated into English, so that everybody can read it; and best of all is the record of his life, which had been devoted to doing good.

Conversion of Britain

by the Sisters of Notre Dame

In the days when Julius Caesar invaded Britain at the head of his victorious Roman legions, fifty-five years before the birth of our Lord, he found the ancient Britons practicing a strange form of religion, called Druidism. It was so called because of its priests, the Druids. The Britons were taught by their priests that there were many gods, but the Druids themselves knew that there was only one God, who would reward the good and punish the wicked in eternity.

The Britons were a brave and simple people, loving their island home very dearly. Their country was invaded by the Romans. The Britons fought hard and suffered a great deal rather than let themselves be conquered. In spite, however, of their courageous defense, the Romans succeeded in making Britain a province of the Empire. Though this seemed a misfortune to the Britons, it was the means of bringing them the greatest of blessings - the true faith.

How and when Christianity was first preached in this island is uncertain. Old traditions say that St. Peter and St. Paul came to Britain. But the truth is that many among the Roman soldiers were Christians, and they would have helped to convert the people around them.

There are many legends about the first apostles of the faith in Britain. One story tells us that St. Joseph of Arimathea came to Glastonbury soon after the Ascension and began preaching to the people. They would not listen at first, so he struck his staff into the ground, begging God to show by a miracle that he taught the true faith. The staff immediately took root, put forth branches, green leaves, and flowers whiter than snow. This miracle converted the people, and a little straw-roofed church was built and dedicated to our Lady, the first in the country which was so soon to become an Isle of Saints. Later on, a fine church and monastery were built at Glastonbury, and this, the mother of churches, or the Second Rome, as it was called, became the most famous shrine in the West of England, the only one that was not destroyed when the Saxons came.

Though Britain was a province of the Roman Empire, the British Christians seem to have been left in peace during the terrible days of persecution. Only during the fourth century do we hear of martyrs suffering for the faith. Despite the favor shown to the faithful by Constantius (the Caesar in the West, and father of Constantine the Great), the edicts of Diocletian were enforced in Britain. Many martyrs gave up their lives rather than deny their faith. We are told of thousands having been martyred in Wales, but the most famous is St. Alban, the first martyr of Britain.

He was a noble pagan of Verulam; and when a holy priest was fleeing from the persecutors, he generously hid him in his house. Some days passed, and Alban, struck by the sanctity of his guest, asked for and received holy baptism. By this time, the soldiers had found out where the stranger was and presented themselves at St. Alban's house. To save the priest, St. Alban changed clothes with him, and let himself be taken before the Roman governor, who at once saw the mistake of his men. He was offering sacrifice at the time, and he ordered St. Alban to join him in the ceremony. On the saint's refusal, the judge commanded him to be cruelly scourged, but as this did not shake his faith, he condemned St. Alban to be beheaded at once on the top of a neighboring hill. Crowds pressed on to see the martyrdom, and as everyone had to pass a bridge over a little stream, the Saint feared that the throng would prevent his receiving his crown of martyrdom before nightfall. So, he prayed that the hour of his triumph might not be delayed, and it is said that immediately a passage opened through the waters, which stood up like walls on either side. The soldier who was to have executed him was converted, and when St. Alban prayed again, a spring burst forth at his feet. He baptized the soldier, and a few moments later both attained the glory of martyrdom.

So many miracles followed that the governor gave orders ceasing the persecution. A famous monastery was built on the spot, and the town of St. Albans grew up around it.

Courage Against Oppression

by the Sisters of Notre Dame

Persecutions Under Septimius Severus, A.D. 202-211. Septimius Severus was at first favorable to the Christians, but in the tenth year of his reign, he renewed all the edicts against them. The persecution raged in Africa, Italy, and Gaul. At Carthage, great numbers suffered, among them St. Perpetua and St. Felicity, who, with three other catechumens, were tormented and then thrown to wild beasts.

Perpetua was a noble lady, Felicity a slave. Perpetua had a little son a few months old.

When she was accused of being a Christian, her father begged her to renounce her faith. But she was firm, and with several others, was thrown into a dark, dismal prison, where they received baptism. Again, her father came to plead with her to yield, but in vain. When these brave martyrs were led before the tribunal, once more the poor old father approached Perpetua, holding her little baby on his arm, and begged her not to bring misery on her child. The judge ordered that he should be removed, and the soldiers struck him as they did so. Perpetua was more grieved at the sight of her father's distress and at seeing him struck than at her own fate, for immediately after being condemned, she was to be exposed to wild beasts. But the people, touched by their courage and modesty, would not let the terrible scene continue, so they were put to death by the sword.

The Emperors who succeeded Septimius Severus were not so devoted to maintaining the Roman form of worship as their predecessors. They wanted to make a new form of religion by uniting several kinds of worship together; thus, the Christians were not so much persecuted. Emperor Alexander Severus was particularly favorable to the Christians, but the lesser officers in Rome often persecuted the faithful when the emperor was away at war. So, despite the peace, many martyrs gave their lives for the faith.

Among other well-known names, none is so familiar to us as that of St. Cecilia. She was descended from a noble Roman pagan family, but had received the faith in her early years, and had consecrated her virginity to god. Her parents had espoused her to a young pagan called Valerian. St. Cecilia told him of her vow and said that she had an angel to protect her. Valerian was so struck with this language that he said he would believe in our Lord if he could see the angel. At St. Cecilia's prayer his desire was granted. St. Cecilia instructed him in the doctrines of the faith, and he was soon baptized by Pope St. Urban. Valerian and his brother Tiburtius were denounced to the magistrate for burying the bodies of the martyrs and were both condemned to death. The night before they suffered St. Cecilia, with several others, visited Valerian and his brother in the prison. Their example and conversation converted the pagan guard, who also underwent martyrdom at daybreak. St. Cecilia distributed her wealth to the poor and devoted her time to converting many, who were then baptized by St. Urban.

The prefect soon summoned her to appear before him. She answered all his threats and questions boldly and was condemned to death.

It was in a vineyard belonging to St. Cecilia that one of the most famous Catacombs was excavated. It contained the crypt in which several Popes were buried, and where St. Cecilia herself was laid after her martyrdom. Her body, still incorrupt, was found there in the ninth century and was then put in a church above ground, where, eight hundred years afterward, it was again uncovered and exposed for the veneration of the faithful.

With the exception of a few martyrdoms, the Christians were left in peace for twenty-four years. This tranquility was disturbed during the two years that Maximin reigned.

Persecutions Under Maximin, A.D. 235-238. This persecution was directed chiefly against the clergy. Emperor Maximin thought to shake the faith of the people taking away their pastors. Two popes were martyred, both of whom are buried in the Papal Crypt. After this short persecution, the Christians again had peace for eleven years.

Persecutions Under Decius, A.D. 249-251. Emperor Decius resolved to destroy Christianity altogether, and to obtain this end, he ordered that all who professed the faith should be cruelly tortured before being put to death. Many who would have bravely met a speedy death recoiled before such horrible torments and renounced their religion. These were known as the "Lapsed." But even so, the number of martyrs was so great that public buildings had to be used as prisons.

St. Agatha was a native of Sicily and a virgin of noble birth. She suffered many tortures because she refused to become the bride of the Roman Proconsul or to adore his gods. The torments she endured were so great that she died in the hands of her persecutors. It was during this persecution that many of the faithful fled to deserts to escape such terrible trials of their constancy. Their example of living as hermits is a practice which afterward became widespread throughout the Church.

Invasion of the Goths

By Helene A. Guerber

During the reign of Decius, new and terrible barbarians, called Goths, came sweeping down from the north. They were tall and fierce and traveled with their wives and children, their flocks, and all they owned.

The Goths were divided into several large tribes: the Ostrogoths, or East Goths, the Visigoths, or West Goths, and the Laggards, so called because this tribe followed the others. All these barbarians spoke a Teutonic dialect, like the one from which the present German language has grown; and among the gods whom they worshiped was Odin.

The Goths met the Romans in several battles and ruined many towns in their path, spreading always farther. Decius marched against them, hoping to punish them for their massacres; but he fell into an ambush, where he was killed with his son. His successor, Gallus, made a dishonorable peace with the barbarians and allowed them to settle on the other side of the Danube.

Gallus and his general, who succeeded him, were both slain by their own troops; The next emperor, Valerian, was the choice of the Roman legions, for he was both brave and virtuous.

Although already a very old man, Valerian directed his son to attend to the wars in Europe, while he went off to Asia to fight the King of Persia. This monarch had overrun much Roman territory and had surprised the city of Antioch while the inhabitants were at the theater.

Valerian recovered Antioch from the enemy but was finally defeated and taken prisoner. We are told that he was treated very harshly, and he died in captivity.

The Last Persecutions

by the Sisters of Notre Dame

Persecutions Under Valerian, A.D. 257-260. Valerian was at first favorable to the Christians, but afterward issued two edicts against them. The first forbade Christians even to go to the Catacombs and ordered bishops and priests who refused to sacrifice to the gods to be sent into exile. The second edict ordered all clergy to be killed, confiscated the property of senators and knights, and exiled all ladies and other noblemen who remained faithful to Christianity. Among the chief sufferers were St. Cyprian and Pope Sixtus II. This holy pope was celebrating Mass in the Catacombs when seized by the soldiers. The Christians present begged to be taken instead, but only the deacons were led away with the pope, who was condemned to death and taken back to the Catacombs to be martyred. One of the deacons was St. Lawrence, who, when asked to give up the treasures of the church, promised to do so. He then collected together all the poor of Rome and presented them as the Church's greatest treasures to the prefect, who, in anger, immediately ordered him to be put to death.

We have a beautiful example of courage and faith in the conduct of a little child called Cyril. His father was a pagan, and, in hatred of the name of Christian, had driven his son from his house. The soldiers brought the child before the governor, who tried gently to persuade him to renounce his faith in order to be restored to his home. St. Cyril answered, "I rejoice to be driven from my father's home; God will give me one much more grand and beautiful." Threats were then tried to frighten him, but neither the sight of the fires nor the sword could shake the courage of the little hero, who begged to die that he might be sooner with God. The bystanders wept when they saw him receive the crown of martyrdom.

Valerian was succeeded by his son, Gallienus. This emperor was the first to issue edicts in favor of the Christians. They were declared a lawful society and were now protected by the State.

Persecutions Under Aurelian and Diocletian, A.D. 274-288. Emperor Aurelian decided to succeed where others had failed. He made up his mind to exterminate the Christians from his dominions. However, he was assassinated eight months after his edicts were issued.

Before beginning the history of the last persecution, it is necessary to glance at the changes which had taken place in the government of the Roman Empire. In 286 Diocletian divided his dominion into two parts, the Eastern Empire and the Western Empire. The Western he gave to Maximian, under the title of Augustus of the West. Six years later, in 292, Diocletian further divided each Empire into two, giving the governors the title of Caesar.

Maximian began to persecute the Christians in his dominions in 286. A revolt broke out near Lyons, in Gaul, and he sent for the Theban Legion, which, according to the legend, was composed entirely of Christians, to suppress it. But instead of using them to quiet the riots, Maximian ordered the soldiers to seek out the Christians and put them to death.

The whole Legion, with their captain, St. Maurice, refused to obey such an unjust command. The Emperor then ordered them to stand in lines and had the head of every tenth man struck off. This only served to encourage the remaining soldiers. The Legion declared themselves faithful soldiers to the Emperor, ready to die in his defense, but continued in refusing to put innocent Christians to death. At last, Maximian, despairing of overcoming their constancy, had them surrounded by the rest of his army and slain as they stood. It is said that six thousand received the crown of martyrdom.

Another celebrated martyr was St. Sebastian, captain of the Praetorian Guard. He was denounced to Diocletian for visiting and encouraging the imprisoned Christians. The Emperor scolded him for misusing the trust he had put in him. Sebastian replied, that, though always faithful to the Emperor, he had long ago discovered the folly of adoring gods of stone. Diocletian in anger called for a company of archers, commanding them to shoot the Saint to death. Covered with wounds, he was left for dead. An old widow came to carry away his body but found that Sebastian still breathed. She nursed him back to life, and a few days afterward Diocletian was astonished to see in his royal court the pale face of the captain of the guards, whom he thought was dead. Furious at such boldness, the Emperor instantly ordered Sebastian to be taken to the hippodrome of the palace, where he was put to death.

Persecutions Under Diocletian, A.D. 303-305. The last persecution did not begin in earnest until 303. A fresh edict was passed in that year ordering all churches to be destroyed and the Scriptures to be burnt.

The severity of the persecution varied in different countries according to the wishes of their rulers. It was enforced with the greatest cruelty in the East by Galerius. In the West, Constantius secretly favored the Christians, though he dared not openly disobey the edicts; so many suffered for the faith – as, for instance, St. Alban, the first martyr in Britain.

Among other glorious martyrs in other parts of the Empire may be named St. Lucy and St. Agnes of Rome. St. Agnes was only thirteen years of age and very beautiful so that the prefect's son wanted to make her his wife. But St. Agnes had chosen Jesus Christ as her spouse and refused all his offers and promises of wealth. She was placed on a funeral pile, but the flames separated without touching her so that the prefect ordered her to be beheaded. The persecution raged furiously until 305, the number who suffered reaching many thousands.

Well may the Church, in her office of martyrs, quote these words from the book of Wisdom:

"Then the upright will stand up boldly to face those who had oppressed him and had thought so little of his sufferings. And, seeing him, they will be seized with terrible fear, amazed that he should have been so unexpectedly saved. Stricken with remorse, they will say to one another with groans and laboring breath, 'This is the one whom we used to mock, making him the butt of our insults, fools that we were! His life we regarded as madness, his ending as without honor. How has he come to be counted as one of the children of God and to have his lot among the holy ones?'"

Division of the Roman Empire

Adapted from the work of Helene A. Guerber and the Sisters of Notre Dame

Emperor Diocletian found that the Roman Empire was too large and hard to govern for a single ruler. He, therefore, made his friend, Maximian, associate emperor. Under the emperors, he then instated two Caesars to further help rule, Gelarius under Maximian, and Constantius under himself. He gave them also a portion of the empire to govern. These four Roman each ruled their own capital; a new epoch began, with Rome no longer the central point of the government.

Diocletian remained the head and was the acknowledged leader and adviser of the other rulers. But his reign was troubled by invasions of the barbarians, a war in Persia, and a persecution of the Christians, –the worst and bloodiest that had yet been known.

A lover of solitude and simplicity, Diocletian soon tired of imperial life. Therefore, when he felt that his strength no longer permitted him to serve the people, he withdrew to a quiet retreat in his native city of Salona, where he spent his last eight years in growing vegetables for his amusement.

As Maximian had retired at the same time as Diocletian, the Roman Empire was now divided between Galerius and Constantius, who were known as emperors of the East and of the West, respectively. Constantius, having obtained the West for his share, went to Britain to suppress a revolt. He died at York, and his son Constantine became emperor in his stead.

Early Apologists

by the Sisters of Notre Dame

Besides the attacks made on the Church by persecution, many of the pagans tried to shake the faith of the Christians by writing all sorts of untrue things against Catholic teaching and accused the faithful of crimes that they had never committed. The Christians were portrayed as atheists because they would not adore the false gods of the Romans; they were also accused of being enemies of the State and of being disloyal to the Emperor, and of many other crimes so grievous that they would have died rather than commit them. The enemies of the Church sought by these accusations to make the Christian religion appear less holy and less attractive to the pagans, hoping to prevent many from becoming Christians.

But God raised up many learned and clever men, who, by their teaching, and especially by their writings, defended the church against these dangerous attacks. These men were called "Apologists." Their writings are known as "Apologies," and are letters addressed to Emperors and others, in which the slanders against the Christian religion are disproved. They also contain instructions on Christian belief and the practice of virtue. Among the most learned of the Apologists were St. Justin Martyr, St. Irenaeus, Tertullian, and Origen.

St. Justin Martyr was born in Palestine. His parents were pagan Greeks, and Justin eagerly studied every system of Greek philosophy but failed to find the truth in any. One day when he was walking on the seashore, he met an unknown man, who told him to study the doctrines of Christianity.

This he at once commenced doing. His longings after the truth were all satisfied by the teachings of the Church, and he became a Christian. St. Justin devoted the rest of his life to preaching and defending the faith. He wore the dress of a Greek philosopher, even after his conversion, because it won him a respectful hearing from the people. In 150 he went to Rome and opened a school of theology. St. Justin wrote two Apologies. The first was to the Roman Emperor, Antoninus Pius, and his Senate. In it he asked that the Christians might not be punished simply because they were Christians, but only if they were guilty of any real crime. This letter was favorably received by the Emperor, who granted his request. The second Apology was written to Marcus Aurelius, who answered it by causing St. Justin to be martyred. He gladly gave his life for the truth he had so nobly defended by his writings.

St. Irenaeus, a disciple of St. Polycarp, and Bishop of Lyons, wrote a refutation of all the heresies of his time, and said that they could all be condemned by the tradition of the Church established in Rome by the Apostles St. Peter and St. Paul. All these early Apologists wrote in Greek, except Tertullian and St. Cyprian.

Tertullian, born at Carthage, 160, was the earliest defender of the faith who wrote in Latin. He had been converted from paganism and was most zealous in using his vast learning in the service of the Church. Unfortunately, he gave way to his fierce temper and fell away from the true faith, and even founded a new sect. Still, his writings have been of much use, and are considered of very great authority. He lived to an advanced age, but it is feared that he was never reconciled to the Church.

St. Cyprian, a native of Carthage, was converted in the year 246. His two Apologies were written some years later. In the second, he proves from Scripture the Divinity of Christ. St. Cyprian became Bishop of Carthage 248 and was beheaded during the persecution under Valerian before the walls of his native city, on September 13, 258.

Origen was the son of Leonidas, who lived at Alexandria. When his father was martyred under Emperor Septimius Severus, Origen wanted to be a martyr too, but his mother hid his clothes so that he could not go out to declare himself a Christian.

Origen was exceedingly learned, and particularly famous for his knowledge of the Bible, of which he had learned a portion by heart every day. He was soon placed at the head of the School of Alexandria, which was renowned all over the world as a great center of learning. Some of Origen's speculative opinions have been condemned by the Church.

Among the most celebrated of Origen's very numerous works, is his "Apology for the Christian Religion." It is specially directed against the calumnies of Celsus, a pagan philosopher. Origen spent twenty-eight years on a work called the "Hexapla," which contained in six parallel columns different versions of the Old Testament. During the Decian persecution, Origen was cast into prison and tortured for the faith. When Decius died, he was released but did not long outlive his sufferings. He died at Tyre in the year 254.

Unit Five: Rise of Christendom, Fall of the Empire

THEME: PERSEVERANCE

THE FIRST CHRISTIAN EMPEROR

Adapted from the work of Helene A. Guerber and the Sisters of Notre Dame

Three hundred years had elapsed since the Ascension of our Blessed Lord. Pagan rulers had done their worst against the Church and had utterly failed. The time was now come when God would deliver His faithful people from such terrible trials and sufferings and would cause His Church to triumph over her heathen foes.

We have seen that one of the Caesars chosen by Diocletian and Maximinian to aid them in governing the Roman Empire was Constantius and that this noble-hearted man would not allow Christians to be persecuted in his province when he could help it. He married a Princess named Helena, who probably was a British lady. They had a son known in history as Constantine the Great. In 306 this prince succeeded his father as Caesar, or Governor, of Britain and Gaul.

The rulers of the Roman Empire at this time disagreed among themselves. Maxentius, the Italian Caesar, declared war against Constantine, who advanced to meet him. Constantine had got as far as Rome, when, at noon on the day before his battle with Maxentius, he saw in the heavens a bright cross of light with the words, "In this sign, you shall conquer." Constantine was so moved by this vision that he made a vow to become a Christian if he won the victory.

Constantine had always used the famous Roman eagle as his standard. Now he ordered a new standard, called a *Labarum*, to be made, which bore a cross and inscription like the one he had seen in the sky; and from this day on, it was always carried before him in battle. The Labarum became the first Christian standard of war ever used.

With this standard at the head of his army, Constantine marched to victory. Maxentius was defeated at the Battle of Milvian Bridge, 312, and Constantine entered Rome in triumph. In memory of his victory, a fine arch was built, which is standing still and is called the Arch of Constantine.

Constantine now reigned over the Western Empire. He at first shared power with the Eastern Emperor, Licinius, but they quarreled on matters of religion. War broke out, and it is said that, when they stood opposite the other, they each loudly called upon their gods.

Constantine won the victory, becoming the sole master of the expansive Roman Empire, and so declared that his God was the most worthy of honor.

He, like his father, had long favored the Christians, even before his famous victory. But, seeing that he owed so much to the cross of our Divine Lord, he took steps to establish the Christian Church so securely that nothing has ever been able to overthrow it since then. He ordered all persecutions to cease. He issued the Edict of Milan, a proclamation granting great privileges to Christians and returning the churches that had been seized. He ordered that the Christians should have full liberty to worship as they pleased. He bestowed the Lateran Palace on the Pope, gave large gifts in money and lands to the Church, and expressed a wish that his subjects should be Christians. Slaves were to be treated less cruelly and could more easily gain their freedom. He also forbade that criminals should be put to death on a cross, as it had been sanctified by Christ; he put an end to all gladiatorial shows, and Sunday was set apart as a day of rest.

All these changes greatly satisfied his mother, St. Helena, who was a devout Christian. In this new age of freedom for Christians, she was able to carry out a mission which she was most anxious to complete; she undertook a journey to the Holy Land in search of the True Cross. Two hundred years before, Emperor Hadrian had ordered that Mount Calvary be covered with earth so that people might forget where it was; but as a statue of Venus was placed on the top, it only served to mark the spot, and St. Helena had no difficulty in finding it.

Three crosses were discovered, but there was nothing to show which was that of our Blessed Lord. So, the crosses were brought to the bedside of a woman in Jerusalem who lay ill of an incurable disease. As soon as the true Cross touched her, she was healed. A portion of the blessed wood was detached, placed in a magnificent reliquary, and sent to Constantine. The remainder St. Helena left under the care of the Bishop of Jerusalem. She had many fine churches built in the Holy Land before returning to Rome. One over the Cave of the Nativity at Bethlehem still stands.

It was only when he became master of the whole empire that Constantine openly declared himself a Christian. At his call, the Bishops assembled for the first General Council of Nicaea. All the learned Christians came together at Nicaea to talk about their religion, and to find out exactly what people should believe and teach. Here they said that Arius, a religious teacher, had been preaching heresy; and they banished him and his followers to a remote part of the empire.

Constantine soon ordered that the city of Byzantium be rebuilt. It received the name of Constantinople, or "city of Constantine." It was dedicated as the new capital of the Roman Empire. Constantine was now at the height of his glory. Because he accomplished so much during his reign, he has been called Constantine the Great, although he was not a very good man, and, unfortunately, sometimes acted in a way that was very wrong, especially for a Christian.

During the latter part of his reign, there were various invasions of the barbarians; and Constantine, who was a brave warrior, is said to have driven them back and treated them with much cruelty. He fell dangerously ill at Nicomedia and is said to have been baptized there in 337. He died shortly after, leaving his empire to his three sons; and his remains were carried to Constantinople so that he might rest in the city which bore his name.

Religious Life in the Early Ages

by the Sisters of Notre Dame

Even in the time of the Apostles, we hear of holy men and women who, to imitate more closely the lives of our Blessed Lord and His Holy Mother, consecrated themselves to the service of God and of their neighbor. St. Paul makes special mention of holy women who were thus spending all their time in prayer and good works.

These widows and deaconesses, as they were then called, lived in their own homes, and served the churches and the poor. St. Agnes, St. Cecilia, St. Dorothea, and St. Agatha were all consecrated virgins, living in the world but spending their lives in good works.

A little later on, in order to be freer from worldly cares, a great number of Christians withdrew into solitary life - that is, they lived each in a separate cell near some town or village, and very often close to a church. They were called anchorites, and for many ages, even when monasteries and convents were founded, numbers of people, both men and women, still embraced this kind of life. In England, for instance, there were anchorites up to the time of the so-called Reformation.

When, during the seventh persecution, Christians were no longer free to exercise their religion, great numbers fled into the deserts - principally of Egypt - either to give themselves entirely to God, or to escape the fierce pains of the tortures prepared for Christians who were brought before the judges. These settlers in the desert were the hermits. The most famous was St. Paul of Thebes, the first hermit. He retired into the desert when very young, in the year 249. For nearly a hundred years he was fed by a raven which brought him half a loaf daily. Just before his death, he was discovered by St. Anthony, the patriarch of monks. This saint had also been a hermit, but so many came to him for help and guidance that a town of solitaries grew up around him. At about the same time, many other towns and villages of hermits were thus commenced. Such a community was called a "Laura." It consisted of hundreds of little cells at some distance from each other, but not very far from a church where all could meet for Holy Mass.

A little later, instead of having separate cells at a distance from one another, the hermits formed into communities, living together under a Superior. Thus, was commenced religious life as we see it now. The Upper Valley of the Nile was the home of these monks and nuns. The men lived in monasteries, the women in convents, following a settled rule of life. The first rule was drawn up by St. Pachomius. The religious spent a great deal of their time in prayer and hard work. They observed strict poverty, both as to food and clothing, but they strove chiefly to excel in obedience and charity. Before St. Pachomius died, seven thousand monks acknowledged him as their superior.

The movement which had commenced in Africa soon spread into other parts of the Church. St. Hilarion introduced it into the East. St. Ambrose, St. Augustine, and St. Jerome all founded convents or monasteries. It was St. Basil who gave the final perfection to religious congregations by causing the members to take vows with the sanction of the bishop. In France St. Martin of Tours was the great apostle of religious life. His rule was carried into Ireland by St. Patrick.

THE HERESY OF ARIUS

by the Sisters of Notre Dame

While Constantine the Great worked at the destruction of idolatry, and at extending the faith throughout his dominions, a new enemy appeared among the members of the Church itself in the person of Arius, an apostate priest. This wicked man taught that God the Son was not equal in all perfection to God the Father, that He was not co-eternal with the Father, but was created by Him as first and greatest among creatures.

St. Alexander, Bishop of Alexandria, called a Synod which excommunicated Arius and condemned his teaching. After this Arius went into Palestine, where he persuaded Eusebius, Bishop of Nicomedia, to adopt his views. This bishop secured for Arius the favor of the Emperor, and that of many bishops of Asia Minor.

The Council of Nicaea – A.D. 325. As the heresy was becoming so widespread, a General Council was held at Nicaea, in Asia Minor, to examine and condemn the doctrines taught by Arius and his followers. St. Athanasius was the chief champion of the Catholic Faith, which teaches that Jesus, the Second Person of the Blessed Trinity, is God, co-eternal with God the Father, and co-equal with Him in all things. The Fathers of the Council chose the word "Consubstantial," proposed by St. Athanasius, to express this doctrine, wrote the Nicene Creed, which contains the exact teaching of the Church about the equality of the Three Persons of the Blessed Trinity. It adds to the general teaching of the Apostles' Creed a definite profession of faith in dogmas attacked by the heretics:

"...and in one Lord Jesus Christ, the only begotten Son of God, born of the Father before all ages, God of God, Light of Light, True God of True God, begotten not made, consubstantial with the Father, by Whom all things were made."

After the Church had thus condemned Arianism as a heresy, Constantine banished its author; but soon, his favorite sister, Constantia (an Arian herself), persuaded the Emperor to allow Arius to return. St. Athanasius would not remove the sentence of excommunication that St. Alexander had passed against Arius, so the Arians made several false accusations against the Saint. Constantine summoned both sides before a court; but though St. Athanasius was declared innocent, his enemies induced the Emperor to exile him from his see to the distant city of Treves.

But the faithful people of Alexandria would have nothing to do with Arius. He, therefore, went to Constantinople, and the Emperor ordered the bishop of that city to receive him in the Church. The bishop knew that he was powerless by himself to prevent the heretic's entrance. He could but pray that God would not permit such a scandal. As Arius was on his way to the church, surrounded by a triumphant crowd, he was seized with a violent illness and died. The dreadful punishment that God inflicted upon this enemy of His Church so impressed Constantine that, when he was on his own deathbed a few months after, he gave orders for the recall of St. Athanasius from banishment. The Alexandrians received him back with great joy.

St. Athanasius was exiled five times in total by Constantine's sons and the emperors who succeeded them, many of whom were furious advocates of the heretics. But he was eventually allowed to return in peace to his diocese, where he remained until his death.

The Heresy of Macedonius. Shortly after the death of Arius, his followers began to teach doctrines quite different from those he had taught them; they became divided into several sects, some of whom taught one doctrine, some another. Thus, from the first great heresy of Arianism arose several others. The foremost of these sects was that of the Macedonians. Arius had attacked the Second Person of the Blessed Trinity, saying He was not equal to God the Father; now Macedonius, Patriarch of Constantinople, attacked the Holy Spirit, the Third Divine Person. His doctrines were quickly condemned, for the Council of Constantinople was called against him in 381.

The Nicene Council had added explanations to that part of the Creed which teaches us what we must believe about Jesus Christ, True God and True Man. The Council of Constantinople did the same to the eighth article, explaining more fully the Catholic doctrine about the Holy Spirit.

The Fathers of the Church

by the Sisters of Notre Dame

In giving the history of the different heresies, we have already named a few of the most illustrious Fathers of the Church. There were, however, many others whose learning and virtues helped to defend the Church against the attacks of heresy and schism. They are generally called the Fathers of the Eastern Church, and the Fathers of the Western Church.

Eastern Fathers

During the fourth century, the principal Fathers of the East were:

1. St. Athanasius
2. St. Cyril of Jerusalem
3. St. Basil, Bishop of Caesarea, in Cappadocia
4. St. Gregory Nazianzen
5. St. Gregory of Nyssa
6. St. John Chrysostom (golden-mouthed), Bishop of Constantinople.

In the fifth century, the foremost Father of the East was St. Cyril, Bishop of Alexandria.

Western Fathers

In the West, the Church was defended in the fourth century by:

1. St. Hilary of Poitiers, surnamed the "Athanasius of the West"
2. St. Ambrose

During the fifth century the most celebrated Fathers of the Western Church were:

1. St. Jerome
2. St. Augustine
3. St. Leo the Great

For the Church to bestow the title of "Doctor" on any of its members she requires:

a. that he be very learned in all matters concerning religion, to be able to teach others;
b. he must be eminently holy;
c. the title must be confirmed by the Pope or by a General Council.

Some of the great saints listed above have merited the title of Father and Doctor of the Church. The term "Father" was, in early times, given to all bishops, but, later on, it came to mean only those writers whose works were of sound doctrine and of great value in the Church, and who had led holy lives; and it is in this latter sense that we have used it.

Julian the Apostate

by the Sisters of Notre Dame

After Constantine's death, the Empire was now held in the hands of his sons – Constantine II, Constantius II, and Constans. Soon after the death of their father, the brothers began to quarrel among themselves. The result was a long series of civil wars, in which two of the brothers were killed. The vast of dominion of Rome was left to the third – Constantius II.

The new emperor, needing help, gave his cousin, Julian, the title of Caesar and placed him in charge of Gaul. As Julian belonged to the family of Constantine, he was, of course, a Christian. He was a very clever youth and had been sent to Athens to study philosophy.

While there, he learned to admire the Greek philosophers so much that he gave up Christianity and became a pagan. In history, he is known as Julian the Apostate, because he abandoned the Christian faith in which he had been brought up. We are told, also, that he spent much time studying magic and alchemy. He gave up his studies with regret, to share the cares of government. While in Gaul, he learned to be an excellent general and drove back the barbarians several times. He soon succeeded his cousin and became emperor.

Julian the Apostate hated the true faith so fiercely that he determined to make the Empire pagan again. As soon as the authority was entirely in his own hands, he ordered that the Christian churches and schools should all be closed and encouraged the people to worship the old pagan gods. He ordered the temples which had been destroyed by Constantine to be rebuilt at the expense of the Christians, who, for this purpose, had to give up all the lands and money they had received for their churches. All the soldiers in his army were forced to give up Christianity, under penalty of being dismissed; Christians were no longer allowed to hold any public offices, and pagans were chosen to fill all places of trust and were granted innumerable favors. The clergy were deprived of their pensions and forbidden to teach even secular subjects. In fact, the Emperor did all he could to throw disgrace and contempt on the Catholic religion. When he persuaded Christians to give up their faith, he treated these defectors with even greater honor than he did the pagans and placed them in the highest posts.

If the Apostate hated Christians, he hated our Lord Jesus Christ still more. He thought he could easily make Christians give up their faith if he could show that our Lord had deceived them by false prophecies. As Christ had prophesied that the Temple of Jerusalem would be utterly destroyed, Julian determined it should be rebuilt with great magnificence.

But hardly were the first foundations laid when a terrible earthquake destroyed all that had been done, and it is said that globes of fire came out of the earth and burnt great numbers of the workmen. Every time the work was renewed this miracle was repeated until at last Julian was forced to abandon his plan. He had only succeeded in proving yet more strongly the truth of the very prophecies he sought to discredit. Far from limiting the spread of the faith, his act became the means of many conversions.

After a short reign of two years, the emperor was struck by a javelin during a battle and was mortally wounded. In his despair, Julian cried out towards heaven, "You have conquered, O Galilean!" The emperor's body was carried to Tarsus, and buried there; and, as Julian had appointed no successor, the army at once gave the empire to one of his officers, named Jovian.

Emperor Jovian and the Downfall of Paganism. The death of Julian the Apostate ended the struggle of paganism against Christianity, for the new emperor Jovian was himself a Christian, and had suffered for his faith under Julian's reign. Jovian's first care was to reopen the churches and to restore the privileges and property of the clergy. He recalled the Christians to the offices from which they had been driven by Julian and his pagan favorites. Henceforward the rulers of Rome were Christians, and the faith spread rapidly throughout the whole Empire.

A good man and a fervent Christian, Jovian quickly reestablished the Christian religion. His reign, however, was very brief, and he was succeeded by two brothers, Valentinian and Valens, who again divided the Roman world into two parts, intending to make a final separation between the empires of the East and the West (364).

Valentinian kept back the northern barbarians as long as he lived, but after his death, Valens was forced to allow the Goths to settle in Thrace. Here they found some of their brothers who had been converted to Christianity. Valens failed to keep many of the promises which he had made to the Goths, and they became so angry that they revolted and killed him at Adrianople.

Saint Augustine and the Pelagian Heresy

Adapted from the work of the Sisters of Notre Dame and by E.C. Donnelly

As St. Athanasius had defended the Church against the heretical teaching of the Arians, so St. Augustine was the champion of the true faith against the errors taught by Pelagius.

St. Augustine was born at Tagaste, near Hippo, in northern Africa, in 354. He was brought up as a Christian by his mother, St. Monica, but was not baptized. Having been sent to a pagan school by his father, he fell in with bad companions and led a very wicked life. For nine years he followed the heresy of the Manichaeans, but the prayers of St. Monica for her son were at last heard, and Augustine received the grace to abandon his sins and become, not only a great saint but also a defender of the faith he had so neglected.

St. Ambrose was an instrument of God in the conversion of St. Augustine, who he baptized in Milan. On that occasion, St. Ambrose composed with his new disciple, the *Te Deum*, a famous hymn of praise in the Church of God. After three years St. Augustine was ordained a priest. Just five years later, he was consecrated Bishop of Hippo.

It was at this time that the heresy of Pelagius arose. At the end of the fourth century, Pelagius went to Rome, where he began to teach that we can save ourselves by our own efforts without the aid of grace and that mankind has not inherited any stain of original sin. When

Rome was sacked by the Goths in 410, Pelagius went to Carthage, where St. Augustine soon discovered the errors of his teaching.

Then Pelagius went to Jerusalem and began to teach. St. Augustine, hearing of this new heresy, brought the question before two Synods, which condemned the teaching of Pelagius.

Later on, a milder form of the heresy of Pelagius began to be taught, which held that although grace is necessary for carrying on good works, man can begin them by his own power. Against this teaching St. Augustine wrote two works to explain fully the doctrine of the Church about grace and free will. Both these heresies soon died out.

For thirty-five years St. Augustine continued to preach and write in defense of the faith. He died in 430, during the siege of Hippo by the Vandals.

St. Jerome. Another great defender of the Church against Pelagianism was St. Jerome. He was born about the year 340 in Dalmatia. He was sent to Rome to complete his studies and was baptized there. After an illness which he suffered at Antioch, St. Jerome went into the desert for four years.

He was ordained a priest in 378 and went to Constantinople, where he helped St. Gregory Nazianzen to get rid of the Arian and Macedonian heresies from among his people. After three years St. Jerome went to Rome, where he assisted the Pope for many years. He spent the last years of his life in Bethlehem, in one of the caves near the grotto of the Nativity. There he directed the nuns of three convents and gave himself up to prayer, mortification, and the study and translation of the Sacred Scriptures into Latin until his death in 420.

Saint Cyril of Alexandria and the Heresy of Nestorianism

by the Sisters of Notre Dame

The next great heresy that disturbed the Church was begun by Nestorius. He taught that there were two persons in Christ and that the Blessed Virgin is not Mother of God, but only of Christ's human person. St. Cyril, Patriarch of Alexandria, defended the glories of our Lady and showed that our Blessed Lady is truly Mother of God.

Nestorius would not submit to the condemnation of his errors by St. Cyril, so a General Council was called finally to settle the question. The Bishops met at Ephesus, to which tradition points as the place of our Lady's Assumption. They condemned the heresy of Nestorius and deprived him of his see. The joy of the people of Ephesus, who had waited all day for the decision, was unbounded when they heard the title "Mother of God" was solemnly acknowledged by the Church. Emperor Theodosius banished Nestorius to Upper Egypt.

An Emperor's Penance

by Helene A. Guerber

Emperor Theodosius was an excellent ruler; and we are told that there is but one stain on his memory, that of the massacre at Thessalonica.

The people of that city once revolted, because the soldiers had arrested one of their favorite chariot drivers, who had failed to obey the laws. In his rage at hearing of this revolt, Theodosius commanded that all the inhabitants of Thessalonica should be killed. But when the deed was done, the emperor repented sorely of his cruelty.

He went to St. Ambrose, who had tried in vain to calm his anger. Humbly begging pardon for his cruelty, he asked permission to come into the Church once more. St. Ambrose, however, would not grant him forgiveness until Theodosius had done public penance for his sin. This, the last great emperor of Rome consented to do, and humbly knelt in sackcloth and ashes at the door of the cathedral of Milan.

Thus, you see, when the Christian emperors did wrong, they were publicly rebuked by the priests, whose duty it was to teach men to do good and to love one another.

Decay of the Empire

Adapted from the work of Helene A. Guerber and the Sisters of Notre Dame

Theodosius was the last of the great Roman Emperors. He was so good a general, and yet still so just, that he soon succeeded in making peace with the Goths, many of whom entered his army and became Roman soldiers.

After years of continual warfare against the barbarians and the emperors of the West, Theodosius became sole ruler of the whole Roman Empire, and thus won his title of Theodosius the Great. During his reign, he induced his subjects to renounce all the pagan gods except Victory, whom they would not consent to give up.

Many reforms were also made among the Christians, the Arians were again said to be heretics, and then the true Christians for the first time took the name of Catholics, which means universal.

Theodosius was the last Roman emperor whose sway extended over the whole empire, and his reign over the united kingdom had succeeded, for a time, in keeping the invaders in check. But when he died in 395, the Empire was finally divided into two; he left the rule of the East to his son Arcadius, and of the West to his son Honorius. Things rapidly went from bad to worse.

For centuries, the great Roman Empire had been gradually falling to pieces. Even so far back as the reign of Augustus, various German tribes had continually invaded the Roman provinces north of the Danube. Though they were always driven back, the enemy gradually grew stronger, while the Empire grew weaker. Sometimes, a German chief with his tribe would serve in the Roman armies as mercenaries and receive a grant of land as a reward – the chief becoming a Roman general or governor. Thus, the Teutons, as we have previously read, began to breach Rome from within, as well as attack from without.

The first Teutonic barbarian invasions into Italy had been due to fear of the Huns. The Goths had been forced over the Danube when their homelands were seized by the Asiatic tribe. They were allowed to remain and settle in Roman territory, but the uneasy peace between Goths and Romans would not last long.

Both sons of Theodosius were mere boys when they were called by their father's death to take reign of the empires of the East and West. For a little while, however, the barbarians dared not invade Roman territory; they had not yet forgotten how they had been conquered by Theodosius.

The empire of the West in time became the weaker and the smaller of the two; for the Caledonians in Britain, the Germans along the Rhine, the Goths and Huns along the Danube, and the Moors in Africa were little by little invading its territory and taking possession of its cities.

As the two princes were themselves too young to govern, the power was wielded by their guardians, Stilicho and Rufinus, who quarreled and finally fought against each other. The national jealousy which had always existed between the Greeks and the Latins was increased by these quarrels; it did not come to an end even when Rufinus was slain.

When the Goths saw that the empires of the East and the West were too busy quarreling with each other to pay any attention to them, they suddenly marched into Greece under Alaric.

The Greeks, in terror, implored Stilicho to hasten to their rescue. He came, and won a victory over the Goths, pursuing them to the mountains and, for that time, saving Rome; but, instead of following up his advantage, he soon returned to Italy. The Goths, seeing this, soon followed him there and laid siege to Milan.

Stilicho raised an army as quickly as possible and defeated the Goths. But the Goths, although defeated, secured favorable terms before they withdrew.

Honorius, the emperor of the West, was a cowardly boy and had been very badly frightened by the appearance of the Goths in Italy. In his terror, he changed his residence to the city of Ravenna, where he fancied that he could better defend himself if they attacked him.

Sieges of Rome

by Helene A. Guerber

The Goths had scarcely gone when some other barbarians made an invasion, and this time Florence was besieged. The town held out bravely until Stilicho could come to its rescue, and then the invaders were all captured, and either slain or sold into slavery.

Shortly after this, however, Stilicho was murdered by the soldiers whom he had so often led to victory. The news of trouble among the Romans greatly pleased Alaric, the King of the Goths; and, when the money which Stilicho had promised him failed to come, he made a second raid into Italy.

This time Alaric swept on unchecked to the very gates of Rome, which no barbarian army had entered since the Gauls had visited it about eight hundred years before. The walls were very strong, and the Goths saw at once that the city could not be taken by force, but Alaric thought that it might surrender through famine.

A blockade was begun. The Romans suffered greatly from hunger, and soon a pestilence ravaged the city. To induce the Goths to depart, the Romans finally offered a large bribe; but, as all the money was not promptly paid, Alaric returned and marched into Rome.

Again, promises were made, but not kept, and Alaric came back to the city a third time in 410. This time, the Goths sacked the city of Rome, and Alaric allowed his men to plunder and pillage as much as they pleased. Then he raided all the southern part of Italy and was about to cross over to Sicily when he was taken ill and died.

THE HUNS

by Helene A. Guerber

Both the Teutonic settlers and the Roman Empire itself were threatened by the fierce tribes of Huns. These Asiatic nomads became a united people under their leader, Attila, their terrible king who was called the "Scourge of God." The Huns overran the fertile lands of the Goths and ravaged the Roman land far and wide. By paying a yearly tribute to these barbarians, the Romans managed for a time to keep them out of the empire and pursue their ravages elsewhere.

But after becoming master of most of the territory beyond the Danube and the Rhine, Attila led his hordes of fierce Huns and other barbarians, numbering more than seven hundred thousand men, over the Rhine, and into the very heart of France. There, not far from Chalons, France, one of the fiercest and most important battles of Europe took place.

Attila was defeated with great loss by the united forces of the Romans, Goths, and Franks. But Attila himself escaped, and the next year, advanced with fresh hordes over the Alps and down into the fertile plains of Italy.

Nothing was done to oppose him by the terrified Emperor and people, and he was crossing the rich plain of Lombardy when Pope Leo the Great came forward to withstand the haughty conqueror. Here, vested in his pontifical robes, the bishop of Rome met Attila and succeeded in inducing him to spare Rome and leave Italy.

The Romans rejoiced at their recovered safety, but soon forgot their deliverer's warning – that they had been thus threatened on account of their wickedness, and that if they did not repent, God's judgments would overtake them. These foreboding words would come to pass all too quickly.

Pope Saint Leo and the Heresy of Eutychianism

by the Sisters of Notre Dame

Eutyches, an aged priest, who lived in a monastery near Constantinople, while opposing Nestorianism, fell into an opposite heresy and taught that Jesus Christ had only one nature, which was a mixture of the divine and human. He was deposed and excommunicated, and his teachings were condemned as heresy.

When Pope Leo the Great heard what had been done, he wrote approving of these acts and explaining the Catholic doctrine about the two natures in Christ. This letter is known as the "Dogmatic Epistle" of St. Leo.

The Emperor of the East tried to undermine Leo's teachings, but when a council of bishops read the Dogmatic Epistle, they all exclaimed, "This is the faith of the Apostles; Peter has spoken by the mouth of Leo!"

But although the teaching of Eutyches was thus condemned by the Church, several Eastern Emperors continued to favor it, and the heresy continued to spread so that it was again condemned at the General Council of Constantinople, 553. After this it gradually died out, except in a few districts where it still exists today.

End of the Empire of the West

by Helene A. Guerber

A few years after the death of the terrible Attila, Valentinian, the Western emperor was murdered. During the next twenty years, nine emperors reigned and there were troubles and wars without end.

The people were very superstitious in those times; and, as their troubles increased, someone suddenly remembered that Romulus, the founder of Rome, had seen twelve vultures. The report was soon spread all over the country that these twelve vultures represented as many centuries, and that, as Rome had been founded about twelve hundred years before, its rule would soon be at an end.

In the course of these twenty years, Genseric, King of the Vandals, another Teutonic tribe, came over from Africa into Italy. Pope Leo's words came true only four years after they were uttered. Genseric captured Rome and allowed his soldiers to pillage it for fourteen days. St. Leo interceded for the people but could only obtain the promise that the lives of the Romans and the most important monuments of the city should be spared. Despite his promise, Genseric's barbarians carried off many beautiful works of art, and as his men were very rough indeed, they destroyed many things which they could not carry away.

The Western Roman emperors at this time were a worthless set of men. The last was named Romulus Augustulus. After his death, the Senate voted that one emperor was enough, and said that Zeno, the East Roman Emperor, should rule over the whole Empire.

But this union was in name only, for Zeno was forced to allow Odoacer, a Teutonic chief, to reign over Italy with the title of *Patrician*.

Thus, ended the great Roman Empire in 476. Rome, which had been founded by one Romulus, was stripped of its glory under another emperor of the same name, after having ruled nearly all the known world for hundreds of years.

The Roman senate, seeing that the empire of the Western was ended, now sent the tiara and purple robes to Constantinople, where the Eastern Empire continued until the city fell into the hands of the Muslim Turks in 1453.

But the old Roman laws and names went on long after the wide Roman provinces had passed into the hands of a number of Teutonic chiefs and had been broken up into small states. These smaller states, however, gradually became new kingdoms, while the old inhabitants were either enslaved or driven away, and the conquerors settled down as lords and rulers. Thus, from the ruins of the vast Roman Empire, arose the modern European states and nations.

THE RISE OF THE FRANKS

by Henrietta E. Marshall

At the beginning of the fifth century, the Franks were among the many tribes of Teutonic origin who helped to dismember the Roman Empire. They took possession of part of Gaul, which, in time, became known as Frankland, and which formed the nucleus of the state which we know today as France. When the Franks invaded the Empire they did so in a manner different from that of the other Teutons. They did not cut themselves off from Germany. They did not wander far into the Empire, making conquests now here, now there. They simply crossed the border and taking possession of a small portion, settled there.

Nor were they like the Goths and Vandals a single people who marched to war in a body. They were made up of various tribes who moved about independently of each other and who settled in various places. Their great strength lay in the fact that they kept their line of communication open. While plundering the Empire they still kept in touch with the great unexploited forces of the heathen world behind them.

The chief of these Frankish tribes were the Salians and the Riparians, who settled in what is now Belgium And it was the Salian Franks which at length became the dominant tribe. Their first king of any account was Clovis. He traced his descent from a mythical sea-king called Merovde, and from that, the dynasty to which he belonged is called the Merovingian dynasty.

Clovis came to the throne at the age of sixteen. He soon set out upon a career of conquest, and in no long time doubled and trebled his kingdom.

At the time of their invasion of the Empire, nearly all the Teutonic tribes were Christian. But they were Arian Christians—that is, they were followers of Arius. It was easier for the uneducated Teutons to understand this doctrine than the more complicated one of the Trinity, and therefore they adopted it.

It may not seem to matter very much what those half-civilized tribes believed. But in the reconstruction of Europe after the fall of the Roman Empire, it had some importance. Although most of the barbarians who attacked the Empire were Christian, some were not. Among those who were not were the Angles and the Saxons, who took possession of England, and the Franks.

Clovis, like the people over whom he ruled, was a heathen, but he married a Christian princess, Clotilda, the niece of the King of Burgundy. And this Clotilda was not an Arian like her uncle, but a Catholic. She was very devout, and she tried very earnestly to convert her heathen husband. But Clovis resisted all her efforts. He allowed her undisturbed to follow her religion, but he was satisfied with his own gods and refused to change. At last, however, Clotilda had her wish.

Clovis was fighting against the Alemanni, and in the Battle of Tolbiac, his soldiers were being beaten. Fervently he called upon his heathen gods to save him, and turn the fortune of the day in his favor. His prayers were in vain, and the Franks fled before the foe. Then, in the agony of defeat, Clovis prayed to Clotilda's God.

"Jesus Christ," he cried, "whom Clotilda declares to be the only true God, aid me. If Thou will grant me victory over my enemies I will believe in Thee and will be baptized in Thy name. I have called upon my own gods and they have not helped me. To Thee alone I pray."

As Clovis so prayed the tide of the battle turned, and when night fell the victory was his, and the enemy fled in all directions. Returning home, the king loyally kept his word. The water of baptism was sprinkled upon him, his forehead received the sign of the Cross, and henceforth he was a Christian. Nor was Clovis alone in his baptism. With him, three hundred of his followers were baptized.

This sudden and wholesale conversion made little difference in the lives of Clovis and his tameless warriors. After, as before, they were barbarians. But much of the king's future success was due to his conversion. For it brought him a powerful friend in the Church and when he conquered the Arian kings of the Visigoths and the Burgundians, the great prelates looked upon him as a champion of the Church. Thus began an alliance between the popes and the kings of France which in days to come had a great influence upon the history of western Europe.

Even the emperor in far off Constantinople honored Clovis. Instead of regarding him as a barbarian enemy, assisting at the destruction of the Empire, he looked upon him as an ally and gave him the title of Roman Consul. It was but an empty title and added nothing to the reality of the Frankish king's conquests, but it pleased him.

Clovis reigned for thirty years. At the beginning of his reign, he had been merely the chief of a petty tribe. When he died he was the ruler of a vast kingdom stretching from beyond the Rhine to the Pyrenees.

Saint Clotilda, Wife of Clovis

by E.C. Donnelly

It is to Queen Clotilda that France owes the peerless and priceless title of Eldest Daughter of the Church. That humble, pious, and fervent queen was the spouse of the pagan king Clovis. She urged her husband to become a Christian and paved the way to that grace by her prayers and good example. At the battle of Tolbiac, when Clovis was on the point of defeat, his troops already beginning to fly before the foe, the king received a sudden inspiration and responded to it. "God of Clotilda," he cried, "if You give me the victory, I will become a Christian." Immediately the tide of battle was turned in his favor, and Clovis was true to his word. The gentle queen, happy in the fulfillment of her dearest hopes, died at Tours in 543.

Saint Patrick

by E.M. Tappan, Ph. D.

A few years before Alaric invaded Italy, a boy was born in Britain who was to become the famous Saint Patrick. It was a wild, rude country. There were bears and wolves and wild boars. It was damp and cold; there was much fog and little sunshine. There were worse troubles than a disagreeable climate, for pirates from Ireland or Caledonia sometimes dashed up to the shore, made savage forays into the country, and sailed away with bands of captives to be sold as slaves. This fate befell Patrick when a boy of about sixteen. For several years he was a slave in Ireland and spent much of his time tending cattle. He had been brought up as a Christian, and as he watched his cattle on the hills, he prayed, some days a hundred times.

At length, there was a chance to escape, and he fled to his home. All his kindred welcomed him and begged him, now that he was rescued from such great dangers, never to go away. Still, his heart was with the Irish. He dreamt one night that a man held before him a letter which began, "The Voice of the Irish"; as he read, he seemed to hear the people who dwelt by the western ocean calling, "Come and dwell with us," and he made up his mind to spend his life preaching to them.

When the time had come that he felt prepared, he returned to the island where he had been a captive. Other preachers went with him, and they traveled up and down the land, telling the people everywhere of the religion of Christ.

Generally, the people were willing to listen to the strangers, nevertheless, the lives of the missionaries were often in danger. The chiefs were always at war among themselves, and it was not safe to go from one district to another without an escort. In one place, the people thought the long, narrow writing tablets of the preachers were straight swords, and that they had come to make trouble. It was some little time before they could be made to understand that the strangers were their friends. There is a story that at one time the missionaries were in danger from Laoghaire, the chief king. At twilight, King Laoghaire went out with his nobles to light the fire of the spring festival. But on a high hill, he saw another fire. It was forbidden on pain of death that anyone else should kindle a fire so long as the king's was burning, and Laoghaire sent men to learn who these daring strangers were and to bring them before him.

The missionaries told the king that their fire was not to celebrate the coming of spring, but Easter and the resurrection of Christ. He listened closely, and finally gave them permission to preach to his people.

For many years Saint Patrick preached and taught and built churches and schoolhouses and monasteries. These monasteries, and others that were founded not long afterward, became the most famous schools of the age. Thousands of pupils came to them from the neighboring countries; and from these seats of learning and piety, earnest teachers and missionaries went forth, not only to Britain but to every corner of Europe. This is the work that was begun by one fearless, faithful, unselfish man.

Unit Six: Light Shines in the Darkness

THEME: HOPE AND LIGHT

Saint Columba

by the Sisters of Notre Dame

The pagan Saxons did not find their way to Ireland, where the faith planted by St. Patrick ever continued to take stronger root among the people. Thus, during the centuries when England was being won back again to the Church, the sister isle had but to multiply her churches and monasteries. These last became so famous that they were thronged by scholars from every land, and it often happened that the inhabitants of a monastery could be counted by thousands, with a still larger number of scholars.

Perhaps the most wonderful work done by the Irish monks was the copying of the Holy Scripture and of other valuable books, in which many of them passed their lives. Their chronicles, too, are of great value, many being written in fine old Celtic verse. Their marvelous skill in ornamenting the sacred volumes they had transcribed excites admiration to this day. The most famous of these manuscripts still in existence is the Book of Kells now in Trinity College in Dublin, Ireland.

Sanctity and learning produced their usual fruit, a great zeal for souls. From Irish monasteries, for more than two hundred years, there poured a continual stream of missionary monks. There is hardly a nation of Western Europe that does not venerate among its first apostles the memory of Irish saints. Central Scotland owes to them its faith; Northern England its restoration to the Church. We have seen St. Columban and his monks at work among the Burgundians, while Belgians, Lombards, Swiss, and the people of the neighboring countries, all owe to them their entrance into the Church.

Still greater works of zeal would have been possible had it not been for civil warfare among the Irish chieftains. It was because of these disputes that the famous St. Columba was exiled to Scotland. Monk though he was, Columba was still a soldier at heart. He had excited his kinsfolk to fight desperately, many had been killed, and Columba was excommunicated. The sentence, however, was shortly after revoked; but Columba was torn with remorse. The monk to whom he confessed his crime laid on him as penance perpetual exile from his beloved Ireland. With twelve companions he set out, and at last settled in the tiny island of Iona - a rocky, barren spot off the coast of the great island of Mull near the western coast of Scotland. Here he established a monastery and received those who came to him for instruction or relief.

Columba's monks went forth into all the neighboring countries, preaching and winning the people to the faith. None was so successful as the saint himself in drawing numbers into the Church. The fierce, hot spirit of a warrior was softened and sweetened into the unconquerable zeal of an apostle whom no danger could appeal. The monks built numbers of small coracles or boats, in which they crossed all the numerous straits and firths of the rugged Scottish coast. They ventured far out to sea, visiting the Hebrides, Orkney, and Shetland Islands. Even the Faroe Isles must have been reached by them, for Irish crosses, bells, and other remains, have been found there. In every important place, Columba built a church, and, of course, a monastery. In each, a fervent band of missionaries would settle, and gradually win the neighboring peoples to the faith. It is said that nearly a hundred old churches can trace their foundation to St. Columba or his monks.

In many of his churches, Columba established Bishops. The Abbot of Iona was supreme over all the dioceses founded by Columba. This form of Church government was set up in nearly all Celtic or Irish sees. Until the end of the seventh century, even in England as well as in Scotland and Ireland, the Abbot of Iona was the Superior, not only of all monasteries but also of the bishoprics. This was because every Bishop was a monk, and they clung firmly to obedience to their religious Superior.

For the good of the monks left in Ireland, St. Columba consented to return to his land, whenever his presence was needed. All the northern Irish monasteries acknowledged his supremacy. On one occasion he was the means of establishing peace between Ireland and Scotland. One of the northern Irish Kings claimed the right of headship over the Scottish chieftains. St. Columba convinced him to give up his demand and to acknowledge the independence of King Aidan the Scot.

The story of Ireland in the next century can be told in a few words. Times of peace are not rich in events, and so though this part of Church history is the most glorious in the pages of Irish records, there is little to tell beyond the constant multiplication of Irish monasteries and of Irish scholars, while the bare list of her saints would fill several pages.

King Aidan, named above, was the first King who received consecration in Scotland. The stone on which Aidan was consecrated in the Isle of Iona has become famous. It was placed in Scone Abbey, and here all Scottish kings were crowned till Edward I carried it off in 1296. It now forms part of the coronation chair of the English Sovereigns and is kept in Westminster Abbey in London. Aidan ruled over the central tribes and was a devoted helper of St. Columba.

Towards the close of his life, Columba made a state visit to St. Kentigern at Glasgow. This great man had been making many converts among the mixed tribes of Scots and Britons who inhabited the country. A fine monastery sprang up, and from it St. Kentigern's monks went forth to convert the people. Like Columba's missionaries, the disciples of St. Kentigern were to be found in all the islands lining the coast. Then Columba, desirous to see a man who had done so much for Scotland, went, attended by a train of monks. St. Kentigern advanced to meet him with all his community. Both sets were divided into three bands, the youthful, the middle-aged, and the aged, among whose ranks the two saints took their places. After discussing the best way of spreading the faith and establishing it solidly among the Scottish people, the two apostles parted.

St. Columba did not survive long. He foretold the time of his death and was found lying before the altar, giving up his soul in peace. It was in 596, just before St. Augustine of Canterbury landed in England. The saint's work was continued by his disciples, but hardly a record of their labor remains. The terrible affliction which befell the Church in England and Scotland at the end of this period - the invasion of the Danes - swept away every trace of the work of St. Columba in Scotland.

The Barbarians and Monasticism

by the Sisters of Notre Dame

The great Teutonic, Gothic, or Germanic branch of the human race, which during the fifth and sixth centuries overran Europe, was made up of several distinct peoples. Little by little they divided among them the broad Roman Empire, but not by any friendly arrangement; each tribe seized what it could and kept possession by force unless driven off by some more powerful newcomers. As time went on, the different European nations began to be formed, and it is possible to say to which tribes each owes its origin, though the countries did not have the same boundaries or names as they have now and the people of today are not necessarily the direct descendants of these old Gothic tribes alone. Indeed, we have only to think of English history to learn how sometimes many nations combine to make up one people.

The principal tribes and the nations they founded are somewhat as follows:

- The *Ostrogoths*, or Eastern Goths, who first occupied the north of Italy, and who later were driven back to Hungary and Turkey.
- The *Visigoths*, or Western Goths, who settled in Spain and in the south of France.
- The *Franks*, who occupied a tract of country comprising the north of France and Germany as far as the Rhine.
- The *Burgundians*, who conquered the south-east of France.
- The *Vandals*, who settled first in Spain and then in North Africa.
- The *Angles* and *Saxons*, who spread over the south of Denmark, that part of northern Germany to the east of the Rhine, and into Britain.
- The *Scandinavians*, or Danes, the conquerors of Norway, Sweden, and North Denmark; and
- The *Lombards*, the last comers, who occupied first Hungary and then advanced into

the north of Italy, from which they drove out the former occupants, the Ostrogoths.

Except for the Franks, Angles, Saxons, and Scandinavians, who were heathens, all the Teutonic invaders were Arians – believers in the heresy that Jesus was not God but was created by God. In the early fourth century, when Arianism was at its height. An Arian Bishop at Constantinople attempted to convert the Gothic people. He invented the Gothic alphabet and translated the Bible for their use. All these bold warriors were therefore converted, not to Catholic Christianity, but to Arian Christianity, and whenever they conquered and settled, they took their belief with them.

The fate of the conquered peoples was not the same everywhere. Where the invaders were pagans, or where they met with fierce resistance, they swept everything before them: the inhabitants were massacred, driven away, or reduced to slavery, churches and homesteads were destroyed, and whole tracts of land were laid desolate. This was notably the case in Britain and the North of Europe. But where the invaders were Arian, they generally settled down among the conquered peoples, leaving them a portion of their goods, and in some cases their form of government also. The newcomers mingled their language with that of the former Roman possessors of the soil and formed a new nation by blending the conquering and conquered nations. The vigorous character of the Germanic invaders, especially where not spoiled by the influence of heresy, their fierce contempt for cowardice of any kind, their respect for law, and their reverence for women, produced their best results when brought under the influence of the Church. Hardly had the invaders settled down in the conquered land than we find apostles busily at work, living saintly lives among them, preaching to them and winning them to the fold of Christ, although in some cases the Arians succeeded for a time, by persecution, in imposing their belief on the conquered people. It is most remarkable how these bold Teutons respected the courage of the missionaries; persecution of the faith is hardly seen through their history, and the martyrs who suffered at their hands are very few indeed when compared with those put to death under the Roman Empire.

Side by side, both the faith and civilization were planted, for the Church has always worked this way. Her missionaries labored to soften the manners of the wild tribes among whom they settled and to teach them all the useful arts of a peaceful life. To turn hordes of savage barbarians into order-loving and civilized nations was, however, in some places the work of centuries. The influence which accomplished this happy change was the monastic institutions and the power of the popes. The revival of learning which marked the sixth and seventh centuries can be attributed to the use of the Latin tongue in the liturgy of the Church. Thus, as one historian said, "Religion made a bridge across the chaos, and linked the periods of ancient and modern cultures."

Saint Benedict

by the Sisters of Notre Dame

After the fall of the Roman Empire, many monastic institutes arose in the West, but the most important was the order founded by St. Benedict, whose rule they all adopted as years went on.

The story of St. Benedict is beautifully told by St. Gregory the Great, himself a Benedictine monk. About the year 480, St. Benedict was born to parents of a high social class at Nursia, Italy. While very young, he was taken to Rome to attend the public schools. It was not long before the boy saw that the lives of his masters and companions would lead him into evil, and he fled from the danger and hid in a desert place about thirty miles from Rome. On the rocky slopes overhanging the little town of Subiaco was a small lake fed by mountain streams, and somewhat higher up, almost inaccessible, there was a deep and narrow cavern. This was shown to Benedict by a monk from a neighboring monastery, named Romanus, who, seeing the fervor of the boy, helped him in his desire of leading a holy and solitary life.

For three years young Benedict dwelt alone in this desolate spot, unknown to all but Romanus, spending his time in prayer and fasting and in resisting the attempts of the Evil One to make him give up his holy purpose. At length, he was discovered. People of every rank and nation flocked to him for instruction and guidance, and gradually the fame of his sanctity spread to distant lands. After some years he was chosen abbot by the monks of a neighboring monastery. St. Benedict consented with reluctance to accept the duty; but before long, he found that the monks were not willing to live according to his views of perfection and sanctity. They were even trying to poison him, so he left them and returned to his solitude at Subiaco.

Here so many disciples gathered around him that he needed to build a monastery to receive them. As time went on, and still more came to follow his Rule, he founded one little monastery after another, till they were twelve, scattered about the heights of Subiaco. The monks themselves labored at the buildings, which were very poor and simple; they tilled the neighboring lands and lived on the produce of their toil. Many persons of noble birth brought their sons to St. Benedict, begging him to educate them. This was the beginning of monastic schools for children.

But it was not until 529 that the most famous part of St. Benedict's career began. Cruel and wicked persecution against the holy monks of Subiaco caused St. Benedict to withdraw with all his monks from the first cradle of his Order, and to settle with them in the mountain region of Cassino. After destroying an idol of Apollo that was still venerated by the ignorant people around, St. Benedict built on the summit of the high hill the celebrated monastery which, frequently ruined and as often rebuilt, exists to the present day. Already some of his monks had carried the faith afar, but it was only after the foundation of Monte Cassino that the actual spread of the Order commenced. Groups of fervent monks were sent out to settle among distant peoples to begin the work of conversion and civilization which has made their name so famous.

It was here that St. Benedict drew up his Rule, the fruit of long years of sanctity and experience. Before his death, St. Benedict had a remarkable vision, in which the future glory of his Order was shown to him, as well as the trials to which it would be exposed.

St. Scholastica. The last days of the Saint were so filled with deeds of holiness and with miracles that it would be impossible even to name them here. Almost the last event that is told of the life of St. Benedict is his meeting with his sister, St. Scholastica, who, wishing to keep him a little longer with her to talk of holy things, obtained by prayer a miraculous storm of rain that forced him to remain that night in the little house where they had met.

St. Scholastica died a few days later, and St. Benedict did not long survive his holy sister. Forewarned of his death, he instructed all to be ready. When the day came, he ordered his monks to carry him to the church. At the foot of the altar he received the last Sacraments, and, supported by his sorrowful spiritual children, he stood praying until his soul took its flight to heaven, 543.

The Spread of Monasticism

by the Sisters of Notre Dame

The spread of the Benedictine Order was very rapid. Monasteries soon covered the land in Italy, Sicily, France, England, and Germany, especially in places where there were no monasteries founded by the Irish Saint Columban. Benedictine monasteries took longer to be established in Spain, but once they were introduced, they multiplied extensively. Wherever the monks settled, they drained the marshes, cut down woods, tilled the barren lands, and built a monastery with its church and schools.

The great Benedictine monasteries were all built on the same general plan, which was only that of an ancient Roman villa, much enlarged and with a church added. The covered peristyle became the cloisters, around which the principal community rooms were grouped, and into which, they all opened. Instead of the magnificent garden of Roman days, with its fountains and statuary, the abbey had its cemetery with a great central crucifix. The monastic enclosure, like the Roman villa, contained workshops, where the monks carried out every trade needed to support and cloth themselves. So, it was that in the monasteries every useful trade and every art known at the time was practiced, every science was studied, and all were brought to high perfection.

Villages sprang up on and around the abbey lands, for in those turbulent times the dwellers near a monastery enjoyed a peace not known on the estates of the great nobles, who were always feuding with one another. On the monastery lands, numerous flocks were raised, whose wool the monks taught the people to weave into cloth, and whose skins furnished the monastery with parchment for books. These were written by hand; the margins of the pages were painted in colors and gold with marvelous skill. Great works, like the Holy Scriptures and the Divine Office, were often bound in covers rich with metalwork, inlaid with enamels, and embossed with jewelry. All the monasteries had well-stocked libraries – for instance, that of Rheims [France] possessed 6,000 volumes, all written by hand. The great library of York [England] was especially famous.

Other monks kept chronicles or wrote learned books. Almost all we know of the history of these times is drawn from the writings of these busy monks of old. Much of this literary work was carried on in a great hall called the scriptorium, where each monk had a little cell to himself to write and study in. The heavier work, such as carving, metalworking, bell founding, sculpting, and the making of glass, was done in the "*Opera*," or workshop. Here, too, music was practiced. Thus, the name we now use for one kind of musical composition recalls the old days when the monks practiced their sacred songs in the great halls of their monastic dwellings.

But this was not all. Every monastery had its school, where the best learning the age could give was to be had by all, and for no cost. Some universities which are still famous in our own days owe their beginnings to these schools. It is said that Oxford and Paris among others, can trace their origin to a Benedictine monastic school.

A guest house was invariably attached to each monastery. Here, travelers of every rank were entertained and lodged, and the poor were fed. The building called the "Abbot's kitchen" was where the food for the guests was prepared, separate from the more frugal food of the community itself.

Monasteries, too, always had their herb garden, in which were grown the materials for the simple medicines used in those days. These were freely distributed at the abbey gates, where the poor flocked for help in their need, both of soul and body.

The power for good of such an Order as the Benedictine may be guessed when we remember that at the time of its greatest development it numbered 37,000 monasteries and colleges; that during following centuries it has given birth to thousands of canonized Saints and martyrs; that innumerable bishops have been trained in its cloisters; and that it has given about thirty popes to the Christian world.

Pope Saint Gregory the Great

by the Sisters of Notre Dame

We have seen what monks did for Europe; it remains to study the work of the popes. The supremacy of the popes was recognized by all Catholic peoples and was of immense influence in bringing order and peace to the nations. The popes never ceased urging kings to govern justly and to be merciful to the conquered. They made useful laws and regulations to restrain the undue use of power by nobles and other superiors; their voice was ever heard in defense of the weak, the poor, and the suffering. Constant communication with Rome was kept up by nations of Europe, and the pope's decrees were received as law by all. If on no other subject there was agreement, yet in faith, and in the language of the Church, Europe was one. It is impossible but that this must have greatly tended to promote the order and peace that are necessary for real progress and civilization.

What the power of a pope for good was will be best seen by following the career of one of the most celebrated of the early medieval pontiffs. Gregory I, now referred to as Gregory the Great, was elected pope in 590. He was of the same noble and wealthy family as St. Benedict. After a brilliant career as Praetor of Rome, he determined to give up the world. He founded seven great monasteries on his estates and placed Benedictine monks in each. He entered the last of his foundations, St. Andrew in Rome. There he lived as a most saintly religious until Pope Benedict I made him one of the Cardinal Deacons of Rome in 575. The next pope sent Gregory as Ambassador to Constantinople, where he remained six years, after which he gladly returned to his beloved monastery, of which he was soon chosen to be the abbot.

It was at this time that the well-known incident occurred in the slave-market which led to the conversion of England. Gregory was so touched at the thought of the sad state of the fair Angle slaves, that with the pope's permission, he started for England with several monks to preach the true faith to those distant islanders. But the Roman people raised such an outcry at finding he was gone that the pope had to send for him to come back.

This pope, Pelagius II, died in 590, and to his intense distress, Gregory was immediately elected in his place. But his sorrow did not prevent him from working hard for the flock committed to his care. It was in a sad state. Arianism reigned throughout all the countries bordering on the Mediterranean. England, Germany, and the lands around the North Sea and Baltic were still pagan. The Franks alone had received the faith, but they were still only half converted. Besides this, the Eastern Emperors continually sought to oppress the Church and harass the popes in the exercise of their sacred duties.

Pope Gregory labored long and earnestly at the conversion of all the heretical and pagan nations of Europe, sending missionaries or encouraging the clergy already at work, writing numerous letters, and sending instructions to bishops and exhortations to sovereigns. He had the happiness of seeing the Lombards, the Spaniards, the Portuguese, and the English enter the true fold. These glorious gains to the Church were the fruit of his zeal.

But this was only a part of his labors. No kind of need escaped his vigilant care. The ill-used slaves, peasantry, and Jews found in him a protector and a friend. His love for the poor was unbounded; he founded orphanages, schools for the poor, and refuges for the aged – the first establishment of the kind we read of in history.

Gregory will always be remembered for his connection with sacred music. The Church's chant, known as the Gregorian, was arranged by him. Men flocked from all nations to the school of music which he founded in Rome, and for ages, the study of sacred song was one of the important parts of a boy's education.

This great pope, the first monk who sat in the chair of St. Peter, promoted the welfare of monastic orders with all the weight of his authority and sanctity. He solemnly confirmed the Rule of St. Benedict and watched over the interests of all the monasteries of the East and the West. To the last day of his life, his one regret was that he could no longer enjoy the peaceful life of the cloister which he loved so dearly.

This life of incessant toil and vigilant care for the whole Church was passed in a state of severe and almost constant suffering. After fourteen years of pontificate, he died in 604. He is truly Gregory the Great, not only because of the lands he conquered for the Church, the power he won for the Holy See, but "for the renown of his virtue, the candor of his innocence, the humble and inexhaustible tenderness of his heart."

Saint Augustine of Canterbury

by Rev. D. Chisholm

Apostle to the Anglo-Saxons

The great Pope Gregory, knowing the sad state in which the Christian religion had been placed in Great Britain since the Anglo-Saxons had obtained the government of that kingdom, decided to send missionaries there who would instruct the people in the law of God. He himself chose forty monks and placed at their head Augustine, the Superior of the Monastery of St. Andrew in Rome.

These missionaries went forth with great enthusiasm; but after a few days journey they became discouraged, for they heard from people on the way of the barbarity of that nation, the difficulties they would meet on their long journey there, and the impossibility of making themselves understood by those who did not know the language they spoke. They hesitated to continue their journey, and begged Augustine to return to Rome, and tell Pope Gregory what they had heard, and beg him not to insist on their undertaking this perilous mission, especially as the success of it was so uncertain.

The pope sent Augustine back with a letter to them, in which he commanded them not to fear on the way, but to persevere with zeal in the accomplishment of the work entrusted to them.

Augustine and his companions, having passed through France, traveled on the narrow strait which separated them from the place of their future labors, and in a short time, they landed on the Island of Thanet.

The Angles and the Saxons, who lived in that part of Europe now called Germany, had become masters of the southern part of Britain, and had divided the country into seven kingdoms; one of these was Kent, which, although not large, was important because of its location. Ethelbert, the first king of that country, was married to Princess Bertha, daughter of Caribert, King of Paris, who had consented to this union only on condition of his daughter having the freedom of living her Christian religion.

Immediately on his arrival at Thanet, Augustine sent interpreters whom he brought with him from France to the king of Kent, as Pope Gregory had told him to do. The French and the Anglo-Saxons spoke a language that they both understood, but Augustine could only speak in the Latin language. These messengers were graciously received by the monarch; they informed him that Augustine had come from Rome to announce to him and his people the good tidings of the Gospel, the knowledge of the true God, and the promise of a Kingdom which would never end.

Ethelbert wanted to have a little time to consider the nature of their mission, and in the meantime gave orders that they should be entertained with great hospitality; this he did more willingly because Bertha the Queen professed the same Faith.

Then the king went into a wide plain, where he could receive them in the open air because he was filled with fear of any magical influence. The missionaries then went forward to meet the king in solemn procession, headed by a cross-bearer carrying aloft a silver Crucifix and a picture representing Our Divine Lord, while they sang hymns and litanies.

When the king had signed to them to sit down upon the grass, Augustine went forward to the monarch, and spoke to him through an interpreter:

"I have come here, O King, to teach you how you may reign after your death, even as you reign now, but in a glory far surpassing all earthly glory, because here on earth you may lose your crown, since you are surrounded by so many enemies, whereas in Heaven you shall have nothing to fear, and your joy will be everlasting."

"That is a beautiful speech, "answered the king, " and these are splendid promises, but as they are very uncertain, I cannot bring myself to trust in them, or to give up the practice which I have so long followed, and which is that of all my people. Nevertheless, since you have come so great a distance, and since, it seems to me, that you desire to share with others the knowledge of what you consider to be the truth, I will not hinder you from receiving into your religion those of my subjects whom you may be able to gain, and it is my will that my people shall provide you with all that is necessary for your comfort and support."

The missionaries having thus received the authorization of the king began their work at once. They imitated the Apostles in their zeal to propagate the truth, and were prepared to suffer, if necessary, for the "Faith that was in them." They entered in procession into Canterbury, the capital of the kingdom, singing these words: "We beseech Thee, O Lord, to turn away Thy wrath from this city, for we have sinned against Thee."

Many of the people, moved by the grace of God and the simplicity and virtues of these apostles of the truth, believed in their words and asked to be baptized. The king himself in a short time was converted and received the Sacrament of Baptism. His example led many others to embrace the Faith, but, knowing that faith is a gift of God, he was careful not to compel anyone to become a Christian unless that person was convinced of the truths of Christianity.

St. Augustine of Canterbury died on May 26, 607.

Caedmon, the First English Poet

by Eva March Tappan, Ph. D.

Churches and convents soon began to rise in England. One of these convents was on a cliff at Whitby, far up on the northeast shore of England. It was the custom at the feasts for each one, in turn, to take the harp and sing verses that he either composed or remembered. There is a legend that Caedmon, one of the dwellers at this convent, felt so disgraced because he could not sing any verses that, when the harp was coming near him, he slipped away and went to the stable. In a dream, he heard a voice saying, "Caedmon, sing!"

"But I cannot sing," he said, "and that is why I came away from the feast."

"You must sing for me," said the voice.

"What shall I sing?" asked Caedmon.

"Sing about the creation of the world," answered the voice.

Caedmon sang, and when he awoke, he found that he had not forgotten the verses. The abbess was told of the wonderful dream, and, after Caedmon had made more verses, she concluded that the new power that had come to him was a gift from God. His poem is about the creation and is a kind of paraphrase of the Book of Genesis. This is, so far as we know, the first poetry that was written in England.

Venerable Bede, the First Writer of English History

by Eva March Tappan, Ph. D.

For the first prose, we must turn to a monk whose name was Bede. He must have been one of the busiest of people, for this convent was also a great school. There were six hundred monks, and no one knows how many other men who came there to study. Bede helped to teach these men; he performed all the religious duties that belonged to a monk, and he also shared in all the work of the farm. He says that he enjoyed winnowing and threshing and giving milk to the little lambs and calves.

With all this work, he found time to write much poetry, and many volumes about science, music, and medicine. At length, the king of Northumbria asked him if he would write a history of the church in England, and so it came to pass that he wrote the "Ecclesiastical History." It is almost the only book that tells us about the early days of Britain. We have to select from this what is probably true and what was only hearsay among a people, who were ready to believe anything if it was only wonderful enough. This is the book that says there are no snakes in Ireland, and it goes further, for it says that the smell of the air kills them and that if a person bitten by a serpent will only swallow a few scrapings from an Irish book, he will be cured.

As Latin was the language of the church and of the convent, Bede naturally wrote in Latin; but he wished to put the Bible into English so that the uneducated people might understand it. He worked on this translation till the last day of his life, dictating the Gospel of Saint John to one of his pupils. At last, when evening came, he closed his eyes in weariness. The young man said, "There is one sentence to write, dear master."

"Take your pen and write quickly," said Bede.

"Now it is finished," said the pupil.

"Yes, it is finished," said Bede. He chanted a few words of praise to God and closed his eyes. It is one of his pupils who tells us the story, and we may believe it to be true. It is a great pity that the translation has been lost, for it was the first piece of prose that was written in England.

Bede is often spoken of as the Venerable Bede. "Venerable" is a title of honor not quite so high as that of "saint." It was probably bestowed upon him sometime after his death, but there is a legend that, when he was old, he became blind and had a boy to lead him about. This boy was full of mischief, and one day he led Bede into a desert place and asked him to preach to a great crowd waiting to hear him. Bede preached, and at the end of the sermon, the naughty boy was badly frightened to hear all the stones cry out "Amen, Venerable Bede! Amen!"

Justinian's Empire

by Henrietta E. Marshall

Justinian, one of the greatest rulers of the Eastern Empire, came to power the year after Theodoric died. He was not content with merely ruling over the Eastern Empire; like the Caesars before him, he had dreams of world dominion, and he longed to gather under his scepter all the lands which had once bowed to Rome. He had great generals at his command to help him to realize his dream, among them Belisarius, at this time a brave and splendid youth.

Belisarius and Narses. About this time the Vandals were quarreling among themselves, and it seemed to Justinian a good opportunity to win Africa again for the Empire. So, Belisarius set out with a great army. In a campaign of three months, he conquered the Vandals. Then, laden with riches, and carrying the captive Vandal king with him, he returned to Constantinople in triumph.

At this time, Italy was also in a state of unrest. Here again, Justinian saw his opportunity, and again Belisarius set forth to subdue a rebel province of the Empire. But to conquer the Goths was by no means an easy matter. The war raged for years, and before he could bring it to a victorious end the jealousy of his rivals caused Belisarius to be recalled.

Two years later he returned to Italy. But he was, he said himself, "destitute of all the necessary implements of war – men, horses, arms, and money." And the emperor, still listening to the envious whispers against his general, was deaf to his appeals. So, the war lingered on, until at length Belisarius was again recalled, and his place taken by Narses, another of

Justinian's great generals.

Narses was no young and splendid hero like Belisarius, but an old man. He was, however, the most brilliant strategist of the day, and he received the support denied to Belisarius. His so-called *Roman* army was indeed merely a conglomeration of Greeks and barbarians, but with it, he swept victoriously through Italy.

It was not far from the ancient city of Pompeii that the Goths made their last stand. Their king, Teias, stood at the front of the battle. In his right hand, he held a mighty spear, and with unerring aim, he dealt death this way and that. Although arrows and javelins fell thick and fast about him, he did not heed them. Yet so many found their mark and remained deeply embedded in his shield that, at length, even his mighty arm could not bear the weight.

So, calling to his squire, he told him to bring another shield. The squire obeyed. But for one moment, in changing one shield for another, the king's side was unprotected. At that moment, a javelin pierced Teias's heart, and he fell dying to the ground. With a wild shout of exultation, the enemies rushed forward, and cutting off his head, placed it upon a spear, and carried it in triumph through their ranks.

Thus, died the last king of the Goths. Yet although leaderless now, his men still fought on, and only night and darkness put an end to the strife. The day dawned and the battle was renewed, but the struggle now was hopeless, and at length the Goths demanded peace. This Narses readily granted, giving the conquered people the choice between remaining in Italy as the subjects of Justinian or departing.

The Goths chose to leave their home. And with their women and children and household goods, they slowly crossed the Alps. They went who knows where? From that time the Ostrogoths vanish from history.

But the campaign in Italy was not yet over. For the Franks and Alemanni – a group of German tribes - had poured like a torrent over the Alps into the plain of Italy, vowing to restore the Gothic kingdom. But these, too, Narses defeated, and only a scattered remnant reached home. Then at length, the harassed, exhausted land had peace, and for the next twelve years, Narses ruled over it as governor for the emperor.

Justinian also attacked the Visigoths in Spain and brought all the south and east of that country under Roman rule once more. Indeed, he reconquered so much of the old Roman Empire that it seemed as if his dream might come true. But in 565 he died, and almost at once, fresh hordes of barbarians overran his newly acquired provinces. The Lombards invaded Italy, the Visigoths rose and expelled the Romans from Spain, Slavs, and Avars, wild peoples akin to the Huns, streamed over the Balkans, while Persians, in a war which lasted twenty years, devasted the eastern boundaries of the Empire. Arabs made themselves masters of Egypt and Roman Africa until at length the Eastern Empire included little more than the countries now forming Greece, the Balkan States, and Asia Minor.

Therefore, it is not for his conquests that we remember Justinian, for his conquests soon vanished away. All through the ages, he has been remembered not as a conqueror but as a lawgiver. His great work was the codification of the whole body of Roman law. To this day, the laws of nearly every country are founded on the laws of Justinian, or the Justinian Code. This is his title to greatness.

The size of the Empire became small indeed after Justinian's reign, especially when compared to the expansive Roman Empire in the days of its strength. But this shrunken Empire would play no small role in the development of Europe; for it formed a Christian bulwark against the future attacks from Asia. While the new Teutonic kingdoms were being formed, it was the Romans and not the Teutons who defended Europe from the danger coming from the east.

Besides being a barrier, the Eastern Empire was also a storehouse of art and literature. In their hands, the learning and the art of old Rome were cast off or destroyed. It would have been lost to the world had it not been kept alive in Constantinople. There, too, the trade and commerce of Europe re-centered in this time of flux. And when, in course of time, the new Teutonic kingdoms settled down and the peoples awakened to the need of learning and art, it was to Constantinople that they turned to find them.

But however useful a role the Eastern Empire played in the development of Europe, the old imperial splendor was gone. New Rome was not mistress of the world, but rather its handmaid. And as the old imperial idea changed, the character of the Empire changed too. It was no longer Roman in any sense, but Greek. Greek became the language of State, and even the later laws of Justinian were written in that language. So, although it was legally the continuation of the Roman Empire, it has come to be called the Greek Empire or the Byzantine Empire, from the name of the ancient city of Byzantium, upon which Constantinople was built.

The Rise of Islam

by Henrietta E. Marshall

About four or five years after the death of Justinian the Great, a little boy was born in Mecca and was given the name of Muhammed, or the Praised. This Arab belonged to a princely tribe who traced their descent to Ishmael. They had in their keeping the Kaabah or sacred temple of the Arabs. Kaabah means a cube, and the name was given to the temple because of its shape, which was square. It had only one window and one door, and until the time of Muhammed, it was roofed only by a great black carpet which hung down on all sides.

This temple was said in legend to have been first built by Adam from a plan sent down from heaven. But it had been restored several times, by Seth, by Abraham, and last by Ishmael. Since that time, the tribe to which Muhammed belonged had had it in their keeping. It enshrined a great treasure, for there was a black stone in the north-west corner of the wall which was said to have been brought from paradise. At that time, it was white, but it had since turned black through the many kisses of the people who came to visit it.

It was therefore in a city already held sacred that Muhammed was born. He would cause it to be held still more sacred to the Arabs and would make the name of Mecca famous throughout the whole world.

Muhammed's father died before he was born, and his mother and grandfather died not many years later. He had many uncles, and as they claimed much of his father's fortune there was little left for Muhammed. So, he began life with no more wealth than five camels and a slave girl. But he was fortunate and prospered well. He was a handsome man, broad-shouldered, lithe of limb, with eyes that shone from his fine face. He seemed born to lead and bend others to his will. Yet he was forty years old before he began the career which made him famous.

At this time many people in Arabia were dissatisfied with the worship of idols and were seeking a better religion. Some of Muhammed's friends were among these. He used to talk much with them, and also with the many Jews and Christians who had settled in the land, and from them, he learned something both of the Jewish and the Christian faiths.

Muhammed pondered over these things, and at length, he announced that he had seen a vision and received a revelation from heaven. One day, he said, when he was in a lonely spot, an angel appeared to him with a written scroll in his hand, and said to him, "Read."

Now Muhammed could neither read nor write and in great fear he replied, "I cannot read." At this, the angel shook him wrathfully and again commanded him to read. Again Muhammed, in great fear and trembling, replied, "I cannot read."

Three times this was repeated. Then the angel himself took the scroll and read it to Muhammed, and the words which he heard were so graven upon his heart that he remembered them ever after, and later, when his holy book was made, they became part of it.

Other visions and revelations followed this first one, and at length, Muhammed announced his message to the world. It was very simple. It was merely, "There is but one God and Muhammed is his prophet."

Thus, a new religion was founded which was, in time, to enslave half the world. But at first, few listened to Muhammed. Indeed, for some years he made scarcely any converts other than the women of his own household. But by degrees, slowly at first, and then more rapidly, his followers increased. And as Muhammed's followers increased, visions and revelations increased also. For when the creed required anything to be added, or when any action of the Prophet seemed to need supernatural support, Muhammed had a revelation. What he learned in these, Muhammed dictated to his scribes, who wrote it down on palm leaves, blade bones of animals, bits of parchment, or anything which came to hand. It was not until after the Prophet's death, however, that they were all gathered together into the Koran, or Book of God of the Muslims.

The Hegira. In time, Muhammed had followers all over Arabia. But the men of his own tribe were filled with wrath against him. For, said they, if this fellow preached that there was only one God, what was to become of the Kaabah and its many idols? If the idols fell into disrepute, the keepers of the temple would be ruined. The thousands of pilgrims who flocked every year to the Kaabah would come no more. All the trade which came in their train, which made both the keepers of the temple and Mecca rich and powerful, would be lost. They decided, therefore, that his mouth must be stopped, and persecution began which ended in Muhammed fleeing with his followers to Medina. This is called the Hegira, or Flight, and with it begins the Muslim era.

It was soon after the Hegira that Muhammed began to preach his holy war. He had taken a great deal of his new religion from Judaism and from Christianity. But unlike these religions, which either did not try to make converts or tried to make them peacefully, Muhammed now decided to convert the world with the sword if need be.

So, Muhammed unsheathed his sword, and in less than eight years, he who had fled from Mecca in secrecy and darkness returned in triumph. He entered the Kaabah and ordered it to be cleared of idols. And as one by one they fell beneath the blows of his followers, he cried in exultation, "Truth has come. Falsehood has gone; for falsehood vanishes away."

But although cleared of idols, the Kaabah remained the holy of holies to the followers of Muhammed, and Mecca is still the holy city towards which every Muslim turns when he prays. For Muhammed quickly saw that unless he preserved the sacred character of Mecca, he could never win his fellow countrymen to his creed. During countless ages, they had worshipped at Mecca, and reverence for it was an important part of their culture. So, Muhammed kept Mecca as his holy city. And when the Arabs found that they could confess the new creed and still worship in the Kaabah, thousands became easy converts.

Thus, he who had begun life with no fortune save five camels, and a slave girl made himself master of an empire. Muhammed found Arabia a mass of hostile tribes, each with its own laws, and perpetually at war with every other surrounding tribe. He found it given over to idolatry. In twenty years, he united the warring tribes and made them monotheistic – believing in one God. In twenty years, he created a nation with a national religion and national laws.

But Muhammed's ambition was not bounded by Arabia. He decided to force his religion on people beyond its borders and, even before Mecca had submitted to him, he had ordered that letters be written to the greatest rulers of the world, to the Byzantine emperor, to the king of Persia, and to the rulers of many lesser countries. These letters he sealed with a great seal, engraved with the words "Muhammed, the Apostle of God." In haughty words, he ordered these proud sovereigns to put away their old "idolatrous" religions and do homage to the one God of the Muslims.

But, as yet, the name of Muhammed was hardly known beyond the borders of Arabia, and his haughty letters awoke no thrill of fear in the princes to whom they were addressed. Some of the lesser rulers answered courteously enough, but the greatest among them, the Byzantine Emperor flung the letter contemptuously aside, while the king of Persia, tore his to shreds in fury, and commanded that the insolent Arab be brought to him in chains. When Muhammed heard what kind of reception his letter had received, he, too, was wrathful. He cursed the arrogant king. "Even as he has rent Thy message, O Lord," he cried, "will

Thou rend his kingdom from him."

Indeed, the time was not far distant when both king and emperor were to tremble at the name of the man they had thought an upstart. But Muhammed himself did not live to see that time, for two years after his triumphant return to Mecca he died. It seemed for a time as if his work had died with him. But it was not so, for he had breathed the spirit of his enthusiasm into others, and he was succeeded by his friend and father-in-law Abu Bekr. He was the first *caliph*, caliph meaning successor.

The Conquests of Abu Bekr. Abu Bekr was filled with as great zeal for the faith as Muhammed, and with an even greater lust for gold and power. So, the triumphant march of the Muslims, or Muslims as they came to be called, through the world began. With sword in one hand and Koran in the other, they set out to conquer and convert the whole world. To all prisoners of war, they offered but one choice – death or the Koran.

Thus, a new danger made all Europe tremble, and for many ages, the cry of Allah, Allah! was to wake fear in the hearts of all who heard it.

The Muslim soldiers were as fearless as they were feared. Death to them had no terrors. It was but the gateway into a new and glorious life; for they believed that if they died fighting for their faith they would at once enter into a paradise of endless delights. If they hesitated, only the pains of hell awaited them.

So, the Arab horde swept onward. All Persia fell before them, from the Caspian Sea to the Indus. Syria, the Holy Land, and Armenia were torn from the Empire. Egypt, too, bowed to the yoke. Yet Constantinople stood firm, and again and again, the Muslim host was pushed back from its walls.

But through the Golden Gate of Constantinople was not the only way of reaching Europe. The Mediterranean lay open to the Muslim ships, and soon the trade routes of the world were in their hands. They sailed at will throughout the whole of the inland sea. They overran the north of Africa. The kingdom of the Vandals, which Justinian had reconquered for the Eastern Empire, became another jewel in the caliph's crown. The conquering Arab marched through Africa until he reached the shores of the Atlantic. There, like some new Alexander, he stood, sighing for more worlds to conquer. Westward lay the Atlantic Ocean. Southward lay the trackless desert. Northward, then, to Europe, the conqueror's eyes were turned.

Across the narrow Straits of Gibraltar lay Spain. The power of the Visigoths had spread until at last they ruled over the whole of what is now Spain, and over a great part of southern Gaul as well. For nearly three centuries, foreign foes had scarcely touched their borders. Yet the Goths did not prosper. For they were turbulent people, and the kingdom was nearly always in a state of unrest. Many of their kings died by murder, many were deposed, revolutions were frequent and bloody.

Roderick and Tarick. Now, instead of uniting against the Muslim danger, they still quarreled among themselves. A noble named Roderick had usurped the throne. But there were many who hated him, among them the sons of the late king, and a certain count named

Julian, to whom he had done a deadly wrong. The Jews, too, of whom there were many in the land, were ready to revolt, for they were cruelly persecuted.

The Arab love of plunder was well known, and it seemed to all these malcontents that it would be well to have their help in deposing the hated king, Roderick. The Arabs would come, thought the Visigoths, defeat and depose their king, and, having plundered him to their heart's content, would depart again to their own land.

So, Count Julian went to the Arab leader and offered to help him if he would but come and free the country from the yoke of the usurper. The Muslims were willing enough, and a young and skillful officer named Tarick was sent to depose King Roderick. He landed at the rocky southwestern corner of Europe which was later named after him, Jebal-Tarick, or the rock of Tarick. It is still called by that name, Gibraltar, although the last syllable has fallen away.

Upon landing, Tarick fortified his camp, and thus more than twelve hundred years ago the military history of one of the most famous fortresses of the world began. King Roderick hurried to meet Tarick, and a great battle began. But when the armies drew near to each other, the Gothic princes began their treasonous plot. They, with their followers, deserted and joined the Muslim ranks, and soon the rest of the Gothic army broke and fled in disorder.

King Roderick had entered the battle as if he were going to be entertained, so disdainful was he of the invaders. Dressed in flowing silken robes, with a jeweled crown upon his brow, he reclined in an ivory carriage, drawn by milk-white mules. But when he saw the day lost and his soldiers fleeing, he sprang from the carriage, and leaping upon his fastest horse, joined their retreat. He fled from the battle, but only to meet a different end. For in trying to cross a river which flowed near the battlefield, he was drowned.

The Muslim victory was complete. But instead of being content with their triumph and plunder, as Count Julian and his fellow-conspirators had imagined, the victorious troops marched further and further into Spain. Everywhere, towns opened their gates to them. Hardly anywhere did they meet with the slightest resistance, and in a few months, the Visigothic kingdom was wiped from the map of Europe. It vanished even as the Ostrogothic kingdom had vanished, and all of Spain, except for a little strip in the northwest, became a province of the great Muslim Empire.

Even then the conquerors were not content with Spain only. They swept on over the Pyrenees, and before long all the south of Gaul was in their hands. It seemed that nothing could stop their conquering march. In less than a century and a half, the Arabs had built up almost the greatest empire the world has ever seen. Now it appeared as if all Europe might bow the knee to Allah and pay tribute to the caliph.

Arab Rule in Spain. Yet it is well to remember that where the conquering Arab passed, he did not destroy as Hun and the Goth destroyed. Beneath the onslaught of the Teutons the art and learning of Rome to a great extent disappeared, and Italy especially was left forlorn and desolate.

It was not so much that the Teutons deliberately set themselves to destroy the splendid monuments of Roman art and learning, as we might imagine. Indeed, many of the chief Teutonic leaders had been trained in the school of Rome and desired to preserve all that was best of Roman tradition. But even so, the Goth and Vandal peoples were so diverse that much that was Roman was bound to disappear.

War was the only art known to the mass of the Teutons when they invaded the Empire. For a long time after their invasion, war was the rule rather than the exception, and people who live in a constant state of war cannot well cultivate the arts of peace.

With the Arabs it was different. At the time of their invasion into Europe, they were already advanced in arts and learning. They brought their learning with them and implanted it in the conquered countries. And for many generations, Spain owed her advance in the arts to the domination of the Arabs.

Saint Boniface

by the Sisters of Notre Dame

The vast countries lying east of the Rhine and north of the Alps remained pagan long after the south and west of Europe had embraced the true faith. Among the Alpine highlands, some tribes had received Christianity in the days when the Romans were masters. Slowly, however, the faith had lost all hold on them. Up to the close of the seventh century, the great mass of the Teutonic people of Central Europe was pagan.

Then the English people with the newborn faith were filled with zeal for the conversion of the peoples which they had looked upon as their own kindred. Bands of noble-hearted young monks went out to convert the tribes still buried in the darkness of idolatry. The earliest missionaries started from the monasteries where St. Wilfrid had established the Benedictine Rule. He sowed the plentiful harvest which God granted to St. Boniface to reap.

Boniface, this great Englishman, one of the most beautiful characters among the Apostolic Saints, did a work for Germany so vast and so lasting that it is hard to realize it could have been accomplished by one man.

Winfrid, as Boniface was at first called, was born in Devonshire in 680, and was of a princely family. When about five years of age he showed so strong a desire to be a missionary that his parents sent him to a monastic school. Later on, he went to Nutcell, an abbey famous for its order and learning. Winfrid soon became remarkable for his sanctity and the influence for good he exercised on all around him; but his first vocation never left him, and after he was ordained a priest, he obtained permission to preach to the pagan Teutons. Winfrid began to labor in Friesland, as the earlier missionaries had done, but met with so many obstacles that he returned to his monastery. Next year he started again and went to Rome. The pope, Gregory II, who is to the Germans what the first St. Gregory is to the English, heartily blessed his missions and sent him to preach to the pagan Germans. Winfrid's hope was to gain his own people, the Saxons, but finding that he could not yet hope for success among them, he began to work in the neighboring nations. On his second journey to Rome, the pope consecrated him Bishop, named him Boniface, and gave him great powers.

The next Pope, Gregory III, made Boniface archbishop and gave him the power to consecrate other bishops. Bavaria was then evangelized, and so rapid and thorough was its conversion that in a few years the whole land was covered with churches, and no less than twenty-nine great abbeys became seats of learning, centers of civilization, and homes of sanctity.

But Boniface had still another work to do. The Frankish nation, though converted, had never really thrown off pagan ideas and customs. Pope Gregory III and his successor, Zachary, entrusted to Boniface the difficult task of restoring the purity of the Catholic faith and of bringing the clergy and people to a Christian mode of living. After much difficulty, Boniface succeeded in introducing some improvement. The real rulers of the Franks at this time were called the Mayors of the Palace. The most famous of these Mayors, Charles Martel, for a long time delayed the good Boniface would have done, for political motives; but at last, when his own power as ruler was established, he aided and seconded the efforts of the saint to restore order. Pepin, his son, and successor did still more for the Church, but this work was only completed by the great German monarch, Karl, or Charlemagne.

The last years of Boniface's life were spent in founding monasteries and convents in his archdiocese. He turned to England for helpers. Numerous monks and nuns hurried to respond to his call. They were of the greatest assistance to Boniface in teaching and civilizing the people among whom they settled.

The work accomplished by this great saint was so thorough that we hear of no relapse into paganism after his time. The finishing touch was put to his work by Charlemagne, as we shall see. The Church in Germany flourished and produced numbers of saintly and learned men up to the unhappy days when a general decay of religion and morality brought on the terrible revolt known as the Protestant Reformation.

Other Missionary Efforts

The Slav converted. The nations of Slavonic origin were converted partly by missionaries from the Western States and partly by Eastern monks. Two Macedonian brothers, Sts. Cyril and Methodius, both religious, and later on Bishops, in the latter half of the ninth century, converted nearly all the Slavonic tribes of South-Eastern Europe. Starting from Constantinople, they first evangelized the Chazars of the South of Russia, then they passed into Bulgaria, where they were invited by Prince Bogoris. The prince had listened with attention to the instructions of the two missionaries, but his conversion was brought about in a singular way. He was building a magnificent palace and having it decorated with pictures. He asked St. Methodius, who, like many a Greek monk in those days, was a good artist, to pain him a subject that should inspire terror. The saint complied and drew the Last Judgement. When the picture was shown to Bogoris and its meaning explained, the Prince was seized with awe and declared he must be a Christian. He was baptized, and though his people at first revolted, he soon reduced them to order, and they followed him into the Church.

Moravians. The saintly brothers, in their great missionary tour passed on into Moravia, where conversions were numerous. Western priests had been preaching zealously for some time but were almost ignorant of the language of the people, which Sts. Cyril and Methodius knew thoroughly. This knowledge was the reason for their success. The two monks invented an alphabet for the Slavonic language and translated the Bible and other books for the use of the people. About this time, the brothers went to Rome, where St. Cyril died in 869. St. Methodius met with considerable opposition in his labors, especially from those who misunderstood the use he made of the Slavonic language in the Office of the Church, but the pope supported him. On his return to Moravia, an incident occurred which led to the conversion of Bohemia.

Bohemians. The young Duke Borzivoy of Bohemia came to the Moravian Court and was graciously received. But at a banquet given by the sovereign, St. Methodius noticed the Duke was not admitted to the table with the Christian nobles, but that he sat on the floor, as the pagans were wont to do, all by himself. The monk was touched with compassion at the slight against the young prince and took the opportunity of speaking to him about Christianity. The gentle kindness of the saint won Borzivoy, and he and his consort became Christians. They and their son and grandson (afterward known as St. Wenceslas) zealously strove to introduce the true faith among their subjects. But the heathen party was strong and had the support of St. Wenceslas's mother. When St. Wenceslas came to his thrown as a duke, the opposition was at its height, and the holy duke and his grandmother, St. Ludmilla, were both assassinated.

The Emperor, Otto I of Germany overthrew the heathen party and kept the new sovereign from open violence against Catholics. Succeeding sovereigns were Catholic, and forty years later, heathenism was banished from the land. Bohemia was instrumental in converting the Lithuanians of Poland, but Russia received the faith from Constantinople, Vladimir the Saint became the first Christian ruler in 988.

The Frankish Kingdom

by Henrietta E. Marshall

The "Do-Nothing" Kings. In the east, Christian Constantinople had stood as a bulwark against the Arab invasion. But despite that, the Muslims had made an entrance through the western gate of Europe, and it seemed as if nothing could now halt their conquering march. Yet halted it was.

Of all the Teutonic kingdoms built upon the ruins of the Roman Empire, the kingdom of the Franks was the only one which was to endure. But for many years after the reign of Clovis, its history was one of turmoil and bloodshed. It was divided and redivided more than once. And over time, the descendants of Clovis, known as the Merovingian line of Frankish kings, lost their vigor and manliness. They became mere figureheads and are known as the *Rois Faineants* or Do-Nothing kings.

Surrounded by luxury and pomp, they sat in their palaces indolently dreaming the time away, while the business of state drifted more and more into the hands of the mayors of the palace. These mayors had been at first little more than the managers of the royal household; in time they became dukes, and at length kings in all but name.

Charles the Hammer. The greatest of the mayors was Charles, called *Martel* or *the Hammer*. It was he who now gathered all the strength of the Frankish kingdom to fight the Muslim foe and roll back the menace of Islam from Western Europe.

The battle in which the Franks and Muslims met is one of the memorable battles of the world. For it was not so much the Franks and Muslims who were arrayed against each other as Europe and Asia, Christianity and Islam. If the Franks were beaten, then all Europe was at the mercy of the Muslims. For behind the Franks there was no power to stop their march. It was true that Constantinople held the gate of Europe in the east. But if the foe made an entry in the west, would that shut gate prevail?

The Battle of Tours. The battle in which the Franks and Muslims met is one of the memorable battles of the world. For it was not so much the Franks and Muslims who were arrayed against each other as Europe and Asia, Christianity and Islam. If the Franks were beaten, then all Europe was at the mercy of the Muslims. For behind the Franks there was no power to stop their march. It was true Constantinople held the gate of Europe in the east. But if the enemy made an entry in the west, would that shut gate prevail?

The fight which now took place between these two great forces is often called the Battle of Tours, but it was actually fought nearer the town of Poitiers, France. Here the fair Teutons of the north, steel-clad, heavily armed, and somewhat slow of movement, met the agile men of Asia. Mounted upon Arab horses, the Muslims, again and again, dashed upon the solid wall of the Teutons. Again, and again they were broken and scattered like waves upon a rocky coast. Yet, undismayed, they returned to the attack, and above the din of clashing steel there rose the shout, "Allah, Allah Akbar!" or "God is Great" in Arabic.

The fortune of the day seemed uncertain. Then suddenly throughout the Muslim army, the cry arose that the Christians were attacking from behind and that the Muslim camp with all its rich treasure was in danger. In a flash, a great body of the Arab cavalry wheeled about and dashed to save the treasure. Their greed cost them the day. With a shout, the Franks charged, and before that mighty onslaught, the Arabs fled like dust before the wind.

The sun went down upon the victory of the Franks. But how complete that victory was Charles the Hammer did not know until next morning when he found the Arab camp empty and deserted. Nor did he at this time follow up his advantage. Seven years later, however, he again attacked the Muslims, and at length drove them out of France altogether. Thus, his name – the Hammer.

By his victories over the Muslims, Charles made a great name for himself; the pope, now Gregory III, sent for him to implore aid against the Lombards, who still troubled Italy. But Charles was friendly with the Lombard king and had no wish to fight against him. So, although he received the pope's messenger with all honor, and loaded him with gifts, he sent him back to Rome without any promise of help. Again the following year, Gregory sent word to Charles, urging him by the true and living God not to prefer the friendship of the Lombards to that of the prince of the Apostles. But again, Charles failed to give the answer which the pope sought, and soon afterward he died.

Pepin the Short. When Charles Martel died, his son Pepin became mayor. He is known as Pepin the Short. By this time the pope had become so powerful, that kings liked to have his sanction to whatever they proposed to do. Before long, Pepin sent an embassy to him to say, "Who ought to be king, the man who has the name or the man who has the power?" The pope thought it reasonable that the man who was really king should also be king in name; and so, it came to pass that no more Merovingians drove up from their farms once a year to sit on the throne for a day. Pepin was made king, and soon the pope traveled all the way from Rome to St. Denis, near Paris, to crown the new sovereign and anoint him with the sacred oil. He was the first king of the Carolingian line.

Charlemagne and the Holy Roman Empire

by Eva March Tappan, Ph. D.

Pepin the Short had done a great deal to unite the kingdom; but when he died, he left it to his two sons, and so divided it again. The older son died in a few years, and now the kingdom of the Franks was in the hands of Charles if he could hold it. First came trouble with the Saxons. They and the Franks were both Germans, but the Franks had had much to do with the Romans and had learned many of their ways. Missionaries, too, had lived among them and had taught them Christianity, while the Saxons were still heathen. It was fully thirty years before the Saxons were subdued. During those years Charlemagne, which means Charles the Great, watched them closely. He fought, to be sure, whenever they rebelled, and he made some severe laws and saw to it that these were obeyed. More than this, however, he sent missionaries to them, and he built churches. He carried away many Saxon boys as hostages. These boys were carefully brought up and were taught Christianity. They learned to like the Frankish ways of living, and when they had grown up and were sent home, they urged their friends to yield and become peaceful subjects of the great king; and finally, the land of the Saxons became a part of the Frankish kingdom.

Charlemagne had only begun the Saxon war when the pope asked for help against the Lombards, a tribe of Teutons who had settled in Northern Italy. The king was quite ready to give it, for he, too, quarreled with them; and in a year or two their ruler had been shut up in a monastery, and Charlemagne had been crowned with the old iron crown of Lombardy.

This war had hardly come to an end before the king led his troops into Spain against the Muslims. There, too, he was successful; but at Roncesvalles, Spain, he lost a favorite follower, Count Roland. Roland and the warriors who perished with him were so young and brave, that the Franks never wearied of recounting their noble deeds. Later the story was put into a fine poem, called the "Song of Roland," which men sang long afterward as they dashed into battle.

In the year 800, a great honor was shown to Charlemagne, for as he was kneeling at the altar in Rome on Christmas Day, the pope set a crown upon his head, and the people cried, "Long life and victory to the mighty Charles, the great and peaceful Emperor of the Romans, crowned of God!" Charlemagne was now not only king of the Franks but the Roman Emperor. This Holy Roman Empire, however, was smaller than the Roman Empire had been in the earlier days, for it included now only France, part of Germany and of Italy, and a little strip in the north of Spain.

Charlemagne had become a great ruler, and other rulers were anxious to win his friendship. Haroun-al-Raschid, or *Harun the Just*, the Caliph of Bagdad, the hero of *The Arabian Nights*, was one of his special friends. This caliph was a poet and a learned man. He founded schools throughout his kingdom, in which medicine, geometry, and astronomy might be studied. Charlemagne did not write poetry, but he was a close student, and he desired the boys of his kingdom to be educated. One of his orders reads, "Let every monastery and every abbey have its school, where boys may be taught the Psalms, the system of musical notation, singing, arithmetic, and grammar, and let the books which are given them be free from faults, and let care be taken that the boys do not spoil them either when reading or writing." When he returned from one of his campaigns, he sent for a group of schoolboys and told them to show him their work. The boys from the poorer families had done their best, and he thanked them heartily. "Try now to reach perfection," he said, "and you shall be highly honored in my sight." The sons of the nobles had thought that as their fathers were rich and of high rank there was no need for their working, and they had nothing good to show their king. He burst out upon them in anger, "You pretty and dainty little gentlemen who count upon your birth and your wealth, you have disregarded my orders and your own reputations and neglected your studies. Let me promise you this: If you do not make haste to make good your former negligence, never think to get any favors from Karl."

As there were few learned men in the Frankish kingdom, the king sent to scholars in other parts of Europe and offered them generous rewards to come to the Franks as their teachers. He collected a library and established a school at his own court; and there the mighty Emperor, his family, and his courtiers gathered around some wise man and learned of him. The Emperor was interested in everything. He often got up in the night to study the stars. Once when the planet Mars could not be seen, he wrote to his teacher, "What do you think of this Mars? Is it the influence of the sun? Is it a miracle? Could he have been two years about performing the course of a single one?"

Charlemagne was a tall, large, dignified man. On state occasions, he dressed most splendidly, but at other times he wore simple clothes and liked best those that were ornamented with the work of his wife and daughters. He was an expert horseman and swimmer, and he taught his sons to ride and to use the sword and the spear. He took charge of his own farms, he built churches and bridges, and he began a canal to connect the Rhine and Danube Rivers. He encouraged trade, making the taxes upon merchants as light as possible. He collected the ancient German songs, he had a grammar of the language written, he improved the singing in the churches, and he even had the coinage of the kingdom manufactured in his own palace. All this was in addition to the fifty or more campaigns that he was obliged to make. Surely he was the busiest of monarchs and the busiest of Germans; for, although the land of the Franks is now France, yet it must not be forgotten that the Franks were German.

Unit Seven: Invasions and Conversion

THEME: UNITY

The Treaty of Verdun
The Beginning of France, Italy, and Germany

Adapted from the work of Henrietta E. Marshall and the Sisters of Notre Dame

Charlemagne ruled as emperor for more than thirteen years, during which time three emperors sat upon the Byzantine throne. Charlemagne endeavored to keep peace with each, sending them embassies, and calling them brother; but it was not until the year 812 that Emperor Michael formally recognized Charlemagne's right to the imperial title.

For hundreds of years following this recognition, there would be two emperors, one in the East and one in the West, each claiming to be the rightful heir of the Caesars. But although in the West the title of emperor endured, Charlemagne's Empire fell to pieces soon after his death; the whole state was filled with discord and violence. For it was built upon no solid foundation but upon the will of one man.

The Sons of Louis the Pious. Charlemagne had many sons, but only one survived him. He is known as Louis the Pious and was more fitted for the cloister than the throne; he was a good man, but a weak prince and Louis's unruly sons tried to rend the Empire from him. He divided his vast Empire among his three sons during his lifetime. and after his death, they quarreled among themselves over their inheritance. The various nations of which it was composed took advantage of the incessant quarrels among these princes to try to recover their independence.

After a time, the two younger of these sons, Louis and Charles, joined together against Lothaire, the elder. At Strasburg, they met together and swore an oath of eternal friendship. The taking of this oath was made an occasion of a solemn ceremony. The two armies were drawn up facing each other upon the plain; in the space between, the kings met, their robes glittering with gold and jewels. Each made a speech, and then, with great solemnity, swore to stand by the other.

Louis, being the elder, spoke first. "For the love of God," he said, "and for this Christian people and our common salvation, as much as God gives me to know and to do, I will aid my brother Charles in all things as one ought rightly to aid one's brother, on condition that he does as much for me. And I will never willingly make any compact with Lothaire which may injure this my brother Charles."

Louis repeated the same words but in another language. The interesting thing about this oath is that it was taken in two languages. It had been the dream of Charlemagne's life to unite all the Germans under one scepter, so that they should be one people, speaking one language, and owning one ruler. Before he died, he had even begun to write a German grammar. But already, less than thirty years after his death, there were two such widely differing languages spoken within the Empire that the Frankish soldiers of Charles and the Saxon soldiers of Louis could not understand each other. So, Louis, speaking to his brother's Franks, spoke their language, and Charles, addressing the Saxon soldiers, used another language. Out of those two languages have grown modern French and modern German.

The Treaty of Verdun. In the following year we see the Empire divided into three parts, which corresponded roughly to France, Germany, and Italy; for all three brothers met together once more and signed a treaty known as the Treaty of Verdun. They agreed that Lothaire, the eldest, should keep the title of Emperor and be given Italy and a strip of land west of the Rhine, running right through the Empire, from the Mediterranean to the North Sea.

The land which lay east of this, now Germany, was given to Louis, and the land which lay west of it, which roughly forms the France of today, was given to Charles. Here we have the beginnings of three great states.

But peace did not follow. Sometimes one of the kings and sometimes another claimed the title of Emperor, with jurisdiction over the others. The princes who ruled were nearly all of the same royal family, the German Karlings.

Exactly one hundred years later, France passed out of the hands of the Karling family by the accession of Hugh Capet. This, the commencement of the Capetian dynasty marks the real beginning of the kingdom of France, which from this time never again formed a province of the Empire. But Italy, which had been an independent kingdom for one hundred and fifty years, was reunited to Germany under Otto the Great, a Saxon Prince, who raised his country once more to the power and rank of an Empire, but with more limited possessions than that of Charlemagne.

Teutonic legacy. Nearly four hundred years had passed since the last Roman emperor of the West had been swept from his throne by an audacious Teuton. And in the turmoil of these centuries, it would seem as if the Teutons had brought nothing in their train but bloodshed and discord and the destruction of art and learning. But as they reformed Europe out of the fragments of the shattered Roman Empire, the Teutons brought something new.

In Rome, the state was everything, the individual nothing. There was a great gulf between the powerful wealthy and the powerless poor, between the slave and the slave-owner. The slave-owner was almighty, the slave merely a piece of property to be used. But among the Teutons, there were no slaves. They were a free people, and each man was conscious of his own worth in the community. The idea of this individual freedom was the Teutonic legacy for future ages.

The Coming of the Northmen

by Henrietta E. Marshall

We have seen the dim beginnings of France, Italy, and Germany. But hundreds of years would pass before these kingdoms became settled. The period following the Treaty of Verdun was one of constant turmoil and bloodshed, for the kings were often feeble, sometimes bad, and their subjects were turbulent and rebellious. Even a strong king had endless difficulties to face.

First, there was the lack of roads. One of the first things the Romans did in a conquered country was to build roads. They knew that roads were great conquerors and great civilizers. But the barbarians who split up the Roman Empire did not know the value of roads, so the wonderful Roman highways were allowed to fall into disrepair. In Saxony, which the Romans had never conquered, there were no roads at all. The difficulties, therefore, of traveling from one part of the kingdom to another were immense, and the transport of an army extremely difficult. And without roads to encourage trade, commerce languished.

Secondly, the king was almost always poor, for the system of taxation was very imperfect. Being unable to quickly travel throughout the kingdom himself, the king was obliged to depute much of his authority to dukes and counts. Having little money, he paid them for their services with land. Their possessions often became so great that they were more powerful than the king himself and rebelled against his authority. So civil wars were constant.

Besides these and other internal disturbances, there were frequent attacks from without to be repelled, and these alone were enough to prevent Europe from settling into peace.

Soon after the death of Charlemagne, the Muslims seized the island of Sicily, overran a great part of the south of the Italian Peninsula, and even threatened Rome itself. Avars and Hungarians from the wilds of Asia swept over Germany and northern Italy, reaching even to the borders of France, and at length settled in the land which is now called Hungary. And lastly, there came the Northmen. They were the last of the German tribes to attack the civilization of Europe, and they left more impression on it than almost any other, although they were eventually absorbed into the peoples they conquered.

The home of the Northmen. Of their early history, we know little or nothing. For, while in southern and central Europe new kingdoms were being hammered out of the old Roman Empire, Europe beyond the Baltic was a region unknown. Until the end of the eighth century, we know almost nothing of Scandinavia. Nearly all the Teutonic tribes who took possession of the Empire came or had traditions of having come, from the far north. They came from beyond the sea where dwelt a mighty people, well skilled in the building of boats; they came "from the edge of the world." But little was known of this far-distant country.

The Northmen as raiders. Hundreds of years passed, and still, people knew little more about this strange northern country than in ancient times. At length, however, towards the end of the eighth century, driven by poverty and the necessity of finding new homes, or merely by the love of adventure, the heathen Northmen began to sail forth from their bays and fjords, and attack the Christian kingdoms of Europe. They came from what are now Norway, Sweden, and Denmark, but in those days, men called them all indiscriminately, Danes, Northmen, Vikings, or men of the bays and fjords. The English chronicles generally call them Danes, the French chronicles generally call them Northmen. But, by whatever name they were known, they made themselves the terror of seaboard Europe for a hundred years.

For the attacks of the Northmen differed from those of any other barbarian people in that they came from the sea, and not from the land. They sailed in long, narrow vessels, capable of holding fifty or sixty men. Bow and stern were alike so that the ship could be steered either way, and they were decorated with the head of a swan or dragon, or some other animal. But the dragon was the favorite. Rowers sat along the sides of the vessels, and there was also one large sail.

Used as we are now to great sea-going vessels, the Viking ships may seem to us but small, and we may marvel how men could venture forth upon the stormy North Sea in such frail craft. But venture forth they did, even upon the pathless ocean, and five hundred years before Columbus, the hardy Norsemen had landed upon the shores of North America.

These dragon-ships became the pest of the seas and a terror to all seaboard dwellers. It was a new terror, too. For hitherto there had been peace upon the seas. Huns, Avars, Bulgars, Goths, Vandals, Franks, Lombards, and all the other lesser tribes which had swept over Europe in turn, had made their attacks by land. Except for Muslim or Vandal pirates, the seas had still remained the peaceful routes of trade. Now that was changed. War and bloodshed came from the sea, just when it seemed as if the beginnings of peace might dawn on land.

The sea was the Northman's element. Yet, although he was a born sailor, he seemed equally at home on land, where he proved himself a skillful, cunning, and coldblooded fighter. They were blue-eyed, fair-haired, tall, and sinewy men. They wore their hair in long plaits and dressed in vibrant colors, scarlet being much loved by them. They wore coats of mail and great horned helmets and were armed with bow and arrows, hatchet, spear, and sword.

They loved war and the ways of war and the weapons of war. Their songs were all about war and the mighty blows of heroes, and in these songs, they gave poetic names to their ships and weapons. But more than any other weapon, they loved their swords, and they gave to them the most poetic names, such as "the lightning of war," "the thorn of shields," "the helmet biter." The hilts and scabbards of these swords were often beautifully inlaid with gold and studded with jewels and were handed on from hero to hero, and prized as no other gift was prized.

Armed, then, at all points, these joyous, blood-thirsty pirates set forth in their dragon-ships. Along the sides they hung their brightly painted shields, ringed and bossed with metal, and leaning upon their spears, they stood in the prow, while the short oars flashed, and the wind sang through the sail. When storm winds blew and others sought the shelter of the shore, the dragon-ship sped still forth, spurning the foaming waves. Then, as day dawned, some sleeping village would hear the Viking battle cry. Then bright swords gleamed, and sparing neither man nor woman, these Northmen plundered at will. At length, their fury and their greed sated, they mounted into their ship once more and sped away as swiftly as they had come, leaving behind them only smoking ruins were, but a few hours before, peaceful homes had stood.

The first of these attacks of which we have any record was upon England, towards the end of the eighth century. But soon England, Scotland, Ireland, France, Germany, Spain, and Italy all knew and dreaded the terrible Northmen. Their coasts were dotted with ruins, the bones of the dead lay on a thousand battlefields, and a new petition was added to men's prayers, "From the fury of the Northmen, good Lord deliver us."

The Northmen in France

by Henrietta E. Marshall

The Northmen as settlers. At the beginning of their raids, the Northmen only came to plunder and did not attempt to settle in the lands they attacked. But as time went on, they came not only to plunder but to settle. And wherever they settled, a change came over them. They were so adaptable that they lost their individuality and became merged in the native population. They settled in England and became Englishmen; they settled in France and became Frenchmen. Later, these Norman-French conquered England and again, in time, became Englishmen.

But before they finally settled there, the attacks of the Northmen on France were both many and cruel. It was not only the coasts that they left desolate, for in their narrow vessels they sailed up the rivers, and towns and villages far inland were laid in ruins. Even Paris itself was threatened by them more than once.

The Carolingian line was, by this time, dying out in feebleness; the weak kings, unable to punish the impudent invaders, paid them gold to depart. The Northmen accepted the gold, but they always returned, each time in greater and greater numbers, ever more greedy, bolder, and crueler than before. With sword and fire, they laid waste the land until there were whole districts in the most fertile parts of France where it was said a man might wander for long days without seeing the smoke of a chimney or hearing the bark of a dog.

"The heathen, like wolves in the night, seize upon the flocks of Christ," wails a writer of the time. "Churches are burned, women are led away captive, the people are slain. Everywhere there is mourning. From all sides, cries and lamentations assail the ears of the king who, by his indolence, leaves his Christian folk to perish."

Rollo settles in the North of France. After a time, some of the Northmen, under their leader, Rollo, took possession of a part of France and settled there. And from this new base, they launched even fiercer attacks on the rest of the country. At length, in the time of Charles the Simple, the French saw that to buy the Northmen off was worse than useless, and to expel them now that they were firmly rooted was impossible. The only thing to do was to change lawless freebooters into law-abiding citizens.

Charles, therefore, sent messengers to the rough, old sea-king, offering him the undisputed possession of all that north-west portion of France in which he and his warriors had already settled. In return for this, he was to become a Christian, be baptized, and declare himself a vassal of the king. Rollo was willing to listen to the king's proposal, but he was not content with the land offered to him.

"The land is desolate and barren," he said, "there is not there the wherewithal to live." So, he demanded more land. Thereupon the king offered him Flanders. For he had a grudge against the count of Flanders. But Rollo would have none of it.

"It is nothing but a waste of bog and marsh," he said, and he demanded Brittany. Now the part of France called Brittany had never really been in the possession of the kings of France. So, all Charles could give Rollo was the right to conquer it, if he could. And this he readily gave.

Matters being thus settled, Rollo had next to perform his part of the pact and do homage as a vassal. Upon the appointed day, the king seated himself upon his throne with his priests and courtiers about him, and to him came the rough old Northman and his warriors. The ceremony began, but when Rollo was told that he must kneel before the king and kiss his feet he started back in wrath.

"No, by Heaven!" he cried. "I will kiss no man's feet!"

"It must be," replied the priests, "in no other way can you hold your fief."

"Then let one of my followers do it for me," replied the proud sea-king.

And as nothing would move Rollo, Charles had to be content with that. So, one of Rollo's followers was bidden to perform the act of homage for his master. But he had as little liking as Rollo for what seemed to him a piece of degrading foolery. He had never bent his knee to any man, and he did not mean to do it now. Striding, therefore, up to the throne, without even bending, he seized the king's foot and raised it to his mouth. So rough and sudden was his action that Charles fell backward to the ground. And thus, amid the loud laughter not only of the rude Northmen but of the Frankish courtiers also, the strange ceremony of homage ended.

After this Rollo was duly baptized and received the Christian name of Robert, and many of his warriors followed his example and were baptized also.

The land which was thus given to Rollo was already known as Northmannie. It soon became Normandy, and its people Normans. They quite quickly forgot their heathen religion and their northern speech and northern home. Normandy, strange to say, became the best-governed part of France, and the exploits of Rollo, the devastator of France, the pillager of monasteries, were almost forgotten in the fame of Robert, Duke of Normandy, the builder of churches, and framer of righteous laws.

Outwardly, wherever the Northmen settled they seemed to disappear and be merged in the native population. In reality, they imbued these populations with something of their own spirit. They were filled with great curiosity, they had a genius for order and government, they were fearless, energetic, and eager, always ready to adventure and to do. Now civilized, they retained much of the old vigor which as barbarian heathens had made them such deadly and pitiless foes. Christianized, they became the passionate champions of the Catholic Church. And the descendants of those Vikings who had refused to bend the knee to any man, and laughed aloud at the humiliation of their overlord, became the great upholders of the feudal system, the impassioned exponents of the orders of knighthood and chivalry.

Leif Ericsson, the Discoverer

by Eva March Tappan, Ph. D.

There was once a Northman called Eric the Red who, for some reason was exiled to Iceland, but in a little while he was in trouble there also. He had lent his seatposts, wooden posts carved into images of the gods, which stood by the high seats at the feasts, and the man who held them refused to return them. A quarrel had arisen, and in the course of it, Eric had slain the man. For this reason, he was now exiled from Iceland for three years.

He knew there was a country lying to the westward, for a sailor caught in a storm had been thrown upon its shores, and he determined to seek it. He found the land and spent two or three years exploring it; then he returned to Iceland. He meant, however, to establish a colony in the new country, and therefore he called it Greenland. "People will not like to move there if it has not a good name," declared this wise colonizer. Probably he had obtained some new seatposts by this time; for the custom was to throw them overboard when land was near, and to settle wherever they floated ashore.

A few years after Eric founded his colony in Greenland, his son Leif, or Leif Ericsson, spent a winter in Norway. There he became a Christian and was baptized. When he was about to return to his home in Greenland, King Olaf of Norway said, "I beg of you to see that the people in Greenland are told of the Christ, for no one is better to attend to this than you."

So, it came about that when Leif returned to Greenland, he carried with him a priest and several other religious teachers. A little later he saved a ship's crew from drowning, and because of this people called him Leif the Lucky, but his father said rather grimly that Leif might have done a good thing in saving the men, but he had done a bad thing in bringing a priest to Greenland. After a while, however, Eric himself became a Christian, and so did his wife, and most of the people followed their example.

Now among those who came to Greenland was a man named Bjarni. On the voyage, he had been blown out of his course close to an unknown land lying to the south of Greenland, and when he finally reached the colony, he told of how he had seen this land. Then Leif and the other young men gathered around him. "What sort of country was it? Were there any people there? What grows in the place? Are there mountains or lowlands?" they questioned, and Bjarni had to admit that he had not gone ashore. "Humph! He was not very eager for knowledge," said the young men rather contemptuously.

They talked a great deal about the unknown lands, and finally, Leif bought Bjarni 's ship and made ready to go on a voyage of discovery. "Do you go with us as leader," he urged his father; but Eric replied, "Oh, I am growing too old for a hard voyage at sea." "But no one else of all our kin will be as lucky as you," pleaded Leif, and at length, Eric mounted his horse and rode toward the ship. Suddenly the horse slipped, and he fell off. That settled the question." It is fated," he said, "that I should never discover any other land than Greenland," and so Leif and his men were obliged to sail without him.

After a while, they came to a shore where lofty mountains rose, covered with snow. This is thought to have been the coast of Labrador, Canada. Then they passed a flat and wooded shore, which is believed to have been Nova Scotia. At length, they reached a coast that seemed to them most inviting. The shores were of white, shining sand; and beyond them were pleasant woods which seemed to stretch far inland. There were rivers full of salmon and meadows covered with rich grass. Leif and his followers carried their beds to land, set up their tents, and made ready to explore the country. He divided his men into two parties and made them take turns in staying by the camp and going out to explore.

One of the older men on the voyage was a German. One day he came back chattering away in his own language. "Weintrauben," he exclaimed, "ich habe Weintrauben gefunden!" The Northmen could not tell what he meant, and at first, he was too much pleased and excited to speak Norwegian. At length, he told them he had found grapes, such as he used to have when he was a boy, and that was what had pleased him so much. It was because of this discovery that Leif named the country Vinland which means "the land of vines." This is thought to have been Rhode Island and the southern part of Massachusetts.

Then the men set to work to gather grapes and hew wood. Toward spring they took their cargo of wood and dried grapes and sailed back to Greenland. This is the story that the Icelandic sagas, or hero stories, tell. The voyage took place in the year 1000, and if we may trust the old saga, Leif Ericsson was the first white man to set foot on the continent of America.

There is a little more of the saga story that ought to be told. After Leif went back to Greenland, a wealthy merchant named Thorfinn Karlsefne went to visit him. On this visit, Thorfinn met Gudrid, one of the shipwrecked people whom Leif had rescued so long ago and married her. She persuaded her husband to go to Vinland to found a colony. The first autumn in the new home their little son, Snorre, was born. Snorre was the first white child born in Massachusetts. When he was three years old, the colony was given up, and the baby explorer returned with his parents to Greenland. It was a rough voyage, but the little American boy lived through it and became the ancestor of a long line of wise and excellent men.

The sagas tell of many later voyages to America, but at length, a terrible plague came upon the northern lands. In Norway many of the people died, and Vinland was forgotten.

Fresh Invasions

by the Sisters of Notre Dame

While the Danes desolated the great kingdoms in the north, various barbarian hordes attacked Europe on every side. In the east came the Slavonians and Lithuanians, while two Asiatic peoples strove with the southern provinces for possession of these fertile lands.

The Slavonic hordes. The last band of invaders were the Slavs, a brave and warlike people descended from the Scythians and Sarmatians of Roman times. They had long occupied the extensive plains which form the Russia of today, but in the tenth century, without abandoning their old home, they pressed west and south and added to their extensive territory all land up to the frontier provinces of the Germanic Empire.

The kingdoms of Bohemia and Poland were founded at this time, the latter by a tribe called Lithuanians. The Slavs also occupied some of the northern provinces of the Greek Empire, Serbia and Dalmatia being settled. A tribe from the Volga advanced into the plain of the Lower Danube took possession without driving out the original people, and gave their name to the land – Vulgaria, now Bulgaria.

Constant warfare was kept up on the borders between the Germanic and Slavonic peoples, and so great was the number of the latter who were taken captive and sold to Western masters that the name *Slav*, which in their tongue meant "speaker," has given us the word slave.

Invaders from Asia: The Muslims. On the Mediterranean shores, the Muslims still endeavored to extend their conquests. They repeatedly attacked Italy without any permanent results, but in Spain they were losing ground. The Christians there had regained several districts, and the kingdoms of Navarre, Aragon, and Castile were founded about the middle of the eleventh century. At this time also the Western caliphate came to an end; but the Moorish dominion in Spain, though not so extensive in territories as formerly, lasted yet five centuries longer. About this time there occurred a terrible persecution of the Catholics in Spain by the Moors.

Magyars. But by far the fiercest of all these invaders were the Magyars, an Asiatic people which from the plains of Asia crossed over into Central Europe, and in 896 first settled on the plains of Hungary. They were heathens, and until 1033 were the terror of the Western States; but they were kept from further incursions westward by the establishment of a border State, or Mark, as it was called. As this was the most easterly province of the German kingdom, it was called the Eastern Mark, in Old German *Oesterreich* – a name which has become modern Austria.

Conversion of Scandinavia

by the Sisters of Notre Dame

Conversion of the Teutons. Nothing contributed so much to the establishment of peace and order in Europe as the conversion of the pagan nations which had been settling down within her borders. The conversion of the Teutons, already far advanced by the labors of St. Boniface and the conquests of Charlemagne, was carried out by the zealous prelates of the frontier dioceses, who, aided by fresh bands of English missionaries, worked long and earnestly, but with varying success, to win to the faith the pagans of the eastward-lying States. Many intrepid Benedictine monks went forth as missionaries to win the North Teutons to the faith.

The piratical habits of the Scandinavians made them most difficult to gain to Christianity. Every summer was spent in predatory excursions, and each winter was passed in living on the spoils of their raids and in preparing for the next. But, undismayed, holy men toiled unceasingly at softening the barbarism of these fierce pirates and at implanting the true faith among them.

Conversion of Norway. Piratical incursions from Norway into England were not infrequent during the ninth and tenth centuries. To two, at least, of the Norwegian chieftains, these invasions brought the blessing of conversion to the Catholic faith. Harold Haarfager and his son, Hakon the Good, were both baptized in England, and, returning to Norway, sought to win their people to their new-found faith. They met with a certain measure of success and were aided by monks both from England and Germany. But when Harold Haarfager conquered the neighboring chieftains and endeavored to introduce the feudal system and make them his vassals, the independent spirit of the Norwegians would not bear his superiority, and though they had accepted the true faith at his hands, they would not submit to his government. Large numbers preferred to emigrate.

Iceland evangelized. They directed their ships northwards and settled in the newly discovered Iceland. There they founded several flourishing colonies, which became the home of the most famous Scandinavian poets and historians. In 1000, missionaries followed the emigrants, and by the middle of the eleventh century, that desolate land had two important bishoprics and several monasteries of Augustinian and Benedictine monks.

Catholic settlements in Greenland. The Icelanders pushed further north and discovered Greenland, where a Catholic settlement was founded with sixteen churches and two monasteries. An old tradition claims for these adventurous mariners the glory of the discovery of America and the establishment on its north-eastern shores of a bishopric in 1121.

Scandinavian settlers in Catholic lands. The Scandinavian pirates who settled in Catholic lands very speedily gave up paganism. Thus, we find Guthrum the Dane accepting the terms offered to him by Alfred the Great and being baptized with all his followers. In France, the Northmen had acquired many small tracts of land on the Loire before 911, when Charles the Simple granted a vast territory to Rollo and his pirates on condition of their becoming Catholic. The offer was accepted, and Normandy, as the newly settled country came to be called, was celebrated for its fervent Church and learned clergy.

The middle of the eleventh century thus found Europe Catholic from Spain to Russia, from Greenland to Italy and Greece. But the same epoch saw the severance of the Eastern patriarchates from the unity of the true Church. The northern plain of the Baltic was yet in pagan darkness, while Western Asia, Northern Africa, and part of Spain were still in Moslem hands.

Egbert, "King of the English"

by Eva March Tappan, Ph. D.

For centuries, England was divided into several districts. At the head of each was a king, or chief, and everyone was trying to get more power than the others. At last, about 829, a king named Egbert, who lived in Wessex, in southern England, showed himself stronger than the rest, and one by one the others acknowledged him as overlord; that is, they paid tribute to him and promised to obey if he called upon them to help him fight. He took the title of "King of the English," and, with a very few exceptions, every sovereign of England from that day to this has been a descendant of Egbert.

England was more nearly united than ever before. More churches and convents were built. These were held sacred, and in all the quarrels that had arisen among the various kings, their property had never been touched. Not only did they have vessels of gold and silver, and finely wrought lamps and censers swinging by golden chains, and jewels and embroidered vestments and beautiful tapestries, and altars covered with plates of gold; but they had, too, treasures of quite another kind, hundreds and hundreds of manuscripts, written on parchment by the monks, for these convents were also schools, and every one of them had its "book-room." There the patient monks and their pupils sat day after day copying books, letter by letter, and painting ornamental capitals in most brilliant colors.

The Northmen in England

Adapted from the work of Henrietta E. Marshall, Eva March Tappan, Ph. D., and the Sisters of Notre Dame

Tidings of the doings of the dreaded Viking pirates had been terrifying the coast people for some time. The evil day came only too soon. Sails appeared on the horizon and fierce marauders approached land. At first, they would make a bold dash inland, plunder the nearest church or monastery, and speed back to their keels. Experience taught them that there was little to fear from terrified people and that monks and nuns were easy prey. Massacres of religious marked every descent of the pirates. The rich spoil of the abbeys, their jeweled shrines and altar vessels, were borne off to Danish homes, while of the churches and monasteries nothing was left but blackened piles of ruins.

King Egbert was able to drive these robbers away and so was his son after him; but in the reigns of Egbert's four grandsons, matters grew worse and worse, for the Danes came in great swarms. There would be an alarm from the east, and before the king could go to the rescue, another alarm would come from the south. Houses were burned, people tortured or killed or taken to Denmark as slaves. If a man planted a field of grain, he had little hope of being able to reap it.

SAINT EDMUND, KING AND MARTYR

Adapted from the work of Eleanor C. Donnelly

During the reign of Edmund, king of the East Angles, the Danes, headed by their ferocious chief Hingar, made an incursion into England. Edmund, who was a wise and just prince, endeavored to repel the rude invaders, and was at first successful in battle against them; but the latter returning to the charge, the Christian monarch and his forces were irretrievably vanquished.

Hingar had vowed an implacable hatred against the faith of Christ, and he now proposed to King Edmund that if he would abolish Christianity in his dominions, he should be rewarded by being reinstated on his throne. Edmund rejected the infamous proposal with indignation and horror. The Danish chief then subjected the holy king to many and painful tortures. He was scourged, and, having been tied to a tree, was pierced, like St. Sebastian, with arrows. Edmund, however, remained constant to Christ and repeatedly pronounced the holy name of Jesus, which so enraged Hingar that he ordered that he be beheaded.

The royal way
To realms above is woe.
Father Adrian Rouquette

THE STORY OF ALFRED

Adapted from the work of Eva March Tappan, Ph. D. and the Sisters of Notre Dame

One bright page breaks the dark record of the second Danish invasion which occurred in the middle of the ninth century. The fourth of the grandsons of Egbert was a young man named Alfred, who was only twenty-two years of age when he became king. He was a great favorite among his people, but they were too wretched to have any rejoicing when he came to the throne.

This second invasion of the Danes was marked by extraordinary cruelty on the part of the pirates. Faster and faster came the Danes. Alfred fought them bravely, but their forces were too strong. The whole land was overrun, and Alfred could no longer remain on the throne. As people looked at matters then, he would not have been blamed if he had left the kingdom to take care of itself and had gone to Rome for the rest of his life, but he had no intention of abandoning his country. He withdrew to a swampy part of England and waited, training his men and planning how to get the better of the enemy.

The Peace of Wedmore. By and by, Alfred had gathered enough men to attack the invaders and then came a fierce battle. The Danes were thoroughly beaten. They agreed to remain in the northeastern half of England and to acknowledge the English king as overlord. The Danish word for "town" is *by*, and there are today many more towns whose name ends in *by* in northeastern England than in the parts of the island where the English lived.

Alfred's work for the Church. Alfred did much for the Church and the education of the people – two interests closely linked in Catholic hearts. How bitterly he grieved over the miseries caused by the Danish invasions and by the sad ignorance of the clergy. But Alfred was not a man to grieve only. He set to work to remedy the evil as far as he could.

Learned men were invited to England to teach the clergy. Churches and monasteries were rebuilt, and communities gathered together as of old, with saintly men set over them to guide them in the ways of holiness and learning. But Alfred loved his people too dearly to let learning belong to the ecclesiastical class only. Monks and priests were taught Latin, so all the lore of earlier days was open to them, but for the people, there must be English books, and Alfred set himself to make them. He translated several valuable works into Anglo-Saxon for them, adding passages containing information which he felt would be useful and interesting to them. He also caused the monks to keep regular Chronicles. Thus, to King Alfred, we owe the first history of England in English.

Alfred's sanctity. But Alfred's private life gives as perfect an example of practical holiness as can be found. His time was always well-regulated and well-spent, his expenditures kept within due bounds, and his religious duties always thoroughly attended to. But his blameless life is still more striking when we learn that all this activity and intelligent zeal for the welfare of his people, his country, and the Church was carried out by a man whose bodily sufferings were keen and constant. No wonder that the memory of Good King Alfred was so cherished by Catholic England, and that the brightness of his fame is undimmed to our own days.

Effects of Danish invasions. The Peace of Wedmore did not end the struggle in England. It was only abated. Alfred's wise government secured peace for Southern England for a long time. But though Dane and Englishmen were becoming one people, the civil results of the invasion were too many and too great to be easily swept away.

During the rest of Alfred's life, he would struggle against the desolation which followed the marauding Danes, and for more than a century after his death, Alfred's successors had many difficulties to contend with. This continued until the Danes came in such numbers that they took possession of the whole land and set up their own sovereigns as Kings of England. In 1016, Canute became one of these rulers. Canute was a wise and good monarch, under whom order and prosperity reappeared. Danes ruled the land until 1042, ending only fourteen years before the conquest of England by William the Conqueror.

CANUTE

Adapted from the work of Helene A. Guerber, Eva March Tappan, Ph. D., and Henrietta E. Marshall

Alfred left worthy sons and grandsons, but the power of the Danes increased. In a little more than one hundred years after his death, the English king was forced to flee to France with his wife and his two little boys; and a Dane whose name was Sweyne sat on the throne of England. Sweyne soon died, and his son Canute became king.

At first, Canute was very stern and cruel, in order to make the people afraid to disobey him, but when he became the King of England, he tried to please his subjects. Many of the Danes were sent home, the English were made his officers, good laws were established, and peace and order reigned throughout the land.

Canute became a Christian and went on a pilgrimage to Rome, to receive the pope's forgiveness for his sins. About ten years after becoming King of England, Canute conquered Norway and because he then ruled two kingdoms, he was regarded as a very powerful king.

Besides being brave, Canute was wise and just, so he had plenty of admirers; and his courtiers, hoping to please him, often remarked that he was sole lord of land and sea. This flattery was distasteful to Canute, so he made up his mind to give his courtiers a lesson.

One day at low tide he ordered his servants to place his throne far down upon the beach; accompanied by his courtiers, in their richest robes, he went down there and took his seat. Grouped around him, and still paying their compliments, these followers kept a watchful eye upon the waves, for the did not wish to get their clothes wet.

When the tide turned, they ventured to suggest to the king that he have his throne set farther up on the beach. Canute carelessly said that he did not want to move and that as they vowed he was lord of land and sea, he would bid the waves stand still. But although he stretched out his scepter and ordered the water not to come near him the waves rose higher and higher till the spray drenched the courtiers' fine clothes and forced them and the king to beat a hasty retreat.

When they were beyond the reach of the tide; Canute gravely told them that God alone was master of the sea and made them feel so ashamed that they never ventured to flatter him again.

From that day too, Canute never wore his crown but placed it upon the figure of Christ in the cathedral at Winchester as a proof of his humility. Many of the Danes were still heathen, but no doubt they very soon followed the example of their king and became Christians too.

Gradually the difference between the Danes and the English passed away. The Danes began to forget that they had ever lived in any other country and lived like Englishmen talking English ways and customs for their own. So once more England became a united kingdom. But this, of course, did not happen all at once. It was many years before the English and the Danes quite forgot their quarrels.

As Canute had other countries to govern as well as England, he felt the need for someone to help him to rule. So, he divided England into four earldoms and placed an earl over each part. These earls ruled the kingdom under the king.

In the year 1035 King Canute died and was buried in the cathedral at Winchester.

The Norman Conquest

Adapted from the work of Charlotte M. Yonge and the Sisters of Notre Dame

Restoration of the Saxon line. Canute left three sons, but one was content to be only King of Denmark, and the other two died very soon. The sufferings the people had endured under Danish reign made them rejoice when a great English nobleman, Earl Godwin, restored the Saxon line in the person of Edward, afterward known as the Confessor. Virtuous and gentle, Edward made himself beloved by the people. He planned with great magnificence the building of Westminster Abbey. The twenty-four years that his reign lasted was a time of peace, such as England had been long unaccustomed to.

Yet, he was too good-natured, as you will say when you hear that one day, when he was in bed, he saw a thief come cautiously into his room, open the chest where his treasure was, and take out the moneybags. Instead of calling anyone, or seizing the man, the king only said, sleepily, "Take care, you rogue, or my chancellor will catch you and give you a good whipping." You may fancy that some would not respect such a king as this, and so there were some disturbances in his time.

Edward had been raised in Normandy and was unwise in his marked fondness for Normans, who were far advanced in learning and manners compared to the homely Anglo-Saxons. The English had forgotten much of what Alfred and his sons had taught them and seemed to be growing duller, and clumsy, and rude. The Normans, however, had learned a great deal in France, and both the Danes and the English thought the Norman-French fine gentlemen, and could not bear the sight of them.

The Saxon nobles were much angered by Edward's love for foreigners and by his placing Normans in positions of trust in Church and State. Think, then, how angry they were when it was said that King Edward wanted to leave his kingdom of England to his mother's Norman nephew, Duke William because all his near relations were still little boys, not likely to be grown up by the time the old king died. Many of the English wished for Harold, the son of Earl Godwin, a brave, spirited man; but Edward sent him to Normandy, and there Duke William made him swear an oath not to do anything to hinder the kingdom from being given to Duke William.

Old King Edward died soon after, and Harold said at once that his promise had been forced and cheated from him so that he need not keep it, and he was crowned King of England. This filled William with anger. He called all his fighting Normans together, fitted out ships, and sailed across the English Channel to Dover. He landed in Sussex and set up his camp while Harold was away in the North. Harold had just won a great battle in Yorkshire when he heard that William and his Normans had landed, and he had to hurry the whole length of England to meet them.

The Battle of Hastings. Many of the English would not join him, because they did not want him for their king. But though his army was not large, it was very brave. When he reached Sussex, he placed all his men on the top of a low hill, near Hastings, and caused them to make a fence all round, with a ditch before it, and in the middle was his standard, with a fighting man embroidered upon it. Then the Normans rode up on their war-horses to attack him, one brave knight going first, singing. The warhorses stumbled in the ditch, and the long spears of the English killed both men and horses.

Then William ordered his archers to shoot their arrows high in the air. They came down like hail onto the heads of the English. Harold himself was pierced by one in the eye. The Normans charged the fence again, and broke through; and, by the time night came on, Harold himself and all his brave Englishmen were dead. They did not flee away; they all staid, and were killed, fighting to the last; and only then was Harold's standard of the fighting man rooted up, and William's standard—a cross, which had been blessed by the pope—planted instead of it. So ended the Battle of Hastings, in the year 1066.

The great Earls of England were not united among themselves, and their quarrels and jealousy had weakened the land. When William the Norman came, there was no one to make a real stand for freedom. Had King Edward been as wise and strong as he was good and gentle, English history would probably have been very different from what it is. All the events of Edward's reign seem a long preparation for the conquest of England by the last of the great tribes which were to contend for the possession of her.

The land had had a great many "conquests" – the Roman conquest, the English conquest, and now the Norman conquest. But there have been no more since; and the kings and queens have gone on in one long line ever since, from William of Normandy down to Queen Elizabeth II.

Feudal Strife

by the Sisters of Notre Dame

During the centuries of constant warfare, we have been studying, a military system of holding lands was prevalent. Every sovereign must have felt the need for as many helpers as he could get. Therefore, when he conquered land, he would grant a tract of it to one of his followers, on condition that the tenant should pay for it by military service, while the lord, in turn, would protect his subject. When the tenant, who was called a "vassal" to his chief lord, gave lesser grants to his own followers, he did so on the same conditions. Lands held in this way were called "fiefs," or "feuds." Hence, this way of holding property is called the "feudal system."

Uses and abuses of the feudal system. This system at first greatly benefitted both rulers and people. By attaching the invading bands to the conquered soil, it helped to put a stop to their roving life and thieving expeditions; by binding lord and vassal together with mutual obligations, it established ideas of law and responsibility. The right of ownership and the love of home and family brought a taste for peaceful pursuits and made men unwilling to risk their little all by continuing a life of warfare.

As time went on, however, the system fostered a continual succession of petty wars between neighboring lords, for the love of fighting in which these men had been nurtured was not so easily got rid of. Every noble, entrenched in his own feudal castle, could go forth at will from within its fortifications to wage war against some neighboring lord to devastate his lands, plunder his tenants, and return laden with booty. To avenge such injuries was considered a matter of honor. Human laws were powerless to check the thirst of these fierce combatants for revenge and so-called glory, and the wretched peasantry, who were the chief sufferers, pleaded in vain for peace.

But this was not all. When lands were granted to the Church, it was on the same terms as when given to lay lords. The Bishop or the Abbot Vassal had to pay homage for his possessions, receive investiture beneath his overlord, and provide soldiers for his lord. Sometimes, even, we find that prelates headed these troops themselves. But, worse still, the lords began to interfere in the election of Church superiors, and too often chose some member of their own family for the post, whether they had any religious vocation or not. At times the Bishop or Abbot named was not even a priest or a monk. Then he simply kept the title and money and named someone in his stead as Bishop or Abbot, paying him a small sum for his services.

It can easily be imagined what kind of care such people would take of the souls committed to their charge. Thus, the feudal system led to another evil, the decay of monastic fervor. The rich gifts made in feudal times to monasteries also became a source of danger. Monks and nuns lost the love and practice of poverty which had kept them so holy and hard-working in the earlier days. Learning, too, was neglected, and this is regarded by some good authorities as one of the principal causes of loss of fervor. Little by little, all kinds of relaxation crept into many religious houses and destroyed their power for good.

Religious and Social Reforms

by the Sisters of Notre Dame

We have seen the dark side of the ninth, tenth, and eleventh centuries. There is a brighter one, which we have now to study – the efforts of the Church to combat the various evils of the day, and the successes with which God blessed her labors. The first attempt at bringing about a better state of things began in the monasteries, which themselves in many cases needed reform.

Up to the time of which we are speaking there was but one great monastic Rule observed in Europe, the Benedictine. Even those Orders which had been founded by other Saints gradually adopted St. Benedict's laws for religious life. But as each abbey was independent of all others, many differences had grown up in their various observances. This did not tend to lessen the abuses spoke of already.

Louis the Mild, Emperor of the West, saw the necessity of putting an end to these troubles and begged St. Benedict of Aniane to try and remedy them in 817.

St. Benedict of Aniane. St. Benedict of Aniane was a monk of extraordinary holiness. He had distinguished himself by his bravery as a soldier in the armies of Charlemagne. One day, in saving his brother from drowning, he almost perished himself. The danger he had run made him conceive so grand an idea of the duty of saving his soul that he gave up everything the world could offer to lead a life of humble penitence. He became a monk, and his example led many others to follow him. Later on, he became Superior, and the fervor which reigned in his monastery caused King Louis to form the project of putting all the abbeys in his dominions under the government of St. Benedict of Aniane.

The Saint undertook the work. He made incessant journeys from one end of the Empire to the other and succeeded by his gentle firmness in introducing a thorough change in the way of living of the monks, and in establishing the same observances in all the monasteries.

Congregation of Cluny founded. But a still greater service was done to the Church by the foundation of the Congregation of Cluny, about one hundred years later, by St. Berno, Abbot of the famous monastery of La Baume, near Marseilles, in which the reformed Rule of St. Benedict of Aniane was observed in all its strictness. Some officers of the pious Duke William of Aquitaine received hospitality in this monastery and told their lord of the wonderful holiness of the monks. The nobleman at once made up his mind to have a community in his domains and begged St. Berno to come and choose a site for the monastery.

The Abbot selected the magnificent wooded valley of Cluny; but it was the favorite hunting-ground of the Duke, who said that the noise of the dogs would disturb the monks at their prayers. "Well, my lord," answered St. Berno, "turn out the dogs and bring in the monks!" The Duke agreed to the sacrifice, and the abbey and church which were raised on the spot became renowned for both the magnificence of their buildings and for the sanctity of the religious.

Many who could not entirely forsake the world retired there for a time to escape from the turmoil of business. Nobles, sovereigns, and popes, even, could be named among such guests, and the monastery became a center of religious fervor whose holy influence spread far and wide. Most of the abbeys of France, Italy, and Spain submitted themselves to the rule of the Abbots of Cluny, of whom the first six became canonized Saints. A large proportion of the Bishops of France and Italy in the succeeding century were Cluniac monks, who labored with great zeal at the general renovation of society.

The "Truce of God" terminates civil feuds. One of the greatest benefits conferred upon Europe was the "Peace of God," a wonderful institution which was the means of putting an end to the continual strife between the feudal nobles, the cause of so much misery. The Bishops and Abbots of Aquitaine, Burgundy, and France united under the leadership of

Odilo, Abbot of Cluny, and Richard, Abbot of Verdun, and succeeded in inducing many of the nobles to promise under oath not to strike a blow in a merely private quarrel, or to attack an unarmed person, or to permit violence or injustice. This attempt at putting an end to warfare was not, however, very successful.

Some years later, by asking less from the war-loving knights, the prelates gained much more in the end. They promulgated the "Truce of God," which only permitted fighting on certain days and under certain conditions. By the provisions of the truce, the nobles were bound, under pain of excommunication, not to fight in private quarrels, or on any festivals, nor during the whole of Lent and Advent, nor from the Wednesday night until the Monday morning of every week during the year. Moreover, all persons were declared sacred from attack whose condition or profession forbade them to carry arms – namely priests, pilgrims, the aged, and women and children; besides which, churches, burial-grounds, and monasteries were regarded sanctuaries, which it was sacrilege to violate, for all who took refuge therein were under the protection of the Church.

When the free exercise of fighting was thus limited, the taste for it slowly diminished, and men had time to feel how much better was a state of peace and security than that of continual warfare. Thus, by the wise action of the Church, the scourge of the early Middle Ages ceased, and respect for law prevailed. More humane feelings gained ground, the weak and unfortunate were protected against the strong hand of injustice. The institution of chivalry, one of the greatest glories of medieval Europe, grew out of the combined influence of a more restrained love of military glory and Christian charity. Though chivalry did not attain its full development until the twelfth and succeeding centuries, its origin can be traced back to the beneficial influence of the "Truce of God."

Abolition of slavery. During the Teuton invasions, slavery, that worst evil of pagan times, which had begun to die out under Christian Roman rulers, reappeared with many of its horrors. Slave-markets existed in almost all great maritime cities. Captives taken in war were nearly always sold into bondage, while in some places the peasantry was reduced to slavery by their conquerors.

The feudal system tended to diminish the number slaves, and the Church worked steadily against the crying evil, and by framing laws in favor of slaves gradually raised their condition, until the peasant, who had been the absolute property of his master, became a serf – tied to the land on which he was born, it is true, but secured in possession of his little holding of cottage and land. He had his flock, his poultry, his harvest, all his own; out of this, however, a small rent in kind had to be paid to the lord in return for his protection, On certain days in the year he was also bound to bring his tools, or his ox and cart, and labor on the estate of his lord. His children might attend the neighboring abbey school, and he, in sickness or want, was sure of assistance from the friendly monks.

In some lands, household servants continued to be slaves, even when all living outside the castle were serfs. Italy and Spain were the last European nations to give up slavery, which they did in the sixteenth and seventeenth centuries.

The Greek Schism

by the Sisters of Notre Dame

The state of the Church in the East was at least as sad as that in the West. A new difficulty arose towards the end of the ninth century, which had the most disastrous results – the complete severance of the faithful of the Greek Empire from the unity of the Catholic Church. As at first no point of doctrine was attacked, the disputes did not end in producing a heresy, but a schism – that is, a breaking away from Catholic unity, not on a matter of faith, but of Church government.

Many causes lead to the sad event. During the repeated heresies that were born in the East, great ill-feeling grew up in the Greeks against the Holy See. For, in these disagreements, the popes always opposed the error, whatever it was, while the Eastern prelates too often defended it. Then several of the Patriarchs of Constantinople thought it hard to have to regard the Bishop of Rome as Head of the Church. They said that, since Constantinople was the chief city of the Empire (as it was until the separation of the Eastern and Western Empires), the chief Pastor of the Church ought to preside over it rather than over Rome. Or they asked that Constantinople might at least be equal or second only to Rome. The popes, with great foresight, opposed all these pretensions, and the jealousy of the Greeks grew stronger.

When the Western Empire was restored by the coronation of Charlemagne by Pope Leo III, another cause of animosity was added. Finally, both Rome and Constantinople claimed jurisdiction over Bulgaria, which had recently received the faith. This was a very difficult question to settle, as the Bulgarian Prince changed his mind on the subject more than once, sometimes wanting to be subject to Rome and sometimes to the Patriarch of Constantinople.

The actual cause of the schism was the question, Who was the lawful Patriarch of Constantinople? The dispute arose in the following manner:

The court of Michael III (856-867) was the scene of most shocking misconduct; every evil was practiced with the approval of the Emperor, the principal leader in iniquity being the young Sovereign's uncle, Bardas. To have more freedom for wickedness, this man persuaded Michael to force his mother, the Empress, and his own sister into a convent. The Patriarch of Constantinople, Ignatius, son of a deposed emperor, refused to receive the vows of these ladies, saying that they were not free in the matter; and he excommunicated Bardas, publicly refusing him Holy Communion. Bardas determined on revenge. He induced the weak Emperor to imprison Ignatius and to name Photius, a clever but wicked layman, in his place. This man consented to the crime and received Orders, each degree on a successive day, the sixth seeing him consecrated Patriarch. This in itself was contrary to the laws of the Church, which does not allow of such hasty proceedings.

Photius, though Patriarch, was afraid that Ignatius would tell the pope how things had gone, and to force him to resign his see, he caused the old man to be shamefully ill-treated in his prison, but in vain. Ignatius escaped, and both parties appealed to Pope Nicholas I. Photius said he was lawfully elected, Ignatius having voluntarily resigned, and he sent a forged document to this effect. Ignatius, on his side, explained the violence he had undergone. The pope sent Legates to Constantinople to see who was in the right. Photius bribed the Legates, who declared in his favor. As soon as the pope learned what had passed, he excommunicated the Legates, condemned Photius, and commanded that Ignatius should be restored.

On this Photius called a Synod and declared himself against the pope. Ignatius was not allowed to come back, and the wrongful Patriarch was supported by the Emperor and by some of the Greek Bishops. Then Photius framed a list of accusations against the Holy See and the Western Church and entered with bitterness into the Bulgarian dispute. The charges which he made against the Latin Church were most insignificant. They could only have been made by one who was determined to raise a quarrel on any pretext. For example, he objected to the practice of fasting on Saturdays, of using milk on fasting days, complained that priests were not allowed to give the Sacrament of Confirmation, and revived an old ground of dispute - namely, that the Latin Church had added the word *Filioque* to the Nicene Creed. The Eastern Church supported Photius in this open opposition to the Holy See, not because they attached much importance to his charges against the Latin Church, but because of the bitter feeling against the supremacy of the pope. The schism was spreading rapidly, when the career of Photius was stopped for a time Michael III died and was succeeded by a man, not of the royal family, named Basil the Macedonian, who from political motives turned out Photius and brought back Ignatius.

The new Emperor asked the pope for a General Council to terminate the disputes and settle the differences between Greeks and Latins. Pope Hadrian II gladly consented, and Constantinople was chosen as the place of meeting. The prelates assembled in 869. It was the fourth and last General Council held in that city. The principal points settled were – that Ignatius was lawful Patriarch, Photius was to be deprived and degraded, and Constantinople was recognized as second in rank after Rome. Eight years later, Ignatius died.

Photius, meanwhile, had been working at gaining the favor of the Emperor and succeeded. On the death of St. Ignatius, Basil raised Photius to the patriarchate and wrote begging the pope (John VIII.) to agree to his nomination. Rather than risk fresh troubles and reopen the schism, the pope said that, provided certain conditions were observed – one of which was that Photius should, in Synod, ask pardon for his misdeeds and acknowledge the authority of the Holy See, especially in the still unfinished Bulgarian dispute – he would acknowledge him. Photius, deceitful as ever, knowing that the Legates did not understand Greek, had the pope's letters mistranslated, the conditions put to him being carefully omitted. He then took possession of the patriarchate. The pope, informed of what had happened, excommunicated all concerned. For a few years, Photius continued to occupy the See of Constantinople, doing his utmost to increase ill-feeling towards Rome. But when Leo the Wise succeeded to the throne, he was deposed and exiled, dying about two years later.

No fresh disturbances arose for one hundred and fifty years, but the old jealousy of the Holy See and the Latin Church lived on. In the middle of the eleventh century, Michael Cerularius, Patriarch of Constantinople revived the old charges against Rome and renewed the schism. The attempt made by Pope St. Leo IX. to settle the dispute failed, and the schism has continued till the present day, nearly all the Russian and Greek provinces still remaining severed from the unity of the Church and the jurisdiction of the Holy See.

The worst evil of this sad period was the state of servitude to which the Sovereign Pontiffs were reduced. Charlemagne and his immediate successors called themselves, and acted as, Protectors of the Holy See. But it was not long before the rulers of Italy came to regard themselves as masters instead of subjects of the popes. The Treaty of Verdun, 843, made Italy an independent kingdom. After the death of its second Sovereign, Italy, like the rest of Europe, was a scene of constant warfare for upwards of one hundred years. She was attacked by invaders from without and torn by contending factions within. The chief Italian nobles struggled amongst themselves for the crown. Rome fell into the hands of first one party and then another. It happened more than once that the section which held Rome named one of its members pope, in hopes of rendering its hold on the city more secure. As often as not the opposing party caused the election of an Antipope, and Rome was the scene of constant strife between the rival powers. At last, the Counts of Tusculum triumphed over other nobles and for fifty years held Rome in captivity and determined the choice of each pope.

The supremacy of Germany in Italy was restored about 950. Adelaide, the widow of the murdered Lothaire, King of Italy, appealed to Otto I of Germany for aid against a usurper who was besieging her. The German monarch went to her assistance and overthrew the tyrant. He afterward married Adelaide, and in 961 was crowned King of Italy. The great duchies were bestowed on German nobles. The position of the popes was hardly improved. Though the Sovereign Pontiff was no longer chosen from one princely family only, Papal elections were not free; the Emperors claimed and exercised considerable power in Rome so that many of the popes were named through their influence, and it came to be considered necessary that the election of a pope should be confirmed by the German Emperor. But the Roman nobles opposed the jurisdiction claimed by the Emperor over Roman affairs, and the clergy and people of the city also asserted their rights, saying that it was by them that the popes should be elected. Many violent quarrels resulted.

After forty years of struggle surrounding the Papacy between the German Emperor and the Romans, two Italian noble families again came into power – first the Crescentii, and once again the Counts of Tusculum. Their dominion lasted from 1002-1048, during which time every Papal election was determined by them. Some historians have spoken strongly against the character of two or three of the popes named during this period, especially of Benedict IX., son of one of the Tusculum Counts, but all agree that even this Pontiff was orthodox in his teaching.

Effect of temporal control over the popes. It may readily be imagined that popes who were forced into the Holy See by political influence would not be loyally obeyed – at least, by their opponents' party. Thus, it happened that the state of the clergy grew daily worse, and a general decline of religion was the result. This time of the degradation of the papacy was one of the greatest trials to which the Church of God has been exposed. But the infallible promise of our Lord was verified even more. Neither persecution nor heresy had prevailed against the Church, and from the greatest danger of all, the servitude of the popes to temporal rulers and the presence of bad men in the Chair of St. Peter, the Church was to come out victorious. When the storm was over, the Holy See was enabled, by the remembrance of the very evils through which it had passed, to attain a power and independence unknown before.

Review of the second period of Church history. Such were the ninth, tenth, and eleventh centuries, a period of disorder in Church and State; yet they were not unmixed with the beginnings of better things. The most hopeful sign of brighter days was given by the change that towards the end of the period took place in the position of the Papacy. Some popes labored earnestly to restore order and were treated with the greatest reverence by the people. There was also the able assistance and strong support of saints filled with zeal for the restoration of virtuous living in clergy and people. During the last twenty years of this period, another point was gained: the popes declared that Papal elections must be reserved to the Cardinals only, though nomination was still admitted.

These centuries are sometimes called the "Iron Age," because the power of the sword was dominant; but the attention of some historians has been so closely drawn to the study of the evil features of these times that they have called them the "Dark Ages." It would perhaps be more just to regard them as a time of struggle between the powers of good and evil, of faith and force, in which the former conquered, and from which broke as from a dark and cloudy dawn, the glorious days of the "Ages of Faith."

Sources

Anecdotes and Examples Illustrating the Catholic Catechism
by James J Baxter, selected and arranged by the Rev. Francis Spirago

Aunt Charlotte's Stories of Roman History for the Little Ones
by Charlotte M. Yonge

A Book of Golden Deeds
by Charlotte M. Yonge

A Book of Discovery: The History of the World's Exploration, From the Earliest Times to the Finding of the South Pole
by Margaret B. Synge

The Catechism in Examples
by Rev. D. Chisholm

Christ in His Church: A Catholic Church History
by Lucius Caspar Businger and Richard Brennan LL.D.

England's Story: A History for Grammar and High Schools
by Eva March Tappan, Ph. D.

Fifty Famous People
by James Baldwin

Fifty Famous Stories Retold?
by James Baldwin

Folk Tales from Many Lands
retold by Lilian Gask

A Garner of Saints: Being a Collection of the Legends and Emblems Usually Represented in Art
by Allen Hinds, M.A.

Heroes of the Middle Ages
by Eva March Tappan, Ph. D.

A History of France
by Henrietta E. Marshall

Jesus of Nazareth: The Story of His Life Written for Children
by Mother Mary Loyola

In God's Garden: Stories of the Saints for Little Children
by Amy Steedman

Leading Events in the History of the Church: Part I. - Christian Antiquity
by the Sisters of Notre Dame

Leading Events in the History of the Church: Part II. - The Early Middle Ages
by the Sisters of Notre Dame

Little Pictorial Lives of the Saints
edited by John Gilmary Shea, LL.D.

Old World Hero Stories
by Eva March Tappan, Ph. D.

Sources

Our Island Saints
by Amy Steedman

Our Old World Background
by Rev. Monsignor Edmund J. Goebel, Ph.D.

Our Country in Story
by the Franciscan Sisters of Perpetual Adoration

Our Island Story
by Henrietta E. Marshall

Our Old World Background
by Charles A. Beard and William C. Bagley

The Story of the Roman People: An Elementary History of Rome
by Eva March Tappan, Ph. D.

The Story of Mankind
by Hendrik van Loon

The Story of the Romans
by Helene A. Guerber

The Story of the English
by Helene A. Guerber

School Reading by Grades: Baldwin's Readers - Sixth Year Book
by James Baldwin; story by Charlotte M. Yonge

Connecting with History Vol. 2 Companion Reader

The Standard Catholic Reader: Volume Four
by Mary E. Doyle; stories by Mother Mary Loyola, by John Lingard and others

Short Stories of Famous Men
by James J Reynolds, Mary A. Horn, and Phoebe Mizell

A Short Sketch of English History
by Henrietta E. Marshall

Short Lives of the Saints
by Eleanor C. Donnelly

Young Folks' History of Rome
by Charlotte M. Yonge

Young Folks' History of England
by Charlotte M. Yonge

CPSIA information can be obtained
at www.ICGtesting.com
Printed in the USA
JSHW061235120822
29194JS00002B/7

9 780578 719665